C

Vision

Cultures

of

Vision

*Images, Media,
and
the Imaginary*

RON BURNETT

Indiana

University

Press

BLOOMINGTON AND INDIANAPOLIS

© 1995 by Ron Burnett

The paper used in this publication meets the minimum require-
ments of American National Standard for Information Sciences—
Permanence of Paper for Printed Library Materials, ANSI
Z39.48-1984.

Manufactured in the United States of America

Library of Congress Cataloging-in-Publication Data

Burnett, Ron, date
    Cultures of vision : images, media, and the imaginary /
      Ron Burnett.
    p. cm.
    Includes bibliographical references and index.
    ISBN 0-253-32902-7 (alk. paper). — ISBN 0-253-20977-3 (pbk.)
    1. Motion pictures. 2. Photography. 3. Visual perception.
I. Title.
  PN1995.B86 1995
  791.43—dc20   94-48674

1 2 3 4 5 00 99 98 97 96 95

for Martha, Maija, and Katie

Contents

Acknowledgments   *xi*

1. Images and Vision   *1*
   A Video Diary   *1*
   Boundaries of Seeing and Feeling   *3*
   The Power to See   *8*
   The Eye in the Photograph   *11*
   Death in Bosnia   *14*
   Out of Focus: David Koresh   *18*
   Rodney King: Community and Communication   *20*
   The Eye and the Ear: In Time   *22*
   The Mirror Can See Forever   *28*

2. Camera Lucida: Barthes and Photography   *32*
   Photographs and Images: The Polaroid   *32*
   Benjamin/Barthes/Berger   *35*
   Avedon's Slave   *40*
   Photographic Images and the Public Sphere   *47*
   Performing the Visual   *48*
   The Photographic Other   *52*
   Clint Eastwood's Magnum   *55*
   Lumière and Méliès   *58*
   Death of a Cameraman   *62*
   Sartre's Memory   *64*
   Toward Projection   *67*

3. From Photograph to Film: Textual Analysis   *72*
   The Disappearance of the Image: Wavelength   *72*
   Is There a Medium for the Message? From Photography to Film   *75*
   Letter to Jane (Fonda)   *81*
   Celluoid-Time/Performance-Time   *84*
   Camera/Text/Frame   *86*
   Wim Wenders and Ozu   *90*
   The Classical Cinema as Paradigm   *95*
   The Classical Disguise   *100*
   The Naturalization of Artifice   *104*
   Why Science? Why Text?   *108*

The Communication of Meaning through Images   110
Tangled Knots of Yarn   116
Through the Lens of Montage   123

4. Projection   127

A Coup in Thailand   127
Reading a Wave   130
Fact Is Always Fiction   132
Documentary Simulations   133
Projection   135
Dreaming the Cinema   138
The Act of Seeing with One's Own Eyes   141
The Purple Rose of Cairo   145
Germany, Pale Mother   149
Narrative—Projection   154
The Topography of Projection   157
The Documentary as Projection: Shoah, Schindler's List   160
Listening to Projections   174
Listening to Hiroshima   178
Insignificance   182
Performance, Projection, and Intention   185
Memories of Identification: Scream from Silence   189
Play-Acting   199
The Body of Projection   205
Inside the Dome of Images   209
Nirvana: The Death of Kurt Cobain   215

5. Reinventing the Electronic Image   218

Prologue: To Be or Not to Be—Virtual   218
Video Activism   224
A Resistance to Theory   230
Video and the Public Sphere   233
Media Theory and the Electronic Image   236
Learning from Video Images   239
Video Politics and Communication   242
Dialogues in Image Form   251
Video Bodies/Video Minds   256
Screens of Subjectivity   261
Challenging Change   270
Community and Communication   274

6. Postmodern Media Communities   278

A Community of Identities   278
Local Travels   285
Visual Media, Ethnography, and Indigenous Cultures   291

Images of a Strike	299
The Marshall Islands	301
The Ceremony	305
Michael Jackson, "Seinfeld," and The Super Bowl	309
The Reflecting Pool	316
Waiting for Baudrillard in Sadie Benning's Living Room	318
The Virtual Printing Press	334
Bibliography	337
Index	349

Acknowledgments

THIS BOOK IS the product of many years of teaching, writing, videomaking, and filmmaking. Through it all I have benefited from the advice and input of colleagues, students, friends, and my family. In many respects, the diversity of issues that I address reflect the context in which I live and work, a place on the borders of America and Canada — Quebec, and within it, McGill University. A sabbatical finally allowed me to bring all of this material together, and financial support from the Social Sciences and Humanities Research Council was crucial to the research on video. Previous research leaves from LaTrobe University in Melbourne, Australia, enabled me to travel to the Marshall Islands and to develop a more profound understanding of the importance of community video to nonwestern cultures. Lectures at the University of Amsterdam allowed me to articulate some of my ambivalences about alternative media and the generally negative attitude of video practitioners to popular culture. A semester-long course, "Television in the Light of Postmodern Theory" in the Graduate Program in Communications, encouraged me to deepen my appreciation of postmodern thought. I am grateful to many of my students for their input, including Haidee Wasson, Scott MacKenzie, Michelle Gauthier, Aurora Wallace, Stacey Johnson, Chandrabhanu Pattanayak, Lynne Darroch, Murray Foreman, Alain Pericard, Marian Bredin, Anne Beaulieu, Cara Pike, and Suzie Fry.

The Dutch filmmaker Johan van der Keuken has taught me more about the documentary cinema and photography than he can imagine. My discussions and correspondence with him have had an effect beyond words. I am grateful to and have learned from Peter Ohlin, Peter Harcourt, Hamid Naficy, George Marcus, Michael Fischer, Will Straw, David Hemsley, Robert Daudelin, Gertrude Robinson, George Szanto, Réal Larochelle, Kass Banning, Janine Marchessault, Kay Armitage, Atom Egoyan, William Routt, Rick Thompson, Tom O'Regan, John Hinkson, John Galaty, Hugh Armstrong, Pat Armstrong, Barbara Creed, Thomas Elsaesser, Merrill Findlay, Patricia Gruben, Dena Gleeson, Marc Glassman, Charles Levin, Paisley Livingston, Mette Hjort, Laura Mulvey, Patricia Mellencamp, Teresa de Lauretis, Kaja Silverman, Bill Nichols, John Richardson, Michael Silverman, Michael Renov, Susan Feldman, Felix de Mendelsohn, Bill Dodge, Lise Ouimet, Brian Morel, Faye Ginsburg, Alain Ambrosi, Joe Clark, Ricki Goldman-Segall, and Nancy Thede.

Before his premature death, anthropologist Roger Keesing and I had many months of fruitful discussion which helped shape the ideas in this book. I am grateful to Hart Cohen, who brought me to the University of Western Sydney for a series of lectures and the many years of friendship which we have had. A year-long e-mail conversation with Andrew Curry has sharpened my understanding of interactive media and has made six years of tinkering with the Internet very worthwhile. My deepest thanks to Shirley Daventry-French and Derek French for their support and for their teaching. I would like to thank Joan Catapano and LuAnne Holladay at Indiana University Press for their advice and support.

Although nearly all of this book is made up of new material, from time to time I have used some parts of the following previously published material: "Video: The Politics of Culture and Community," in *Resolutions: Essays on Contemporary Video Practices*, ed. Michael Renov and Erika Suderberg (Minneapolis: University of Minnesota Press); "Video Space/Video Time: The Electronic Image as Found Object," in *Mirror Machine: Video in the Age of Identity*, ed. Janine Marchessault (Toronto: XYZ); "Dreaming the Cinema," in *Responses: In Honour of Peter Harcourt*, ed. Michael Dorland, Zuzana M. Pick, Blaine Allan (Ottawa: Responsibility Press); "The Frontiers of our Dreams Are No Longer the Same: Quebec Nationalism from an Anglophone Perspective," in *Boundaries of Identity: A Quebec Reader*, ed. William Dodge (Toronto: Malcolm Lester Publishers); "Video/Film: From Communication to Community," in *Video in the Changing World*, ed. Nancy Thede and Alain Ambrosi (New York and Montreal: Black Rose Books); "Between the Borders of Cultural Identity: Atom Egoyan's Calendar," in *CineAction* 32; "Camera Lucida: Roland Barthes, Jean-Paul Sartre and the Photographic Image," in *Continuum* 6.2, ed. John Richardson; "Toward Media Anthropology," *Commission on Visual Anthropology Review*, Spring 1991; "These Images Which Rain Down into the Imaginary," *The Canadian Journal of Film Studies* 1.1; "The Eyes Don't Have It: Video Images and Ethnography," *Continuum* 3.2; "Lumiere's Revenge," *Borderlines* 16; "Micro-Chip Video," *Copie Zero* 26. I would like to thank the editors and publishers of the above for their permission to use extracts from work which first appeared in their pages.

To my parents, Sophie and Walter Burnett, and my sister Sandy and her husband, George, thank you for being so understanding and supportive. To my wife, Martha, and our daughters Maija and Katie, my deepest appreciation and thanks for your support and love during the long months of writing and research. This book is dedicated to Martha, who never wavered in her belief that it could be written and whose input and love made it all possible.

1 | Images and Vision

A Video Diary

In 1992 a major statue of one of the founders of Canadian confederation (Sir John A. Macdonald) was decapitated in a local park in Montreal. Although the statue was rusty and neglected, the decapitation provoked a major outcry from Canadian federalists. To make matters worse, the decapitated head was stolen. Two years later no effort has been made to replace the statue or repair it. Pigeons now roost on the remains, and the statue has deteriorated further. From time to time journalists have commented on the loss, and some private citizens have banded together to raise funds to have a new head made. But the symbolism of the gesture will never be forgotten, nor will this symbolic death of the federal spirit in Quebec simply disappear if and when the statue is restored. In a sense this sculpture, both in its full and fragmented form, stands for historical realities that transcend its status as an object and are a clue to its transformation into an image. The aura of the statue (negative or positive) seems to bring history, the former prime minister, and notions of the nation state into a synoptic grid, from which many different meanings can be drawn.

So complex is this interplay, so naturalized are its underlying premises, that the task of "writing" about this history of the image of Sir John A. Macdonald will be richly endowed from the start. It will move through a number of sometimes contradictory and sometimes connected levels of meaning, creating a sphere of relationships in constant need of interpretation and reinterpretation. The process will oscillate between the micro-historical and the macro-historical, and the terms of that interaction will produce new and different relationships dependent on the context of analysis and the subjective choices of the interpreter. In other words, the statue is at once a powerful presence and an incidental component of what we do to it, the basis for a hierarchy of interpretations, and the reason we tear at the statue's foundations.

"The attempt to grant a statue an apprehending ear, a voice, even a motivated silence of its own, can become an occasion to redream the possibilities of speech. That attempt puts language and silence (as well as the statue) on trial; it lets us examine what piety or care, what violence or emptiness, words can carry, what bonds or estrangements they create, what they make us blind to, what they can make us remember or forget."[1]

Although headless, the statue of Sir John A. MacDonald retains all the qualities that allow it to be identified with its human predecessor. As a focal point in the debate about the future of Canada, it matters little whether the head is there or not. Yet as an image, the loss of the head brings the arguments of history into the forefront and suggests a rather paradoxical situation in which image and history are one, in which the visual and the material coexist through the absence of the eyes of one of the founders of modern-day Canada.

This process of decay and reconstruction has been paralleled in recent times in Eastern Europe. As the Communist dictatorships fell, crowds of men and women rushed into the streets of cities and towns. One of their first acts was to topple the giant sculptures of Lenin, Stalin, and local figures who had supported or run the state apparatus. The images of these statues falling to the ground remains one of the most powerful reminders of the frailty and strength of monuments created to support a symbolic, ideological, and social order. Numerous films and videotapes have explored the graveyards in which these statues are now stored. One of the most poignant was made as a video diary for the BBC by Ylli Hasani, an Albanian doctor. "The Man Who Loves Gary Lineker" won the top prize at the equivalent of the Academy Awards for the documentary film in Britain in 1993. One of the scenes in the video takes place in a warehouse where the statues of the former Albanian dictator Hojda are stored. We see people pulling at the nose of the dictator as the camera scans the shattered pieces of his body lying on a dirty floor. History is brought into the foreground as a tangible object, not just a discursive construction. Hasani talks over the images and is ecstatic. The entire video comes together at this moment, symbolically exorcising all of his pain as a witness to, and victim of, the poverty and despair in his country. It is this movement between the symbolic and the imagistic, the discursive and the real, that sustains the power of the video and that points toward a new and powerful strategy for interpreting everyday life through images. Hasani is both the subject of the video and a witness to the historical process. He is simultaneously in front of the camera and the cameraperson. He watches himself and is seen. He stands on both sides of a divide with radically changed boundaries: he recognizes how visual representations can create moments of historical expression that can be controlled by the spectator and the videomaker. Images are not cast in stone.

The iron or stone from which the monuments have been cast represent a moment in which historical meaning has been redefined. The presumably natural link between the visual and the symbolic falls apart. A recent exhibition in

---

1. Kenneth Gross, *The Dream of the Moving Statue* (Ithaca: Cornell University Press, 1992), 148.

New York in the Courtyard Gallery of the World Financial Center played with the paradoxes of this situation. Here are two examples of what artists would do with the now useless sculptures. "Scherer and Ouporov propose a mass ceremonial procession of the statues and monuments. The procession would culminate in their actual burial. John Murray envisions burying the states of former leaders, so that their heads and shoulders stick out of the ground, thereby simultaneously demystifying their former exalted status (by equalizing the viewing plane) while rendering the experience of gazing into their eyes all the more terrifying for being so intimate."[2]

The fictions of history are foregrounded, and the status of the image as a representation is thrown into question. In Hasani's case his video diary slides between the anger and truth of oppression and the images he creates to exemplify his reality. The power of the video lies in the contradictions of being within and outside of the very moments he wants to record. This paradox both permits and encourages dialogue, situates his images as historical, and encourages their projection and appropriation by other cultures and individuals.

Boundaries of Seeing and Feeling

> *In devising a story, therefore, the first thing that comes to my mind is an image that for some reason strikes me as charged with meaning, even if I cannot formulate this meaning in discursive or conceptual terms. As soon as the image has become sufficiently clear in my mind, I set about developing it into a story. . . . Around each image others come into being, forming a field of analogies, symmetries, confrontations.*[3]

This book explores the many fascinating aspects of Western culture's relationship to images, vision, and human understanding. Much of the discussion in this book is devoted to a study of photography, to the cinema and video, and to questions about vision, discourse, language, and the sociocultural context of modern media. The book proposes that the Western relationship to images is not as dependent on the activities of seeing or listening as we often presume. The assumption that to look means to see, or that to see means to understand, is derived from models of mind which for the most part conceive of human consciousness as a mirror of the world we inhabit.[4] It matters little that we

2. Lawrence Weschler, "Portfolio: Slight Modifications," *New Yorker* (July 12, 1993): 61–62.

3. Italo Calvino, *Six Memos for the Next Millennium* (Cambridge, Mass.: Harvard University Press, 1988), 89.

4. W. J. T. Mitchell's effort to deal with the contradictions of this strategy are outlined in *Picture Theory* (Chicago: University of Chicago, 1994). See his discussion on pages 50–51. Also see Claude Gandelman, *Reading Pictures, Viewing Texts* (Bloomington: Indiana University Press, 1991). See chapter 12, "Oculocentrism and Its Discontents."

have long ago abandoned the idea that the mind is a tabula rasa at birth or that learning follows a predictable developmental path from early childhood on. At a cultural level, the idea of the image implicates the mind in a representational process defined and measured through reflection and linearity. In part, this is a question of power—the subjective power to control "sight" and to locate the "seen" discursively, within or as a part of the everyday language we use. It is also about efforts to drive the process of seeing into an anatomical and physical sphere, however metaphorical that might finally end up being, and thus to anchor vision in the "real" world of human thought, perception, experience, and practice.

The interaction of visual metaphors with language and power is explored by Marcel Danesi. He developed a list from which it is worth quoting:

> I cannot *see* what you're getting at; There is more to this than meets the *eye*; That is my *point* of *view*; That's the way I *visualize* it; It all depends on how you *look* at it; *Seeing* is believing; I cannot quite *picture* that; That idea is really *out of sight*; I do not *see* the point of your argument; Please *look* your idea over; They always *focus* on the same concept, etc.[5]

This list could be expanded through the use of words or phrases like *insight*, *hindsight*, *oversee*, *scan*, *keeping an eye on*, *looking down on someone*, and so forth. The intimate linkages between thought and vision, suggested by the complementary aspects of these discursive characteristics, will be explored in greater detail throughout this book. The emphasis on the eye as the "site" of perception, thought, reflection, communication, and representation suggests that more is at stake with regard to the above inventory than might initially seem to be the case. What stands between the eyes and knowledge? What makes a world seen, a world understood? Or do these questions promote the all-too-easy conflation of vision with thinking?

At the heart of this debate, itself part of a broader philosophical and cultural argument about the relationship between subject and object, are a variety of quandaries and contradictions about the many different and complex relationships between vision and knowledge. What are the distinctions between observation and looking, for example? Is a glance the same as a stare? When we study an object or a person, is that the same as reading? Do similar principles of comprehension and explanation come into play in all of these processes?

A central trope for the activities of seeing in the modern and postmodern era is the *window*, as an object that frames and mediates the possibilities of vision. "The condition of the window implies a *boundary* between the per-

---

5. Marcel Danesi, "Thinking is Seeing: Visual Metaphors and the Nature of Abstract Thought," *Semiotica* 80. 3/4 (1990): 221–38.

ceiver and the perceived. It establishes as a condition for perception a formal *separation* between a subject who sees the world and the world that is seen, and in so doing it sets the stage, as it were, for that retreat or withdrawal of the self from the world which characterizes the dawn of the modern age. Ensconced behind the window the self becomes an observing *subject*, a *spectator*, as against a world which becomes a *spectacle*, an *object* of vision."[6] Why is this argument so pervasive and so familiar? It is often used with respect to technologies like the cinema and television, but it was also a dominant aspect of the initial critical response to photography during the 1850s. Is it the case that windows separate us from the world? Are they the condition upon which the activities of spectating are based? Why and how does the world become a spectacle? Can windows become a place for contemplation, a place where energy is gathered to create an imaginary and sometimes real union of the seen and the seer? Can they be like a landscape painting, which in the first instance proposes a separation in time and space between the scene and the canvas, but then leads the viewer back to a real and/or fictional Provence or Arles, or the windswept cliffs and skies of a Turner ocean, an English sea?

Romanyshyn's argument is seductive. It freezes the very relationships that his otherwise excellent book explores in great depth. To him the world becomes "a matter of information," "a bit of data, observable, measurable, analyzable and readable as a computer print out" (Romanyshyn 42), because what he pictures as a spectator is a self divided off from knowledge and from awareness, a passive actor in the world. This notion of the window as a place where sight rebounds against itself and viewers lose their senses of touch, smell, and hearing—this is the dystopic argument that has been applied to most modern media. It is a position in which the body devolves into the eye, and vision shifts from exploration to consumption, from the insecurities of watching to a fixed gaze. It is an approach that relies, sometimes correctly, on highlighting the increasing levels and complexity of mediation, the distance of our bodies from experience, the use of media to explain and reflect the world as if our implication in it can be negotiated from afar as observers.

It will be one of the contentions of this book that we need to look very carefully at the implications of this approach. Although, for example, I am but a distant witness to the tumultuous changes in South Africa, the 1993 election of Nelson Mandela to the presidency of the country left me in tears. The images I "watched" felt as close to me as the people with whom I shared the experience, which was as much of a physical and emotional experience as other more "direct" and less mediated instances during that very same day. Cultural analysis must be careful indeed in asserting that the windows people use can-

6. Robert D. Romanyshyn, *Technology as Symptom and Dream* (New York: Routledge, 1989), 42.

not be smashed. Media-tion must be thought about as multileveled with as many gray zones as clear ones. My perspectives on the world are never as immobile as the metaphor of the window suggests. More often than not I imagine myself to be beyond the constraints of the frame. Sometimes I succeed in stepping outside of the boundaries to which I am accustomed and other times I fail.

The work that follows tries to build on this ever-changing foundation. It takes into account that time is a crucial element in the viewing experience and that at no point do media spectacles freeze viewers into positions that they cannot control or change. In fact, notions of spectator and spectacle need to be recast as instances of oscillation between the control implicit in acts of seeing and the parallel loss of control in every act of watching. This simultaneity of power and loss creates the possibility, the openings for the imaginary. It is our imaginations that permit us to wallow in the images of violence we abhor and to transcend those moments with a thought, a daydream, an intuition. Our senses and our bodies don't disappear because the television is on. We are not the victims of what we watch, feel, listen to, although we may wish to alter how we see the world, may wish to open the window and check or validate the truth of the images that we come in contact with. Even in those instances when we cannot, a friend, distant or close, may come to our aid. We may turn to other media, to other forms of communication and to our own experience of the world, to enhance or negate what has been presented to us.

This then is the crucial shift of twentieth-century media, which are defined by their incompleteness, by their incapacity to totalize, to fully represent the world they both form and respond to. Even in those situations of monopoly most fully represented by the former Communist nations of eastern Europe, state media failed miserably in their efforts to conquer the spirit and thoughts of their citizens. By way of contrast, a case has been made that the media in the West conquer through subtlety, through the twists and turns of processes invisible to the population at large. This is the window forever closed, the window that endlessly keeps its citizens from grasping the reasons for their desires, their needs. It is the argument of Herbert Marcuse, Neil Postman, and Christopher Lasch.[7] Together, these authors see a dystopia in which the public, the citizenry wander through life dependent on false needs, false ideas which they hunger for, don't really understand, and cannot control. The pessimism of this stance often seems justified when the windows to knowledge are indeed closed in those more obvious instances of war and exploitation and oppression. But I

---

7. Herbert Marcuse, *One-Dimensional Man* (Boston: Beacon Press, 1966); Christopher Lasch, *The Culture of Narcissm: American Life in the Age of Diminishing Expectations* 2d. ed. (New York: Norton, 1979, 1991); Neil Postman, *Amusing Ourselves to Death: Public Discourse in the Age of Show Business* (New York: Viking, 1984).

will argue that we are dealing with a complex constellation of relationships from which much can be drawn and much can be lost. The range is so broad here that most of the dichotomies that we have comfortably used to explain mediation to ourselves in the latter part of the twentieth century are no longer applicable.

It is my own feeling that out culture is some distance from understanding how the media are used to make sense of daily life, but perhaps the most important step that can be taken is to disavow the simplistic causality that would see the media as responsible for people's actions. We need models that recast the window precisely as mediated, that is, as multidimensional, as a membrane dependant on us, that has no status outside the use we make of the window to see, to feel, and to imagine. It will be crucial to subjectify the window, to give it a personality, to recognize the productive consequences of our pragmatic manipulation of its form and shape and content. In a sense, the window must be seen as just one part of a house in which there are doors and hallways and rooms and other windows providing us with unpredictable views of the world, unpredictable experiences both of ourselves and our neighbors. Yet even as all of these experiences remain ephemeral, even as our memories work with our visions and against them, the impulse to explain and elucidate the processes of vision suggests that we are dealing in a temporal sense with a continuum for which there are not many markers.

Thus all of our efforts to spatialize, to talk about windows as frames, houses as metaphors for consciousness, to create forms that will represent vision are unlikely to provide us with an explanation. It is this *breakdown* of the supposedly rational encounter between language, thought, and seeing that continuously nourishes understanding and the need to both create and attribute meaning to the paintings, photographs, films, videotapes, and television images we produce and view. Seeing and listening are only two of the many facets of an embodied process—bodies, so to speak, at work—creating and recreating the cultural, political, and personal categories that we use in our efforts to define who we are. We cannot talk about vision without also talking about gender, ethnicity, class, and sexual preference. But, as I will argue below, we also have to develop hypotheses independent of categories that we are struggling to explain and understand. At no point must the arguments around the status of the image or the role of the viewer freeze time in order to conveniently pump up the theoretical parameters that cultural analysts have come to depend on. I am skirting at the edges of a classic argument in cultural studies between diachronic (temporal) and synchronic (atemporal) approaches to cultural analysis. My strategy will be to mix the two, to find as many gray zones as possible, to chip away at the binarism that would divide the synchronic and the diachronic from each other. Neither personal nor public forms of historical discourse and experience implode as conveniently as the terms would suggest.

In fact, time as such remains a fragile abstraction as dependent upon social convention as any other cultural construction—mathematical notions of time, notwithstanding. In a sense, the arguments around time are about cultural categories that take on an absolutist character and begin to play an almost theological role in constraining the range of interpretations that individuals and communities make of their daily lives.[8]

The Power to See

Yet, even given what I have just said, I would argue that there are autonomous processes at work in the human mind that form at least part of the foundation(s) upon which perception, cognition, and comprehension are organized. These may have no direct relationship to the experience of seeing or listening or the more generalized sense of what we mean by feeling. They may act separately and/or together, to both encourage and constrain not only the way we see, but the way we articulate our (in)sights. Gerald Edelman has put it eloquently: "parts of the brain (indeed, the major portion of its tissues) receive input only from other parts of the brain, and they give outputs to other parts without intervention from the outside world. The brain might be said to be in touch more with itself than with anything else."[9] Or as Jonathan Crary has explained: "Once the objects of vision are coextensive with one's own body, vision becomes dislocated and depositioned onto a single immanent plane. The bipolar setup vanishes. . . . subjective vision is found to be distinctly temporal, an unfolding of processes within the body, thus undoing notions of a direct correspondence between perception and object."[10] I would like to bring Edelman and Crary together. They are in any case more closely related than I imagined. What follows then is implicitly a dialogue between two rather different approaches, although I would caution the reader that many of the claims I make are my own.

Vision—the cultural approach to seeing and thinking—privileges the objects of sight, as if they will provide some clear answers to the dilemmas of viewing and understanding, as if the questions, indeed possible contradictions of autonomy, need not be addressed. For example, hallucinations and dreams are sights not in the control of the conscious mind. It is more difficult to trace

8. I would refer the reader to Stephen Kern, *The Culture of Time and Space 1880–1918* (London: Weidenfeld and Nicolson, 1983), and in particular his discussion of the late nineteenth century and the debates that took place around the normalization and standardization of time measurements.

9. Gerald M. Edelman, *Bright Air, Brilliant Fire: On the Matter of Mind* (New York: Basic Books, 1992), 18–19.

10. Jonathan Crary, "Modernizing Vision," *Vision and Visuality*, ed. Hal Foster (Seattle: Bay Press, 1988), 35.

their origin because they suggest autonomy without specifiable external or experiential causes. This could be reason for excitement, visible evidence, so to speak, of the mind reconstructing and redeveloping conscious and unconscious relations. Instead, autonomy, which I am not suggesting is the only process at work here, is more often than not recontextualized into an objectivist language of description and analysis. In fact, the sense of estrangement attributed to hallucination or dream cannot be divorced from the hesitations we feel in describing the "inner" workings of vision—the often obvious way the reflective autonomy of thought challenges preconceptions of order and disorder.

Once again the sense that control is necessary alters the parameters within which any analysis can be made of why one form of vision would be seen as interior and another as exterior. Crucially, as Crary suggests for the early nineteenth century and which I believe is just as applicable today, the body is quite capable of reincorporating the visual as a physiological, psychological, and discursive process. As a result, the opaqueness of the eye with regard to the mind is overcome by language, but never to the point where language and vision become one. This has led to a nostalgic desire for the eye to be dominant and an often-times paradoxical feeling that although language is posited as the royal road into consciousness, this is somehow really achieved through the act of seeing. The penchant for describing the activity of watching a film or television or any visual phenomenon as "reading" is the best example of this cultural ambiguity at work, although another and perhaps more forceful example is the hysteria around violent images, from the photographic to the televisual, which supposedly have a transformative effect on consciousness. The problem is in the way we view the mind, arbitrarily creating a material universe of physiology and cognition when that suits the events being described, and other times invoking a metaphysical notion of consciousness, within which there is no room for the body at all.

The exemplary pivot for these contradictions is found in descriptions of some visions as epiphanies—events outside the control of language or the eyes —and consciousness as inclusive, the inner both revealed and somehow still mysterious. To see then transcends the body of the visionary and stands as a reflection of a higher order, with the messages of sight originating in a universe outside of the control of the messenger. This theological impulse continues to exercise great influence, but now the gatekeeper is the media. Power resides yet again in a place beyond the control of those who are proposed as its victims. Yet the activities of seeing are never as innocent as that, never bound to the moment of sight within a temporal or historical vacuum. The body continually reasserts a primacy that even the most optimistic proponents of the image as virtual cannot do away with. The power of sight is not equivalent to the power of belief. Yet it is possible to work with the contradictions of the seen and in so doing rediscover levels of connection to experience and to the known, which the metaphors of distance cannot allow for. As much as we may try to design the future of our own perceptions and to instrumentalize the effects of the apparatuses we use, the power to control what we see remains a cultural myth. It is the strength of this myth that is so interesting, for it encourages us to continue to tell stories, to use images, to create new technologies devoted to seeing, hearing, and other forms of embodied experience.

I am interested in exploring spheres of thought and reflection not easily situated in rational mental activities (recreating then the paradoxes of control and the loss of it). What I find exciting about images is the sense of excess I get from my experience of them—the feeling we are dealing with an almost endless poesis, an eruption of meanings upon which we have to exercise restraint, into which we have to project structure and generate discourse, but from which much more is drawn and created than is "present." That is perhaps why much of the literature on images looks to dreams as evidence of an internal process at work not in the control of consciousness that may still refer to the images one watches or the experiences people have.[11] The effort to understand vision as a rational process and to therefore think of the mind as an ordered place, within which certain experiences fit and others don't, encourages the notion that "what" we see is directly linked to how we think.[12]

Yet, as I hope to point out, all the boundaries remain vague, and distinctions of internal and external, thought and vision are more often than not tools of interpretation. Seeing, as I will argue, is part play, part work. The various processes of substitution and replacement that constitute the activities of seeing are situated in the stories about the "eye." There is not one continuum within which sight operates; often many contradictory continua are involved. None of the relationships are linear, nor are they direct. The eye and the body are in constant conflict, with unity appearing to be just around the corner in a space and time with and without markers or signs. Human beings are at one and the same time many bodies and many eyes.

11. Miriam Hansen's comments on Hugo Münsterberg's early efforts (1916) to discuss the psychology of viewing point out that film images were seen as evidence of "the free play of mental experiences." This notion tied in with the assumption that filmic images encouraged the suspension of "spatio-temporal laws." This also meant that the imagination could be freed from its conventional parameters. In the final analysis Hansen concludes that Münsterberg's approach was too behavioral. His book remains one of the most interesting examples of the recurring difficulty that the analysis of images poses if the underlying model suggests that mind and sight are directly linked. Hugo Münsterberg, *The Film: A Psychological Study* (New York: D. Appleton, 1916; rpt. Dover, 1970), and Miriam Hansen, *Babel and Babylon: Spectatorship in American Silent Film* (Cambridge, Mass.: Harvard University Press, 1991).

12. Hansen explores the contradictions of this approach with respect to the cinema and maps out a different direction by using the arguments of Alexander Kluge and Oskar Negt (in large measure derived from Jürgen Habermas's work) in relation to the public sphere. I will comment in greater detail on this argument in chapter 4.

Seeing and feeling are not separate; both traverse and are traversed by desires. What does it mean to see one's own heart beating? Or to hypothesize the look of our skeletons beneath our skins? Or to gaze fondly at a lover? Why remove the other senses from sight? Do our memories dominate the present-tense sensations of seeing? And if they do, what do we mean by the present? Might it be the case that vision operates through a series of accidents (what is described as intuition)?

The crucial point here is vantage point. No one is ever, so to speak, beyond the mind that sees, and sight is not a property of mind to the exclusion of the consciousness that is seeing. There is as a result no objective moment within which postulates can be developed that are somehow outside of the many strategies we have to categorize and explain why one vision works and another doesn't.[13] For example, "to be seen" refers as much to a subjective state of mind as it does to the fact that someone is looking. An "Other" can watch this interplay of subjectivities, watch the interaction of two people, as both observer and participant. He or she operates as the third person of a "scene" bound by expectations and norms and conventions, desires and feelings not reducible to the looks being exchanged. In other words, the argument that people are objects of vision or that a look can objectify collapses these complex processes into a deterministic chain that eliminates the very vantage points needed to understand how and why a "look" can have so much power, so much effect. A relay of looks jumps between the physical act of seeing and processes of thought, between self and self-definition, along a speculative line that is never direct and that sustains itself with great difficulty. The many interdependent links between thought and vision cannot be divided into a set of easily describable parts. How can all the possible meanings attached to the look of one person at another be unpacked? And what happens when we are the third person, looking at a scene that we neither control nor influence? This question can also be asked with respect to images. What does it mean to look in on a scene we have not created but which we nevertheless want to witness and control?[14]

The Eye in the Photograph

There is an empty space between Georges Bataille's *Story of the Eye*[15] (which invests every look with fantasy and converts every fantasy into a series

13. I would refer the reader to Richard Rorty's analysis of these contradictions from a philosophical point of view in *Philosophy and the Mirror of Nature* (Princeton, N.J.: Princeton University Press, 1979).
14. An excellent essay by Hamid Naficy, "The Semiotics of Veiling and Vision: Women and the Cinema," *Arena* 1 (1993): 145–60, explores the different strategies of non-Western cultures to vision which Naficy relates to radically different conceptions of subjectivity.
15. Georges Bataille, *The Story of the Eye* (London: Penguin, 1982).

of images[16]) and the technological determinism of László Moholy-Nagy (a member of the Russian constructivist movement of the 1920s): "Photography, then, imparts a heightened, or [in so far as our eyes are concerned] increased, power of sight in terms of time and space. A plain, matter-of-fact enumeration of the specific photographic elements—purely technical, not artistic, elements—will be enough to enable us to divine the power latent in them, and prognosticate to what they lead."[17]

For Moholy-Nagy the activity of taking photographs and looking at them encourages the human eye to evolve into a new state, with radically new goals. Moholy-Nagy proposes close parallels between the technological language of photography and such terms as abstract seeing, exact seeing, rapid seeing, slow seeing, intensified seeing, penetrative seeing, simultaneous seeing, and distorted seeing. To him these terms exemplify new configurations of human sight generated out of the relationship of technology and human activity. The camera, so to speak, is woven into the eye, and it is Moholy-Nagy's contention that the eye must change as a result. A direct line is established between picture-taking, the image, vision (as response), and thought. This is in part why Moholy-Nagy privileges the scientific importance of photography and trivializes its artistic role. In contrast to Bataille, for whom the word and the image are located in the imaginary and for whom the imaginary is, so to speak, located in the eye, Moholy-Nagy seeks truth as the epistemological grounding for what is acceptable and what isn't acceptable *as* image: "the real photographer has a great social responsibility. He has to work with these given technical means which cannot be accomplished by any other method. This work is the exact reproduction of everyday facts, without distortion or adulteration. This means that he must work for sharpness and accuracy. The standard of value in photography must be measured, not merely by photographic esthetics, but the human-social intensity of the optical representation" (Moholy-Nagy 56).

This quote must be understood as one of the key assumptions in the description of photography as a medium, the melding of scientific and aesthetic

---

16. Bataille's comments on pages 69–70 of *The Story of the Eye* as a postscript to the narrative are suggestive. He sees two photographs and is able to recall an important moment in his life. This is followed by further detail on his past, including the fact that his father was blind when Georges was conceived. The photographs recede into the background to be replaced by more and more complex levels of fantasy. Jean-Luc Nancy has commented on the meaning of Bataille to him. It is worth quoting from since it comes very close to my own feelings about the communication of meaning through images: "Bataille immediately communicates to me that pain and that pleasure which result from the impossibility of communicating anything at all without touching the limit where all meaning spills out of itself like a simple ink stain on a word, on the word meaning. This spilling and this ink are the ruin of theories of communication, conventional chatter which promotes reasonable exchange and does nothing but obscure violence, treachery, lies, while leaving the power of unreason no chance of being measured." Jean-Luc Nancy, "Exscription," *Yale French Review* 78, ed. Allan Stoekl, (1990); 47.

17. Richard Kostelanetz, ed., *Moholy-Nagy* (New York: Praeger, 1970), 52.

concerns around ideas of representation, the attempted fusion of technology and the eye. Moholy-Nagy anticipated the pivotal role of photography in generating scopic regimes that would validate cultural presumptions of truth. He could not have anticipated the way photography would evolve as a distinctive marker for temporal shifts, as an integral and strategic respondent and creator of historical discourses. Yet he would have been aware that he was in fact creating a context for the photographic image that locates its truth value in the power of its reproductive aesthetic and its instrumental role. And he would have known that he was following the Cartesian imperative to rid the world of its optical illusions, to find truth in the visible, and to make the visible truthful. For Moholy-Nagy, the mental, the physical, and the real gain their strength from the image. The image becomes that schematic point of reference allowing technology to transcend the inconsistencies and weaknesses of the human eye. His was as much a technical as a pedagogical imperative. The aim was to use the image to teach some basic truths about the human condition, to strip away those categories of seeing which the "eye" of everyday life imposes on human subjectivity. In positing such a direct link between knowing and seeing, Moholy-Nagy makes use of a model of mind that enframes knowledge as visual and that constructs the mind as a mirror of the world around it. That model continues to resonate with some power in present-day discussions of images, particularly with respect to the role of images in the media.[18]

The reasons why Moholy-Nagy's approach would become culturally dominant will become clearer in a moment. Just as there is a need to dialogue across the divide separating Crary from Edelman, so there is a need to examine the potential links and conflicts between Moholy-Nagy, Georges Bataille, and Gerald Edelman. Bataille was as obsessed with images and vision as Moholy-Nagy, and as concerned with the cultural and social role of new technologies as his contemporaries in the art and architecture movements of the 1920s and 1930s. In a statement not dissimilar to the claims made by Edelman in the book from which I quoted, Bataille says the following: "What you are stems from the activity which links the innumerable elements which constitute you to the intense communication of these elements among themselves. These are contagions of energy, of movement, of warmth, or transfers of elements, which constitute inevitably the life of your organized being."[19]

To Bataille, consciousness is governed by autonomy and indeterminacy. Edelman, coming from a neurobiological perspective, says that "for systems that categorize in the manner that brains do, there is macroscopic indeterminacy" (Edelman 169). The rather vulgar materialism of Moholy-Nagy pales in

18. Joel Snyder dissects the ideology that underpins this conception of the image in "Picturing Vision," *The Language of Images*, ed. W. J. T. Mitchell (Chicago: University of Chicago Press, 1980), 219–46.
19. Georges Bataille, *Inner Experience* (Albany: State University of New York Press, 1988), 94.

the light of these debates. To Edelman, all of the various categories that we use to explain consciousness, memory, and vision are not in any way fixed. The all-too-easy relations of causality and effect built into notions of technological determinism fall by the wayside. There are levels of unpredictability built into all of this, which as Edelman suggests, are "never free of affect" (Edelman 170), and in much the same way, Bataille suggests: "Life is never situated at a particular point: it passes from one point to another (or from multiple points to other points), like a current or like a sort of streaming of electricity. Thus, there where you would like to grasp your timeless substance, you encounter only a slipping, only the poorly coordinated play of your perishable elements" (Bataille 1988, 94).

Knowledge, and our awareness of what we know, generally exceed the parameters of the models we put in place to explain relations of understanding and perception. Edelman balances biological and scientific arguments around consciousness with an equal if not greater concern for subjectivity, for interiority. He avoids the mechanistic approach of Moholy-Nagy by emphasizing the role of time, memory, and history (Edelman 168). It is this contrast between mechanistic and nonmechanistic strategies of explanation with regard to consciousness that is marginalized by Moholy-Nagy. But this in itself is part of his faith in technology, in the potential of machines to contribute to human progress. Increasingly, as the camera eye has come to stand for, if not stand in for, the human eye, the perspective of Moholy-Nagy has taken root as one of the fundamental assumptions of industrially advanced societies.[20]

Death in Bosnia

In a recent photograph from the *New York Times* we see a Bosnian soldier facing the camera and begging for his life. He is a young man. He has curly hair and a smooth face. His arms are outstretched. Behind him stands a Serbian soldier, rifle cocked and ready. As the caption "Death in Bosnia" suggests, this man's pleas were answered with his own death. He is staring at the camera as if it will provide him with refuge, as if the photographer will somehow intervene. The photograph cannot anticipate history, but the caption can. The prisoner pushes against the camera—he is pleading for help. Yet without the caption, his "story" and the interpretations we could make of it would be en-

20. See Merritt Roe Smith, "Technological Determinism in American Culture," in *Does Technology Drive History? The Dilemma of Technological Determinism*, ed. Merritt Roe Smith and Leo Marx (Cambridge, Mass.: MIT Press, 1994), 1–36, as well as Leo Marx, "The Idea of Technology and Postmodern Pessimism," 237–58 in the same volume. The latter essay describes of the rise and fall of technological utopianism and the shift from an optimistic to a pessimistic view, as a further, but more complex form, of technological determinism.

tirely circumstantial. In this case, the written word acts as an arbiter for the event and tries to intervene in our interpretation. But even as I say this, the photograph slips away. This anonymous man's torment is as silent as the paper it was printed on. It would take an imaginative projection on my part to overcome the gaps created by his death as written and as image.

It is this tension between image and word and the spaces between language and the photograph that Moholy-Nagy wanted to overcome, but which remains a continual question mark with respect to all images. Nevertheless, I can, by an act of imagination, partially place myself in that man's position. It is this act that allows me to at least think I can feel his fear and pain. My argument remains ambiguous because I have simply taken the image and used it to my own advantage. Whatever applications I want to make of the knowledge I have about the Bosnian war can be invoked in an arbitrary fashion. This instability is a source of tension. It drives the image into a sphere quite different from the original moment when it was taken. What then is the value of my appropriation of the image? In Moholy-Nagy's terms, the eye, which he saw as an optical instrument, and the technology of photography, which he championed along with other formalists of the early 1920s, made the photographic print the result of a superior process of vision. The frailties and ambiguities that I have just described can be transcended through the proper use of the technology, he suggested (a pedagogical role as important to the formalists as their experimentation with aesthetics), and the contradictions of subjectivity can be overcome.[21]

"In a photograph a person's history is buried as if under a layer of snow."[22] The antipositivist stance of Siegfried Kracauer, commented upon by Miriam Hansen,[23] stands in stark contrast to the ideas of Moholy-Nagy. Kracauer distinguishes between the photograph of a person and the memory-image. The latter is what is left when the photograph is viewed outside of the time when it was taken. This distinction is a crucial one. It temporalizes the photograph and in so doing heightens the role of discourse: what is said and what isn't said about images. No photograph escapes the contradictions and potential excitement of temporal dislocation. There are so many movements in space and time, so many moments within which history must be rewritten, that the conceit of truth must be understood not as an ontological basis for interpretation, but as a site where memory is reinvigorated, even when memories slip from fact into

21. Abigail Solomon-Godeau comments on these issues in her article, "The Armed Vision Disarmed: Radical Formalism from Weapon to Style," in *The Contest of Meaning*, ed. Richard Bolton (Cambridge, Mass.: MIT Press, 1992), 86–110.
22. Siegfried Kracauer, "Photography," tr. Thomas Y. Levin, *Critical Inquiry* 19.3 (1993): 426.
23. Miriam Hansen, "With Skin and Hair: Kracauer's Theory of Film, Marseille 1940," *Critical Inquiry* 19.3 (1993): 437–69.

fiction and back. The pleasures of seeing in this instance are invested with desire—to make the memory real, to generate truth, to manufacture a narrative.
The truth becomes a metaphor just as quickly as the image disguises its sudden
transformative power. The snow melts, and there is a dissolution of memory,
although the photograph remains suggestively encouraging—as if no historical
moment will ever again escape its simultaneous role as event and image, memory and potential arena for debate.

Vivian Sobchack captures these ambiguities: "In the still photograph, time
and space are abstractions. Although the image has a presence, it neither partakes of nor describes the present. Indeed, the photograph's fascination is that
it is a figure of transcendental time made available against the ground of a lived
and finite temporality. Although included in our experience of the present, the
photograph transcends both our immediate present and our lived experience
of temporality because it exists for us as never engaged in the activity of *becoming*."[24] At the same time, Sobchack makes the claim that the photographic
image is in itself meaningless: "it does not act *within* itself to choose its meaning, to diacritically mark it off" (Sobchack 60). Clearly, no object can ever engage in marking off its own boundaries with respect to meaning and communication. Sobchack moves from this "emptiness" to the conclusion that "like
a transcendental consciousness, the photograph as a transcendental structure
posits the abstraction of a *moment* but has no *momentum*" (Sobchack 60). Yet,
to begin with, the photograph is never like consciousness. There is no basis of
possible comparison here. Temporal frameworks cannot transcend subjectivity,
and subjectivity is never, so to speak, within the photograph. Although her
work is far more sophisticated at a theoretical and historical level than that of
Moholy-Nagy, Sobchack nevertheless falls prey to some of the same problems.
The many levels of mediation that go into the production, creation, and interpretation of photographs suggest a great deal about how we categorize and
make judgments about sight. But images are not the markers for this, not the
place within which this process drives toward a result. The tensions here don't
resolve themselves into some sort of ontological sphere that produces either a
radically different subjectivity or a dramatic shift in perceptual ability. The
gaps are enormous, and they are characterized by an attribution of power to
the image process that cannot be dismissed, since at a cultural level this process
is what continues to legitimize the role of images as tools of communication.

It is also important to note that the contrasting positions of Kracauer and
Moholy-Nagy are located in Kracauer's desire to challenge the Modernist tendency to search out and then catalogue the supposedly inherent characteristics
of any medium. This debate, which is crucial to practitioners, situates meaning

24. Vivian Sobchack, *The Address of the Eye: A Phenomenology of Film Experience*
(Princeton, N.J.: Princeton University Press, 1992), 59.

in the properties of the technology being used and is in part another aspect of the drive toward an ontological approach. I will comment on this point in greater detail during my discussion of film and television.

Let me suggest that photographic images neither illustrate thought, nor are thoughts illustrated by the pictorial. Photographic images are silent, blind, unseeing. They don't listen to us nor do they change when viewed. They are not the source of a magical emanation from which the seeing eye draws inspiration. They rarely display the hand of the photographer who has created them, and for the most part leave no traces of the chemistry that has produced them. This is not simply a matter of arbitrariness, of meanings lost and then gained, of part-whole relations floundering in confusion. Photographs cannot rob the subjects they portray, since as I will try to discuss below, photographs never have subjects—men, women, and children—"imprinted" upon them. What is in play here is the very language used to describe and explain the "sight" of an image: the categories, words, and labels that have been applied to the miniature worlds we peer into, anthropomorphize, recreate.

These tiny strips of paper contain within them the history and residual consequences of post-Renaissance cultural activity, a movement from notions of artifice in painting to assumptions of transparency in photography (the machine produces what we see and not the cameraperson). The photographic image is not the platonic world of illusions, that place and space within which the real is somehow transformed into a shadow or worse, the shadow becomes the real. Like a theatrical stage, the photographic image foregrounds the mise-en-scène of a hypothetical world, but unlike the stage, everything is reduced until what is left are pieces of paper, flattened, unmoving, which subsist on our yells and screams, on our invocations to the image to speak and on our desire to be heard and to be seen. The *"enjeu"* here is desire, which can remain embedded and unexpressed, but for which no fantasy is the final outlet and for which no image or discourse provides a simple or complete answer. The hypothetical world made possible by images is not a place within which viewers control what they see. Rather, and as has become clearer with the rapid growth of digital images, the question is, what do we mean by viewer and why the focus on sight? There is a strong argument for disengaging the term "viewer" from its conventional and cultural roots, at least temporarily, in order to explore the complexity of hypotheses about the experience of images.[25]

There are moments within which fantasies operate as if the very notion of

25. Kaja Silverman uses Jonathan Crary, Jacques Lacan, and a film by Hroun Farocki (*Bilder der Welt und Inschrift des Krieges*) to examine some of the problems that I am referring to. Silverman offers a particularly creative analysis of Lacan's distinction between the gaze and the eye in order to reexamine the role of visual apparatuses such as the camera in theories of representation. Kaja Silverman, "What is a Camera? or: History in the Field of Vision," *Discourse* 15.3 (1993): 3–56.

sight seems redundant, as if our preconceptions that to see means to understand will dissolve in the face of the theories needed to explain why the obvious never seems so simple. We end up blaming the object or the image for what *we have done to it* (projection) and then feel guilt for importing feelings or sensations or thoughts we cannot control (as if the outside and the inside have become one). This phenomenon suggests that the activities of seeing are never as static as the image itself proposes. In fact, the opposite is true: the ephemeral aspects of seeing are themselves built into the image. The many different layers operative here are as personal as they are socially and culturally constituted.[26]

Out of Focus: David Koresh

Waco, Texas—Spring 1993. The image of God is only as strong as "his word." Reading from the Bible, David Koresh prepares his followers for death with pictures of a world gone mad. (The images of Koresh lecturing his followers fill the television screen. In the background, a voice-over describes Koresh's power over his audience. The images come to us via an Australian television network.) The only place of order is Koresh's universe, into which believers must plunge, and from which there is no exit. The mind here fits into the geography of a Faustian suburbia in which all pictures become literal, where the word, the thought, and the image turn into a blazing inferno of oneness. The mass death in Waco comes at a time when what we say and what we believe can only be united and dispersed through the various uses we make of images. But this is not simulation; rather, these are images quickly punctured, flimsy, fragile, like the wooden buildings Koresh burned in a final act of defiance against the police and the world. Koresh's words may have worked to ensure his vision. Yet, it was clear as we "watched" image after image of Koresh taunting his interviewers that he was performing the role of cult figure. He enjoyed his notoriety. He built on the foundations his fame created for him. His words were those of an image, and that made him all the more dangerous since he saw no distinction between word and image, between hallucination and truth. When he spoke, it was as if he was in a trance. This trancelike state made him even more powerful to his followers, who attributed the trance to god, who saw Koresh as the conduit for a deity's words. They energized him to believe that the words were divine, and he in turn took their worship as a sign that god had in fact spoken to him. How can this reciprocity be broken?

26. Martin Jay discusses these issues in an early part of his new book. Martin Jay, *Downcast Eyes: The Denigration of Vision in Twentieth Century French Thought* (Berkeley and Los Angeles: University of California Press, 1993), 23-25.

It is, as with all images, built on a flimsy foundation, but that only strengthened Koresh, encouraging him to become larger than life, an enlargement.

As the fire spread, the first images on television were telephoto pictures of buildings in flames. The distance and the heat produced a wavy, opaque effect—the dissolution and recreation of the image—a loss of substance, as if the crematorium were the figment of somebody's bizarre imagination. More than anything else, the idea, let alone the reality, of mass suicide could not be brought into the status of a "real" image. Rather, as the telephoto suggests, the event makes distance essential, because these "sights" are not for human eyes. They represent ideas and events which can't be viewed—the cult as a laboratory for a culture that has lost its ability to "see." The telling irony here is the almost medieval belief in a world controlled not by rationality and human choice, but by deities. Any claim can be made for what cannot be seen, and the unseen can act as a dark shadow harassing those who disbelieve.

The photographs reproduced in newspapers the following day were also "out of focus." The justification for such restricted access was the heat of the inferno and the fears of police that the fire might injure journalists who wanted to get closer. At the same time, the photographs were surrounded by articles puzzled at the decision of the cultists to die. Death cannot be shown though it is not without some irony that NBC put on an instant fictional retelling of the history of Waco a few months later—evidence of the need to reconstruct, to tell a story of mass death in the present tense. This effort at fictionalization was not an accidental recuperation. It can be thought of as cultural analysis. It was an effort to move from the event to an interpretation, to find subjectivity where none had been apparent—a ritual way of taking control of events that seemed to be unintelligible. It was also a strategic response to the darkness of Waco, to its invisibility.

This was an event that seemed to be so close that it required the dream, the daydream, the painting or the screen. More than anything, NBC transformed Waco from an image into a symbolic construct and in the process validated the need for the poetic, for the fictional. Waco finally lost its specificity but its historical importance became clearer. What would happen if the invocations by religious extremists were the expression of precisely the mythic underpinnings of civilized America? What are the social implications of the claim to be God? Or even to be the messenger of God? It is easy to disavow, to dismiss, to dispel the role of the religious Right in American life. It is much more difficult to find the images that will reveal its weaknesses, its dependence on metaphor, its desire to save people in the same way that David Koresh did. So, although the firestorm was more about the death of innocent children than about the parents who fathered and mothered them, it was also the clearest manifestation of the pitfalls that can occur when symbolic hypotheses move from the realm of theory to practice.

Rodney King: Community and Communication

Rodney King. The fury at King's first trial—at the acquittal of four officers whose actions had been captured on video was based on a presumption of guilt even before the trial had taken place. Putting aside for the moment any consideration of truth, why was the video image so effective? This question was certainly not asked by the vast majority of viewers who rioted or by the media in general. The crucial point is not whether the event happened but how to interpret it. Arguments against cause and effect seem to fall apart here, as if earlier and widely discredited theories of the media as a hypodermic needle could indeed be justified and validated by the intensity of the rage at the verdict. But that, crucially, is the paradox. The verdict, although steeped in the contradictions created by the presence of the video, relocated the image in a process far more complex than the television transmission of the beating—the crucial differences between information and communication.

Communication is social and community based. There is of course a symbiotic relationship between communication and information. But there is one crucial difference. Information can exist, so to speak, without being placed into the public sphere. In other words, the books lined up in the stacks of a library retain their status as information until they are used. When a book is taken out of the library a communicative space is opened up, but even this remains hypothetical and contingent until the book is read, glanced at, talked about, and so forth. Of course the book was produced in the context of a social and public space, and its purpose is communicative. But I am emphasizing the importance here of use—the pragmatics of the movement from written word to public debate.

The Rodney King video was information until it was broadcast. Once it hit the airwaves the transformation was immediate. As with most images it was used in many different ways. Information can be highly codified but communication cannot.[27] The broadcasting of images encourages interpretation and inevitably increases the circulation of many different viewpoints. This further develops the need to generate consensus and to find a way of accommodating differences. But if information and communication are collapsed, the very idea of consensus seems impossible. The truth seems to be "in" the information and not in relations of communication and understanding.

A "viewing" of the video images establishes the environment and the possible premises for an act of communication, but it is not the translation of the

27. These issues are debated in great detail in Umberto Eco, *Interpretation and Overinterpretation* (Cambridge, England: Cambridge University Press, 1992).

codifications that were built into the shooting of the video or its subsequent broadcast (within the context of news shows). What we are dealing with is a variety of interpretations within the framework of a subjective context that is both community based and individual. Consequently, the argument is not whether Rodney King was beaten (information), but to what degree and with how much intensity the communication of the event would be appropriated (for many different reasons) by the communities and individuals who watched.[28]

The level of appropriation will inevitably vary from community to community and from individual to individual. The degree of variance will depend on sometimes predictable and often-times unpredictable circumstances. The interpretive strategy chosen to deal with these contradictions will contribute to the formation of community and to its potential dissolution. At the same time it is possible for a highly localized communicative framework to be created not necessarily dependent on the original historical processes at work in the event or in the creation of the images about the event.

This movement beyond a "source"—this dispersion—makes it very difficult to account for intentional relationships, to specify cause when effect seems so apparent and visible. The term that helps to explain this is diffusion. Diffusion spreads the subjects of communication around an ever-widening public sphere that actively legitimizes and delegitimizes itself as a variety of hypotheses and actions are tested in the community. Some fail and some succeed. Clearly, as the buildings burned in Los Angeles we were witnessing a rage that unified, albeit briefly, a community whose experience of oppression left it with few alternatives. The word *riot* tends to suggest homogeneity of purpose, combined with loss of rationality. But, another way of "seeing" this event would be to understand the violence as a concrete expression of Rodney King's dilemma. He knew that he had been beaten, and his body displayed the results. He watched the video as further evidence of police brutality on the natural assumption that information and experience combine into communication and truth, as well as forming a base for understanding why events unfold as they do. Although this rather formulaic approach has all of the appearance of logic to it, the paradox is that truth communicated through the image doesn't gain legitimacy unless there is some consensus to back it up. What was so frustrating for the black community in L.A. was the sense that the truth had been

28. A special issue of the magazine *High Performance* elicited the responses of over one hundred artists, writers, teachers, children, parents, and gangmembers to the Rodney King verdict and the subsequent uprising in Los Angeles. This is precisely one of the ways in which consensus is built and through which communities develop a more global understanding of their role and potential. *High Performance* 15, Special Issue, "The Verdict and the Violence," 1992.

validated through the video, and that this consensus was being denied its legitimacy. The gaps here are enormous and deeply scarring. The question is, was the image a valid starting point from the outset?

The foregoing may not explain why the Rodney King verdict went against common sense logic (and reflected the racist agenda of the defense, as well as the confusion and racism of the jury), but it suggests that information can *always* be manipulated to suit goals and assumptions that have little to do with the image. If the image is taken as the *only* arbiter of the process, chances are that we will continue to confuse information and communication as if they transparently reflect the same level of organization and structure, the same intent and meaning.

Debates of a similar kind arose when photography was first used in trials as evidence of a crime. Many questions were raised, not the least of which was possible tampering with the image. The point here is that the image can be challenged in a courtroom to the same degree and using similar premises to the challenge thrown out at a witness. Similar levels of subjectivity can be suggested. And as the transcripts of the first King trial reveal, the credibility of the image can be attacked. Essentially, the defense toyed with questions surrounding information and communication by introducing so many levels of interpretation to the image that the jury was dissuaded from taking the beating at face value. Yet this is precisely the paradox and the motor force of communicative processes through images. They can be taken at face value or not. In the final analysis, a jury could not have settled this question and consequently, it was left up to the community to prevail—a necessary yet brutal form of popular justice.[29]

The Eye and the Ear: In Time

Often, to speak of photographic images is to say, "there was my mother," or "I looked beautiful as a child." The plasticity and the physicality of the image collapses. Distinctions between memory and sight and photographic print temporarily melt into each other. This entanglement is cultural and is also representative of a history (histories) of desire, a history that links the invention of photography to the legitimation of the image as a tool of communication and that prioritizes directness, the explicit, the transparent, as formless expressions of truth. In this entanglement is also one of the roots of the nostalgia that haunts relations between family imagery, photography, and memory. As the plasticity of the photograph recedes into the background, its

29. For further detail on the Rodney King debate see, Judith Butler, "Endangered/ Endangering: Schematic Racism and White Paranoia," *Reading Rodney King/Reading Urban Uprising*, ed. Robert Gooding-Williams (New York: Routledge, 1993), 15–22.

transitory nature becomes more and more important. It takes an act of will to keep all of these connections from simply splaying off into many different directions. Because of this, photographs are always in transition and at the same time they are held in tow. This process, this tension partly results from the manner in which photographs come from the past and must be converted into the present. Artifice transforms the photographic image into a representation needing little connection to the original experience from which the photograph was drawn.

David Freedberg has commented upon the long-standing belief in the power of the image to both inspire and pervert (as if without form). Thus, well before the invention of photography, the image played a paradoxical role: as information, as an icon of worship, and as a vehicle for the imagination. This history was most poignantly played out in what Freedberg describes as the *tavoletta*.

> What comfort could anyone conceivably offer to a man condemned to death, in the moments prior to his execution? Any word or action would seem futile, and it would be as nought beside the inner resources or human weakness of the condemned person. But in Italy between the fourteenth and seventeenth centuries, brotherhoods were set up to offer a kind of solace; and the instruments of consolation were small painted images. . . . Each *tavoletta* was painted on both sides. On one side was a scene from the Passion of Christ; on the other side, a martyrdom that was more or less relevant to the punishment to be meted out to the prisoner. This martyrdom the brothers would "relate" in some inspirational way to the actual plight of the prisoner as they comforted him in his cell or prison chapel during the night before his morning execution. On the next day, two members of the brotherhood would hold one of the pictures before the condemned man's face all the way to the place of execution.[30]

It is thus crucial to think about the attribution of "a transparent effect" to photography through a general cultural history of images. Photography may have appeared as a new technology during a significant moment of the Industrial Revolution, but the insertion of photography into the history of images must be examined within the carefully defined parameters of its relationship to painting, for example. The shift in mediums did not necessarily change the assumptions governing the use and interpretation of images. Photography added its technology to the cultural spheres of influence already in place. The dynamics of the movement from painting to photography may have enhanced the attribution of power to the photograph (though this was not the case in the first instance), but this power could not have been proposed without the firm yet contradictory beliefs and suspicions that had always surrounded im-

30. David Freedberg, *The Power of Images: Studies in the History and Theory of Response* (Chicago: University of Chicago Press, 1989), 5–6.

ages. As much as painting changed because of photography, so too did cultural assumptions about the image. More and more it was the case that painters and photographers had to take responsibility for their creations. In a sense they had to show intention when it wasn't clearly there (the idea of the snapshot) and justify their choice of subject in order to prove that artistry was behind the impulse to photograph. In a stylistic sense this imperative drifted into painting through the impressionists and post-impressionists who became bolder and bolder in their use of paint strokes. The residues of their artistic work were imprinted on the picture and came to have as much meaning as the subjects they painted. What interests me is the formal and historical reciprocity between photography and painting, a reciprocity governed by notions of intention and artistic control. It took until the middle of the twentieth century for photography to overcome the stigma of its technological base. This would not have been possible without the advent of the cinema.

Although there is also the history of art photography, modernist and post-modernist, that tries to foreground itself as aesthetic practice (e.g., photomontage) and thus reveal its plasticity, these are creative engagements that see themselves framed through an oppositional struggle with culturally dominant conceptions of the image. The problem is that these dominant conceptions are grounded in discursive practices which link language and sight as if the two processes are not always and inevitably contesting each other, as if, although inextricably bound, they are not also the site of ambiguity and confusion. There may be no better time than now (with virtual technologies inching closer to realization) to rethink *what* we mean when we talk about pictures and what we are capable of *saying* about the pictures we create. One of my aims then, is to discuss strategies for renaming and redescribing (thus reinterpreting), not only the pictures themselves, but circular processes of interaction, the relationships between images, thought, language, and subjectivity.

Images are bound to the perceptual and cognitive activities of subjects. Although images have a material existence outside of the use made of them, it is through an examination of the interactive processes of comprehension that we will gain a deeper understanding of them. This understanding shifts the analysis of images toward the human body and away from the reductive linearity of "effect" and "impact." It also moves the examination of vision into the contingent sphere of memory and desire.[31] We need to look "beyond" the pictorial, so to speak, and in so doing reopen the boundaries, the very geography within which we travel as we examine the images which surround us.

Human memory doesn't operate within the restrictions of photographic time, just as consciousness displays no immediate temporal reflection of what

---

31. See Jonathan Crary's discussion of the shift in nineteenth-century thinking with respect to vision and materiality in "Unbinding Vision," *October* 68 (1994): 21–44.

we say when we talk about it. What is described as that place within the human psyche—the inner—is a mixture of sensations, feelings, thoughts, desires, abstractions, all of which can be isolated by language into discrete units, none of which can be described in isolation of the other. It is this symbiosis (and the organicity that underlies it) that links experience with learning, but makes the translation between experience and learning neither solely dependent on language nor somehow outside of the linguistic, neither of the image nor beyond it. Efforts to quantify human vision into units or to create normative rules to constrain or funnel visuality into a particular set of categories (e.g., proposals that the human mind operates like a computer) cannot account for the complexity of memory, its arbitrariness, its unpredictability.

The "outside" of language has always been described as imagistic. In poetry, for example, words combine to produce an image, though this is clearly an idea of image that must be translated into prose in order to make sense. Obviously the idea has no firm location in space. It is made tangible through language, yet it feels as if it has come from somewhere else. This is often the feeling I get when reading the poetry of Elizabeth Bishop or T. S. Eliot. I locate my feelings in what I say about what they have said, yet the process itself exceeds the parameters of language, theirs and mine. This excess repeats itself with images never fully present through the language of description and interpretation—the boundaries of the image dissolve in the face of what is said about them. There is a wonderful unpredictability here that overwhelms the specificity of what I say (the desire to point to a picture and transparently link meaning and language), which potentially transforms every encounter between images and myself into a novel situation. How then do we learn to deal with this endless reiteration of the new? Is this what encourages us to learn and unlearn the lessons brought to us by what we watch? Or must we find a dramatically different way of describing viewing and spectatorship?

A balance has to be struck here between the way the mind is modeled in language (usually through such words as *reflection* and *representation*) and a recognition of the complexity of consciousness. Any effort to somehow reduce this complexity because it will be easier to unpack the often contradictory relationships we have with images (seduction and rejection), simplifies if not elides the interactive processes through which we categorize and organize our experience(s) of the visual. Of course the cognitive figures in here as one element in the perceptual, one of many stresses and strains between the operations of consciousness and our interpretation of the results. So varied and interactive are the interconnected strategies that we use to make sense of what we see, that it is no wonder the perceptual is drowned out in a chorus of words. But to see an object, for example, does not mean that its "name" or its properties have simply been translated from vision to language. It is precisely this relationship that has to be made, brought into a coherent structure through which the sensuous, that which is "felt," can be labeled, even if it is described as a "sight." Linguistic categories are a necessary and integral component of this relationship, but they are not the objects per se. Neither are they representations in the fixed sense of signifier-signified relations. The simple duality of object and sight falls apart here, as do all the other binary formulas that transform vision into a function of the perceptual or the linguistic.[32]

The dualism of viewer and image is one of the problems because it forces us to look in often oppositional and divisive terms at a staggered process. It suggests a movement in stages across a horizontal axis toward the visual, toward that which can be understood developmentally, as if consciousness is itself some sort of computational network within which there are connections soldered together by experience. The irony is that we know so little about how or even why our minds are capable of creatively engaging with so many different, sometimes recognizable and sometimes unrecognizable processes. We may need the dualism to make sense of sight and to confirm to ourselves that our minds are not the center of the universe, but we cannot continue to experiment with cognition as if it can be packaged into neatly constructed modules within which learning, vision, and language are essentially treated as homologous, parts organized into a puzzle, the whole already known well before the process has begun.

It may be more useful to think of the relations between mind and vision as a series of hypotheses leading to destinations that randomly connect and disconnect, constructs more dependent on temporal distortion than linearity. The time of vision may not link up to the time of thought or understanding. All of these points in the process may be endlessly divisible and the possible combinations of meaning impossible to count. This richness has been subsumed under the endless rubrics of mechanistic and Cartesian dualisms: perceiver and perceived, sight and object, mind and body, signification and representation. In most cases the sensate body disappears into the head as when the syntax of a language is equated to the structure of the mind or when perception is described as a labyrinth of mirrors, as if the visual cortex reproduces the objects transmitted from the eye to the brain. To some degree these are popular conceptions necessary perhaps to legitimate the operations of the visual as a function of experience and mind, but great care must be taken in how these are applied to the tasks of interpretation and the analysis of images.

We move through an infinite number of *hypotheses* about the visual at the same time as we try and apprehend what we see. We visualize an object in many different and often unpredictable ways. We create and recreate maps, which themselves may already have been transformed by thought and fantasy

32. For an interesting discussion of these problems see the anti-Kantian work of Richard Wolheim, *The Mind and Its Depths* (Cambridge: Harvard University Press, 1993).

and dream. This produces a sometimes chaotic interplay between the basic elements of a process which we don't have to understand to engage in. Yet these are not processes lacking coherence as a result of all the variables; quite the contrary, we are able to temporarily unify the parts and in so doing articulate defined moments in which certain categories of explanation work or in which an interpretive strategy is acceptable. At each moment, if we grant the temporal a central place, a variety of new and potentially radical associations arise that yet again transform what had seemingly been fixed.

Crucially, it is also our memories that are in play here. They are not slots into which all of this fits—memories of the visual and the oral lose their way, the many paths of memory and thought diverge almost as soon as they are articulated. The gaps in almost all of these instances arise because the conditions under which thought, vision, and hearing operate must continuously be rethought, and we are not necessarily in charge of the rethinking. It is like an endlessly expanding amoeba within which there are so many layers that no one part can survive without the other, and all of the parts constitute the organism—any one piece is the whole, though all await the consequences of reorganization and the many unpredictable combinations giving life to the process.

On the surface it appears as if there is order and constraint. The postmodern term that begins to describe this is *hypertext*. Even this concept, which aficionados of computerized technologies see as a liberating jump from linearity, is dependent upon fixed categories which an interpreter moves around in an infinite number of ways. In speaking about vision we are dealing with a structure that defies patterns of organization because it is constantly in motion and nevertheless remains functional. The best way to think about this is to question what we mean by the word *awareness*. An awareness provides us with a subjective sense of knowledge without the objective constraints of codification. To be aware may or may not refer to an understanding of an object or a thought. It is a way of generalizing about perceptions through an interplay of interpretive strategies. To be aware of the body allows us to generalize while resisting specificity. These are sensations of wholeness without the precision of location. The body knows, yet it is difficult to explain what this means. At all stages we can replace the body with the mind or generate a metaphor in which both are envelopes within each other. This flexibility means that the categories of knowledge with which we normally operate are never fixed, nor are the subjective evaluations of these categories a simple duplication of the thoughts or events we attach to them. If, to some degree, consciousness organizes *itself*, then notions of subjectivity are in constant flux even as we argue with the process of categorization, and even more so as we face the consequences of shifts that we cannot explain.

It is the paradox of our use of images that we attach to them a quality of concreteness which our own thought processes about them contradict. This paradox then raises the question as to whether we can attribute communicative properties to the image, whether what we describe as "code" or meaning—an object with characteristics and its own explanatory power—refers more properly to a *projection* by consciousness onto a world in need of categories and explanation. Although the first few chapters of this book do not deal with this idea, I explore the conceptual basis of projection, both as a way of thinking and as a way of seeing and hearing, in chapters 4 and 5. We need to replace the term *image* with *projection* in order to more fully implicate ourselves in the multifarious ways we design, redesign, and recategorize the world around us. There has to be an understanding here of the rich creativity at the heart of cognition and of the profound unpredictability of perceptual and intellectual processes. I am not returning, in this argument or in those following, to a nineteenth-century vision of human consciousness as the center of the world. Any effort on my part to deny the empirical reality of history or the complex ground on which the social polity is built would go against the basic thrust of my discussion. I am however trying to recapture a way of thinking about subjectivity that will make allowances for the impact of intentionality on the way images are conceptualized. I am therefore looking for the authority in authorship, while at one and the same time proposing that intentionality is itself a projection, a desire and most importantly a crucial element in the maintenance of certain forms of subjectivity and identity.

The Mirror Can See Forever

Imagine yourself in a rather narrow hallway with two large, although not life-size mirrors. The mirrors are on opposite walls, one slightly higher than the other. Until you step in between the two mirrors they reflect each other, ad infinitum. Then, when you interrupt this timeless stand-off, you become part of it. Your image travels through you from one mirror to the other in increasingly smaller frames that nevertheless retain the original proportions of your body to the mirror. This happens even though the image you see is always partial and your body fragmented.

You have not created nor can you change the mirroring effect, although you must interact with the mirrors to confirm whether or not your "vision" has happened. Metaphorically, "you" are split into many parts even as you remain visible. Questions of identity are not answered or constrained by this process but are constantly being developed and redeveloped (constructed, deconstructed, reconstructed?) Words such as *construction* point toward hierarchies, layers, bound together by architectural design, a scaffolding of parts linked for a purpose and once complete, seemingly beyond change. Yet the self in the mirror, now receding into the background, exists in both a time-bound and a timeless continuum. The reflection-effect is stable, but this is precisely why the subjective relationship to it is so unstable. The body floats in an ethereal universe, just out of grasp and thus outside of the architectural configuration which she or he inhabits. This contradictory flow, being inside and a witness looking *in* from the outside, destabilizes the self in the mirror and puts the status of the mirror itself in question. Neither the words reflection nor representation adequately express or explain this endless juxtaposition of meanings. The very idea of a source disappears and although the mirror does not, the challenge is to articulate, if not hold onto, the sliding movement of significations. Thus the mirrors do not provide some absolute point of entry or a controlling moment for the relationship. They reflect only what the viewing subject chooses as important—in other words, the in-between is always a point of mediation, not resolution, a projection, not an object.

Put another way, looking in from the outside "we" (the reader of this book or spectator of this scene) see a subject looking in a mirror—they never, in the simple sense, see their own reflection. The mediations in this instance suggest that the act of seeing involves a trilogue that operates through a relay of relations for which the mirror as object is not the only source. There are endlessly circumscribed interpretations and commentaries possible here, and it is this triangularity that opens the space for reimagining the role of subjectivity in the activity of viewing and may provide us with an useful strategy for reinterpreting otherness.

Donna Haraway has put it this way: "The topography of subjectivity is multi-dimensional; so, therefore is vision. The knowing self is partial in all its guises, never finished, whole, simply there and original; it is always constructed and stitched together imperfectly, and *therefore* able to join with another, to see together without claiming to be another."[33] Your image is split between the subjective sense you have of "being" in the hallway and the interaction between and across the two mirrors. But the exchange, so described, is not complete. There is a plurality to the process of interaction that travels through identity, gender, class, ethnicity and transforms the image by splitting the experience of viewing into many fragments. This "topography" of experience aestheticizes the surfaces of the mirrors and paradoxically makes it appear as if they hold within them some sort of clue to the subjective experience of viewing. It is here that we draw upon distinctions between the perceptual and the mental, suggesting that it is the sense of sight that apprehends the "fact" of the mirror's relationship to us and that our ideas about that relationship happen in a "different time." In other words, we see and then we think, or to put it in more popular terms, we are affected by what we see and then think about it. Yet, this is a moment dominated by various and different kinds of conflicts

---

33. Donna Haraway, "Situated Knowledges," in *Simians, Cyborgs, and Women* (New York: Routledge, 1991), 193.

about the possible set of relationships between self (selves) and mirror(s). This isn't a codified space between two parts of a process somehow locked into place but a sliding and sometimes very uneasy ground in constant need of revision and explanation.

The mirroring itself is timeless. Once you have looked, you can turn away, but to all intents and purposes the only way to make sense of the experience is to more closely examine the image and the splits produced. In order to stare at your own receding image you must look in such a way so as not to interrupt the interaction of body and mirror. You have to bend over and look upward into one of the mirrors in order to see the effect. Two mirrors, many images, one body reproduced infinitely. All you control is your perspective on the image. Yet that perspective is never complete, always shifting and changing as a result of the relationship between vision and comprehension, perception and thought (themselves processes not as easily divided as my terminology would suggest). It is here that a fantasy of the mirrors and their effect comes into play. In the mirrors your body floats in a universe of optical mirages that challenge "sense" and where the only way the fragments can be organized is through an imaginary activity that cannot in the simple sense be reduced to conscious experience. The body sees itself as an Other, so to speak, and the conventional distinctions between sensation and thought disappear. The narcissism of this activity never fulfills itself, but the crucial point is that the narcissism seems somehow to be separate from the person staring into the mirrors. It is that person floating in the mirrors who doesn't meet the expectations of the viewer, and it is precisely because unity can never be achieved that the experience is almost immediately relegated to the status of a memory.

Time is present, but somehow time also seems to be absent. Metaphorically, the space between the mirrors comes to stand for a potential set of meanings that the viewer can produce. But there is the lingering sense that the relationship between the mirrors continues to produce meaning without the need for a subject to be present. This is not a play of opposites. The oscillation, mirror to sight, to imagining both, is one of the grounds upon which fascination with images in general is built—a continuum where the effect of infinity in the mirrors, for example, remains constant even as the *perception* of infinity reveals itself to be a projection of the human psyche, as the experience takes on the quality of a voyage through a labyrinth or a maze.

The "magic" of images is embedded within these paradoxes and in the claims that have been made for their transformational abilities and effects. As the mirrors themselves recede in importance, the particular moment in front of the mirrors shows itself to have been a memory almost from the start, because although I have been located in an endless regression of mirror-images, a slight movement of the eye destroys the effect (I therefore try to remember what happened.). There is thus no single surface on which this drama of the image plays itself out in a complete way, since the mirror has proven itself to be as unreliable *as* my own relationship to it. Nevertheless, the claim can be made that the mirrors are a constant in this process of exchange if only to provide some coherence to our use of language and the discourses upon which the experience depends.

The notion that there might be a constant must here be recognized as an effect of subjectivity and a desire to create a ground upon which to make sense of the experience of viewing. The regression of the images in the mirrors seems permanent, like the permanence of a photographic print. But the effect, as we have seen, is impermanent, and the mirrors in the hall suggest little about the relationship that we will have with them. In the final analysis the phenomenon as such will depend on a constellation of subjective factors which our knowledge of the mirror effect will only partially explain.[34]

This example begins to explore the shifting movement among observation, perception, comprehension, and interpretation with respect to images and projections. Below, I will explore the relationship among these constitutive processes with an emphasis on photography and cultural notions of vision.

Why do discourses on vision and images use photographs as the fulcrum for their explanations of the relationship between sight and meaning? My claim will be that sight cannot be divorced from the discourses that we use to interpret both *what* and *how* we have seen. In some senses as Roland Barthes argues in his book *Camera Lucida*, the activities of seeing are less closely linked to the sphere of objects than our discourse about them would suggest. Yet what is fascinating is the strategic use of the object (e.g., the photographic print and/or what it pictures) as a pivot for explanation. In his short but prescient essay on the history of photography, Walter Benjamin makes an important point to which I will return. For Benjamin the caption under a photograph says a great deal about our need to "textualize" the visual. "This is where the caption comes in, whereby photography turns all life's relationships into literature, and without which all constructivist photography must remain arrested in the approximate."[35] The conflict between the approximate, the contingent, and the textual is where I would like to begin a discussion of Roland Barthes and his work on photography.

34. See "Insomnia" by Elizabeth Bishop, *Elizabeth Bishop: The Complete Poems 1927–1979* (New York: Farrar, Strauss and Giroux, 1991), 70.
35. Walter Benjamin, "A Small History of Photography," in *One Way Street and Other Writings*, (London: Verso, 1979), 256.

2 | Camera Lucida
Barthes and Photography

Photographs and Images: The Polaroid

> "One day, quite some time ago, I happened on a photograph of Napoleon's youngest brother, Jerome, taken in 1852. And I realised then, with an amazement I have not been able to lessen since: I am looking at eyes that looked at the Emperor."[1]

The eyes of the emperor's brother once looked straight into a camera, in this case "manned" by a photographer whose duty it was to take pictures of the rich and powerful. Jerome's eyes had been privileged enough to look into Napoleon's eyes. The photograph as described by Roland Barthes allowed him to establish a relay between Jerome (in the 1850s) and the modern readers of *Camera Lucida*. This juxtaposition of time and space is at the root of Barthes's meditation on photography in *Camera Lucida*. Barthes provides us with the social and cultural matrix at the heart of his activities as a viewer and as a cultural analyst. *Camera Lucida* is part analysis, part theory, a personal examination of the role of photography in Barthes's life, and an homage to Jean-Paul Sartre's book, *The Psychological Imagination*.[2] An extraordinary number of essays and articles have been written about *Camera Lucida* and Barthes's work. My purpose here is to interrogate the photographic image in historical and cultural terms. Barthes is a focus, but this chapter is designed to raise a primary distinction between photographs and images. My premise is that this distinction will allow us to more clearly understand the role played by the viewer in the experience and interpretation of images.

One of the aims of the project[3] of *Camera Lucida* is to discover whether there is an interpretive space *between* image and photograph that will allow for if not encourage new ways of thinking and seeing. Barthes tests many

1. Roland Barthes, *Camera Lucida*, tr. Richard Howard (New York: Noonday Press, 1981), 3.
2. Jean-Paul Sartre, *The Psychological Imagination* (London: Methuen, 1972).
3. The book is far from being the literary exegesis that some commentators have suggested. Its playfulness with regard to form, its lack of commentary on the many photographs to which it refers, and its use of photographs that are not even reproduced, suggest that Barthes was as worried about the "word" as he was about the image.

strategies of interpretation with regard to photographic meaning, but much of the book is governed by an emphasis on death—the death of his mother, the death of photography as a form of cultural expression, the death of the interpreter. "If photography is to be discussed on a serious level, it must be described in relation to death. It's true that a photograph is a witness, but a witness of something that is no more. Even if the person in the picture is still in love, it's a moment of this subject's existence that was photographed, and this moment is gone. This is an enormous trauma for humanity, a trauma endlessly renewed. Each reading of a photo and there are billions worldwide in a day, each perception and reading of a photo is implicitly, in a repressed manner, a contract with what has ceased to exist, a contract with death."[4]

This theme has been researched and commented on by a number of writers,[5] but my sense is that Barthes is exploring the meaning of death at the symbolic and imaginary level. Death in this instance speaks to the frailty of memory, but most importantly, Barthes follows the writings of Bataille in recognizing the silence of the photograph in the face of all that is done to it. "Death is a disappearance. It's a suppression so perfect that at the pinnacle utter silence is its truth. Words can't describe it. Here obviously I'm summoning a silence I can only approach from the outside or from a long way away."[6] The distinction then between image and photograph will allow me to speak about the cacophony of voices that engulf the silent photograph. My position will be different from Barthes. He is worried about loss and absence. My concern is with the rich discourse arising from the human encounter with images and the creative use made of photographs as they are placed into different contexts.

There is a further emphasis by Barthes on the Sartrean ego, the one who is both the master of his or her identity and destiny and also its victim. "In front of the lens, I am at the same time: the one I think I am, the one I want others to think I am, the one the photographer thinks I am, and the one he makes use of to exhibit his art. In other words, a strange action: I do not stop imitating myself, and because of this, each time I am (or let myself be) photographed, I invariably suffer from a sensation of inauthenticity, sometimes of imposture (comparable to certain nightmares)" (Barthes 13). The relationships that Barthes establishes here between the "I" and the "eye," between the

4. Roland Barthes, *The Grain of the Voice*, tr. Linda Coverdale (New York: Hill and Wang, 1985), 356.

5. In particular, Mary Bittner Wiseman, *The Ecstasies of Roland Barthes* (New York: Routledge, 1989), and Stephen Ungar, *Roland Barthes: The Professor of Desire* (Lincoln: University of Nebraska Press, 1983).

6. Georges Bataille, *Guilty*, tr. Bruce Boone (Venice, Calif. The Lapis Press, 1988), 7.

dream and the "sense" of oneself both as image and as reality can be better understood if one begins to think of the image in general terms as a "place" of subjectivity. Thus what is important with regard to Napoleon's youngest brother is that he has an identity that has been sculpted by Barthes from the photograph as raw material. The "clay" in this instance is Barthes's imagination, which suggests that the photograph is never outside of the subjective, never outside of strategies of interpretation and analysis. Photographs are rarely about anything new. They can startle, shock, inform, but they only offer a hint of what can be done to them. Images, which represent the activities of human intervention and interpretation, which are an amalgam of photographic intentions and subjective placement, are part of a process that is embodied, the result of a "labor of relation."[7]

This is to some degree represented by a Polaroid photograph in the beginning of *Camera Lucida* that W. J. T. Mitchell has described as a veil[8] but that I interpret as a curtain over a photographic window, as, in other words, the potential place from which a large number of "sights" can be inferred or given the right circumstances, constructed. Mitchell refers to Barthes's dislike of Polaroids and of color photographs in general (Mitchell 302–303), but I see the Polaroid as an apparatus that encourages the imaginary, that frees the cameraperson to explore his or her experiences. In some senses Polaroids are the precursors of small-format video, which produces an instantaneous result to the creative use of imaging technologies. The notion of instant development, the instant print, runs counter to the "value" of the photograph as a vehicle of preservation, as a special moment during which an event or person has been captured for the family album or the art museum.[9] As a result of Barthes's ambiguous feelings about photography, the Polaroid comes to stand for, if not legitimate, the contradictions of vision, the perpetual sense Barthes has that more is being taken away than is being given. The curtains highlight the levels of mediation that both encourage the imaginary and prevent us from "looking outside." The Polaroid is a "throw-away," but what exactly does it offer us?

7. I have borrowed this phrase from Anthony Wilden's book *System and Structure*. He makes the comment about "labor of relation" in a discussion of Jacques Lacan. He critiques Lacan's dependence on language, on the symbolic, and Lacan's use of linguistic signification to explain the imaginary and its relationship to subjectivity and identity. Anthony Wilden, *System and Structure* (London: Tavistock, 1972), 473.

8. W. J. T. Mitchell, "The Photographic Essay: Four Case Studies," *Picturing Theory* (Chicago: University of Chicago Press, 1994), 302.

9. Rosalind Krauss makes the important point that the discursive space for photography has shifted from informal settings to the museum, to a place of exhibition, and this has transformed the aesthetic expectations surrounding photographic images. Rosalind Krauss, "Photography's Discursive Spaces," in *The Contest of Meaning: Critical Histories of Photography*, ed. Richard Bolton (Cambridge, Mass.: MIT Press, 1992), 287–301.

Is it the same as all other kinds of photographs? What happens to the photographer if he or she can see the result of his or her intuition or reaction or sight of an event immediately after it happens? What effect does all of this have on the subjects being photographed? The temporal collapse here could be described as one of the breaking points between modernity and postmodernity. The sharpness of this shift should not be underestimated. The Polaroid is more like a found object in the sense developed by Marcel Duchamp and encourages a radical reappropriation of the world as image, now being realized to an even more sophisticated degree by digital technology. This movement to a dramatically different level of appropriation was not achieved in the cinema until video appeared. Multimedia computers and CD-ROM promise to change the parameters even more. Did Barthes anticipate all of this with the Polaroid at the beginning of *Camera Lucida*? That would be stretching my point. He did however sense the depth of the change which the Polaroid process engendered. And much of his discussion of time and death in *Camera Lucida* anticipates the reversals and transformations of instant photography and video. What is even more interesting about Polaroids is the way they challenge simplistic notions of referentiality, the way the Polaroid camera encourages shifts in framing and takes the photographic process away from the extraordinary, the special event, the birth, the marriage. As a result of the Polaroid, everyday life can be transformed into an image without any pretense, while at the same time all of the pretensions of photography as an art form can be marginalized.

Benjamin/Barthes/Berger

The title of Barthes's book is also a play on "camera obscura" and as such refers to the history of the medium of photography, to its origins as a device that transformed the three-dimensionality of the "real" world into a flat surface. The deliberate ambiguity of the term *Lucida* allows Barthes to "look" at photographs both for what they are (he provides the reader with many descriptions and analyses of photographs and they punctuate his arguments throughout the book), and as triggers for bringing out the "inner" light of thinking and interpretation. *Camera Lucida* plays with questions of "lucidity" and proposes no clear answers to the now commonplace arguments concerning the relationship between between photographs and reality. Suffice to say that Barthes's book represents an important "site" of the intense debate about images and their role in the development of cultural theory and history. The personal nature of the book contributes to its significance as an exegesis in which the biographical, the historical, and the pictorial come to represent the personae of Roland Barthes and his significance in the intellectual world.[10]

Camera Lucida is characterized by contradictory statements and by theoretical debates which Barthes makes no effort to resolve. "Whatever it grants to vision and whatever its manner, a photograph is always invisible: it is not it that we see" (Barthes 6). By this Barthes means that the referential power of the photograph overwhelms its status as a medium. Barthes is torn by the desire to foreground the operations of the image *as* image while at the same time wanting to gaze at the photograph as a "primitive, without culture" (Barthes 7). This tension, which the book never resolves, is a far more cultural one than Barthes acknowledges. It lies at the heart of our culture's ambivalence about images, an ambivalence located in the seemingly transparent nature of a medium that nevertheless forms and deforms what it portrays. Yet, the difficulty is not with photographs per se, but with the process of engagement, with the transformation of the photograph into an image, with the movement from one level of meaning to the next. The primitive in this case is Barthes's mythological Other. The primitive represents an innocence that precludes sight. This then is one of the other major themes of *Camera Lucida*: to *see* is itself an ambiguous way of rendering the irresolvable conflict between appearances and truth. Although Barthes often suggests that appearances can be punctured in order to go further, the paths opened up are themselves in conflict because no direct reading of a photograph is possible.[11] Mitchell puts it well: "Barthes emphasizes what he calls the 'punctum,' the stray, pointed detail that 'pricks' or 'wounds' him. These details (a necklace, bad teeth, folded arms, dirt streets) are accidental, uncoded, nameless features that open the photograph metonymically onto a contingent realm of memory and subjectivity" (Mitchell 303). In this strategy, which carries an aesthetic and ideological weight to it, Barthes joins with Walter Benjamin in looking beyond what the eye immediately sees (and I should add, what the ear hears), for what John Berger says is that which "overflows the outline, the contour, the category, the name of what is" (Berger 219). Susan Buck-Morss mentions Benjamin's concern for the transitory, for the relationship between technology, which represents progress, and the imaginary, which neither affirms or denies its own mythic underpinning.[12] The transitory in Barthes can be translated into the instantaneous. To Barthes, photographs are glued to the real because their first effect on the viewer transcends their status as an image. This is not too different from Benjamin's dis-

10. Jacques Derrida explores the emotional connection that he had with Barthes and the impact of Barthes's death in an essay entitled "The Deaths of Roland Barthes," *Philosophy and Non-Philosophy Since Merleau-Ponty*, ed. Hugh J. Silverman (New York: Routledge, 1988).

11. Barthes would, I think, agree with John Berger who says, "Clouds gather visibility, and then disperse into invisibility. All appearances are of the nature of clouds." John Berger, *The Sense of Sight* (New York: Pantheon, 1985), 219.

12. See Susan Buck-Morss, *The Dialectics of Seeing: Walter Benjamin and the Arcades Project* (Cambridge, Mass.: MIT Press, 1989), and in particular Benjamin's discussion of the "wish-image."

cussion of the effects of Paris of the nineteenth century upon him, the feeling that he was immersed in a phantasmagoria that overwhelmed his senses and left him with the feeling that all of the mediators for his experience had disappeared.[13]

In alluding to the camera obscura in an historical and theoretical sense, Barthes is also putting the agenda of the viewer or observer in the forefront of his book. As Jonathan Crary has remarked, the history of the camera obscura as a technology is really about a "philosophical metaphor" that dominated the seventeenth and eighteenth centuries, a metaphor for "how observation leads to truthful inferences about the world."[14] Crary's work is exemplary. He shows how the dominant metaphors used to explain the camera obscura changed in the nineteenth century: "In the texts of Marx, Bergson, Freud, and others the very apparatus that a century earlier was the site of truth becomes a model for procedures and forces that conceal, invert, and mystify truth" (Crary 29).

It is in the space between these two approaches that Barthes operates. The camera remains an object capable of creating the links between reality and vision while at the same time inverting if not distorting the simplicity of that relationship. It is this ambiguity and tension between rationalist and nonrationalist approaches to understanding how photographs communicate meaning that Barthes discusses. At the same time Barthes tries to avoid the notion that there is a systematic base to the way photographs operate as purveyors of meaning (rejecting the more scientific aspects of his earlier work in *Elements of Semiology*), and yet he makes the effort to catalogue their constituent elements in order to bind photographs to their own specific characteristics. This becomes an entry point into historical and interpretive analysis and for Barthes, particularly with respect to a photograph of his mother as a young child, a meditation on the ability of the image to keep the dead (or meaning) alive.

The difficulty is that *visual media* resist being defined with that kind of specificity, because as objects, what we say about them is the result of a *relation*. The relationship will always be *contingent*, a space in between, without the properties normally attributed to subject or object. (Crary mentions the profoundly different approach taken by John Locke and Arthur Schopenhauer:

13. Bernard Comment discusses the shift in Barthes's approach from his earlier more formal analyses in *Elements of Semiology* to the more phenomenological strategy in *Camera Lucida*. He attributes this to an increasing effort on Barthes's part to eliminate all forms of intentionality from the photograph. This contributes to the sense that what photographs as a medium encourage is an instantaneous apprehension of meaning. Comment calls this approach "magical." Bernard Comment, *Roland Barthes, vers le neutre* (Paris: Christian Bourgeois, 1991), 120.

14. Jonathan Crary, *Techniques of the Observer: On Vision and Modernity in the Nineteenth Century* (Cambridge, Mass.: MIT Press, 1991), 29.

"Unlike Locke and Condillac, Schopenhauer rejected any model of the observer as passive receiver of sensation, and instead posed a subject who was both the site and producer of sensation"[Crary 1991, 75].) My choice to describe a contingent relationship here will hopefully enable me to talk about a subject not fully in control of vision nor completely out of control, where consciousness is neither a reflection of what has been seen nor the progenitor (dreams that turn into hallucinations which then become real). To me the emphasis has to be on relationships and on the discourses produced out of them. These discourses may not be entirely dependent on the binary division between discourse and picture. More often than not, they exceed, if not overturn, the very idea of that division. At the same time contingency allows for a discussion of daydreams and dreams—relations situated in the tensions between the symbolic and the imaginary, which are in my opinion a necessary part of any analysis of images. The contingent allows us to challenge the notion that there is a direct relationship between the "time" of seeing and the "time" of understanding. It brings into play, most importantly, questions of power. "Vision is *always* a question of the power to see—and perhaps of the violence implicit in our visualizing activities. With whose blood were my eyes crafted? These points apply to testimony from the position of 'oneself'. We are not immediately present to ourselves" (Haraway 192).

Barthes's effort to generate a set of observable characteristics that will delimit the medium of photography is itself part of this creation of a contingent "relationship." The potential problems with this approach only come into play when that delimitation of boundary is shifted to the ontological level. I will address the impact of contingency as a strategy for textual analysis later. Suffice to say that for the moment the crucial point is that contingency has an effect on how visual media can be interpreted. What must be kept in mind is that although the observer and the text are to some degree "visible" as parts of a complex process of exchange (in the same way that two people talking to each other can be observed by a third person), the relationship between those parts is not. Instead, it is the discursive, performative, and interpretive *consequences* of the *relationship* that take on a textual quality and for which a variety of analytical strategies can be developed.

Contextual arguments are themselves contingent, often arbitrary, and dependent on the position of the observer or analyst. They are more often than not hypotheses that do not drive toward some *conclusive* testing of their premises. This of course has always been promoted as the fundamental difference between artistic and scientific activities. In some respects *Camera Lucida* is an unveiling of the history of this tension and difference, but it takes it one step further by implicitly exploring notions of conventionality and codification. For it is through those semiotic and interpretive presumptions that the *idea* of cultural norms has arisen. The normative argument makes its strongest appearance in arguments about genre and canon, and while I will not delve into this at the moment, it is important to note that *Camera Lucida* was Barthes's last book and came after a long intellectual career during which he argued for the normative (in his work on fashion, advertising and literature—*S/Z* and *Systéme de la mode*) and against it (in *The Empire of Signs* and *The Lover's Discourse*). These divisions don't sit in simple opposition to each other. They crisscross Barthes's work and in some respects provide the intellectual energy for *Camera Lucida* (and I would suggest for the shift by Barthes from a structural to a poststructural position), but at another level Barthes doesn't seem ready to confront the impact of these divisions on his own praxis as a critic and analyst. It is within the arguments around contingency that one can begin to pose questions about the connections Barthes develops in relation to politics, context, and historical analysis. It is an important and often overlooked fact that much of *Mythologies*, for example, was written as a series of articles for a newspaper in France. This provides a context for the book that its appropriation as cultural theory has elided.

Camera Lucida is a return to an earlier *politique* but makes no effort to foreground that history. Ironically, this is part of the contingent approach so characteristic of Barthes. His work remains unsure of its purpose, bound to, as Richard Rorty has so beautifully put it, a "tissue of contingencies."[15] I should add that part of my emphasis on the notion of contingency is related to Walter Benjamin's concern to situate photography within the textual, the imagistic, and the mythic. For Benjamin the photographic image both takes away and confers new insights in the ongoing relationship between vision and understanding, but the tensions here are steeped in a set of nonnormative and nonprescriptive contingencies that lack the permanence often attributed to the image. The struggle between permanence and impermanence, between the role of images as potential focal points for the expansion of thought and vision and the often dystopic and negative perspective on their effects is a central thematic of *Camera Lucida* and of Benjamin's work on images.[16] At the same time Barthes and Benjamin supported the idea that photographic images extended if not redefined the cognitive experience of the viewer while also contributing to the denigration of meaning, to the simplification of perception and understanding.[17] This tension (in Benjamin's case in the late nineteenth century and in Barthes's at the cusp of the computer age) also expressed itself through con-

15. Richard Rorty, *Contingency, Irony, and Solidarity* (New York: Cambridge University Press, 1989), 32.
16. See Martin Jay, *Downcast Eyes: The Denigration of Vision in Twentieth-Century French Thought* (Berkeley and Los Angeles: University of California Press, 1993) for an extended description and analysis of this tension.
17. Susan Buck-Morss's summary of Benjamin's analysis emphasizes the distorting influences of capitalism as a factor in undermining the potential of photography. Susan Buck-Morss, *The Dialectics of Seeing: Walter Benjamin and the Arcades Project* (Cambridge, Mass.: MIT Press, 1989.)

ceptions of the popular, notions of mass entertainment, and the role of high art in a time of shifting concerns about the impact of new technologies on traditional conceptions of cultural activity. To a large extent these concerns remain relevant today, and they are premised on the difficulties of attributing some kind of cause to the use that viewers make of images.

As we shall see, the photographic image rarely enframes or constrains what is said about it and this may be one of the sources for the frustration felt about the form, but it is also one of the most provocative reasons why intentionality and authorship seem to disappear. This is a further source of tension with respect to the image—the sense that authority has been removed and replaced with the fluidity of subjectivity. But in a reversal, the anger for this loss is channeled into the technology. The camera, for example, becomes responsible for a loss of authority and intentionality, which is then transferred to the viewer as a crisis of subjectivity. (As we shall see this is one of the reasons for Baudrillard's dystopic vision of modern technologies.)

However, it seems to me that the opposite has happened. The camera rarely appears in photographs that individuals take, a fact that in effect transfers the power to the viewer who can attribute intentionality to the image or not depending on the context of viewing and the potential use that will be made of the image. The technology will bear as much responsibility as one wishes, since "it" cannot answer for its actions. In the final analysis the tensions of attribution here are sources of creativity and not the reverse. Benjamin recognized this when he prioritized the dream as an integral part of the role human desire plays in the construction of meaning in relation to images. These desires play themselves out in a variety of ways and only a consensual agreement among a wide variety of viewers ever fixes (and even this is only temporary) the attribution of effect and meaning to images. In this sense the photograph never belongs to anybody. Barthes quotes Sartre: "The persons in a photograph drift between the shores of perception, between sign and image, without ever approaching either" (Barthes 20). It is this territory, this space without a fixed shape but nevertheless with borders, that opens up the potential for exploration and discovery and that moves the photograph from print to image. "The photograph itself is in no way animated (I do not believe in 'lifelike' photographs), but it animates me: this is what creates every adventure" (Barthes 20). It is as if understanding and interpretation are conflated into a notion of instantaneous recognition and comprehension, an epiphanous moment of effect and affect.

Avedon's Slave

Throughout *Camera Lucida* Barthes claims that the eye is only capable of seeing if the subject who is looking has mastered an understanding of his or her inner thoughts or inner vision (a difficult task but one that must always be pursued, he suggests). The act of seeing is defined by Barthes as a product of the tensions between the image as external and thought as internal. Barthes raises fundamental questions about the subjective and discursive sphere within which the experience of viewing images is articulated.

> I think again of the portrait of William Casby, "born a slave," photographed by Avedon. The *noeme* here is intense; for the man I see here *has been* a slave: he certifies that slavery has existed, not so far from us; and he certifies this not by historical testimony but by a new, somehow experiential order of proof. (Barthes 79)

There are a number of important elements to this quote that warrant examination. The first, which Barthes himself says very little about, is that the portrait is by Richard Avedon, one of the most important commercial photographers of our time. (Avedon photographs the covers of *Vogue* and *Self* magazines and directs the television commercials of such companies as Revlon, Calvin Klein, and Chanel.) Although Barthes mentions Avedon in an interview reproduced in his book *The Grain of the Voice*,[18] it is to assert that Avedon is simply one of the contemporary photographers he has decided to use in *Camera Lucida*.

In a highly critical article Richard Bolton[19] quotes Avedon with reference to a series of photographs about the modern American West published in 1985: "everything embodied in the photograph simply happened . . . . the person in the photograph was always there . . . was not even in the presence of a photographer."[20] Bolton feels that Avedon plays into the worst tendencies of photographic documentary practice: He decontextualizes the subjects he photographs:

> Avedon's photographs owe their effectiveness to his style, to an approach established through years of photographic encounters with the beautiful and the well known. Avedon eliminated evidence of specific locations in the West by placing his subjects in front of a seamless studio backdrop; he diminished the sculpturing effects of light by photographing his subjects in shadow. Three-dimensionality was also reduced through the use of narrow depth of field, while the surface of the subject was emphasized through the use of an 8 ×10 camera. The subject was exaggerated further through elaborate print-

18. Roland Barthes, *The Grain of the Voice*, tr. Linda Coverdale (New York: Hill and Wang, 1985).
19. Richard Bolton, "In the American East: Richard Avedon Incorporated," in *The Contest of Meaning: Critical Histories of Photography*, ed. Richard Bolton (Cambridge, Mass.: MIT Press, 1992).
20. Richard Avedon, "Foreword," in Avedon, *In the American West 1979–1984* (New York: Harry N. Abrams, Inc., 1985), n.p. quoted in Richard Bolton, *The Contest of Meaning*, 264.

ing, and the negatives were even opaqued (with red lipstick, of all materials!) to remove even the slightest tone from the white backgrounds. The final prints are large, and some are gigantic, calling still more attention to the photographic effects. (Bolton 263)

I am far less concerned than Bolton with the moral framework for the artifice Avedon used. This seems to me to be a matter of degree. No photograph escapes a variety of strategic creative and aesthetic choices that inevitably move the image beyond a transparent relationship to what has been pictured. I am on the other hand fascinated by the extent to which Avedon went in trying to alter the photographic prints that he shot. These are not minor stylistic changes. Rather, they are attempts to bring the body of the photographed subject into the foreground. They are not dissimilar to the heightened artifice of a Robert Mapplethorpe. The photographic moment becomes the premise for a further sculpting of shape, look, and figure. In working against the transparent requirements of time and in showing photographic time to be radically different from print time, Avedon has actually increased the flexibility available to the interpreter of his photographs.

Bolton is also very concerned with Avedon's assertion of realism, really a claim that the photographic subject somehow evades the impact of the camera upon them. It is of course crucial to ask whether context as such can ever be removed in the manner suggested by Bolton, because in the final analysis it is what viewers *do* with the photograph that counts. Bolton goes on to discuss the way Avedon reproduces stereotypes, even quoting and then adopting a typology suggested by the art critic, Adam Gopnik. My concern here, however, is with Barthes's uncritical use of the Avedon portrait and his presumption so similar to Avedon's and Bolton that "the thing [or subject] has been there" (Barthes 76). "There is a superimposition here: of reality and the past. And since this constraint exists only for Photography, we must consider it, by reduction, as the very essence, the *noeme* of Photography" (Barthes 76-77).

Barthes is suggesting that whatever or whomever has been photographed *has* been there. It is this sense of presence and of reference that Barthes discusses in the Casby portrait as evidence of the "essence of slavery" (Barthes 34), which as he subtitles the Avedon portrait means that "the mask is meaning, insofar as it is absolutely pure (as it was in ancient theatre)" (Barthes 34). This transforms the photograph into speech, "the *object speaks*, it induces us, vaguely, to think" (Barthes 38). Barthes is drawing an ambiguous equation between image and language. Reference becomes a pivot for questions about what is seen and what is said. Built into Barthes's statement is an hypothesis about the way photographs transcend the limitations of their own "objectness"—photographs are in other words transformed into the other side of a dialogue, responding to the viewer or initiating the encounter itself. Clearly, there are no rules for this encounter and this would suggest that the viewer approaches the activity of looking and thinking about a photograph as if each encounter is a new one. But the "dialogue" is between the differing levels of the viewer's own relationship to what he or she has seen. The dialogue is premised on the ability of the viewer to generate the terms of the relationship. It is dependent upon the discursive and intellectual creativity of the spectator and on her ability to speak from *both sides*, to incorporate, or not, what is important, or not, about what has been seen and understood. The fascinating thing is that Barthes creates a dialogue with William Casby. Casby is Barthes's creation, just as, at one time, Casby was Avedon's creation. In both instances Casby is a projection: an object of desire and the focal point for the imaginary.

It can be asserted that nothing remains of Casby, and paradoxically the technology of the camera and the act of taking a picture seem to support this contention. A photograph taken at 1/250th of a second exists so far beyond or outside of time that on one level it is pointless to suggest that the person or object has been "captured." But why in the first place even talk about photography, using the argument that in order to be "photographed" Casby at least had to be there? It seems clear that the time of portraiture supplies almost no information about the moment itself. This is perhaps the greatest irony of the photograph—not that it is part of a world of simulacra but that on the contrary it cannot be a simulation. The notion of simulation suggests copy, imitation, resemblance, and these are then adopted as the terminology for representational processes. But were it not for the presence of a written caption, Casby would not carry the weight assigned to him by the statement that he was a slave who was photographed. It is necessary to override the limitations of the technology with language. A space is provided within which dialogue can take place, though this in no way produces a simple equation between perception and discourse, language and the photograph. This symbiosis of the written, the verbal, and the photographic placed into a context of potential appropriation by a viewer, produces *a* Casby, not the man himself. Thus the question of what he may have been experiencing when he was photographed is as much of an hypothesis as the contingent discursive framework into which he was placed when Barthes set about interpreting the importance of his life through the photograph.

To make things even more complex the contradictions of this process may preclude the possibility of coming to grips with the way meaning is then generated through the interaction. But this very ambiguity also suggests that the photographic image may not be axiomatically related to the print as a *site of the visible* nor even as the site of the discursive (which I believe is linked to another elision by Barthes of Casby's significance as an African-American). It may not be possible to talk about the staging of meaning through a preconception as to the referential qualities of the image or what "it" is supposed to be saying. What is visible may not be legible. The assumed duality of visible/image may be transformed into a set of relationships that signify a *disjuncture* between perception, thought, signification, and representation. As one part of a circuit, the image may inhibit language and expression, the verbal, the written, precisely because it cannot illuminate the schisms it generates nor clarify the operations of legibility.[21]

This may suggest that photographs encourage the viewer to displace the conventional parameters of language use in order to create a new context for the articulation of meaning. A radically different conceptual framework may be initiated that does not, in and of itself, permit the easy use of either the verbal or the written for descriptive or interpretive purposes. The conflation of language into the image (proposing that the photograph "speaks," for example) may inhibit the discourse that might reveal the differences between language and the image. It seems clear that descriptions of photographs fit all too neatly into arguments about literacy and that the silence of the spectator in relation to the image is often proposed as evidence of "not having seen" or "not having understood," or having understood too quickly, or being silenced by the power of the visual. The pressure to turn the photograph into a written text and to create an equivalence between the visible and the legible is partially responsible for that pedagogically conservative term, "visual literacy."

Let me put Avedon, Casby, Barthes, *Camera Lucida*, and Bolton together for a moment. In all of their comments the photograph is assumed to carry within it the subjectivity that has been applied to the image—in other words, irrespective of context, a mirroring process has been put in place that creates the sensation, if not the presumption, that the object has something to say. This "transference" may be a useful strategy, but in the Casby photograph it is a good example of mystification. The puzzle is that although Casby the slave has been plucked from among many different faces and given prominence by Avedon, "he" doesn't exist unless the viewer of the photograph is ready to both agree with and confer some reality upon him. As photograph he is subject to the whims and fancies of the viewer, and although this may be "unfair" to his legacy and to his history, these personal points of his story are only of marginal consequence to the rather arbitrary use to which his photograph can be put. (In Saussurian semiotics, arbitrariness has been attributed to signification, to multiple breaks between signifier and signified. I am in effect asserting that these breaks and gaps are the result of subjective movements and are not necessarily inherent to the way images operate.)

If we return for a moment to the example of two mirrors facing each other

---

21. One of the most dangerous results of confusing the legible with the image is the use of the word "reading" to describe the relationship that the viewer develops with images. This is a classical instance in which understanding, interpretation, and vision are collapsed into one apparently seamless process.

in a hallway, Casby is both the subject in between and the image being looked at. This combination of positions creates the "third" space of viewing which, so to speak, tries to interrupt and then recreate Casby's status as an image. The viewer does not substitute herself for him nor does he simply continue to exist as a simulation of the real Casby for which his photograph has become the representation. "He" does not exist within the terms of a dialogue for which he would otherwise bear some responsibility, because the "dialogue" is else-where—in that third space made possible by relationships of projection and image. Even the designation "third space" here cannot do justice to the fluidity of the boundaries, to a mapping that continuously repositions Casby, that em-bodies and disembodies him. Yet this is precisely why interpretive strategies can be so rich, why the circle of meanings opens and closes as it is explored further and further, and why it is so necessary to reexamine the categories of interpretation normally applied to the analysis of images. "Unlike memory, photographs do not in themselves preserve meaning. They offer appearances—with all of the credibility and gravity we normally lend to appearances—prised away from their meaning. Meaning is the result of understanding functions. 'And functioning takes place in time, and must be explained in time. Only that which narrates can make us understand.' Photographs in themselves do not narrate."[22]

A photograph is a metacommunication about an event or a person or an object. It is not simply acting in place of, standing for, replacing what it seems to be picturing. Often photographs are described as windows or mirrors of the real. The power of these metaphors lies in their equation of the visible with the communicative. But what is visual and oral can only be communicated to someone (or to a number of people), which means that the window will never be static and that the mirror will not enframe the boundaries of meaning crea-tion or discourse. A photograph opens up many questions about degrees of communication, about levels of replacement, and about the various sites within which substitution can occur, but substitution as such only operates within the realm of the subjective. A photograph cannot replace what it pic-tures but a human subject certainly can imagine that it does.

While it is true that we must believe that pictures communicate quickly and quite universally, those characteristics tell us very little about the depth of the relationship a viewer develops with a photo, or even whether a portrait of a black slave could cross the boundaries from personal history into the public sphere. Photographs don't just exist for recognition but play a rather complex

22. John Berger, *About Looking* (New York: Pantheon, 1980), 51. Berger quotes Susan Sontag, *On Photography* (New York: Anchor Books, 1989) without giving the exact refer-ence. But Sontag's and Berger's emphasis on time is in sharp contrast to Barthes's notions of the instantaneous. *On Photography* initially appeared in 1977, and Barthes dialogues with it throughout *Camera Lucida*.

role in relation to identity and knowledge. Thus the home photo album is as much a source of storytelling as it is a pivot for the illustration of memory. But what it comes to exemplify is not simply what we recognize in it but the capacity we have to produce a narrative in relation to its contents. Often there are hints of this circular self-reflexivity in the photographs themselves, as when a smile is missed or a frown is caught. The artifice of making the photographic appear natural contributes to its aesthetic, as if the photo can transcend the subject it pictures. This need not be framed as a negative effect of the medium. The limitations of the act of taking a photograph are precisely that it puts in question the possibility of subjectivity, which is in part why it is scary to be photographed. At the same time, subject, photograph, and photographer share a relay of voyeurism difficult to uncover, let alone display at the aesthetic level. The photograph communicates about itself and about its viewers, but crucially neither part of this process can be isolated from the other, though both can be quite easily elided from the image.

A photographed face is a face that *has been* photographed, which means that from the outset the viewer has to generate his or her own sense of time. This potential conflict of meanings encourages the intervention of the spectator. As a result, the viewer has to produce the illustrative qualities of the photograph, confirming or denying an aesthetic with which she may or may not be pleased and over which she has had no control in in the first place. The photographed face immediately exists at a different level from the face to which it seems to be referring. However, if the referential process is itself subject to a variety of contradictory constraints, then reference may be the least important aspect of what is from the beginning a transformative relationship. This inevitably prioritizes communicative exchange over reference and puts into question the relationship between information and communication. Crucially then, a photograph of William Casby, for example, has at best a very distant connection to the real man. The various levels of signification that constitute his image (slavery, Avedon's appropriation of his history, Barthes's shock that there is a modern photographic portrait of someone who had been a slave) pivot not around his absence, but around the impossibility of his presence in the form suggested by the photograph. In that sense, a photograph doesn't replace him but is merely part of a vast system of signification and discourse into which he is constantly placed, that precludes the possibility of Casby ever coming to life as an exemplification of what he supposedly signifies in image form.

In this sense he is merely one part of a performative context of appropriation and recreation. There need be no fixed point of entry into a study of his image, no encyclopedic set of assumptions to guide an interpretation of his history—in other words, the Casby portrait may carry none of the weight suggested by the semiotic notion of codification. The result is not a message without meaning. Quite the contrary, the practical outcome of the relationship of Casby to Barthes is a metacommunicative sphere that can be explored with a variety of interpretive tools, in part centered on the use to which the portrait will be put (i.e., the difference between Avedon's Casby and Barthes's Casby) and the public and private context into which it will be placed.

Photographic Images and the Public Sphere

Barthes is very concerned with the general relationship images have to the public sphere, to that "place" where differing sets of conventions buttressed by social, economic, political, and cultural processes try to "fix" meaning in a particular way. Barthes resists the idea that images are locked into place by unchangeable meanings (this resistance comes through in the autobiographical style of *Camera Lucida*), yet he proposes to struggle with the way photographs come to stand for, to represent, what they depict (this is a strategic choice which he converts into an ontological one, creating as a result precisely the fixity he wants to avoid). So he chooses to accept the notion that photographs have at least a partial relationship to the world they "capture" in image form. He solidifies this notion into a structural constraint (with superstructural characteristics, hence ideological impact), and then proposes to unmask the implications of a choice that he needn't have made in the first place, but that he suggests viewers make all of the time.

The fundamental question of whether images and what they depict are related in some manner to the "reality" they seem to contain within them presupposes a need to search for the origins of meaning in a place "outside" of the photograph. But just as reality is never fixed other than when the decision is made to narrow if not eliminate the options we have to interpret and change it, so the photograph and the image are in constant flux, neither referring to a specific moment nor a specified configuration of meanings in the "real." In saying this, I am not promoting the highly unsatisfactory binary contradictions between truth and illusion, reality and nonreality, artifice and the absence of construction or presence of constraint. Rather, these oppositions have little value in explaining how images can provoke unpredictable combinations of meaning, not a sur-real, but an endlessly transposed and transposable interaction of significations. The danger always is that specificity will fall by the wayside, but that is precisely the allure of the photographic, which I would propose is a site of contestation around representational and ontological issues (thus even the most explicit of photographs opens up a debate as to its truth-value—what I am suggesting is that this creates a cultural moment of interpretation and discussion, which in the final analysis is more important than whether the photograph is true or not).

The trap here is seeing that contestation as if it is dependent on the "real" and thus to belittle the desire to transform the photograph into a vehicle for debate and discourse (as in, "That is a photograph of Roland Barthes," which creates an indexical relationship but eliminates the more serious and potentially richer question, "Is that Roland Barthes?"). Barthes falls prey to this when he says, "The photographic image is full, crammed: no room, nothing can be added to it" (Barthes 89). Yet, as I have suggested, photographs are never locked into their borders. Even as Barthes meditates on a photograph of his dead mother when she was young, even as he suggests that nothing in the photograph can transform his grief, he is setting the scene, precisely, for that transformation. Although time seems to be arrested, the point is that time can never be stopped. Even the assertion that the photograph was shot in 1903 means very little. Time cannot be reversed to satisfy the subjective desires of the viewer. Inevitably, the time of viewing *is* the time of the photograph, and although we may then decide to legitimize or validate its historical authenticity, we have not returned to the moment when it was taken. This is for Barthes and for Sartre the crucial axis for a profound sense of loss. Rather, I would suggest, the feelings of loss contribute to the process of interpretation. The loss is one of the sites of subjective intervention. The history being referred to is the history being made.

This brings up the crucial question of context. If the image is the fulcrum for a context-dependent interpretation of the relationship between seeing and understanding, then images lack a narrow specificity. They are the "site" of a continuous process of reinterpretation produced out of the historical context of presentation and performance. This "instability" at the heart of postmodernist reflections on the variability of meaning in all texts foregrounds images as processual—there is no *fixed* moment of projection or apprehension. (This would have a dramatic effect on the notion of the photographic archive and on presumptions of photographic truth.) However, my concern here is not to elevate process (as a concept and heuristic tool to explain change) to a point beyond which any constraints operate. It seems to me that little can be resolved here if we accept as a given the notion that images operate in a sphere without history. Crucially, it is history itself and historical discourse that encourages an almost endless set of permutations in the events it purports to describe. I say this not in order to promote the idea of "open-endedness," but to reinvigorate the way in which we approach positionality.

Performing the Visual

Let us for a moment imagine the photographic scene that Barthes described above in relation to Napoleon. Jerome goes to a studio or perhaps the photographer comes to his house. The photographer experiences a fair degree of discomfort, for indeed, there is power in those eyes, and a glance in the wrong direction could be misinterpreted. Some days later Jerome sees the photo and declares that "it is not me." To what degree are Jerome's reflections on his photograph the result of a difference in perception between himself and the photographer? Jerome obviously has a self-image that does not match the image produced—the photograph has increased the gap between image and self, at least in the eyes of the man who has seen the emperor.

Could William Casby have requested a new photograph from Richard Avedon? Clearly not, and what this answer clarifies is that power relations are at the heart of the photographic activity, not only a result, but a necessary imperative for taking a picture. Ironically, Avedon initiated a process over which he had decreasing control as the photograph spread further and further into the public sphere. This contradiction (which the written caption and the identification of the photograph as a portrait by Avedon try to dispel) ends up reconfiguring the points of entry for analysis. The importance of the photograph is its link to slavery, to the way white colonial history has marginalized the black experience. Yet this very discourse is clearly "outside" of the picture and describes a place where aesthetics and history are incommensurable, where the practice of linkage either to author or to the act of taking the photograph elides the margins as a strategy of recuperation.

Barthes's description of his shock when he saw the photograph didn't lead him into a historical analysis of slavery. He wasn't moved enough to search further. This self-imposed restriction, however, shouldn't be attributed to Avedon. Instead, it says a great deal about a Eurocentric analytical framework which may not want to more fully explore the consequences of linking Casby to slavery in the first place. What does the photograph exclude? To what degree are generalizations about slavery embedded in Casby's look? What historical discourses are available for relating Casby to his past? How would *he* have captioned the photograph? Yet what must be recognized here is that these questions are themselves strategic, and they are premised on the interpretive tools that I want to put in place. The photograph of Casby is one part of the focus I have chosen, but it is not the *only* part. A web of meanings comes into existence, a hypertextual and thus three-dimensional confluence of significations, all of which are triggers for further exploration. One example, to what degree was Avedon influenced by the television miniseries, "*Roots*," when he took the photograph? This tantalizing question may lead to many avenues of exploration. In a sense, the Casby photograph becomes the "starred" text of *S/Z*, except I would take the process even further, which is why I used the term *hypertext*. The Casby photograph has the potential to unsettle the relationship between Avedon and photography in general because so many discourses can interact around an image that is itself at the center of a process of historical displacements.[23]

Does the absence of finality here suggest an endless proliferation of mean-

23. For further details on the discursive linkage between Eurocentric conceptions of cultural difference and national identity see Partha Chatterjee, *Nationalist Thought and the Colonial World: A Derivative Discourse* (London: ZED Books, 1986), 36–53, and Edward W. Said, *Culture and Imperialism* (New York: Alfred A. Knopf, 1993), 169–90.

ings? With regards to interpretation are we dealing with a metacritical task circumscribed by discourse and dependent on a process for which lack is the defining metaphor? In a sense, as the boundaries of the photograph expand, "it" becomes a trigger, not for a specific repertoire of already given meanings, but for a *performance* of meaning more oral than visual (in the sense that the photograph must be "spoken" about—the visual must be given a verbal explanation). It may be the case that to see means to listen, both to one's own verbal explanations and those of others. This conversational model doesn't end up replacing the photograph as one of the loci for discussion but encourages a process for which the photograph may not be the main focus. The performative context is always a contingent one, as a result of which meaning changes, evolves, and can comment upon itself. The notion of an original meaning designed to provide the hinge, upon which all future discussions will depend, disappears. It is as if time is reintroduced into what is usually thought of as an atemporal process. This temporally bound set of relations diminishes the authority (and author-centred concepts) of the pictorial and would, I suspect, lead to a revision of the platonic notion of illusion. It may also explain why Barthes's proclamations about the death of the author reflect a desire to reinsert time into highly contingent interpretive analyses. It is of course clear that we are not dealing with either/or propositions here. There always is an author just as what the author creates has an existence outside of his authority: as text, as picture, as painting, as photograph. The crucial point, it seems to me, is how all of these relations are performed within a context that is discursive but for which there is no moment of completion. The "talk" and the talk about talk never ceases. These performances don't have to follow a narrative form or even a carefully structured processual framework.[24]

The meaning of an image is "more" than text (written or photographic), more than words (spoken or heard), and it is only through an exploration of the gap between self-image and photograph, that is, between identity and comprehension, that one can begin to understand the interpretive flexibility needed to discuss a photograph. This lack of specificity (almost equivalent to a lack of "objectness") makes the dilemma of talking about photographs both open and closed—a contradiction paradoxically as postmodern as it is primitivistic. Barthes spends much of *Camera Lucida* worrying about this tension, about the innocence of a face captured without the knowledge of the subject, which gives that individual "life" but also rips away "their" thoughts and produces a visual object without content. Thus, as much as we might desire it, the

---

24. See Jürgen Habermas, *Moral Consciousness and Communicative Action*, tr. C. Lenhardt and Shierry W. Nicolson (Cambridge, Mass.: MIT Press, 1990), 135–36. Habermas discusses the process of intersubjective communication and ways of reaching agreement discursively between different parties to a discussion. He emphasizes the role of the performative in all of this.

photograph does not see, although it is somewhat convenient to look at Jerome's eyes *as if* they have seen Napoleon's. Yet clearly it would have been possible to generate that image with one's eyes closed, to see "in" the imagination, to be in control of the look through desire and daydream. In fact, the photograph of Jerome's eyes foregrounds not some ineffable moment in need of recovery but the rather easy way in which claims can be made about photographs in general. Thus Barthes can create a narrative around a memory of a photograph of Jerome, a story which by its very nature undermines the almost singular purpose of the original portrait. In this way, he both invents his identity and that of the fictional Jerome. Though all of this is done through the paradoxes of a medium that can never stand on its own, it is culturally situated as if it does.

Jerome is a vehicle for Barthes to create a discourse that can explode the presumptive link between image and referent (there is nothing in the portrait to suggest that Jerome ever saw Napoleon). In this way, the photograph comes to life as contradiction. And although this contradiction might have led to a radical break with traditional notions of simulation, reproduction, and representation, Barthes falls back in *Camera Lucida* to a perceptual model dependent upon similitude, and he does this because he still adheres to the earlier versions of image analysis that he undertook, notably in his piece about advertising images entitled "Rhetoric of the Image." I will not explore this article in great detail here except to say that the choice to create an inventory of meanings around an advertising image, in which as Barthes mentions, intention is so self-evident, begs the issue of photographic meaning. It is an altogether too convenient a referential tool. "Why? Because in advertising the signification of the image is undoubtedly intentional; the signifieds of the advertising message are formed *a priori* by certain attributes of the product and these signifieds have to be communicated as clearly as possible. If the image contains signs, we can be sure that in advertising these signs are full, formed with a view to the optimum reading: the advertising image is *frank*, or at least emphatic."[25]

Barthes does qualify this assertion by saying that any description of a photograph is always a metalanguage, but he disregards this insight in the actual text. In fact, the effort to talk about the photograph as language and to invest images with discursive properties transforms his analysis and interpretation into a mechanical task. The photograph becomes encoded, and the viewer acts to decode its elements. The semiotic slippage here is into precisely the opposite of what I have been talking about up until now, because the result is an elimination of discursive richness. The image becomes its message—a reversion to the ontological status that Barthes had earlier wanted to contradict (and this interesting though untheorized adoption by Barthes of Marshall McLuhan, is

25. Roland Barthes, *Image-Music-Text*, tr. Stephen Heath (London: Fontana, 1977), 33.

later taken up by Jean Baudrillard in *The Evil Demon of Images*).[26] At one level *Camera Lucida* moves beyond this and debates important issues situated interestingly enough in questions raised by the imaginary. At another level, however, *Camera Lucida* takes a similar stance to the "The Rhetoric of the Image," continuously looking for a concreteness that photographic images may not have.

The Photographic Other

Photographs and images—the former, at a cultural and social level, pivot on the relationship of sight to object, verification, and truth. The latter are produced through an act of consciousness and are therefore subject to a different, though related set of processes that center on interpretation, that need not rely on the photograph for verification. The former must be *seen* to gain status, though as Barthes suggests, a photograph "is always invisible: it is not it that we see" (Barthes 6).

Although photographs were historically described as inevitably linked to an object or subject ("A Photograph is always a photograph of something which actually exists"[27]), and although this linkage is presently being challenged by the reconstructive and transformative abilities of digital and computerized photography, it seems clear to me that the claim for linkage was always misplaced.[28] I don't intend to frame this assertion within the context of an already tired debate about whether photographs are real or not or whether there are varying degrees to their realism (or not, as the case may be). Rather, I would suggest that from the moment it became a mass medium the photographic process was profoundly transformative, and that the difficulty has been with the movement from the photographic to the imagistic, from the object to a recognition of the role played by human consciousness in constituting the *idea* of the photographic. The reliance on the object is a dilution of the subjective—a conscious and often unconscious choice to conflate the photographic print with perception and to create a causal link between the print, and its comprehension and interpretation. The photograph becomes *an Other* responsible for initiating a process it could not have started and is unlikely to end once the print ceases to be the main concern of the viewer. In other words, the photographic print may not be the source for what is attributed to it, although it seems to provide a representational space within which attribution is emphatically suggested as necessary and inevitable. This is of course what is

26. Jean Baudrillard, *The Evil Demon of Images* (Sydney: Power Institute, 1984).
27. Kendall L. Walton, "Transparent Pictures: On the Nature of Photographic Realism," in *Critical Inquiry* 11 (1984): 250.
28. W. J. T. Mitchell explores these issues in great depth in *Picture Theory: Essays on Verbal and Visual Representation* (Chicago: University of Chicago Press, 1994).

interesting about photographs. The transition from photographic print to image parallels, but may not be equivalent to, the movement from perception to discourse.

It is to Barthes's credit that *Camera Lucida* undermines and then foregrounds these ambiguities and contradictions. However, it is not the case, as Barthes suggests, that the photograph freezes the self, the id, one's subjectivity. "But each time that, as writer or 'public' man, he enters the *Maché* of languages, each time he thus finds himself exposed to Images, the question of his idiosyncrasy resurfaces: it is like military service; I am obliged to comply with the Image. I cannot be 'exempted.' " *Fort/Da*: each time he is obliged to enter the public arena, Barthes must abandon his "creation of self," be "frozen," become an Image, in short a "non-person," a figure of fashion: "Fashion affects the body. By fashion I return in my text as farce, as caricature. A kind of collective 'id' replaces the image I thought I had of myself, and that 'id' is me."[29]

If we move this quote away from its overly existential elements and instead focus on the way the photograph shifts the parameters of private self-image into the public arena (a similar move might be from the daydream to exposition, both verbal and written), then the discursive elements used to displace subjectivity cannot be located either spatially or temporally within the photograph itself, although the assertion that the photograph is responsible may create that illusion.[30]

In this sense images cannot claim the autonomy of photographs. Images can never be separated from vision and subjectivity (in other words, photographs can be put into an archive while images cannot). Images are part of a mental process, the result of an interaction between photographs and viewing subjects. Images operate within the realms of perception and thought, conscious and unconscious, looped in a spiral of relationships that are continuous—a continuum. Time, in this loop, does not rely on the movement of a clock but is instead located in the physical periodicity of the photograph. Jerome is seated in a chair that "comes" from the 1850s and this "location" of meaning allows Barthes to assume that history is present, though clearly the photograph plays only a fragmentary role in this presumption. The "chair" may, in the discursive strategy we take to the photograph, refer to the period in which it was created as long as we recognize the use-value we are making of it and as long as we are willing to *close* the circle of possible interpretations that could be made of the chair *as image*. In other words, a claim could be

29. Réda Bensmaïa, *The Barthes Effect: The Essay as Reflective Text* (Minneapolis: University of Minnesota Press, 1987), 88.
30. See Rosalind E. Krauss, *The Optical Unconscious* (Cambridge, Mass.: MIT Press, 1993) for more discussion of this issue, especially pages 217–20.

made that the chair comes from the period when the photograph was taken. But as image there are many possible interpretations that grow out of this claim and that need to be carefully distinguished from any definitive assumptions made about the history being referred to. So, at one and the same time specificity may be present, but only as a consequence of the transformation of the photograph into an image, that is, into a premise and vehicle for discursive, imaginary, and practical use.

The point is that neither the photograph nor the image exist outside of a very contingent set of relationships as much defined by context as they are enframed by the seeming absence of time. Although Barthes asserts that the photograph reproduces one moment in time, something that has "occurred only once" (Barthes 4), he cannot make that assertion from within the time of the photograph. He is as a result referring to the relationship between his moment of viewing and interpretation and the hypothesized moment of the photographic act. It is the assertion of fixity in the former that leads to the assumption of referentiality in the latter. This is a common fallacy in the analysis of photographs—the idea that an object can be viewed from within both present and past, as if "it" has somehow evaded the consequences of its own movement from one moment or period to another and its subsequent appropriation by many different subjects.

This is a fascinating problem. Modern photographs can be given an historical look by bleeding sepia colors into them. The reference here is not the past as such, but the idea of yellowing, parchment, paper exposed to the ravages of time and by extrapolation to the movement of history. But clearly, an "old" photograph has been interpreted and looked at many times. Somehow the photograph is meant to retain an original or authentic moment within the parameters of the print. The fact that it can be faked suggests that it always could have been. This looseness or flexibility could allow for the writing of another kind of history and could provide viewers with a variety of entry points into a constellation of interpretations. Instead, the effort to restrain this shifting movement often allows the photographic to overwhelm the image, creating as Barthes himself mentions over and over in *Camera Lucida*, an existential bind that places the viewer in the unenviable position of never being sure whether she has seen anything at all. I will return to this point when I discuss how postmodernists have grappled with the same problem (which is usually classified into an opposition between presence and absence).

The argument about time could be applied with some interest and effect to ethnographic photographs, particularly those taken in the late nineteenth century as evidence of cultural specificity (or as was more often the case, primitive otherness). The transparent links established between the images and the cultures they were meant to depict turns out in revisionist analyses to have been blatantly imperial. Not only did the photographs generate stereotypical inventories of Westernized presumptions about tribal cultures, they contributed to the process of colonization. "Outsider use of early photographs of Samoa, like that of Asian and African photographs, can be seen as representing Western efforts to classify an unfamiliar culture in terms of Western values and systems. Photographs of Samoa were made, distributed, and used by Westerners to reinforce stereotypes of the South Seas, often limiting outside knowledge of the place to clichés of palms, sunsets and beaches, sexually compliant women, barbaric chiefs, and the needs and opportunities for Western religion, education and economic development."[31]

On the one hand Nordström's interpretation has a ring of validity and truth to it. There is a clear attribution of intentionality, history, and specificity. There is also a correction of the position from which the original photographs were taken—a reinstallation of colonial ideology and recovery of an interpretive space that the photographs themselves, in Nordström's terms, disavowed. On the other hand there is nothing to suggest that the photographs haven't changed with time in order to open up a different discursive field and that it wasn't possible from the very first instance to inform them with an historical meaning now seemingly recovered as if it had been absent.

This claim does not stand up to close scrutiny. I will raise one major point with regard to Nordström's analysis. The ethnographic privileging of the Western voice over all others, the discourse of the ethnographer who speaks for the Samoan must be interrogated and unveiled for its political, historical, and social implications. With this I have no dispute. Yet the question of how the Samoan will herself respond to and analyze both the past and the historical revisions of her past both with regard to image and self-image, cannot be framed in these terms. The machinery of cultural appropriation simply installs another reading as if it is more historically accurate. The photograph is not necessarily a special site for this, but if history is to be understood differently, the question is, from which vantage point?

Clint Eastwood's Magnum

Often the assumption is made that photographs have an existence outside of the exchange between viewer and object. "Unlike any other visual image, a photograph is not a rendering, an imitation or an interpretation of its subject, but actually a trace of it. No painting or drawing, however naturalist, *belongs*

31. Alison Nordström, "Ethnography and the Photographic Image," a paper delivered for the Graduate Program in Communications, McGill University, Montreal, November 1992.

to its subject in the way a photograph does."[32] This hypothesis, a central one in all discussions of photography, is based on the idea of possession—the notion that there is a reality outside of the photograph for which the print becomes the representation. Berger extends his argument with the assertion that a photograph "*fixes* the appearance" of an event. In the movement and flow and flux of everyday life, the photograph preserves and reveals what the eye might otherwise not capture (a point which Benjamin also makes in his essay on photography).

At this point I would argue that image and photograph must be seen as dramatically different. For although the photograph has an existence separate from the viewer it can never be removed from the process of interpretation. The idea that the photo can capture a moment in time happens to be a specific ideological statement born out of, and sustained by Western cultural conceptions of representation. This has as much to do with notions of the observer and the observed as it does with the presumed relationship of an apparatus to reality. Thus the fact that a close-up of a flower shows details invisible to the eye does not necessarily elevate the photograph outside of the constraints of which I have been speaking. What is brought forth are further layers of meaning, and these can be proposed as scientific, but that is itself merely an additional level of interpretation.

The question I am asking here is not what the difference is between the real and the photographic, but to what degree, if any, the photograph initiates a temporal and spatial break between consciousness and the process of depiction. Clearly, what interests an observer of a photograph is the way she can manipulate time, not simply look at a moment torn from a continuum. Control is the key here, and unlike Sontag or Berger, one must approach the way a viewer marks out the aesthetic boundaries of the photograph in order to deal with the consequences of the "taking." This must be carefully linked to the desire to manipulate memory.

Culturally, images are seen as "sources" for meaning, their ever-present cultural role constituted not by a reversible process of interpretation but by a set of intrinsic characteristics to which viewers supposedly respond—the idea of effect. At the same time then, the image "leads" by example, refining its helmsmanship as it presumably gains more power, while also representing the culture within which it operates. Suggestions about effect must be seen for

32. John Berger, "Uses of Photography," in *About Looking* (New York: Pantheon, 1980), 50. Berger quotes Susan Sontag: "A photograph is not only an image (as a painting is an image), an interpretation of the real; it is also a trace, something directly stencilled off the real, like a footprint or a death mask." The Sontag quote is itself derived from the André Bazin's *What is Cinema?* tr. Hugh Gray (Berkeley and Los Angeles: University of California Press, 1967), 9–16. Many of Barthes's concerns in *Camera Lucida* are derived from Bazin's discussion.

what they are: interpretive responses to both the experience of viewing and to the institutions of image creation and distribution. And this must be understood as the kind of process that provides our culture with the ideological framework for the production and reproduction of meaning in nearly all media.

The question of effect, however, generates an even greater confusion in which the image becomes an "object" whose visible properties are equated in a literal sense to the "furniture of the world." This argument presumes that the image converts what it has appropriated into pictures, leaving intact those properties of the world of "things" automatically retrieved by the camera. (This is a further extension of Bazin's arguments.) Thus in the simplest sense, the name of an object is not transformed as it mutates into an image. This would then suggest that there need be no conflict between its use in everyday language and its appropriation as a photograph. The image as a result is defined as an amalgam of the real and the representational, as a kind of bricolage between different modes of signification. But what are the criteria that can be used to compare the image and the object? Can one make sense of those criteria by privileging the meaning of the object upon which it is then assumed the image relies? And if the object and the image are always to some degree "representational," then at which point does the image intervene to confirm that a process of signification has taken place? If the image merely translates the already given set of representations conferred upon the object, does that exhaust the possible range of meanings that can be attributed to the image and the object, once it takes on a photographic form?

Photographs are seen as carriers of meaning, an argument used to explain the referential power of the picture. Without reference the photograph would not *mean*, yet clearly, the object named "gun" is dramatically different from the image we decide to name and explore as gun. The naming, the classification, is not the same in both instances. For example, there is a photograph of Clint Eastwood carrying a Magnum which originated with the role he played in the film *Dirty Harry*. As image, it stands for Eastwood's public and private persona as well as for the violence in American society. This set of discourses creates more than a simple equation between reference and the language of interpretation. The gun, its use, the context into which it has been placed, the function it has in the film, the history of Eastwood's previous roles, have all been foregrounded, and this rather complex discursive field exceeds, transforms, even renames the object and the photograph of it.

This excess is the site upon which we build our sense of the image. It is this discursive field that makes the connections between object and image arbitrary. There is no pure moment of the gun as photograph that escapes its placement and the use to which it has been put. In this sense, there need be no synonymity between photograph, language, and object. If there were, the actual work of interpretation would simply rely on a presumed unity of reference, discourse, and representation. An objection could be made here that a gun is after all a gun. But it is precisely the desire to negate the significance of discursivity, of enunciation, that leads to the *conflation* of discourse and image.

Images cannot exist outside of their context of use. That context may dramatically alter the way an image fits into the referential categories established in our culture. This process may also upset the criteria used to establish reference in the first place. The contrast then between object and image is a fundamental one and is similar to the difference between photograph and image. The gun as image must be validated, whereas the gun as photograph doesn't necessarily have to be.

"The photograph is vaguely constituted as an object, and the persons who figure there are certainly constituted as persons, but only because of their resemblance to human beings, without any special intentionality. They drift between the shores of perception, between sign and image, without ever approaching either."[33] Crucially, the photograph is often confused as *the* site of perception, as if it has qualities that evade the glance in its direction. As soon as there is a spectator for the photograph an image results, but the discursive boundaries of the encounter cannot be predicted. Thus the image is never able to dilute its continual role as a pivot for processes of substitution. This is being realized to its greatest degree through the convergences of text, computer, photography, and video in the hybrid medium of hypermedia.

Images operate at a level of autonomy, which does not bind them to a set of predetermined referential properties. However, the status of reference as a property cannot be eliminated. We can then begin to talk about autonomy and reference coexisting and the image being partially stripped of its referential qualities. What purpose is there in drawing an equation between photograph and image and language? Reference tends to become pinpointed as the term of an inevitable identity when it is precisely the site of a process of argument and negotiation around meaning.

Lumière and Méliès

Photographic practitioners both initiated and sustained an *institutional* structure to uphold the idea of the *memory trace* (as a way of simplifying the transformative qualities of image-taking processes)—a concept not born in an ontological sense from within the properties of the medium itself. Crucially, it is vantage point that is the central raison d'être for the conceptualization of

33. Jean-Paul Sartre in *Camera Lucida*, 20.

the trace since it is founded on a Cartesian perspectivalism that makes it possible to theoretically envision a moment outside of subjectivity. Yet the photograph never functions with that kind of intrinsic autonomy. What must be recognized here is that the photograph is a subset of the image. At the institutional and cultural level there is nothing to prevent the photograph from being separated from the image. The choice, once it is made, tends to transform the observer's gaze into a function of the photograph, which as Barthes has so eloquently argued, *naturalizes* the artifice of the exchange. The result is a reversal of image and photograph with the latter taking precedence over the former in a chain of relations then described as representational. In other words, the process of thinking, which is simultaneous to the act of viewing, is subdivided into an opposition between representation and depiction. The viewing subject becomes a *witness* to representation, as if he has not created the interaction. In this sense the photograph comes to signify an absence, but it is not so much the real that is missing but the viewers themselves.

Let me return to the example of Jerome who "saw" an image of himself he didn't like. In other words he saw himself as if the photograph was not filled with a specific or expected meaning. He looked through, in the Barthesian sense, at an absence and created a presence. Yet he claimed the photograph was at fault—that the photograph was incorrect, and not his vision of it because he wanted it retouched. In part, he confused the relationship of image and photo. In the "royal" sense he assumed his perception was correct and the photograph was wrong.

This act of replacement where the photo takes on a life of its own and thus a power separate from the eye that views it confers a status upon the object that in fact eliminates the power of the eye. Thus it is not so much the photograph that disappears but the capacity of the viewer to reflect upon his or her relationship to the picture. Consciousness, sight, and photograph are seen as one, and the process of *visualization* is presented as dramatically different from the many different ways all of these relations are imagined over and over again. It would be interesting to speculate on the impact of virtual reality images on this argument and the notion of being "wired"!

Though Jean-Luc Godard quite wisely inverted the following opposition between the Lumière brothers and Georges Méliès, it remains at the heart of debates around the production of meaning in images. For Lumière, an image was photographic if it matched the requirements of human vision, that is, if it had something like a recognizable form so that the screen (in the case of the cinema) or the photographic print would display the needs of the "eye" within it. To Méliès, on the other hand, the eye was impoverished and conditioned by everyday life to exclude the real source of its capacity to "see," which was the imagination. The durability and longevity of this opposition has, along with other factors, conditioned discussions of realism with regard to images. For our purposes, however, images are in need of a quite different set of definitions and thus the opposition suggested above—illusion versus reality—connotes a rather complex bind from which it may not be possible to generate any clear conceptualizations. Godard's assertion that Lumière was a creator of fantasy and Méliès was the true realist does not confront the possibility that the polarity may not exist within the framework put forth by the filmmakers themselves. Godard's inversion may fall prey to the very ideology he was trying to avoid. The dichotomy here between two parts of what may be a continuum (the illusory and real meshing at all times) will be discussed in greater detail in when I talk about Godard's film, *Letter to Jane*.

Barthes takes up this debate by asserting that photographs are never, in a general or immediate sense, distinguished "from their referent." "Thus it is not impossible to perceive the photographic signifier, but it requires a secondary action of knowledge or of reflection" (Barthes 5).

Barthes via Sartre: "To determine the properties of the image as image I must turn to a new act of consciousness: I must *reflect*. Thus the image as image is describable only by an act of the second degree in which attention is turned away from the object and directed to the manner in which the object is given" (Sartre 1).

This assertion of a primary and secondary level to the act of perception is in Sartre's case related to an activity of inner reflection. Barthes has transposed this reflection to the photograph and in so doing has made the photograph a part of consciousness—photo to eye. The viewer is able to engage in a secondary act as a result of the way photographs carry their meanings within them. The idea that the "photograph carries the referent within it," sine qua non, means that the viewer has not engaged in a process of construction of meaning in the first instance, just as the photographer has only been an accessory to a process over which he or she has had no real control. This presumption assumes that a photograph of a house carries the meaning of "house" with it. But the argument can be made that there is no logical necessity for the house to be so named nor for the photograph to be dependent upon the external meaning, house. The drift between internal and external is crucial here. For while the photograph establishes a boundary that marks off the "real," it also disavows its own limitations. As the photograph is transformed into an image, those limitations expand or contract through the language used. But what would happen if the photograph of a house were described as an image of a lion sleeping on the veldt in Africa? There is an explosion of possibilities, a surreal juxtaposition of potential constructs which reveal that the photograph changes into an image at the instant it is "apprehended"—that is, subjectivity *replaces* the photograph.[34] The representational effect is not "There is a house!" but "I just saw a lion sleeping on the veldt in Africa." What has been named is the subject, what has been described is subject position, and this challenges the presumption that the photograph can ever contain within it—as object—any likeness of the house outside of the strategic cultural efforts to validate its meaning. There is a conflict here between an intention to name "house" through the image and the potential subjective sphere in which the arbitrary movement of meanings is not just a possibility, but the basis upon which meaning as such is negotiated. I think the concept of negotiation has to be kept in the forefront. It moves us away from thinking in global or inclusive terms. The negotiation of meaning repositions the overlapping boundaries of vision and comprehension. It strengthens the arguments, not for an ever-fluid or overly dominant notion of subjectivity, but for the continual subjective work involved in the recovery of meaning, in the marking out of the creative relationship between discourse and knowledge. It points toward sites of struggle and contestation where the aim is not to deny linkages of meaning but to broaden the scope through which they are created and maintained.

The fascinating thing is that arbitrariness is often assumed to be a negative characteristic of relations of signification, a process to be overcome so that potential contradictions of meaning can be resolved. It seems obvious, however, that without the arbitrary characteristics of the image and the photograph, we would be locked into a representational system of predictable messages with equally predictable responses and interpretations. The desire to eliminate many of the ambiguities of reference suggests that meaning must be looked for *in* the photograph, which as a result becomes a container filled, as it were, with the traces of the signifying properties of the objects or subjects it enframes. Here, vision becomes an accessory to what has influenced the process of depiction—the unsteady eye is replaced with a truthful picture—an image produced by technology suddenly makes the activities of viewing possible.

Paradoxically, because of this, the photo can at once be a vehicle of debasement and/or an arena of scientific activity A crucial assumption is invoked: to understand a photo means distilling what is visible, that is, "visualizing" in the most concrete way possible those elements that presumably communicate information. Fundamentally, the photograph takes on the qualities of a subject and generates processes of interpretation through *its* mapping

34. This was of course a central argument within the Surrealist movement. It was taken up by Walter Benjamin as a strategy for talking about dream-work. The hallucinations of everyday life become the premise for artistic activity and at the same time reinform the everyday with the creativity needed to create new forms of political action. This aesthetics of politics and history was the centerpiece of André Breton's approach to art and a crucial element in Benjamin's fascination with images in general. See Peter Osborne, "Small-scale Victories, Large-scale Defeats: Walter Benjamin's Politics of Time," in *Walter Benjamin's Philosophy: Destruction and Experience*, ed. Andrew Benjamin and Peter Osborne (London and New York: Routledge, 1994), 62–67.

of a referential structure, and this produces the paradoxical notion that photographs have a language. The suggestion is that their meaning is organized along linguistic lines, which of course is only possible—even if we have the most reductive notion of language itself—if the photograph has a consciousness (and that is only possible if we decide to project that idea *into* the photograph).

Death of a Cameraman

The ambiguities in photographs lie with the paradoxes of materiality and loss, the *simultaneity* of presence and absence, though all of these relations are not dichotomous. The following example illustrates this. When Neil Davis, an NBC cameraman, died in Thailand during an abortive coup in 1985, his camera continued to run. His death, according to the news media that used the footage, was recorded by him. Of course, that is an impossibility. But, what it points out is a fascination with visualizing what can never be seen, preserving the process of dying as if life and death can be materialized through the image. To "see" death in a photograph, or for that matter, on a screen, one must see the death of *an Other*. But what then is one seeing?

The photograph of Neil Davis, which was on the front pages of many newspapers, showed his body in the arms of his sound man. But, even as I say this my language simplifies the complexity of the relationship between the newspaper picture and the work of interpretation and analysis. I saw Davis's dead leg and lifeless torso. His leg was twisted into an impossible position and then frozen. I didn't see his face because he was holding onto his camera. Yet this description only hints at the profound sense of disgust that I felt at the way his death brought to life my own fears, at the need I felt to personalize an event that had taken place many thousands of miles away from my home. In so doing, I located his death within the confines of the photograph for an instant, in order to confirm my narrative of his pain. To return to a previous point, this is why the photograph seems to slip out of the control of the viewer even as she reasserts control by placing the meaning back into the photograph. The narrative seems to be authored elsewhere. Yet the struggle to regain and define authority *continues* within the viewer.

During the Vietnam War, Buddhist monks burned themselves in front of television, movie, and still cameras. It was an act of supreme sacrifice, supreme protest. But it remained, once preserved in the form of a photograph or on the screen or on television, not the record, not even the preserved etchings of death, but the death of our separation from the act itself. One saw, through an empathy for those men, what it meant to be *seen* dying. The monks knew that the substance of their protest was visual, spiritual, and political, but they also understood better than anyone else that "seeing" death was only possible from within life, and even then there was no guarantee that anyone would mourn. Thus the act of preserving their self-immolation photographically was itself an activity of death because the "visualizations" provided by images cannot be reduced to the convenience of the image as a representation. And what the image replaces is not the reality from which it has been "taken" (Does the camera remove some part of the real onto celluloid? Is the piece of reality that the photograph appropriates replaced or returned after it has been taken? Or is reality in any case merely an image awaiting some form of recognition by the camera?). Rather, what is replaced is the viewer, who is seen as an appendage to a set of givens that seemingly delineate for him or her the boundaries between cognition, fantasy, and the visible.

Thus my conversion of Neil Davis into a dead body is as much an act of the imagination as it is a recognition of the event itself. And the possibility that the real and the imaginary can act together at the same time to produce my experience of Davis's death suggests that the photograph may be playing a far less significant role in the networks of meaning that I put in place to understand my experience of it. In the same sense, the photograph of a monk burning provides me with an entry into an event but not much else. In order to personalize what I see, I must introduce the present tense into the relationship. I do this by transforming the immolation into a combination of thoughts and reactions, a process whose outcome I cannot predict—I have to play within and with my memories. This is both the pleasure and the pain of using the present tense. It allows me to cohabit with a set of contradictions over which I must exercise some power, through which I identify my position, and as a consequence of which I negotiate the seen and the said as well as my memories of the deaths I have experienced.

Teshome Gabriel summarizes these contradictions in a piece entitled "Ruin and The Other: Toward a Language of Memory."[35] He talks about memory as a ruin, as a place within which our thoughts about the past are nomadic. "Here, nomadism refers to a state of mind with reference to a style of thinking and of signification. Moving through time and space along a varying path, this form of discourse rejects fixed positions. It is a form of discourse that does not accept the notion that there is only one narrative or one truth. The nomadic sensibility, as a form of discursive strategy, thus acknowledges and accepts undifferentiated histories and narratives" (Gabriel 217). Gabriel's notion of the ruin is itself taken from Benjamin, who borrowed the concept from Freud. Surrealists took up the idea as well because it suggests that mem-

---

35. Teshome H. Gabriel, "Ruin and the Other: Towards a Language of Memory," in *Otherness and the Media: The Ethnography of the Imagined and the Imaged*, ed. Hamid Naficy and Teshome H. Gabriel (Langhorne, Penn.: Harwood Academic Publishers, 1993), 211–20.

ory, death, and the imaginary are inextricably linked. Gabriel is talking about opening up as many doors as possible while at the same time never finding the stability of the center. The margins become a metaphor for repeated intrusions of the contingent into strategies of interpretation. Memories are the medium for this, for a recognition of the imaginary as the river within which consciousness of self swims. It is this sense of past and present coexisting within the embodied mind and spirit of the imagination that the dying Buddhist monk symbolizes. One of the most extraordinary things about the protest was the dignified silence of the men as they experienced the most excruciating pain imaginable. Their bodies represented the ruins of the civilized world—the death of memory, even as the protest itself suggested that a future was possible.

Sartre's Memory

"I look at a portrait of Peter. Through the photograph I concentrate on Peter in his physical individuality. The photograph is no longer the concrete object which gives me the perception; it serves as material for the image" (Sartre 21). So arbitrary is this relay of relationships that the notion of convention is often used to explained the repetitive appearance of what Sartre describes as the "indifference" of the object to what it signifies. The photograph appears over and over again millions of times, creating an associative network of meanings. However habitual, conventions are only as solid as the cultural and social institutions that sustain them. The relative impermanence of the photograph is the reason why it can function as an accessory to memory but never be memory itself. Memories are a function of consciousness and not of the photograph. The family album doesn't inform the viewer about the past as much as it makes possible a narrativization of memory by many different members of the same family.

The moment of the photograph can never be repeated which is at the heart of the nostalgia felt for the events or people depicted. Any resemblance between Peter and his photograph can only be posited or proposed if Peter exists within the moment of his image, forever. This suggests that we are inevitably dealing with various levels of approximation, which paradoxically tends to harden the notion of convention and thus of representation. "The entreaty to perceive Peter has not disappeared, but it has entered into an imagined synthesis" (Sartre 23).

This imagined synthesis is based on presumptions of truth. Whatever the constraints, the assertion will always be, "that is Peter." There is an irony haunting this relationship between truth, representation, and image, and it has come to the fore with notions of the postphotographic. It is now the case that most photographs can be digitally altered through computer technology. This movement from the chemical to the electronic has provoked some serious questions about the photograph as a representational device, particularly with respect to photojournalism.[36] The paradox is that as computers allow for a complete redefinition of photographic representation, the argument that surfaces is that chemically based images were somehow more faithful to what they depicted. The postphotographic construction of meaning becomes the site for precisely the same kinds of questions that have always haunted photographs, questions centered on whether or not truth is present. The beauty is that digitally remastering if not digitally producing photographic prints merely points out what has always been the case. Photographs have always been subject to design and redesign, to constructivist and deconstructivist practices that have made truth the playground for the imagination with images as the prop, a theater for fantasy as André Breton and Georges Bataille recognized and as was put into practice by people like Mapplethorpe and Avedon.

Sight is a mental construct, since the connections between seeing, perceiving, and knowing are at best only available to us through hypotheses about the results of their interaction. When we speak then of seeing, are we speaking of a process? Or of the products of that process? And as the word *process* suggests, the maelstrom of visual activities accompanying the viewing of a photograph cannot simply be reduced to the technological instance represented by the print. The desire to make the print the pivot for all of this says more about the desire of the viewer than it does about the photograph itself. The visual properties of a photograph are quickly enhanced and often reduced by the activities of viewing, which transform photographic prints into images. Meaning is in large measure defined by the context in which the image is viewed and isn't only a result of the aesthetic, ideological, and philosophical constraints initially put in place by the photographer.

This process not only creates the possibility of substitution (I substitute myself for what I see), but also transforms the objects of sight (what I see is no longer separate from me, thus, I only hear what I have said). The activity of viewing allows the spectator to engage in projecting as well as transforming the image into a site of meaning. What we have then are not simply photographs—they do not represent the activities of perception within them. They can only be understood as *instances* of viewing, or if one were to give them a topographic description, images are found between print and spectator. This does not mean that every image is different for every viewer. Rather, it means that what is shared by an audience, and there is much that is shared, cannot be located outside of the exchange process which in an endlessly circumscribed fashion establishes, denies, and reestablishes the limits of spectating.

I would suggest that there is very little permanence to the photographic

36. Fred Ritchin, "Photojournalism in the Age of Computers," in *The Critical Image*, ed. Carol Squiers (Seattle: Bay Press, 1990), 28–37. Also see the work of W. Mitchell in *The Reconfigured Eye: Visual Truth in the Post-Photographic Era* (Cambridge, Mass.: MIT Press, 1992).

print. It merely permits a viewer or viewers to speak (or write) about image-based configurations subject to almost continuous interpretation and reinterpretation. This lack of fixity seems to be in direct contradiction with the status of the print itself. But as image, a print merely provides a context. It does not have the status of language, does not speak to the viewer. The spectator, in speaking to it, generates the potential for reference which is in part what Godard recognized when he claimed that the magician, Georges Méliès, was a documentarian.

In other words, Jerome's eyes see nothing other than hypotheses of himself as viewer. He has not looked into Napoleon's eyes, even though, through an imaginary jump, Barthes proposes that he has. Can we gain access to what Jerome is thinking by looking at his photograph? Obviously we can in some respects, though in so doing the photo becomes part of a wider field of meaning—image—the derivations of which are both arbitrary and ambiguous—his thoughts are my own, though I confer the act of possession upon him. Jerome as such does not enter my consciousness in a direct sense. The image however, does permit an endless narrativization of Jerome's potential thoughts—stories within stories—the reason *Camera Lucida* is an essay written in the first person *as if* it is about to become a fiction. This tone of contingency is at the heart of Barthes's project—an analytic strategy in which representation and signification are never fixed, although this lack does not preclude or prevent the creation of boundaries.

What is at stake here is how we can talk about the production and reproduction of knowledge in our society. As well there are important questions about the objects we wish to study. An overemphasis on the visual characteristics of the image often results in a kind of *detached* definition of meaning and comprehension. Thus, images are often labeled as a sites of fantasy and illusion, and this naming is meant in a pejorative sense, as if images stand outside of our culture while at the same time producing it. The further suggestion growing out of this is that specific images have a determining effect on the way viewers think and act. There is then a power source, so to speak, which seems to be coming from a place beyond the social and cultural relations which are at its very raison d'être. What interests me is not whether images have an effect but why so much power is imputed to them. The image (in order to function, to work) always breaks away from the technology that produces it. The result is not simply an "object." Ironically, the viewer is engaged by a time-bound moment of communication simultaneously framed and unframed, magnified, flat, ghostlike, which to be experienced cannot simply be observed. The validation for the experience must be found in a relationship and not simply in the object.

Herein lies the problem and it is one which Barthes explores in great depth. It is always easier and convenient to conflate Jerome with the idea that he was the brother of Napoleon. It is seemingly more concrete to talk about the photograph by prioritizing its content. To do so gives a presence to Jerome that makes his otherwise more ambivalent status as image transparently dependent upon his status *outside* of the image. It is the received history of Napoleon which acts upon Barthes, and it is those texts with which he is engaged. There are an infinite number of things that Barthes could have said about the photo and yet he chose to mention his own shock at the historical connection to Napoleon. It is not an accident that of all the photographs in *Camera Lucida* the one which is missing is the photo of Jerome, as if the centerpiece for his opening argument in the book doesn't need the validation which the photograph might provide.

Toward Projection

"Let us consider this piece of paper on the table. The longer I look at it the more of its features are revealed to me. Each new orientation of my attention, of my analysis, shows me a new detail: the upper edge of the sheet is slightly warped; the end of the third line is dotted . . . etc. No matter how long I may look at an image, I shall never find anything in it but what I put there" (Sartre 7).

Sartre's subjectivism with all of its phenomenological roots is taken up with a vengeance in *Camera Lucida*. There clearly is a need to place some mediators between the discourse of the imaginary as it is externalized by a subject and the piece of paper or the photograph. "The range of that which suggests itself as really photographable for a given social class (that is, the range of 'takeable' photographs or photographs to be 'taken', as opposed to the universe of realities which are objectively photographable given the technical possibilities of the camera) is defined by implicit models which may be understood via photographic practice and its product."[37] Bourdieu goes on to discuss the cultural norms he feels are at play when a photograph is taken. These norms, he suggests, are class based, and this is perhaps the least interesting element of his argument. Most useful for our purposes is Bourdieu's development of a clear argument for the social and cultural configurations that he feels constrain the popular imaginary from conceiving of the photographic act in anything but the most limited of ways.

The contrast here between a phenomenological and objectivist approach is most pronounced in the following quotation from Barthes.

"In 1865, young Lewis Payne tried to assassinate Secretary of State W. H. Seward. Alexander Gardner photographed him in his cell, where he was

37. Pierre Bourdieu, *Photography: A Middle-brow Art,* tr. Shaun Whiteside (Stanford: Stanford University Press, 1990), 6.

waiting to be hanged. The photograph is handsome, as is the boy: that is the *studium*. [*Author's note*: Barthes's term for a process of perception that doesn't have an immediate effect; meaning is not apprehended in an instant.] But the *punctum* (the opposite of studium—immediacy, almost shock at the recognition of meaning) is: *he is going to die*. I read at the same time: *This will be* and *this has been*; I observe with horror an anterior future of which death is the stake. By giving me the absolute past of the pose the photograph tells me death in the future. What *pricks* me is the discovery of this equivalence. In front of the photograph of my mother as a child, I tell myself: she is going to die: I shudder, like Winnicott's psychotic patient, *over a catastrophe which has already occurred*. Whether or not the subject is already dead, every photograph is this catastrophe." (Barthes 96)

Thus, as Sartre has also suggested (Sartre 23, 24), the image is a place within which endless additions can be made because the activity of "observation" is immediately enriched by the imaginary. But for Barthes the question of the *death* of Lewis Payne somehow brings the photograph to another level. He is able to confirm the death although he will never "see" it, able, that is, to bring history into the argument at the same time as he poeticizes both his discourse and the event. As an additional example, he sees his mother as a child and anticipates her death. The visible then pivots on the photographic in much the same way as the photographic anticipates its relationship to the historical moment it is forever creating and denying.

Let me reverse the terms of the argument for a moment. How then does an image become a picture? It would be difficult to talk about an image without also talking about the pictorial. The pictorial is a quality that one attributes to the image. It would be incorrect to assume that the pictorial is based in a simple sense on the visual. If there is a picture in an image, it acts somewhat like a proposition, proposing, that is, the relationship between a concept and a visual trace. A trace, however, doesn't have to have a relationship with what it is designating. A visual trace can have a life of its own but it is ultimately a performative device fitting into a context of communication and exchange. Its structure is not sequential; that is, a series of traces need not be related, one to the other, for there to be meaning. A visual trace pivots on the space between meaning and communication. In that sense its materiality will not be the result of any one cause. Its materiality can in fact be produced by the absence of the photographic.

It may be necessary now to refine the concept of the image and to talk about *projection*, a process that performs the visual, disrupts linearity, and undermines the presumed equilibrium between signification and representation. The performance of the visual produces a series of traces, and what results is an "afterimage." That describes very little of what happens to the pictorial when it is transformed into an impressionistic configuration of shades, which alter what at "first sight" seems to be immediately accessible. First sight, lost sight, memory of sight—the indicators of displacement and replacement. The traces of which I am speaking here are not signs, but lost sights. Their power lies in their contingent nature and their incompleteness.

One would have to introduce here a variety of different questions. Is there a difference between an image that is succinct and one that is not? Can one talk about an image as a schemata? Can the inherent plurality of the image be disengaged long enough to discover its parts? Is there a system that organizes visual traces into coherent expressions? Can the boundaries of the image be clearly and easily established in relation to the viewing process?

For Edison and for Lumière, in the late nineteenth and early twentieth century, the image was a scientific instrument that could research the real by capturing its essence. In part this was done so as to be able to see what the eye could not. Ironically, the fragmentation of space, the stopping of time, and the reduction of movement to a pattern of visual traces became vehicles for seeing more, not something different, thus expanding vision, going beyond the real to a level that could explain and simultaneously duplicate it. The desire to make patterns of movement intelligible (the galloping of a horse, the running motion of a human being) made it seem as if science and image were natural partners. History was also subsumed under the same process and newsreels were not accidently named. The play on the words real and reel (as in "newsreel") reflected the need to constantly assert truth, in a sense to force truth into and onto the image. To produce truth meant to duplicate reality, that is, to replace projection with reproduction.

Yet, if we are ready to accept that images do not simply reconstruct the real or just recontextualize its properties, then we must also accept the reciprocal effect that the transformational qualities of the image confer on reality. The projected image represents a relationship among a number of different levels of meaning. And it is the stresses and the strains of that relationship which produce the *idea* of the photograph. Acting more precisely at the level of a relation, the image is the clearest evidence of the difficulty that photographs have with replication. Meaning will not be found as a result in reality or in the image or in processes of projection, but in the manner in which all of these elements interact, in the very "site" created by their interaction. None of these parts of what is an *endlessly* divisible whole are the privileged site of truth, because they can never claim to be outside of the links uniting theme nor outside of the divisions separating them. As a result, images do not depict a real that is absent from the photograph and then brought to life by interpretation or viewing. The process is neither mechanical nor linear. There are no prior moments outside of the image, no history that doesn't at one and the same time declare itself as image and as discourse and as event.

Clearly, the relationship between images and reality is one of interdependence, but that is precisely why a photograph, for example, does not *display* reference. Photographs taken in the home for example have to be contextualized by the life narrative into which they are placed. What they display are the traces of a process both descriptive and interpretive. A photo is a metacommunication about an event, a person, an object. It is not simply "acting in place of," "standing for," "replacing" what it seems to be picturing.

Crucially then, a photograph of Clint Eastwood, to extend my previous example, has at best a very distant connection to the "real" man. The various levels of signification that constitute his symbolic existence pivot not around his absence but around the impossibility of his presence. In that sense a photograph isn't a substitute for him but is merely part of a vast system of signification into which he is constantly placed and which precludes the possibility of Eastwood ever coming to life as an exemplification of what he has come to signify. It is in this sense that he is both a production and a projection. Interviews with the "real man," newspaper articles about him, films in which he acts—all of these merely confirm a continuing spiral away from the simplicity of reference into a mosaic or constellation of meanings.

The distinction between signification and the real, especially as it is applied to the image, produces a division between reflection and reproduction. Yet significations are precisely the material upon which the real must also be built or constructed. For as soon as the distinction between the real and signification is introduced, the material world is "represented" as having greater significance. The connection is then reintroduced as a function of duplication, which tends to stress the power of the symbolic over the real. In both cases either the real produces the properties of the symbolic or the symbolic explains and produces the logic of the real. Yet clearly neither can exist without the other. The notion of reflections denies relations of meaning and creates a context in which a neutral technology generates a neutralized content. Thus reflection strips the visual of its conceptual framework while asserting that concepts can be expressed and explained through representations.

The image in and of itself does not name what it depicts. It merely sets in place a process of potential identity. The visible in an image is therefore merely a fragment of what is signified. Take the ironic name, newsphoto (which is related to newsreel). The name softens the effect of the disjuncture between information and picture, and an aura of truth is created around that disjuncture. The truth may be in the way that disjuncture, with all of its contradictions and divisions, is suppressed. The picture of that suppression can only be included in the photographic with great difficulty. It becomes possible for a representation to represent a representation and so on. What is important is where we choose to place the boundaries (though Jean Baudrillard would assert that the boundaries have long ago disappeared). The boundaries of the photographic print are in part shaped by the distance of the spectator from it.

The closer one gets to the print, the more the boundary is disrupted. The print has not changed but our relationship to it has. There is here, potentially, an endless series of relationships. The pivots for meaning will be found not in some "pure" visual apprehension, but in the conjuncture of boundaries chosen to produce the visual, that is, the way the conjuncture is understood, related to, constructed.

Barthes, confronted by all of these paradoxes, collapses the contradictions into the theoretical proposition that the photographic act and the apprehension of meaning are imbued with a kind of "madness" that various institutional, social and cultural processes attempt to control. The madness is situated in the lack of control that viewers have over their relationship to understanding, because for the most part the photographic process drains as much as it confers. In the end he returns to an argument that denounces the lack of authenticity produced out of this process and calls for the abolition of the image.

I will not conclude this chapter with a wrap-up statement to explain Barthes's anxiety or provide an easy answer to resolve the dilemmas he describes. Suffice to say for the moment that Barthes anticipated the arguments of Jean Baudrillard in the latter part of *Camera Lucida* and in so doing returned to the existential tradition outlined by Sartre in *The Psychology of the Imagination*. The image and the photograph become the bearers of loss and yet remain subjects of discussion. It is precisely this "endless" flow that must be grappled with in a continuum of image production, which will always be responding to paradox as well as generating contradiction. I see no need to confront the breaks as if they must be soldered together. Rather, and with *jouissance*, I embrace the irony that we must never give up learning why all of these "breakdowns" are a necessary condition of our use of images.

3 From Photograph to Film
Textual Analysis

The Disappearance of the Image: *Wavelength*

At the end of Michael Snow's film *Wavelength*, a photograph visible at a distance but obscured comes into view. This is after forty-five minutes of slow movement from one end of a long room to another, generated by the telephoto movement of a camera locked into a fixed position. Incrementally, as it fills the frame, the photograph reveals itself to be an image of the ocean taken from a cliff. As the film ends, the photograph fills the screen. The waves are still, frozen in time.

Wavelength is about the time and space of images, about the way images can simultaneously be everywhere, irrespective of the conventional constraints we place on what they picture or how we relate to them. The film interweaves time into this picture of arbitrariness—such that sequence and duration, essential to the integrity of storytelling in the cinema, are unveiled as formal devices. Formal in the sense that they are the product of a melding of technology with aesthetic concerns—formal because they represent structure without a fixed signifying architecture. It is this capacity to engage movement, stillness, time, and space, to mix them up and rearrange their very premises, that distinguishes film as a medium from photography. *Wavelength* theorizes about the impact of that separation and in so doing plays a game of cat and mouse with film history, film practice, and image theory.[1] "A persistent polarity shapes the film. Throughout, there is an exploration of the room, a long studio, as a field of space, subject to the arbitrary events of the outside world so long as the zoom is recessive enough to see the windows and thereby the street. The room, during the day, at night, on different film stock for colour tone, with filters, and even occasionally in negative is gradually closing up its space as the zoom nears the backwall and the final image of a photograph upon it—a photograph of waves. This is the story of the diminishing area of pure potentiality."[2]

---

1. Some of these issues are examined by Regina Cornwall in *Snow Seen: The Films and Photographs of Michael Snow*, (Toronto: PMA Books, 1979).
2. P. Adams Sitney, "Structural Film," *Film Culture Reader*, ed. P. Adams Sitney (New York: Praeger, 1970), 332.

Wavelength was hailed as a brilliant avant-garde film when it came out in 1967, because it challenged the norms in place for the creation (and one could say, analysis) of images since the cinema's inception in the late 1890s. Gilles Deleuze has characterized this shift as a movement (in the literal and figurative sense) through space in which space itself becomes the subject matter of the film. "the shadows, the whites, the colours, the inexorable progression, the inexorable reduction, elevation plane, the disconnected parts, the empty set: all come into play here."[3] For P. Adams Sitney, "structure becomes form" and this phrase became a rallying call for what Sitney and others described as a new genre of experimental cinema which they named structuralist. *Wavelength*, which has a soundtrack made up of machine voice, and live sound from the room in which it was shot, also challenges notions of sequence and duration. No particular moment in the film need follow from the next. Everything is reversible—including the zoom of the camera. All filmic images play with time, but in Snow's case time takes on a shape and form, as if it can be touched, as if images encourage a concreteness that their own projection tends to negate.

Wavelength examines the boundary markers for meaning in the cinema and in particular how and whether the frame operates as a potential point of exploration for analysis and interpretation. It examines time and then shows the frame to be a fuzzy boundary between the experience of seeing and interpretation. It questions the link between the photographic and the cinematic by shifting the debate away from the simplicity of that opposition. Most importantly, Snow, as he does with his film *Presents*, wades into the theoretical discussion about how to analyze and interpret the experience of images. What is at stake here is not whether there is a system to film form, but to what degree and with what emphasis form can be a vehicle of communication. Is there a moment beyond words, beyond the conventional parameters of vision and hearing (because the film is dominated by a high-pitched sound) for which we have no clear discursive tools?

Let me return for a moment to a discussion of photography in order to more fully explore the questions Snow raises. Photographs produce framed boundaries between prints and "scenes." The relationship between photographic meaning and the boundary markers of print and picture will be affected by the *use* to which the photograph is put and by the way its signifying properties are described and interpreted. This happens at a number of different levels of comprehension, description, analysis, and interpretation, with the result being a multilevel process that recasts and restructures the pictorial content of the photograph and gives new meaning to its aesthetic organization. This restructuring affects the meaning of the photograph as it is viewed and

3. Gilles Deleuze, *Cinema 1 The Movement-Image*, tr. Hugh Tomlinson and Barbara Habberjam (Minneapolis: University of Minnesota Press, 1986), 122.

also transforms its identity as an object of communication. Although to some degree the photograph then "disappears" into a discursive form, this in no way eliminates the pictorial nature of the photograph which generally opens up many potential arenas of thought and explanation. Rather, the relationship between the pictorial and the discursive is unveiled as a contingent one dependent on the context into which the photograph is placed. This process pivots on the interactivity of signification and viewing, but there need be no particular point of departure and no obvious end to the approach taken. The frame of a photograph sets out a *hypothetical* space within which an infinite number of arguments can be developed and deployed. As Snow reveals, photographs become images when they lend themselves to the general and the specific at the same time. Thus, to see a photograph of the car one owns may encourage a movement from the personal to the general and back depending on the choice of discourse. It can be a Honda, my Honda, the Honda my uncle crashed, the Honda that was a lemon, and so forth. The choice of boundary here will momentarily enframe this activity but not put an end to it, which is of course one of the fundamental differences between photographs and images.

Framed photographs can be appropriated for any number of different uses, can be talked about in so many different ways, that the link between the pictorial, communication, and interpretation is almost entirely context-dependent. Talking or writing about a photograph never exhausts the many strategic choices that can be made with regard to understanding its meaning. Although a photograph refers to a particular and sometimes quite specific moment, it is the axis upon which a variety of different explanations and interpretations can be developed. This has long been recognized by artists whose appropriation of the photograph dissolved the notion of the original so as to make any number of interpretive, discursive, and visual reconstructions possible (e.g., pop art, in particular, Andy Warhol).

Recent experiments by German photographers have taken this principle and moved it even further. Sigmar Polke, for example, takes photographs of Goya paintings and reworks the images to create a blend of possible meanings that play with history and notions of the original.[4] As the original disappears, so do the boundaries of time built into the pictorial. The photograph loses its purity, its uniqueness, and dissolves intentionality into a mix of attributes derived from viewing and the chain of discourses developed as the images travel from one context to another. This means that we are dealing with a constant flux of meanings that produce hybrids, networks, webs, from which any number of possible significations can be drawn. This flux has often been described

---

4. See his "Goya (The Old Women)," (1984), part of an exhibition at the Guggenheim Museum entitled *Photography in Contemporary German Art: 1960 to the Present*, held in 1993.

as intertextuality but as we shall see below, attributing the notion of text to the results of this process seems to dilute not only its complexity, but simplifies the possible points of entry for analysis as well as unnecessarily framing the visual with the textual.

My first viewing of *Wavelength*, as with many other experimental films of that period (late 1960s) by Stan Brakhage, Paul Sharits and Hollis Frampton among others, left me with the feeling that the images were peripheral to what I was doing to them. I was the sprocket hole struggling with my daydreams and thoughts as I drifted from the film performance into myself and back again. Yet I was always able to translate the experiences, always made the effort to give or take away meaning, to, in a sense, transform the images into a voyage. This was a hint to me that narratives can be generated from any picture, a hint also that intentionality finds its place, not so much in the authority of images but in the imaginary dialogues we establish with them.

So much of what is "not there" (Calvino 1988, 91) can be attributed to the filmmaker and to myself. The various associations we develop with images drift into and out of what Calvino calls the possible and the impossible. What interests me are the links, the connections between various levels of thought and fantasy. Linkages enable us to create and recreate our experiences of viewing. The links are a "place" in which we can practice what Calvino calls a "pedagogy of the imagination" (Calvino 1988, 92). Elsewhere, Calvino has commented on the task of the critic: "Every true book of criticism may be read like one of the texts it deals with, as a web of poetic metaphors."[5] It is the webbing I found myself in while "watching" *Wavelength*. Yet I wasn't caught, nor did I find myself without potential points of exit and reentry. Calvino again: "Each meaning faded into the next, and on the walls the rain was soaking the election posters, suddenly aged, as if their aggressiveness had died the last evening of the political battle among meetings and billposters, the night before last, and as if these posters were already reduced to a patina of paste and cheap paper, where, layer upon layer, the symbols of the opposing parties could be read, transparently. At times the world's complexity seemed to Amerigo a superimposition of clearly distinct strata, like the leaves of an artichoke; at other times, it seemed a clump of meanings, a gluey dough."[6]

Is There a Medium for the Message? From Photography to Film

Photographers, particularly those most heavily linked into the use of photographs for describing and transmitting information about the cultures and

5. Italo Calvino, *The Uses of Literature*, tr. Patrick Creagh (New York: Harcourt Brace Jovanovich, 1986), 59.

6. Italo Calvino, *The Watcher*, tr. William Weaver (New York: Harcourt Brace Jovanovich, 1971), 7.

events they photograph, try to limit and constrain the interpretive and discursive boundaries into which the image is placed. They operate on the other side of the photograph/discourse distinction, presuming that the discursive is a limitation, if not a weakness, in the links among meaning, expression, and comprehension (the idea that what you see is instantly understandable). The links and possible contradictions among seeing, discourse, and interpretation are devalued in favor of a vaguely theorized notion of information. A fascinating example of this is the work of Sergei Mikhailovich Prokudin-Gorskii, who was a pioneering photographer in Russia at the turn of the century. Prokudin-Gorskii "developed a system of producing three-part colour photographs that could be projected simultaneously. Using a small folding hand camera of the type designed by Mieth, he photographed three exposures of the same subject, made at about one-second intervals on a glass plate approximately 84–88 mm wide and 232 mm long, which was mounted vertically into the camera. The plate dropped to a new position after each exposure, and the image was captured through three different colour-separation filters. Because of the need to take the same picture three times, Prokudin-Gorskii was limited to subjects that would make no movement. Thus much of what he recorded consisted of fixed subjects."[7]

Prokudin-Gorskii was driven by the desire to document the changing urban and rural landscape of imperial Russia. His photographs were commissioned by the tsar, and his aim was to create a vast photographic archive for future generations. The colors he managed to produce were spectacular with an unimaginably rich set of hues—the result of his inventiveness as a chemist and the three-plate process mentioned above. The truth was crucial to him, and although his photographs often have the look of paintings, he insisted on their "naturalness." I mention Prokudin-Gorskii here not to attack the naiveté of his propositions about the natural nor his assumption about the ability of images to replicate what they capture. Rather, I am interested in how a range of possible interpretations narrows when images are almost entirely related to the scenes they are meant to picture. For Prokudin-Gorskii history is in the photographs. The boundaries of meaning are within (yet his photographs also represent a site of experimentation with chemistry. This is, in the first instance, what makes them so attractive). To me, although the frame is fixed, it is *through* the photograph that a viewer appropriates the elements necessary for the construction of meaning about the scenes depicted.

I will suggest as this chapter goes on that these debates and ambiguities have been applied to the analysis of the cinema and that the notion of the image itself has been transformed to fit the constraints of the frame. This is very

7. Robert H. Allshouse, ed., *Photographs for the Tsar: The Pioneering Color Photography of Sergei Mikhailovich Prokudin-Gorskii* (New York: The Dial Press, 1980), xiii.

much a consequence of the presumption that films and in fact all images are naturally linked to photography and share a similar process for the actualization of the real, for the construction and communication of meaning. I will examine the link between the photographic, the filmic, and the textual, which together form a triumverate of categories used in the analysis of *moving pictures* (most libraries still archive books on the cinema in the moving-picture category).

For example, the framed image extracted from a film,[8] either for purposes of illustration or quotation, valorizes the pictorial and is really the sign of a crisis, the crisis of how to reconstitute processes of visual communication and experience for the purposes of analysis, description, and interpretation. Films are converted into a series of photographs as if they are a text ready to be "read." Images are connected to each other by a system or by a code which can, so to speak, be extracted from the continuum that governs their projection. The code comes to stand for the images not only constraining their meaning but governing their interpretation. The difficulty with this approach is that few distinctions are drawn between text and film, among notions of textuality, projection, and performance.

The practice of textual analysis in film approaches these problems of representation and signification by assuming (a) that film is a text; (b) that the text represents an apparent unity; and (c) which then means that it must be broken up to discover the hidden relationships among its parts. This, it must be noted, is radically different from the hypothesis that representational systems produce meaning through a series of independent and autonomous systems which must then be brought together (the illusion of their separateness demystified) to reveal the inherent unity of all the parts.

Textual analysts[9] like Christian Metz assume that the frame is the central photographic unit of the cinema, a part or fragment of a whole and that its properties can not only be recovered, but can be described. Frames are used for illustrative as well as empirical reasons, constituent elements of shots and mise-en-scène. The composition of the frame can be described in much the same way, using the same interpretive language, as a photograph, or even a painting. The position of a character and for example, his or her dress, the location of various objects—all of these elements can be given significance by pulling the frame away from the film and describing it much as one might describe a pho-

---

8. It would be unusual for a book on the cinema *not* to have pictures derived from the movies under discussion as an important part of the text. This use of stills either derived from celluloid or from promotional photographs issued by the production companies is linked to a desire to quote from the films being examined.

9. Here I am referring to the work of, among many others, Christian Metz, *The Language of Film* (New York: Praeger, 1972), and Christian Metz, *The Imaginary Signifier: Psychoanalysis and the Cinema* (Bloomington: Indiana University Press, 1982).

tograph. There are important questions that must be raised regarding this strategy. Should the critical discourses used in relation to the cinema and photography be the same? Do they in fact share a similar historical genealogy? What is the effect, common since the invention of the cinema as a technology, of reproducing stills from films as if they represent a shot or a scene or even the entire film?[10]

Is the frame a unit of celluloid or a unit of what passes by on the screen? If it is a unit of celluloid, then the rules for its combination are of a different order than the rules for its presence on the screen. For the purposes of projection, frames are units of time. For the purposes of editing, frames become constituent elements in a projected set of relationships, which are both temporal and spatial, defined in large measure by the technology of the editing table.

Time passes in the cinema as a direct result of the number of frames projected. Through the exigencies of projection and interpretation, through the relationships established in the film theater, frames change into images. Cinematic images are permutations of what has been embedded in the celluloid, but because they are part of a circuit that involves viewing and comprehension, the relationship between an image and a frame is rather more arbitrary than that suggested by textual analysts. Strictly speaking, in projection, frames have no meaning. Except for the animated film, movies are not shot as a series of frames. For the purposes of textual analysis, however, the frame, now a still photograph, becomes an instance of signification and enunciation. The desire to produce a discrete unit, paradoxically rendered boundaryless by projection, is of course a function of the interpretive system applied to the whole film. (I will discuss digitalization at a later stage in this book; suffice to say, that my discussion here is limited to the more traditional technologies of cinema production which, as time goes on, are becoming more and more obsolete. Many of the principles of narrativity and textuality that characterize film form continue, however, to govern the newer productions coming out on CD-ROM and videodisc.)

However, if the "notion of photograph, by a sort of implicit synecdoche, designates in certain contexts the ensemble of figurative images obtained by mechanical means,"[11] then the frame becomes an instance of expression most fully dominated by what is *recognizable* in it. Metz is suggesting that meaning is found in an already constituted form in the photograph by virtue of its prop-

10. The effort by Alfred Guzzetti to break Jean-Luc Godard's film into its constituent parts essentially through the use of the script and photographs from the film ends up representing the film instead of presenting it. I am grateful to Hamid Naficy for pointing this out to me. Alfred Guzzetti, *Two or Three Things I Know About Her: Analysis of a Film by Godard* (Cambridge, Mass.: Harvard University Press, 1981)

11. Christian Metz, *Language and Cinema*, tr. Donna Jean Umiker-Sebeok (The Hague: Mouton, 1974), 229.

erties of stillness, and as a result the meaning can be extracted for analytical purposes. To assume that the frame simply introduces potential motion to a photograph and thus that the frame will reveal what motion hides, transforms the signifying structures of the cinema into a linear combination of pictures understood to operate as messages. The contextual factors influencing the way the framed photograph is classified and identified are immediately related to the film as if, for example, the temporally determined viewing relationship established by the spectator and the analyst can be given empirical force through quotation. But even a series of still photographs from a film cannot represent the way time has effected the development of meaning within the context of a projection. My claim will thus be that a frame is not a photograph and little is served by extracting a frame from a film for the purposes of analysis and interpretation. For example, the film *The Flicker*[12] tells its story not within the parameters of the frame but in the space between them. The film highlights the fact that frames, by themselves, tell us very little, and this meditation on the space in between tends to undermine the notion that the image must be visible in order for there to be meaning.

The aims of textual analysis are to isolate a set of discrete units. The resulting establishment of an identity between interpretation and enunciation becomes another way of reinscribing denotative referentiality as the base upon which visual expressions have to build their meanings. Thus, a frame becomes an instance of denotation. In textual analysis, the construction of unit relationships points toward a more complex web of connotation. What is suggested then is a causal link between a simpler level of meaning and a more complex one. David Bordwell has characterized this strategy in the following way: "textual analysis reveals the film's "unconscious," its repressed material that may surface in the slightest details of form and style."[13] Although Bordwell clearly uses the unconscious in a metaphorical sense, that is not the way Raymond Bellour, to whom he is referring, and Thierry Kuntzel make use of psychoanalysis. In particular, Bellour's article on Hitchcock's *North by Northwest*[14] subdivides the film into shots, for which he provides photographic frames, to empirically show how the hero of the film validates his paternal hold over the woman he loves. Bellour's approach is archeological not in the sense of Fou-

---

12. *The Flicker* was made by Tony Conrad in 1966. The film has been described as "imageless" by Ken Kelman, because Conrad used alternating frames of black and white of varying lengths to create a strobelike effect. "*The Flicker* built from relatively simple slow alterations of dark and light, to an overpowering effect where waves radiated over the audience as if some cold sun had risen in the theater." Ken Kelman, "Anticipations of the Light," in *The New American Cinema: A Critical Anthology*, ed. Gregory Battock (New York: Dutton, 1967), 31. Clearly, the film was not imageless.
13. David Bordwell, *Making Meaning: Inference and Rhetoric in the Interpretation of Cinema* (Cambridge, Mass.: Harvard University Press, 1989), 87.
14. Raymond Bellour, "Le blocage symbolique," *Communications* 23 (1975): 235–350.

cault, but of Freud, mediated by Jacques Lacan. It is not "just" a symptomatic reading of the film as Bordwell suggests; rather, the strategy is to confirm *a* reading, to make the film reveal its latent synchronic structure. The central aim is to provide a fixed thematic umbrella for which there is *visual proof*.

There is some difficulty, however, in applying textual analysis to a quickly moving camera where one frame reveals streaks of motion in the manner of an abstract-expressionist painting. The more abstract, the less figurative, the less likely that a determinate relation can be established between frames, either as units or as fragments of some greater whole. In other words, a priori, the analysis of still frames from a film focuses on those elements that can be *seen*, and this almost inevitably creates an hierarchical relationship in which the denotative is equated to the pictorial and the connotative represents the realm of ideas. It is rare for textual critics to work on more experimental images because these resist conventional definition and are continuously challenging the pictorial, are in fact raising serious questions about the very nature of the image. (This is in large part the challenge posed by the art video movement, but has been a longstanding characteristic of the experimental cinema as well. The work of filmmaker Maya Deren is a good example.)

The reduction of the cinema to a series of frames from which meaning can be distilled and then extracted collapses image relations into the equivalent of written texts. Cinematic specificity comes to be represented by the manner in which the stills taken from a film can express or exemplify a logical structure with the systematicity of grammar. The textual endeavor is then directed toward finding a "key" for the production of meaning, a formula to explain for example the repetition of a theme or of an action. Textual analysis is an attempt to generate a set of deterministic equations that reveal order and continuity within the discontinuous. The qualities of nonlinearity and instability are difficult to include. The key will be a revelation of unity—the narrative as an example of unity. Once the key has been put in place, it comes to represent and even name its original object of investigation. Of central importance here to further discussions in this book is the manner in which symbolic processes are reduced not only to the visible but the way in which time—filmic, historical—is elided so that the cinema's production of meaning seems to take place outside of the performative context, which is its very raison d'être. (At a minimum a performative approach tries to take account of voice, sound, cinema architecture, the ethnography of audiences, even the role of food in the experience of filmgoing, and so forth.)

Any analytic procedure inevitably reduces and constrains the boundaries of time if only to more fully grasp and discriminate among the differing levels of meaning available for study. But this does not mean that the reduction must become the site of meaning itself, outside of the relationship between the discursive and the performative. This point needs emphasis. Criticism maps sometimes similar and often contradictory elements into a coherent whole. This is not just a tendency of theoretical work; it is its very purpose. This process attempts to "visualize" that coherence[15] even as it claims that the map is merely an hypothesis and not a series of fixed points from which interpretations can be drawn. The map on its own becomes an object of and for criticism. There would be nothing wrong with this were the further claim not made that the territories of map and film, for example, are the same.

Letter to Jane (Fonda)

One might begin then to argue against the simplicity of the Godard-Gorin film, *Letter to Jane* which seems paradoxically to support the notion that a frame taken from a film will reveal a significant set of meanings which can then retrospectively be applied to the whole film in question. Their critique of Jane Fonda centers on her look, her gaze, as she tours a war-torn North Vietnam. They jump between the still image of her face in *L'Express* magazine to the presumably similar gaze of actors and actresses in a variety of Hollywood films. In particular, they use still frames of Fonda in *Klute* and *Tout Va Bien* and Henry Fonda in *Grapes of Wrath* and *Young Mr. Lincoln*. They compare her film-photo-frame with similar expressions they have found in other films and journals. They see it as the pain of a look that can project no solutions to the crisis upon which it is gazing, the pain of a look that detaches itself from its own role in producing history.

> The camera took this photograph from a low-angle. Actually in the history of the cinema this low point of view cannot be considered an innocent one. This fact has been emphasized technically and socially by Orson Wells in his first pictures. The choice of frame is not neutral or innocent either. The frame is composed in relation to the actress who is looking, rather than in relation to what she is looking at. She is presented in the frame as if she were a star. . . . The following page shows photographs of what she saw at other moments, but not what she was looking at in this photograph. As far as we are concerned these are the same type of pictures that now flow automatically through the channels of TV and newspaper publications in the free world.[16]

I would argue with their interpretation and with the simple deduction that we are getting a clue to the expressive quality of an image hitherto unnoticed in

15. See the schemata chosen by David Bordwell to represent "textual structure" and "a cognitive model of critical interpretation," in *Making Meaning*, 171 and 203. Also see the discussion of time and the visual by Johannes Fabian in *Time and the Other: How Anthropology Makes Its Object*, (New York: Columbia University Press, 1983).
16. "Excerpts from the transcript of Godard-Gorin's *Letter to Jane*," *Women and Film* 1. 3–4 (1974): 48.

the films to which they refer. They suggest that their interpretation reveals the presence of codes, but for Godard and Gorin *codes* become a set of ahistorical rule-based systems dominating the production of meaning at all levels of discourse and performance. It specifies particular expressions or gestures as fixed. With the photo as their base, Godard and Gorin are thus able to argue as if they have, through an empirical process, discovered meanings that appear not to be in the images to which they refer. Of course what is interesting about *Letter to Jane* is that it is a film, and the filmmakers use the medium to make an argument about the cinema in general. Their conflation of the history of cinema into a series of gestures is precisely at the heart of the decontextualization I have been discussing. Crucially, they made the film when frame analysis was introduced into film theory and into the theory of images in general in 1972. They make a fetish of the visible and in so doing make no room for Fonda's voice, for her response to their accusations.

Their argument, that they are reintroducing the historical, is stripped of significance by their emphatic formalism. The codes they discover are merely entry points for their own interpretive grid. Their description of *the look* sounds more like an explanation of a natural law. (I must stress that this is not an accidental outcome of the approach they chose; rather their elevation of the codic to law confers authority upon their own interpretation. The result is a taxonomy of looks and gazes that rises above the history of the cinema, let alone of Jane Fonda, and becomes a determining factor in the production of all films and a methodological grid into which all photographs and images must fit.) Their reflections on Jane Fonda's image-picture-expression in *L'Express* paradigmatically come to stand for all such expressions in film (as if the still from the magazine is no different from the way in which the cinema produces images). For the purposes of illustration, they extract still after still from other films and compare each to pictures in journals and newspapers. The role of each medium, the particular role of each expression, the exigencies, historical and otherwise, that affected the production of a cinematic image and/or a newspaper picture are all put aside in a privileging of an empirically fixed meaning. But why, one may well ask, would Godard and Gorin, at that stage staunch Maoists, be pushed toward empiricism? To a certain degree they were caught by a rather mechanistic view not only of the image but of the way audiences react to images. They didn't suggest that Fonda's image might have a probable effect—to them the picture confirmed an inevitable outcome to any reading of it. Their reductiveness turns the interactions of expression and understanding into predictable processes. More important here is the status given to the history of the image in Hollywood which for Godard and Gorin is synchronous. Jane Fonda's gaze and those of so many film stars before her become part of a static pattern of meanings which are fixed, permanent, held in place by a transparently causal relationship between the industrial structure of the cinema, its star system, and the spectator. They never explain their historical model nor do they give any place in the film to a discussion of determination. The power of their critique comes not from the evidence that they so smugly uncover, but from the aggressiveness of their polemic which often borders on misogyny.

Their movement from what is observable to what isn't presumes a jump to theory and history. But, and this is also a central characteristic of textual analysis in film, they presume that the generalizations they are making are homologous with the laws that govern meaning production in the cinema. They generate an isomorphic relationship between the image and their theory of it and in so doing collapse the distinction of model (an abstract construction) and text (understood to be empirical). This collapse allows them to explain the links joining a variety of different photographs of different people as predictably similar. The very history of each photograph, their letter to Jane, does not uncover any new relations of meaning. It simply narrativizes the way they have gathered their information.

There is a substantial difference between constructing a model designed to prove that meaning will be produced from a specific combination of constituent elements, and a model concerned with the wider set of probable processes that develop out of the continuous circulation of meaning in any setting. Theory and the construction of paradigms always alter the complexity of the phenomena they examine, and this is a necessary feature of theoretical inquiry. For both Godard and Gorin the activity of critiquing Jane Fonda is really a programmatic way of designing and redesigning their own filmmaking and locking the viewer into an intentional structure from which the viewer can't escape. As a result their approach comes very close to being antitheoretical. It is also a way of containing what they see as the fundamental disorder that filmic meaning production puts in place through performance. The connections they construct are meant to have both a theoretical and practical outcome. Not only will our view of Jane Fonda change, but their new history may also programmatically affect the approach filmmakers take to the stars whom they use for their films. For our purposes what is important here is the degree to which celluloid-time overwhelms the historical time of a film's projection performance. The condensations that make time possible in the cinema need not be part of the representational process. For example, the apparent unity of a narrative film must be recognized as a strategic response to disorder, to the numerous ways in which the cinema's transformational characteristics generate meanings that cannot be anticipated by referring to celluloid. This leads to the arbitrary historical reinscriptions practiced by Godard and Gorin, a process they paradoxically want to restrain under the guise of demystification.

Celluloid-Time/Performance-Time

An important question arises at this point. How can one grasp hold of the image for the purposes of criticism and analysis in order to analyze it more fully? Is it not valid to subdivide a film into parts and thus be able to assign different meanings to those fragments and then to extract a frame as a marker and example—to be able, in a sense, to quote? I think that both questions have to be answered in a qualified way, keeping in mind that the movement from celluloid to projection to text means not only that time is being changed, but that the historical axis upon which the analysis depends will also shift. Changing the performance of a film into a text will alter the way certain qualities are attributed to the film, and will become the primary interpretive screen through which the film itself will be viewed and re-viewed. Another way of thinking about this is that the system of classification that necessarily links the parts chosen for analysis with the whole will transform the way the whole is then treated.

The analyst becomes a spectator of her own creation, introducing another and more complex temporal restriction to the work. This restriction historically situates the new object that analysis and interpretation has produced. I once attended a lecture in which thirty minutes of *Marnie* were projected one frame at a time. At certain points the teacher-critic would intervene and the still frame sat on the screen for many minutes as he lectured about its characteristics. As he edited more and more, he didn't produce the starred text of Roland Barthes's *S/Z*; rather, it felt like a series of transparencies were being added to the film as he traveled further and further away from projection to photograph. There would perhaps be little harm in this were it not for the fact that he extrapolated a whole host of meanings from the stills to *Marnie* as a whole. The evolution of meaning in the cinema is temporal, and time cannot be ripped away in such an arbitrary fashion.

The aging of the main character in, for example, *The Elephant Man*, reveals the arbitrary splitting of time, the designation of time as a function of make-up within the specific constraints of a narrative. In this case continuous connections must be developed between a visible past and a visible present. Time must be materialized in the face of the main character. This can only be achieved by fragmenting the conventional markers for time by distorting the intervals that permit one moment in time to be connected with another. Yet this process retains a large measure of order to it, a simultaneity of unity and fragmentation. Can this unity be broken up into individual parts? Can the fragments be extracted for analysis? To some degree an analytical strategy will always focus on those elements or parts central to the project of interpretation. Crucially, some distinctions will have to be drawn between part and whole and these will be dependent on the definitions made of the object under study. But great care must be taken with any claims that systematize the relationship between the parts as if time is *merely* one of the many formal constraints within which the meaning of images will be found.

If the distinction between celluloid and projection is valid, then how can the photographic meaning of the frame be quoted? Are we dealing here with increasing layers of discourse from which few claims can be made regarding the photographic truth of the frame? Can a match be made between the visual and what is said or written about the visual? Should the effort of interpretation be directed toward establishing that equivalence? It may be that real time does not exist in the cinematic projection process with the result that the *idea* of the photographic acts as an anchor for interpretation. Each time a film is projected it repeats its temporal structure. This would suggest a dynamic system where there need be no symmetry between the time of shooting and the time of projection, nor with the time of viewing. The equation does not read that *The Empire State Building* (Andy Warhol's film that uses a static camera and films the building for a whole day) projected for eight hours equals the real time of the filmmaking, nor does it mean that eight hours of a day have passed and we are viewing that passage. Rather, time in the cinema, once printed onto celluloid, never changes. Against all odds time is preserved. But this leads to indeterminacy, because projection happens in qualitatively different times (this is commented upon and then built into the narrative of *Lightning Over Water* by Wim Wenders). As such, the preservation of time by celluloid is a condition upon which the history of projection depends. But in the cinema the preservation of time is also a necessary condition for the shifting parameters of the photographic, the performative, and the dissolution of time. The movement of a character across the screen is both a movement in space and time, which means that present and past are reversed, become reversible. It is possible to break a glass and reconstruct it, possible to depict the destruction of nuclear war and reprint the film to reverse the horror. It is precisely this arbitrariness that makes the notion of the still so attractive for analysis, since the result is a set of manageable boundaries applicable to the seemingly endless variations in play during the performance of a film.

It might be useful here to briefly examine *Insignificance* by Nicholas Roeg, which is about Albert Einstein, Marilyn Monroe, Joseph McCarthy, and Joe DiMaggio and plays with a whole variety of definitions of historical and filmic time. The movement of day to night and night to day becomes screened by memory, which in the cinema makes the past and the present interchangeable. The character who plays Einstein has a watch that has not moved from 8:15 A.M.—the moment when the first nuclear bomb was dropped on Hiroshima. The watch itself stopped ticking when, as a child, he electrocuted it. Thus, the convergence of that moment with Hiroshima is a necessary condition of the present for him. For each of the characters a particular moment of the past continuously reappears to contextualize the present. Time can only be represented through memory, which means that time present and time past must be re-presented as mental constructs.

A character glances away from the screen toward a mental construct (Hiroshima in flames) also on the screen, also filmed. But here a kind of nonequilibrium is introduced between the way time passes and memory: a dissymmetry of time, repetition, and the timeless. Simultaneously, one of the main actresses in the film, Teresa Russell, can be herself, Marilyn Monroe, the mythic image of Monroe, cover girl, actress, scientist, and victim. She can also be thinking of herself as a little girl and acting out her thoughts. And there need be no necessary causality to unite all of this except that the various levels will alter as the story develops. History and historical reconstruction lose their anchors in a past seen as somehow devoid of the future, but locked into the imaginary.

Insignificance, as its title suggests, plays with significance and the way history becomes meaningful, as well as the many ways time disappears as the historical is reconstructed through the cinema, through the image, and through the activity of viewing (It would be interesting to test the assumptions of the film against those of various documentaries made about the nuclear age.). But as the above analysis suggests, a particular discourse, interpretive and descriptive, was needed to disengage at least some of the elements of the film. There need be no particular causality to the approach, no necessary link between the film and the discourse produced in response to a viewing. The result is that interpretation plays with multiple levels of meaning, and claims can be made that those levels are located in the film, but those claims are themselves the result of a further set of interpretive strategies. As we shall see, textual analysis applied to the cinema tries to overcome this last phase as if it were a problem to be solved. The textual approach drives toward something more rooted in the text, something that transcends the pitfalls of interpretation and that can at a minimum make assertions about the "presence" of meaning in a specifiable "place."

Camera/Text/Frame

"In a film, the frame is not simply a neutral border; it produces a certain vantage point onto the material within the image. In cinema the frame is important because it actively defines the image for us."[17] There is no doubt that the position of a camera will produce a specific framing of whatever is being filmed. But that framing does not produce a still frame, which is clearly what

17. David Bordwell and Kristin Thompson, *Film Art* (Reading, Mass.: Addison-Wesley, 1979), 109.

distinguishes the making of a movie from the taking of a still picture. For the practitioner of textual analysis the real of the frame becomes that which it pictures. The problem with Bordwell and Thompson's suggestion that the frame offers a vantage point for analysis and experience is that it presupposes links among the screen, projection, and viewing which can only be arrived at by the extraction of the frame from the entire film in much the same way as Godard and Gorin approached the analysis of Jane Fonda. So, for example, it is Jane Fonda *in* the photo of *Letter to Jane*. She becomes responsible for her expression. Though she did not take it, though her image was produced by a male photographer who may have desired her pose, may have waited not to catch it (the metaphor here of the photograph as snare simply supports the argument that it is "catching" the real as it is) but to create it, Fonda must take responsibility as if she were not only a representation but as if she has transcended the limitations of herself as photograph. Celluloid, photographic paper, cease to mediate the representations etched onto them. The sign becomes an object, meaning without difference. For the sign to become an object it must exist in a relation of overdetermination with cinematic reality allowing little leeway in the meaning it produces. This lack of flexibility may suit the interpretive project of Godard and Gorin, but it cannot come to grips with the obvious ambiguity that sign-object relations generate in the cinema.

This is best illustrated by the difficulty that arises in trying to describe an object that has appeared on the screen. More often than not a descriptive phrase of some length is needed that will include the context of the object's use and the rationale for its appearance, a situating of relations. In *The Shining* by Stanley Kubrick, the hotel so named cannot be so simply described. The evolving context of its use as a metaphor must be explained. The hotel represents the unconscious of the main character. The bridge between fantasy and reality collapses for him throughout the film, and metaphorically Jack Nicholson plunges into further and further levels of insanity. This is symbolically represented by the elevator shafts in the hotel bleeding until Nicholson is effectively overwhelmed by a pool of blood. But for the spectator new bridges must be opened that challenge and reawaken the need to draw some coherence from his fantasies. To see the hotel in this fashion, as a living, breathing entity, may allow the film to be classified as a horror film, but what is more important is the way all of these facets of cinematic expression are worked upon. In fact, much of the film dwells on the image of Nicholson. It is this complex and rather rich interaction that the film itself comments upon, since so many of the other characters are themselves playing the role of spectators. How can all of this multiplicity be constrained? Should it be? How does the cinema "picture" the unconscious of a character like the one played by Nicholson? This is a challenge to discourse both within the film and from the point of view of the spectator. And the results need not be tied to the film in a strict sense.

A filmic image is never simply just out there on a screen awaiting a description. It has already passed by, been projected, and as a result the discourse constructed around it is faced with the urgency of understanding memory, of exploring memory and experience. And since there need be no synonymy among projection, discourse, and memory, the result is at best, hypothetical. Yet, it is precisely this flexibility that transforms what is pictured into a hybrid of meanings, which makes it possible for an object to become a subject, for an hotel in *The Shining* to take control of its occupants. The loss of the third dimension in the cinema is also about loss of significance, about a whole host of strategies to replace that loss and about the necessarily *contingent* relationship of signification, projection, and subjectivity.

This raises the important point that for celluloid to be projected, a significant percentage of it must be black, as differentiation is created by frame dividers. This is well understood by the avant-garde and experimental cinema where the struggle with meaning often includes a concern with absence—the absence of the flicker that frame division creates (e.g., David Rimmer and Stan Vanderbeek). However, the difference between a projection and a photograph is as strong as the difference between a pictorial sign and a verbal sign. A projection disperses the pictorial while a photograph carefully constrains that dispersal (the difference between a cinematic screen and a photographic print). The photographic may not be the material base upon which meaning is built in the cinema. Strictly speaking, is a black screen with sound a film? I would argue that it most surely is.

It is no wonder then that close frame analysis depends upon a particular technology in order to dissect the films it examines. The special projectors that show a film one frame at a time, or the editing table designed for the study of a film, emphasize the stability of the pictorial. They produce a particular language of description and analysis that reinforces the hypothesis that images can be *read*. Each frame acquires the status of a unit, self-contained, yet related to the entire structure of the film, individual, but at the service of broader narrative constraints. The broader question is, can there ever be units of this kind in the cinema? Yet it is precisely those constraints that produce wide variations in meaning, and the copresence of structure, order, and disorder. Frame analysis proposes a conjuncture between the units it extracts and the wider narrative of which they are a part. The unit comes to retrospectively stand for a continuum, to illustrate a flow of meaning. What is stressed is the illustrative and empirical role of the pictorial. Neither the ambiguity of the pictorial nor the potential contradictions of the language of description can be included in the approach.

Why, for example, do terms drawn from the professional context of film production dominate the way different frame-units are described? Terms like "pan," "tilt," "tracking," supposedly provide the analyst with a springboard into understanding how a frame organizes its constituent elements into a meaningful whole. Is there not a distinct difference between such elements as the process of shooting a shot many times, reformulating it into a single shot within an edited sequence, and its final projection onto the screen? While a cinematographer sitting on a specially designed dolly may call the movement of his or her camera "tracking," how can that be similar to the position of the critic or spectator in front of the screen? The projection does not simply reproduce the original tracking. But more importantly, how can a frame indicate or even provide the trace for the original tracking motion of the camera?

The transfer of technical terminology to the critical and interpretive process tends, however, to justify, in a rather tautological fashion, the presumably concrete effects of a film upon the viewer. This is a classical instance where the desire to make the image concrete supercedes the mediations produced by viewing and comprehension and most importantly by performance. Even in those films reliant on a self-conscious play with the technology, (e.g., *Wavelength*) the challenge they put forth is precisely *how* to articulate the point of view of the spectator from hypotheses about camera position. Yet, the idea of point of view is itself a rather static notion. Metaphorically, it suggests a spectator who scans with a camera eye. It reinforces narrow conceptions of linear communication. It supports notions of singularity and vision as geometric.

One could perhaps reproduce one hundred or two hundred frames from a particular cinematic sequence in an effort to describe background changes in a series where the foreground remains relatively static. This shifting relationship could perhaps indicate a hypothesized camera movement. Of course what we are getting is proof that movement has signifying characteristics. There might be greater complexity to the motion than the term "tracking" allows for. But more importantly, the assumption here is that motion is being reproduced directly from its original conditions of production to the screen. Paradoxically then, the premise that film is a device of reproduction is reinscribed anew, but this time at the level of its formal and technical constraints *as if* a naturalized principle has been established. This is the sign of a crisis, both with respect to the interpretive and historical tools we have for examining the film production context, and to the analytical strategies that can be applied to the study of cinematic projection. I am deliberately using the word "crisis" here because with regard to motion in images, what differentiates movement as a physical characteristic of a moving camera from its projection onto a screen? What then also differentiates the various levels of understanding applied to those projections within the context of a film theater? How does time factor into all of this? More importantly, how do we deal with sound for which the image provides no specifiable location? (For example, the term "synchronous sound" can be used with respect to the editing table but cannot be easily transposed into the film theater. Dubbing is the best example of all of the variables at work here.)

"In certain circumstances, our view (meaning, the spectator) may be explicitly identified with that of the camera itself. A bumpy, jiggling image usually implies that the camera was hand held, that the operator did not anchor the machine on a tripod, but instead trusted his or her body to act as the support" (Bordwell and Thompson 1979, 123).[18] The presumption that there is a line of vision between the critic-spectator and the screen, and that it is relatively unmediated is in part brought about by the approach used in the stilling of the projection itself. This reduction has the effect of neutralizing the ambiguity of the signifying process and of making the image adhere with seemingly extraordinary clarity to its referents. Thus, the qualities of *cinéma-vérité* that the authors are referring to in the above quote are based on how well the camera reproduces the scenes being filmed. The distance between the image and that to which it refers must be lessened, decreased, to the point where knowledge appears to be graspable, since the image is full and complete as a representation, and therefore need only be *seen* to be understood. But how does the identity between the camera's "view" and that of the spectator manifest itself? The links here are at best tenuous. The formalism inherent in Bordwell and Thompson's approach is itself challenged by the way images in the cinema are always intimately linked to sound, which tends to dilute the location of meaning and make relations of camera to image to projection far less transparent.

Wim Wenders and Ozu

In the film *Tokyo Ga* by Wim Wenders, a meditation on the image and the many ways in which the image can be seen and understood (while also being a travelogue and an homage to Ozu), Wenders, who is the narrator, says that he would like to use the camera as a human being uses his or her eyes. He just wants to look without having to attach any meaning to the activity. This desire for absence, for nothingness, is really a desire for purity, for a recovery of innocence. Most importantly it betrays a misunderstanding of the relationship of vision to thought and of speech to vision. The links between looking— looking through a camera and looking at a screen—can only be established hypothetically, and they are in any case separate activities. Each operates at a different level with the screen representing a process that doesn't simply dupli-

18. For even greater detail see Janet Staiger, Kristin Thompson, and David Bordwell, *The Classical Hollywood Cinema: Film Style and Mode of Production to 1960* (New York: Columbia University Press, 1985).

cate the camera's view. This is clearly the case in *Tokyo Ga*, where Wenders's narration tries to "fix" what the image cannot, tries in a sense to provide a solution to the difference between screen and projection. The camera's viewer is the director, which is most forcefully brought out during a scene with Ozu's cameraman. He shows Wenders where Ozu normally positioned his camera. But of course it is Wenders's camera that is the center of activity, Wenders's directorial position that his narration organizes into a performative role. And so Wenders, because of the documentary style he chose for his film, lessens the distance between sight and image and knowledge, a distance he describes as fundamental to Ozu's cinema. Paradoxically, Wenders collapses projection into the operations of the camera with his narration, guiding us through the present tense of his experience. Wenders's search for innocence is really an attempt to join filmmaker and viewer, to collapse the differences among meaning, performance, and projection. Yet this is classically the position of the auteur, the stance of the author who wants to control the polyphony of meaning upon which he or she depends for his or her creativity, but which they want the spectator to disavow. This is fertile ground for exploration. It may be the case that media like the cinema represent precisely the ambiguity between control and its loss (hence Wenders's fascination with Ozu) and that projection situates that loss as an inevitability. This may explain the deep frustration of filmmakers who face audiences with so many divergent understandings of their images that the reaction is often to try and tighten the technical framework for the production of the images. It may also explain why film schools overemphasize technology, heightening the need to discover even more sophisticated strategies of intentionality, even as projection loosens the hinges, so to speak.

In reaction to the ambiguity of projection, close analysis proposes that the frame of a film becomes that which it depicts.[19] The language of description voids itself of any immediate concerns with interpretation, allowing the single frame to become that which it was intended to be. Authorial power is used to justify the construction of the elements within the frame. Frame analysis tends not to probe the conjuncture of meaning and communication. It presumes that semantic relationships can be extrapolated from the frame-to-frame encounter that the critic chooses to highlight. It must be remembered here that the choices are extremely limited. If a critic tries to pull a particular sequence out of a film, he must choose between the 1,440 frames that pass by in one minute. Highlighting ten frames out of a sixty-second shot is the product of more than a simple "reading." Paradoxically, the critic is reediting the shot sequence and

19. See Leo Braudy, *The World in a Frame: What We See in Films* (Garden City, N.J.: Anchor Press, 1976), and Louis Giannetti, *Understanding Movies* (Englewood Cliffs, N.J.: Prentice-Hall, 1983, 1990) for examples of this approach.

carefully articulating those elements which best serve her purpose. Thus it can be argued that frame analysis produces a carefully constrained metareading strategically created as proof of the text's dominance over viewing.[20]!•

This weight of the text allows Bill Nichols, for example, to reduce the role of the viewer to an adjunct of a cinematic category that he calls "camera cutting." "During this sequence [from *The Birds* by Hitchcock] we literally pivot at the window of the town cafe as the camera cuts back and forth from Melanie Daniels inside the cafe to what she sees outside."[21]!Of course we do not "literally" pivot, nor does the camera cut. Nichols backs up what he says with photos of eleven frames. The problem is that we cannot counter his choices, nor even examine the context within which his selections were made. It is editing that produced the original cuts, and it is hardly an error of phraseology to highlight the camera—rather it is fundamental to the approach, fundamental to the notion that the viewer has become the camera.

Yet what Nichols is also doing here is suggesting a particular strategy to, if not articulating the very nature of, the viewing process. The screen, a site of potential exchange, of potential communication, becomes the reflected instance of viewing, now situated within it. This is the effect of collapsing technology and subject, of equating sight with consciousness as if both can be found *within* the screen. Perhaps recognizing this, Nichols tries to change his approach somewhat in a later essay. He examines Magritte's famous painting of a pipe (*Ceci n'est pas une pipe*) and explains how meaning is "conferred" upon it by a viewer in order to decode what would otherwise be information as "noise." The "sensory impressions" are there, but meaning must be assigned to them. This is then described as a process of decoding. Meaning can then be pinned down such that a variety of "answer keys" will be found. Once these keys are in place they come to reflect the organization of the image. But decoding is only possible if the conventionalized properties of a film, for example, have put in place a pattern already coded. The question is whether there is a preestablished harmony of screen and viewer (keeping in mind here that the filmmaker is also a viewer), and whether there is any validity to the opposition of noise and information. The tension between Magritte's caption-title and the image remains conflict ridden irrespective of an interpretive decision to assert the primacy of "pipe." The space opened up by the contradiction is precisely at the heart of a challenge to interpretation. It is also crucially a challenge to processes of representation.

A recurrent term in Nichols's work is "recognition," which is meant to

---

20. See the effort by Alfred Guzzetti, which ends up providing a paper version of a Godard film. *Two or Three Things I Know About Her: Analysis of a Film by Godard* (Cambridge, Mass.: Harvard University Press, 1981).
21. Bill Nichols, "The Birds At The Window," *Film Reader* 4 (1979): 125.

explain the relationship of meaning and expression to comprehension. As a qualification, Nichols mentions how difficult it is to isolate discrete units and pin down their meanings. "For methodological purposes we may try to single out the more from the less expressive aspects of an image but there is ultimately no binding rationale, no court of appeal, to uphold the choice."[22] But ultimately, even though there "is no remedy for this other than to speak as precisely as possible, while recognizing that this very precision is fundamentally alien to the analog codes to which it is applied" (Nichols 48), the problems created by the approach he is using will not go away.

We are not dealing in any image with analogical processes unaffected by the rather intense metaphorical and performative framework upon which they depend. (And here I am in agreement with Metz's position elaborated in detail in *Language and Cinema*, where he places a great deal of emphasis on performance, hinting at but not elaborating a pragmatics of cinematic communication.) In fact an image proposes a metaphorical context that is both its foundation and its undoing. What must be remembered here is the intensity of that stress and the many different gaps that stress puts in place. Though Nichols points out how textual analysis creates a new object, a "moiré" or new pattern of meaning not necessarily dependent on its original constituents, it is the cinematic object itself that is the base upon which he builds his assumptions. Yet it is the function of projection to also create a moiré, otherwise the juxtaposition of meanings necessary for the creation of meaning in the cinema would be predictable. This would tend to suggest that textual criticism intervenes at another and more distant analytical level where *the text becomes that privileged unit of study*, which demarcates the object, organizing for us what is representational or nonrepresentational, what can be recognized as lifelike and what cannot. The assumption here of shared information, of significance and meaning already present in the object (thus waiting for extraction), reduces both the spectator and the critic to articulators of a predetermined set of meanings. The mixture of concepts at the heart of Nichols's intuition that a moiré somehow exceeds and recontextualizes the elements that constitute it, cannot be realized within the semiotic framework he proposes, because his major concerns remain centered on images as textual.

It then becomes clear how we could "literally pivot" as a camera while watching a scene from *The Birds*. Both the spectator and the film become examples of coded, preprogrammed devices, there for the purposes of information exchange. This objectification of the subject and collapse into objectness is characteristic of close frame analysis. As the object comes to represent the consciousness viewing it, so too does the cinema become the privileged site of

---

22. Bill Nichols, *Ideology and the Image* (Bloomington: Indiana University Press, 1981), 47.

a fixed relation between conventionalized meaning and its apprehension. One must then ask with great care where the line or slash can be drawn between signification and understanding, between enunciation and comprehension. The impulse to "punctuate" a continuum (Nichols 1981, 45), to separate by opposition, tends to reinforce the parameters of a division that may not operate as "difference" along the lines of signifier/signified or even within the boundaries of screen/subject. There may be a need here to radically reconsider the way we map relations of meaning into and out of the context of performance. This reconsideration would have to take into account both the presence of the screen as a device upon which many different forms of expression and enunciation have been inscribed and the extreme variability within which communication, in all of its forms, operates.

"The signifier/signified splitting, like figure/ground or sign/referent (and self/other), refers to the fixation of meaning upon persistent objects or qualities even when sensory impressions or social encounters vary (over a limited range). The bar or boundary represented by a slash (/)—marks a division of realms" (Nichols 1981, 45). The very notion of realms, however, will effect the boundaries being established. The definition of splitting will qualitatively alter the emphasis placed on one or another side of the punctuation. Moreover, the very qualities of what one might consider to be "fixed" will become the context for opposition or similarity. The question of textuality and the way meaning is produced through stylistic choice and aesthetic organization is usually referred to as a play between spectator and enunciation. The slash (/) in this sense is the marker for an already mapped-out gap between the dyadic pair of viewer and screen. This presumption is situated in what is understood to be the uniqueness of the cinematic spectacle, its separateness—the cinema as a place and palace of dreams.

For the textual critic the demystification of that uniqueness is perhaps best represented by the argument that the cinema produces meaning by stapling or suturing relations of enunciation such that the process of constructing meaning is hidden or naturalized. From this vantage point edits flow into each other as if they have ceased to be there. To arrive at an understanding of what isn't there one must decompose the text to produce a new enunciation that reveals absence. My argument here is not with the suggestion that edits disappear when projected but with the notion that they must be visible in the first place. The difference again is between the craft work on celluloid and projection. The two in one sense cannot be separated. However, the final print of a film has ceased to be edited (the terminological confusion here derives from the collapse of two different levels of meaning creation into one), has instead been transformed into a series of projections, where the flow of meanings is defined by spectacle and performance. This is why the now familiar thesis that the showing of a film is a one-way process (feedback will supposedly not change the film) cannot account for the way any spectacle is the site of reconstruction, the continual site, that is, of discovery and innovation on the part of the spectator.

The Classical Cinema as Paradigm

Stylistically, the classical cinema has constructed a framework generally known as the continuity system; this system involves the familiar rules for linking shots and achieving a smooth narrative flow: the axis of action, screen direction, eyeline matches, and so on. Similarly, the camera placement creates the optimum framing of the narrative action, both in terms of distance and angle; camera movement either follows action or ends by revealing a narratively significant element. As David Bordwell has pointed out, a classical framing typically places the subject in the upper central portion of the screen; if the subject is centered the elements will generally be in balance. The result is a de-emphasis of the frame as such; the illusion of the depth and real space within the frame becomes more prominent than the graphic qualities of the composition on the flat screen.[23]

Continuity produces and controls the even flow of narrativity, but it is not there for the spectator to see. There is rather an illusion of real space, a linkage of which we are unaware, an eyeline match peripheral to viewing but nevertheless fundamental to its functioning. The vanishing point of perspective vanishes to produce meaning and to create a similarity between film and the real, or rather a similarity between the real and our understanding of it. The argument thus presented produces the following proposition. For a filmic text to be real or realistic, whether it be a fiction film or a documentary, the viewer must be duped by the strategy of the text to the viewer.

The other side of this argument might go as follows. The cinematic flow of meaning is discontinuous. It is viewed in a context of noise and misinformation. It can hardly ever get its message across. Narrativity is characterized by the struggle to achieve order, which if accomplished is quickly broken by disorder. The differences between representation, enunciation, and projection are barely graspable, sliding as they do over a number of different levels of comprehension and errors in understanding. Discontinuity is the base for a lack of homogeneity. What Roland Barthes describes as the multiplicity of possible connotations for an enunciation is evidence of the infinite number of possibilities that any given set of projections generates. It is possible for the expression of meaning to be contradictory ad infinitum. It is equally possible for those contradictions to be produced in a context of self-reflexivity. The supposed illusion of the real in the cinema is, to paraphrase Godard, the reality of

23. Kristin Thompson, *Eisenstein's Ivan the Terrible* (Princeton: Princeton University Press, 1981), 54–55.

the illusion. Cinematic projections are not the site of an exclusion, not the place where the viewer is kept away, so as to forget self; rather, projections are always a site of contradiction and disbelief. The narrative does not conceal its arbitrary "constructs" because the arbitrary is its lure, its attraction. It is precisely because at any given moment a film can shift from the clear to the unclear, from coherence to incoherence, that characters for example may die and close their eyes after death—all of this is not only illusion, but performance and play. Rather than being the product of an interaction designed to dupe, the viewer is part of a process of stress and strain that makes copresent, communication, breakdown, contradiction, and exchange. I have of course taken an extreme position here. But I do this in order to review the debate on narrative, to look again at the multifarious ways viewers reconstruct their experiences of images, not to match some mythic intention, but to better place themselves, to better understand their attraction for images.

Does the category of the classical help in the understanding of processes of meaning and projection which combine both pattern and disorder? Are the products of this activity as ordered as Thompson suggests? As the frame disappears and as edits are supposedly sutured over, does this generate an illusion of homogeneity, of a narrative somehow in control of its elements? Isn't the materiality of the screen always in question? How does the theatrical context of a film's presentation create a context for viewing? Rather than assuming, as Thompson does, that there is a link between the screen and the viewer, it would be necessary precisely to construct a theory to explain that link. The notion of the eyeline match, or the concept of the Renaissance code as constituent elements of the classical cinema need to be recast as hypotheses, rather than being presented as interpretive categories with a fixed character.

The terms "recognition," "fix," "place," "perceptual code," "subject position," and so forth, are the natural outcome of a process of categorization as opposed to one of hypothesis building. Underlying so many of these normative categories is the desire to produce a science of the text and of the way texts generate meaning (to justify the creation of a canon). But there is no necessary (until proven) connection between the elaboration of textual properties and the viewer or spectator who watches a text. While recognizing that the text is the construction of the critic, theorists like Thompson and Bordwell make the jump to the viewer as if paradoxically their new object provides a reflection of the viewer's comprehension of the film itself But even there, the "subject" remains unaware of this process; "the one thing we normally do not comprehend is this very constitution, a self-awareness of our own construction as subjects (Nichols 1981, 53). What Nichols is saying is of course at the very heart of the debate on realism and its effects. I don't propose to enter into that debate here. Suffice to say that a careful set of distinctions would have to be drawn to avoid collapsing notions of the unconscious with conscious activity. Once again a theory of the way a text hides meaning is not necessarily a theory of the way a viewer deals with the problems of exchange and meaning construction. The circularity of posing the text as a site of meaning and the spectator as a resident of that place—a sign-system dweller within a high-rise of rule-based flats with each providing distinct levels of order for the inhabitants—that circularity inevitably must conjoin with notions of regularity and control (even, as is often the case, Nichols disavows precisely that kind of reductiveness). Thus, while I agree with Nichols that the "subject" is not fully aware of who she is, this cannot be the basis upon which a theory of viewing can be constructed. The lack of evidence here works both ways.

The repeated and pervasive presence of what film theorists label as the classical system of narrative organization may contain within it enough levels of discontinuity and breakdown to suggest that its efforts at concealment are not so much the result of repetition or convention as they are a response to the crises and cleavages caused by representational and performative systems themselves. Part of the problem here is with the process of definition which tends to limit the boundaries of investigation prematurely if it becomes categorical.[24] Take as an example the following definition of the "classical, (dominant, Hollywood) cinema" by E. Ann Kaplan in her book entitled *Women and Film*: "A feature length narrative sound film made and distributed by the Hollywood studio system. There is ambiguity about the precise dates for the classic period (people agree on roughly 1930–50). What is important is the concept of a classical model with fixed conventions of film practice that are repeated from product to product and that the audience comes to rely on and to expect."[25]

An important feature of the definition is the parallel concern with the spectator. Repetition establishes a pattern, and this is then the pattern audiences come to expect. While clearly the question of genre and style is crucial, the underlying definition of what constitutes a repeated and repeatable pattern is equally central to the argument. For a pattern to come into existence there must as a rule be a number of tests, a testing out of what might prove to be workable or not workable as pattern. Furthermore, the suggestion about expectation on the part of the audience is also a suggestion about the process of learning, about how certain patterns become fixed and are then held to as valid. Generalizations are applied to accommodate difference, which leads in-

24. This is commented on by Roger Odin in a short polemic highly critical of the self-imposed limitations of the classical model. Roger Odin, "La sémio-pragmatique du cinéma sans crise, ni désillusion," *Hors Cadre* 7 (1988–89): 77–92.
25. E. Ann Kaplan, *Women and Film* (Methuen: New York, 1983), 11.

evitably to a very limited system of classification. A taxonomy is created into which a whole series of subdivisions can be introduced. Thus the classical cinema as category produces with it further sets of subdivisions that seem to legitimate its normative character.

For a particular genre to have gained the dominance suggested by this definition, a variety of quite tentative approaches must have been made to construct the possible "field" within which the films could have operated. These tentative strategies coalesced into a pattern which, as a consequence of repetition, evolved into genre. Yet even within what are suggested as genre patterns there are numerous conflicts and contradictions. For example the often-made suggestion with regard to *film noir* is that the genre seeks out a variety of meta-discursive strategies to its production of meaning, to its use of certain themes, locales, and styles. Why seek to be self-reflexive if the strategy of communication you have established works well for you? After all, the self-reflexive approach will inevitably infringe upon the genre, altering its boundaries and establishing new and different sets of concerns. As it turns out many of the best examples of *film noir* are steeped in an awareness of the precariousness of genre, of storytelling, of language. *Letter From An Unknown Woman* is distinguished by its play with problems of sight and understanding, as if the director, Max Ophuls, was as concerned with absences of meaning as he is with their presence. It helps to know that the scriptwriter for the film was Stephan Zweig, whose work as an essayist and novelist was profoundly influenced by Bertolt Brecht and Sigmund Freud. Zweig clearly wanted the film to play with the ambiguity of writing, with the many different ways letters work to both reinforce and undermine their own communicative effectiveness. In addition, the capacity of various genres to survive their appropriation of other styles and forms suggests that conflict is one of the ways a genre sustains itself.

The supposedly simple circularity of meaning exchange suggested by Kaplan's definition of the classical tends to reduce the importance of the performative and the self-reflexive and limits the strategies that can be chosen for the analysis of one's own position as spectator. There are further problems related to how we theorize and analyze relations of dominance and submission, of how we talk about trial and error, and whether any given genre or film is ever capable of producing the homogeneity suggested by the definition. Underlying the use of the term *classical* is a simultaneous concern with narrative as a site of coherence, as a place where contradictions are resolved, where the circularity of beginning, middle, and end (proposed as the basic structure of classical narrative films) combine to provide a resolution of contradiction and a smoothing over of narrative effect. The classical narrative becomes a puzzle into which we fit a quite limited number of analytic solutions. But the very "self-containment," the "unity," the logic of a space now narrativized, now held in place, "without gap or contradiction"—the very order of the preceding list is an imaginary one. It is precisely a tautological depiction of the narrative and communicative process. For rather than providing a sense of closure, the sense of an ending, cinematic narrativity *struggles* with closure, with suitable devices to interlock sometimes disparate and contradictory elements.

In a general sense the struggle to *find* order is the struggle of narrative, primarily because narratives do not exist in isolation of the performative context into which they enter in a film theater. There is a continual tension of context, of contextualization. Narratives structure, try to put in place, an argument. They also try and construct a set of relations that will encourage viewing and comprehension. In a broad sense, narratives try to produce a process of consensus. But narratives may or may not work because of the plurality—the heterogeneity—created by the context of exchange within which they operate. Some narratives are of course quite homogeneous, but this doesn't necessarily create an equilibrium between the tensions of order and disorder. Nor does this mean that narrativity in the cinema is inevitably predictable either as to content or effect. Although David Bordwell makes the effort to include many of the above elements in his description of the narrative cinema,[26] he relies so heavily on the classical model to establish a series of "norms" (read *conventions*) for cinematic expression that the more flexible elements he proposes regarding performance fade into the background.

Storytelling in the cinema is described by Kaplan and Thompson as a site of misrecognition. The spectator is inscribed within an unambiguous sphere, pinned down, as it were, caught in a complicit act of cooptation. From this viewpoint cinematic projection becomes a site of tremendous power. Narrativity as such becomes an example of the insufficiencies of a spectator caught in the act of an identification with the lie of the story. But the lie may well be one which the spectator has to rectify. A narrator may contradict herself, be violent in a scene and gentle in her depiction through words of it. She may speak of love and narrate memories that make love an act born of an existential angst (*Hiroshima mon amour*) and which she doesn't understand, but about which the viewer develops a number of complex hypotheses. These hypotheses make the act of viewing quite unpredictable. There need be no structure to this unpredictability, and it may not create the kind of equilibrium suggested by notions of the "classical." The performative context can remain quite coherent in the face of all of these contradictions and inconsistencies.[27] It may be the case that it depends upon them for its existence and legitimacy.

In a narrative film, lies may reveal truths, and the narrator may dupe her-

---

26. David Bordwell, *Narration in the Fiction Film* (Madison: University of Wisconsin Press, 1985).
27. See Ilya Prigogine and Isabelle Stengers, *Order Out of Chaos: Man's New Dialogue with Nature* (London: Heinemann, 1984), esp. pp. 13 and 14 for an interesting discussion of the way order and disorder are not necessarily in opposition to each other.

self or himself effectively enough to render everything she or he says illegitimate. This may be the premise for the construction of another level of truth by the spectator, yet all of these relations may be completely unstable. The point here is that we may learn at the beginning of a narrative how the ending may never come or even that the beginning never began, and yet there clearly must be a beginning and an end. We may, as Peter Watkins's films try to point out, rearrange our own supposedly logical premises, our very rationality, to overwhelm the narrative and replace it with a different sense of the role we play as viewers. (Examples from Watkins's work include *Privilege*, *Culloden* and *Punishment Park*). To view the cinema as a place of exchange one must also recognize how narrativity has to be negotiated and that the "direction of meaning" a film takes orients the sphere of a discursive interaction—the traces of a possible set of experiences—the patterns of which may not be found in the narrative as such.

The Classical Disguise

Kaja Silverman, in her book *The Subject of Semiotics*, makes the crucial point that the term *classic text* refers to an idealization, a constructed model "derived from a process of abstraction from numerous textual instances, much the way that *langue* can only be derived from numerous instances of *parole*."[28] Silverman goes on to say that the model is of necessity abstract and thus is set off from the real text, which always contains a surplus of meaning, an excess. A crucial problem here is that the model must, if it is to be activated, exist prior to the analysis that will be undertaken. A model is after all a construct, a systematic tool: it has instructions and methods built into its very organization. In fact, to construct a model is also to engage with another kind of, though perhaps at a different level, argument. This does not mean that there are an infinite number of paradigms working in a regressive fashion toward a particular level of truth. Rather, the construction of a paradigm involves the interaction of many different concepts and practices, in order to arrive at a carefully schematized hierarchy of ideas. This is oriented toward information and evidence and makes a number of transformative bridges possible between theory and practice.

If we examine the classical in relation to the avant-garde or the experimental cinema some of the problems with the former as a mode of classification become clearer. The concern in the avant-garde movement with revealing how meaning is constituted and through what means, is contrasted to the homogeneity of texts that can use paradox, even ambiguity, but inevitably cast them-

28. Kaja Silverman, *The Subject of Semiotics* (New York: Oxford University Press, 1983), 242.

selves as noncontradictory (i.e., classical). The existing cultural order is up-held, supported, carefully limited to avoid contradiction. In order to do this the text must present itself as real in opposition to the experimental which has few such concerns. In this sense the viewer can feel as if he or she is mastering meaning, controlling their experience, while in actual fact being unaware of the control the text itself is exercising. Yet the problem here is once again with where the markers for the opposition are placed. Are we dealing in a strict sense with two realms divided and opposed to each other? If the boundaries are more fluid than that (I am reminded here of a seminar given by the avant-garde filmmaker, Stan Brakhage, in which he asserted with some degree of pride that his system of editing was classical) what effect will the construction of the classical as paradigm have on the debate? Should the function of the paradigm be to explore the way various texts produce meaning or should it simply validate the premises of its own exposition?

Silverman works with another set of oppositional terms: writerly vs. read-erly; consistency vs. multiplicity; stability vs. flux; coherence vs. incoherence (Silverman 246). Do all of these oppositions produce the abstracted instance that Silverman suggests as methodologically crucial? I think not. Her analysis remains programmatic. It is not necessarily the case that an inventory of the characteristics of one type of textual production will move the analysis to a level of abstraction which could be considered as paradigmatic. Her references to abstraction refer, I believe, to the necessary distance between the task of critical analysis and the text itself. She premises her description of the classic text on a set of rules that guide, at a systemic level, the production of meaning. Those rules, the real arbiters of meaning are hidden, as *langue* is hidden from *parole*. Or said another way, we may use grammar to speak but need not be aware of grammar in order to produce speech. The classic text conceals its rules, its system, and produces meanings, enunciations, which the reader or spectator cannot gain direct access to via the experience itself.

"The readerly (classic) text thus attempts to conceal all traces of itself as a factory within which a particular social reality is produced through standard representations and dominant signifying practices" (Silverman 244). The task of interpretation becomes the substitution of one text by another. Thus, the interpretation comes to stand for, to represent, that which is being interpreted. There need be no synonymy between the two texts. However, the problem is that the original is, so to speak, not there, which would perhaps be acceptable if it were not referred to as a site of the classical, a place of restricted and restrictive conventions. How does this concealment take place? In the first in-stance Silverman assumes that there is an intention to conceal and with it the creation of a particular set of rules not visible to the viewer. But at an episte-mological level the rules need not suggest anything about the viewer. It is vir-tually impossible to extrapolate from the rules to the way viewers interact with images. There need not be a causal connection. And if the choice here is to suggest causality as a possible road into viewing, can we extrapolate from that into the unconscious of the spectator?

The production of meaning pivots on the context into which images are placed. Thus almost from the moment of enunciation, images cease to have anything but a multiply-tiered, pragmatically oriented position (as much for the critic as the viewer). This then is the inevitable instability that Silverman sees only in the nonclassical cinema. The argument around classicism makes it appear as if that which coheres fixes corresponding sets of interpretations to enunciations. Or, put another way, images she always refers to as texts come to hold within them the programmatic guide for their decoding. Now the question here is whether that process of concealment operates as a rule-based system and with consistency. If it does then we will be able to predict, more often than not, the way the classical cinema constructs its meanings and the way those meanings will be understood. In order to discuss the characteristics of the classic text as she does, Silverman must accept the notion that the text has a finite set of meanings, all of which contribute to a homogeneity that precludes and prevents the possibility of a "productive, rather than a consumptive capacity" (Silverman 246).

The nonclassical text "opts for heterogeneity rather than unity, and instead of the familiar it looks for the alien and the unpredictable. Finally, far from striving for transparency, it attempts to foreground the traces of its cultural inscription" (Silverman 246). How does the classic text escape the "traces of its own cultural inscription"? There are so many possible relations any text makes possible. Those relations may interrupt, even destroy linearity and predictability. For the purposes of paradigm construction however, it may be useful to posit specific and quite limited relations of meaning. Thus, the paradigm, by its very consistency, will act to restrict the number of possible substitutions that one set of meanings can make for another. In the light of this, one can suggest limits, and those limits can be systematized. The paradigm so constructed can also have its own rules. It may evolve and change according to those rules.

Observation, however, does not provide the theorist with the structural laws that lie hidden in the paradigm. The empirical moment is only one facet of a complex set of patterns, and the problem is whether one can move via induction from the observable to the nonvisible. Clearly for the paradigm to be one realm and the text to be another, for them to be distinct yet related, means that the laws governing both are inherently in them. The error that can be made is to produce the text as a mirror of the paradigm, to link the paradigm and text as similar. There is no pretheoretical moment that will permit the understanding of the text without a paradigm. But in the process the text does not become the paradigm. There would then be little purpose in constructing the latter. The model of the classic text falls prey to this problem, especially in film, because the model is used as a practical means of applying certain quite limited interpretations to a specific body of films. As a result, the circle of closure attributed to the classical cinema must be carefully distinguished at the paradigmatic and textual levels. The contradiction is to suggest a model of textual organization over many films and to inscribe that model as a characteristic of the films themselves.

This particular argument so confuses what it believes to be the tautological moment of classicism that it sets up the avant-garde or experimental cinema as the contrasting opposite to the whole process. Having asserted this unified and closed narrative form, having elevated it to the level of a category, the next step is to demystify, to unglue, to break apart, to fragment, in other words, to follow some of the suggested strategies of the avant-garde, and segment that unity into its constituent parts. This activity isolates signifying units from each other to impede linear progression. The activity of segmentation can then reveal the codes at work in the text and foreground their operative effect.

"It is important to note that segmentation not only demystifies the classic text, but enriches it enormously. The starred text has been expanded to four or five times its original size. Its play of signification now occurs in slow motion, and it accommodates endless digressions and interpolations. These digressions and interpolations open up a whole new field of meaning—one which was there all along, but whose existence was hidden behind the linear organization of the text" (Silverman 248). If the classical text has this rigidity, then how is it so able to submit to segmentation? The narrative closure, the puzzle with all of the fitting pieces, describes an object of inquiry lacking precisely the plasticity that the critical intervention proposes. Rather, the dialectic of unity and disunity must be in the paradigm, must belong to the hypothesized set of structural constraints organizing that class of properties regrouped under the term *text*. Those structural constraints are rule based, but they are not frozen. It is quite possible for a rule-based system to generate a wide variety of contradictory and ambiguous meanings. It is even possible for rules that appear to be at the level of the paradigm to generate meanings that appear *not* to be rule based. At the same time the new field of meaning opened up (there all along) should not be ascribed to the text—certainly not to a text hiding behind the linear progression of its own narrative structure. Why? Because the relationship between a rule and the way it governs meaning does not indicate a homology between the two levels. The starred text is in reality a hypothesis about potential sets of meaning. To suggest that it is an expanded paraphrase, and a revelatory one at that, creates a taxonomy of presumed absences which the paradigm is uncovering. Paradoxically, the meanings are already given by virtue of their placement in the context of classicism, of which they are meant to be the illustration.

There is a further danger and that is to overdo the generalizations the model suggests may exist in the texts to which it is referring. In that instance the generalizations overwhelm the texts, destroying in the process the very possibilities of theory. This does not mean that there is some real text the critic is attempting to uncover. Rather, the very systems that the critic wishes to reveal by using of the model will in turn be affected by relationship between the model and the text. A number of films may by their very organization suggest a variety of systems that their textuality cannot reveal. However, the reconstitution suggested by the work of textual analysis, the very construction as Christian Metz suggests (Metz 1974, 73) of the underlying systems of meaning that the text provides is produced by a process of differentiation and similarity. In other words, while clearly a metareading, the question of how to use a given set of semiotic material is not solved, as Metz again suggests by "a description [that] hopes to establish the system which organizes this realization: the structure of this text and not the text itself. The system is nowhere clearly visible in the actual unwinding of the film: a system as such is never directly attested" (Metz 1974, 73). The movement from film to system has an already constituted paradigm working to provide the critic with the tools to do the critical reconstruction. For the system to be invisible in the actual unwinding of the film means that whatever is selected to reveal it will inevitably also reveal another model at work. The circularity of this process which Metz fails to confront permits him to contrast the work of the semiotician with that of the "naive" viewer.

And it is here paradoxically, that the "other" model so forcefully used in textual analysis becomes startlingly self-evident. For it is that naive viewer who, by her lack of awareness, reveals systems at work designed to support the absences in the text themselves. The viewer does not know, which must then mean that the film does not reveal. The emphasis here is on the word *know*, because even if we were to grant that the viewer being spoken about is an idealization, the model of viewer being suggested is converging with textuality to produce a system derived from a mirroring of text and viewer. Each in a reciprocal fashion reflects the other. But the starting point for the analysis is a rather clear preconception about viewing. "The semiotician's reading is a meta-reading, an analytic compared to the 'naive' reading (in fact the cultural reading) of the spectator" (Metz 1974, 74). The emphasis then on what a film hides is derived from a well-developed model for viewing, a model based on exclusivity, the role of the critic, and crucially on the perceived realm that constitutes the discipline known as textual analysis.

The Naturalization of Artifice

The movement in textual analysis from a reliance upon the paradigm of the classical cinema to a critique of the effects of that cinema (and its images) upon the spectator, is bound up with a desire to expose and criticize the role that dominant ideologies play in relation to viewing. Since the naive viewer misrecognizes the way a film works and since that misrecognition contributes to a dehistoricizing of the viewer's relationship to the image, a trick has been played. The illusion so produced must be demystified if the viewer-consumer is not to fall victim to the text. "What the world supplies to myth is an historical reality, defined, even if this goes back quite a while, by the way in which men have produced or used it; and what myth gives in return is a 'natural' image of this reality."[29]

The circularity of this argument (and note Barthes's particular use of the term *image*) rests on the supposition that the spectator is mirrored in the text and vice versa. The naturalized text both hides this process and makes it work. It is thus the pivot upon which a lie is perpetrated and the medium through which that lie is communicated. The text comes to reveal what has not been understood, because history has been emptied (historical meaning has been removed) and replaced by "nature," "a perceptible absence." The paradox then, that a discourse seen as naturalized is understood to be a powerful agent of control, a site where human complexity has been abolished. The naturalization of meaning results in readerly texts, producing readers who are essentially intransitive and unable to gain "access to the magic of the signifier." Readerly texts are, for the most part, classical ones, suggesting "a world which is without contradictions, because it is without depth, a world wide open and wallowing in the evident, it establishes a blissful clarity: things appear to mean something by themselves" (Barthes 1972, 143). The cultural, for example, ceases to be understood as cultural, and this results in signifying systems not having the appearance of being in control, either of their own processes or the communicative network they have entered. Naturalization blurs the boundaries and constraints acting upon human subjects, making cultural conventions and their rules appear to be without immediate or direct effect. Their presence is only known through their absence. This binary play between emptiness and presence, between absence and fullness, between what is visible as meaning but seemingly without determination, produces a system that it is suggested cannot be understood as historical by the viewer. At the same time meanings are also produced that conceal their apparatuses of enunciation. Plurality is reduced to singularity.

"Since there are people who have not yet learned to watch films skillfully, the aim of criticism may also be understood to be a making of the forms of art perceptible to those for whom they are too defamiliarized. The critic may deal with a difficult film by showing how the complex structures within it function, thereby enabling a less experienced viewer to comprehend what was hitherto

---

29. Roland Barthes, *Mythologies*, tr. Annette Lavers (London: Jonathan Cape, 1972), 142.

an undifferentiated tangle" (Thompson 52). The natural, the naturalized, seen as the absence of the fabricated in texts as the elided, the hidden, begins with a conception of the reader, the spectator as naturalized object, as empty and without knowledge. "We can now understand why, in the eyes of the myth-consumer, the intention, the adhomination of the concept can remain manifest without appearing to have an interest in the matter: what causes mythical speech to be uttered is perfectly explicit, but it is immediately frozen into something natural; it is not read as a motive, but as a reason" (Barthes 1972, 129).

What is frozen here is a paradigm that centers on certain levels of discursive production as self-contained. Formal interrelations are proposed as the site of a rationality which then shapes a conception of the human subject as limited. We live facing a mirror we cannot see. We fail to recognize ourselves in the meanings we use. We speak a hypostasized language that displaces us from within. Motives are removed and intentions are covered. The natural, which began as a metaphor for signifying processes hiding their artifice, is converted into an empirical fact, descriptive, explanatory, and paradigmatic, all at once.

For Barthes, the mask of naturalization needs a radical act to unmask it. And though clearly the emphasis here on praxis is an important one, a trap has been set. Praxis itself is not divorced from the workings of the symbolic. Language does not evaporate, nor do its meanings, through revolutionary activity. Proposed this way, the site of the natural is also the place of its undoing. The text unravels not meanings its classicism hides, but semantic configurations inevitably produced by the approach taken. The crucial problem here is not with the text itself but with the strategic choices made by the metalanguage. And unavoidably that metalanguage will clash with the text. Strategically then, to suggest that the text is *preventing* an understanding, is really an indication of the metalanguage's status. Any attempt to see the text as the cause of its own mystification confuses the relationship between the work of interpretation and the text as an object for analysis.

To further his argument here, Barthes maps out two sites of semantic activity. One where contradiction is an active guiding element in the production of meaning and another where contradiction is hidden, producing as a result a subject unable to see contradiction. The suggested parallel here is between the way *langue* is not a visible component of the speech act and yet determines its syntactic organization. In the same way myth takes on the status of a *langue*, constricting the possibilities of expression, of *parole*. Paradoxically the very diversity that might grow out of all forms of speech, a diversity that might even contradict itself, is only and ever a transformation of speech into form, cutting off then the potential of speech, and "robbing it" of genuine meaning. Barthes then eliminates the potential relationship between mythic speech and politicized speech. By valorizing, quite arbitrarily, one form of speech act over another, Barthes elevates one to a status that eliminates contradiction, and the other to the side of contradiction. He leaves no room for precisely the metalanguage that could, by reflecting on itself and on its relationship to action, change the parameters of subjectivity.

Within the context elaborated by Barthes and pursued in an uncritical fashion by film theory, it is the denotative instance (in the dyad of denotation and connotation) that is the most fully naturalized. Denotation is a site of immediacy—representations represent without seeming to—and thus a place bound more fully to referentiality than the realm of the connotative. Connotation is characterized by a relationship of further signification to a more primary one. That is, denotation provides the base upon which and through which connotation can be grasped. The denotative acts, in the literal sense, as that which underpins a more complex and hence second-order level of meaning creation. I don't propose to enter into the debate around the validity of the categories themselves. What concerns me is the oft-repeated use of a model that presumes that processes of representation hide their real meanings in a play of absence and presence, a play of veils and masks for the critic to unveil, to unmask.

I am not suggesting that the structural constraints that necessarily operate to make possible an enunciation (e.g., grammar) are in a simple sense, present. Nor am I suggesting that the meaning of a cultural artifact reveals itself and the ideological framework within which it is operating, via a simple process of mirroring. If as Barthes suggests, connotation is the place where ideology operates to hide and justify the workings of a set of dominant values, then the crucial question becomes how does it do so? As much as in one sense connotation becomes the place of ideology, it also becomes the place of plurality. For Barthes this contradiction of restraint and freedom is never really resolved. And I would suggest it cannot be within the model chosen by Barthes to explain the production of meaning in the classical text. The presumption of the classical as a place, as the expression of an ideal, establishes an a priori homogeneity which analysis then cracks into pieces. This is radically different for example, from a materialist perspective which proposes that before unity there are parts, such as the law, the economy, which appear to be autonomous and must be analyzed to reveal their inherent and necessary unity.[30] Sahlin's suggestions have some immediate relevance to my argument because the strength of the classical paradigm is found in the rather global fashion it is applied. The model suggests a causal relationship between a structure of presence and one of absence with the truth being *conferred* upon the sphere of absence. Thus the

30. Marshall Sahlins, *Culture and Practical Reason* (Chicago: University of Chicago Press, 1976), 4–5.

classical text hides what is essential to its functioning. It naturalizes not only the effects of its own structure but the manner in which that structure communicates about itself. But a serious problem arises here. The configuration of meanings hidden, so to speak, from the medium nevertheless inhabit its form. For without the relationship of absence and presence there would be no text. But clearly the emphasis on a structural absence is also a statement about the text and is itself textual. So the boundary between absence and presence is actually a very fluid one and dependent upon the interpretive choices of the critic. Of equal importance are strategic decisions concerning the surface, since it supposedly contains the signs or symptoms of that which must be read—a distorted instance of what is not immediately apparent as meaning.

"The structure and its effects are separated; the structure existing behind and beyond the forms of the given it establishes as their truth and raison d'être. The given which the structure establishes becomes the inessential, the dross of visible forms in which the essential of the structure hides itself."[31] In being naturalized the structure, so to speak, disappears. It becomes the task of criticism to reconstitute what is not there, to construct another text that reveals the original text not present. The contradiction here is from which vantage point the entry into the text is possible. If naturalization does not permit entry, then what does? Barthes describes the natural as that illusion which must constantly be denounced—that alibi which the social majority uses to legalize its own activities. Criticism becomes the task of the outsider, a task of transgression, continuously constrained by the difficult if not impossible fantasy of breaking the hold that naturalized ideologies have on unsuspecting subjects.

Why Science? Why Text?

Obviously the strategic choice of the critic will be governed by a desire to resolve this crisis. It is thus not without consequence that the project suggested by Barthes and reenforced to a large degree by the work of close analysis in film, supplemented in part by the investigations of Umberto Eco, is to generate a *science of textual analysis*. The danger is to move toward that science by using models of systemization that remove the heterogeneous elements from processes of signification, representation, and communication. In my opinion, signifying operations reveal a paradoxical play of experimentation and testing punctuated by order and disorder. However, the metalanguage chosen to examine the markers for that punctuation must carefully avoid reducing the numerous ambiguities at the heart of the practice of communication. Otherwise a tautology can be put in place, which quite conveniently advocates an equilibrium that analysis must then set about dismantling.

This potentially dangerous error is related back to the problem of vantage

31. Paul Hirst, *On Law and Ideology* (New Jersey: Humanities Press, 1979), 78.

point mentioned earlier. What kind of cultural analysis starts from a presumption of equilibrium? How are supporting facts and suppositions arrived at? Where does the notion of equilibrium gain its strength? The roots of this approach lie within structuralist strategies to the analysis of history, where one of the central purposes is to look for synchronous levels of meaning that have sustained their logic and purpose across a diverse number of cultural, political, and social activities.[32] Part of the strength comes from the ease with which criticism can then proceed. If all of the elements of a given cultural equation are stable, disorder is seen as an effect of subjectivity upon an object or constellation of meanings.

"What *are* meanings, where do they come from, how exactly do they become inscribed upon material objects or social practices?"[33] Herbert's question challenges the unavoidable stability introduced when textuality takes on an ontological status within the study of culture. This move toward the normative reflects, as John Mowitt has suggested, conflicts within the discipline of linguistics about its relationship to literary studies, with the latter attempting to take on the status of the former.[34] The effort to construct a science of signs and representations, to move from the metaphorical to the empirical of the text, eliminates the difficulties of searching for vantage point. If all of culture and in effect all of society are textual, then what is the status of subjectivity? If language and subject are coextensive (which to some degree they have to be) then how do individuals embody the text within them? How does a cultural configuration embody the subjectivity of its members? The danger is that the textual comes to stand for a predictable arrangement of meanings that in effect act to constrain conflict and change.

The circularity of suggesting, for example, that there are a set of fixed conventions of expression in the cinema leads, as we have seen in the quote from E. Ann Kaplan, to notions of the spectator as a mirror reflection of already precoded narratives. The model then becomes the arbiter of how meaning works at the level of text and viewer, and a rather simplified and rigid conception of stability is introduced. As a result a dual and quite contradictory hypothesis arises. The classical cinema supposedly exemplifies the cognitive processes used to comprehend it, while also producing a viewer who misrecognizes the way those images and narratives affect him or her. The model of classicism becomes a tool through which a taxonomy can be constructed, and the taxonomy stands for, is the sign of, structure. As much as the model points

32. For a sophisticated critique of the impact of structural thinking on the social sciences, see Stephen Tyler, *The Unspeakable: Discourse, Dialogue, and Rhetoric in the Postmodern World* (Madison: University of Wisconsin Press, 1987).
33. Christopher Herbert, *Culture and Anomie: Ethnographic Imagination in the Nineteenth Century* (Chicago: University of Chicago Press, 1991), 18.
34. John Mowitt, *Text: The Genealogy of an Antidisciplinary Object*, (Durham: Duke University Press, 1992), 13.

toward signifying and representational strategies, it also exemplifies the structural constraints that empty the films of meaning because the model predates the projection of the images.

The history then of the classical cinema develops into a discourse of recovery and loss. It reveals the relationship between a layer of fixed meanings in the taxonomy and the cinema as a discursive and performative vehicle that responds to structural regulation. Because the surface of this discourse is naturalized the taxonomy becomes the privileged fulcrum through which meaning is uncovered. In order to explore this point more fully, the following section examines an approach to meaning in the cinema dependent on the relationship between frames, shots, and sequences. I will be looking at John Carroll's approach to structural relations in which the use of the classical model in relation to the narrative cinema leads him to equate the operations of meaning in film with natural language.[35] I will also examine the work of Marie-Claire Ropars and Pierre Sorlin.[36] I consider both of these approaches to be significant examples of dominant modes of thought in the textual analysis of images. The cinema is privileged here because as a medium it poses challenges to critical and theoretical inquiry while also having been the discipline to take up "textuality" with the most fervor.

The Communication of Meaning through Images

Carroll is ready to accept the notion that in a metaphorical sense, film as language is useful for the study of the cinema. For Carroll, the acceptance of the metaphor is an entry point into the study of how the cinema produces meaning. "The slogan film is language is as old as cinema theory itself. Its fundamental justification is purely intuitive: film sequences seem to have a syntax" (Carroll 1). In order to justify the above statement, Carroll describes the following three images.

i. A close-up shot (i.e., face only) of man, A, smiling.

ii. A medium-shot (i.e., from the waist up) of two men, A and B, engaged in conversation.

iii. A long-shot (i.e., revealing both men completely) of the two men A and B parting; they wave to one another as they walk off. (Carroll 1)

Carroll then goes on to suggest that a conversation has taken place between A and B and that the smiling gesture of A is what initiated it. The order of the above also suggests "A's overall satisfaction with meeting B." If all of the above

35. John M. Carroll, *Toward a Structural Psychology of the Cinema* (The Hague: Mouton, 1979).

36. Marie-Claire Ropars and Pierre Sorlin, *Octobre: ecriture et ideologie* (Paris: Editions Albatros, 1976).

were reordered, they would have a different sense; hence his suggestion that we are dealing with a syntactic arrangement.

Any reordering of these shots will render them incoherent. Or as Carroll puts it, will transform them into visual nonsense. Carroll's concern here is with intentions. The shots have been constructed with a particular aim in mind and in an empirical sense, as image, they reveal their meaning. Aside from the problems of equating the descriptive sentences he uses with their visual counterparts (a problem derived from the fact that Carroll confuses the relationship between scripts as written language and images as performance and elides the many layers in between, such as the production context and editing), Carroll is also creating a set of boundaries as arbitrary as the images he describes. Fundamentally, the question is whether each of the shots he has extracted function as units. If they do, then the cinema can be segmented into its constituent parts, much as we might break a sentence up into subject, verb, object. Images then become equivalent not only to what is written about them, but they turn into a *form* of writing.[37] The attraction of this approach is that it weans the interpretation of images away from contradiction and ambiguity. Yet the problem of markers cannot be done away with so easily. Where are the markers between different shots? What determines the choices made by the critic? Are there similarities between the syntax of a natural language and the organization of images into a narrative form?

Carroll justifies his particular use of textuality by reference to Sergei Eisenstein. For Eisenstein the visual, semantic, and syntactic coherence of a film sequence depends upon an interplay between its shots. Crucially, that interplay is held together by the illusion of real time (without which the story would have no coherence). The sequence is edited in order to move from the shot fragment to the narrative structure. This movement, in Eisenstein's terms, produces ideas out of images. For example, a statue in the film *October* is attacked and torn to pieces by a rampaging crowd. If that were the only reading of the sequence then the montage would not be successful. Raising the denotative meaning of the sequence to the conceptual level is Eisenstein's aim. The actual historical event, its reconstruction, and the montage together form three tiers of a process that also brings out the symbolic meaning that the event on its own could not. All of these elements must be produced through the montage, which becomes the overriding factor in the construction of narrative coherence.

The notion that a combination of shots produces an idea is based on Eisenstein's overall premise that a universal visual competence governs the way pic-

---

37. This is a position strongly supported by Marie-Claire Ropars in *De la litterature au cinéma: génèse d'une écriture* (Paris: Colin, 1970), which is indebted to and dependent upon the work of Jacques Derrida.

torial language is understood. Carroll takes this up with the following statement drawn from Noam Chomsky's theories of generative grammar. "Perhaps
the human mind defines and manipulates the structure of complex sequences
of symbols in narrowly proscribed universal ways" (Carroll 4). If the mind
does this, then an abstract model of the process will reveal the finite limitations
of the grammar upon which the relationship between comprehension and perception is based. This model then extends the film as language premise into a
paradigm of mind. Although it is not entirely based on a reflection model, any
effort to use human language as a system of systems to explain relations of
thought, perception, and understanding with respect to the image (which goes
far beyond the carefully delimited aims of Chomsky's theories of grammar) is
an argument for the elimination of subjectivity.

Let me explain this crucial point. Introspection allows us to develop hypotheses about our experiences. We may talk to ourselves, think, daydream,
write, and we may do all of these activities at once or separately. Introspection,
however, cannot be described as an empirical process. There is no way of validating either the truth or falsity of what we say about what we have thought
or whether there is even the remotest connection to what we have seen. This
subjective state, which can often be foregrounded, even corrected or enlarged
upon through communication with others, remains bound to language, but
not systemically. In other words, as John Searle says, "we can't see consciousness."[38] As a replacement for this dilemma and because it seems ridiculous to
talk about the visual as if we have seen nothing, the text or the film or the
image is substituted for the ongoing relationship between seeing and thinking.
The substitution gives coherence to the idea that meaning will be found outside of the mediations that make it possible in the first place. The result is a
kind of subjective void with regard to images, in which what we say comes to
stand for what we have seen and meaning is lodged in a system of relations
determined by the text. There is an endless regress of reflected instances in
which the image comes to stand for if not to duplicate the mind's operations.

Clearly though, seeing and perception are not similar processes, just as
thought and speech, though interdependent, are not homologous. Thought
and sight don't necessarily operate in tandem, although if we follow Carroll's
arguments, it would seem that they do. Now, with regard to film, the subjective
experience of the cinema may or may not be the result of a strategic approach
to editing, to the linkage of one set of shots to another within the context of
a narrative. We just can't be sure. A number of aesthetic assumptions can be
drawn from the repetition of certain practices that segment meaning into fragments. But this is merely one step in the interpretive process and has little to
do with intention. A distinction must be drawn between the production strate-

---

38. John Searle, *The Rediscovery of the Mind* (Cambridge, Mass.: MIT Press, 1992), 96.

gies of a filmmaker or imagemaker and the multiplicity of interpretive analyses that a viewer can make. Given the narrowness of the Carroll-Eisenstein approach, which nevertheless remains widespread in a variety of media, it is no wonder that the postmodern reaction to this has been to declare the author dead. Intention so configured gives so much weight to the image and its form that the viewer, and the critic for that matter, simply become appendages to a set of givens that they merely validate or critique from within a set of inflexible norms.

Why then did Eisenstein move with such force toward segmentation? He acknowledges that "each sequential element is perceived not next to the other, but on top of the other."[39] But that blending of movement and spatial relations seriously affects the denotative power earlier ascribed to the pictorial construction. Also the effectiveness of the units so carefully constructed to justify certain editing procedures is in fact contradicted by the process of superimposition. "For the idea (or sensation) of movement arises from the process of superimposing on the retained impression of the object's first position, a newly visible further position of the objects" (Eisenstein 49).

The crucial premise here is that the denotative strength of the image never disappears. Thus it is in response to the blending of all of these elements that segmentation must be introduced. Ironically, segmentation suppresses precisely what Eisenstein saw as the heterogeneity that prevented clear ideas from being transmitted with speed and accuracy. If, as I have suggested, the cinema communicates in an ambiguous and rather unclear fashion, and if it is indeed different from photography (not a series of pictures relating to each other in a linear and static fashion), then what strategy can be used to produce the kind of instant clarity Eisenstein searched for? In response to this problem, Eisenstein formulated the idea of collision at the level of image and idea. Different shots would collide producing ideas but not shattering the unity of the editing as a whole. Until the advent of digitalization this idea became central to most forms of editing both in film and television. The presumption is that as long as the material is well organized it will reflect structural and thematic integrity.

Paradoxically, as Eisenstein refined these ideas he moved away from film *as* language, to film *is* a language. Thus, editing, montage, the drive to fragment and unify, which must be seen as aesthetic strategies, were transformed into a system, and that system was a mirror reflection of the relationship grammar has to speech in natural languages. Carroll's conception of grammar is far more complex than Eisenstein's, but he nevertheless presumes that the cinema produces meaning in much the same way as a sentence does. If English language speakers are capable of recognizing sentences from nonsentences intuitively, then it follows that shot sequences can also be divided into acceptable

39. Sergei Eisenstein, *Film Form and Film Sense* (New York: Meridian Books, 1957), 49.

and unacceptable forms, and for Carrol, the comparison is based on the fact that we are using similar thought processes to understand both. Carroll's book is an attempt to characterize that body of intuitions that will allow the viewer to distinguish between segments that are correct and those that aren't. While the hypothesis of a grammar tends to point toward a systematic level at which a variety of sometimes competing intuitions are organized, Carroll's notion of grammar is not all that different from the following formulation presented by Eisenstein:

> Piece A (derived from the elements of the theme being developed) and piece B (derived from the same source) in juxtaposition give birth to the image in which the thematic matter is most clearly embodied. Expressed in the imperative for the sake of stating a more exact working formula, this proposition would read: Representation A and representation B must so be selected from all the possible features within the theme that is being developed, that their juxtaposition—that is, the juxtaposition of those very elements and not of alternative ones shall evoke in the perception and feelings of the spectator, the most complete image of the theme itself. (Eisenstein 11)

Eisenstein does not adequately define what he means by "piece," but we can assume that it is close to the term *scene*. While he is searching for an evocation of a particular theme, he is also making assumptions about what a correct sequence is and how it will work with regard to the spectator. His premise is that just as grammar can predict the correct syntactical form that a sentence must take, so too must the organization of image relationships properly reflect a set of structural constraints, which will guide the viewer through the labyrinth of visual experiences characterizing cinematic enunciation. "In typically phallic rhetoric Eisenstein characterized successful montage as a 'series of explosions of an internal combustion engine.' Though Eisenstein thought long and hard about what he called 'vertical montage' and the 'synchronization of the senses,' he tended to apply a graphically derived model of montage to voice, music, and noise with surprisingly little sensitivity to the heterogeneity of sonarific signifiers" (Mowitt 168). I would add that picturing the film image through a "graphically derived model" (represented in Eisenstein's writings by his recourse to sketches of shots and camera position) does more than affect the sound; it produces precisely a cartography of significations. And this mapping, in a temporal sense, is meant to precede the creation of the image, control its production, and enframe its reception. The "signs" of this process are then confused with representation in the cinema and in the image.[40]

"A linguistic grammar provides a theory of sentence structure; it defines the sentence in terms of its internal structure. Analogously, a cinema grammar

---

40. This problem is clearly present in the work of Raymond Bellour. See in particular his "Le texte introuvable," in *L'analyse du film* (Paris: Editions Albatros, 1979).

(of the sort countenanced here) provides a theory of scene structure, and defines the scene unit in terms of its internal structure" (Carroll 60).

The internal structure so defined by Carroll presumes that there are, as with natural language, operational relationships within scenes and between scenes, which a viewer will recognize as acceptable or unacceptable. He points toward examples provided by practitioners of continuity editing without which few commercial narratives would make sense. Carroll quotes and supports an assertion by Karel Reisz; "the sort of unacceptability that arises when actions are not matched during a cut: an actor begins an action in one shot, during the action there is a cut to a new camera position, and then the action is completed in the second shot" (Carroll 67).

The problem here, as with Eisenstein, is not only in the easy conflation of structure and sequence (so that there is an assumption of structure just because one scene follows another) but in the quite problematic notion that "the very best data is on the cutting-room floor" (Carroll 68). At no point does Carroll deal with the rather complex relationship among editing, celluloid, and projection. The former is not simply mirrored in the latter. And, crucially, the former is not in a direct sense the cause of the latter. By staying on the cutting-room floor, Carroll is able to say, for example, that "intrashot composition must be consistent with the narrative to which the scene corresponds. For example, jitter and shaking of the camera can only be acceptable when motivated in the narrative; lighting, lighting differences, and shadows must be consistent with facts about the narrative situations" (Carroll 71). He uses a number of examples from what he considers to be the classic cinema, and justifies the above as a rule or principle that must be followed. Using diagrams derived from Karel Reisz's book on editing he tries to show how an unmotivated jitter is basically unfilmic. So not only will montage produce structure, it will also prescribe the conditions of acceptability that govern projection and viewing.

Constrained as he is by a reliance on the commercial cinema, Carroll's hypothesis is from the outset a truncated one. For example, he suggests that student films, or rough-cut versions of commercial films, would be good examples of unfilmic data. This is presumably because they do not follow the rules for the production of images, which he has essentially naturalized into atemporal codes. No mention of the experimental cinema, no mention even of someone like Jean-Luc Godard because, as it were, those examples would challenge precisely the patterns that he extrapolates from the commercial cinema.

Both Eisenstein and Carroll do not distinguish between the staging of an event for the camera (production context) and the subsequent performance of that staging on the screen. There is a difference between, for example, a gesture produced in any moment of film production and the transformation of that gesture onto the screen. The emphasis on editing *as* structure decreases the number of possible interpretations that can be made for a particular scene.

"A scene consisting first of a close-shot of a man followed by a more encompassing long-shot of a man hitting a ball seems to be a paraphrase of a scene consisting first of a close-up shot of a ball, followed by a long shot of a man hitting the ball" (Carroll 85).

Is there then a continuity between the language used to describe a filmic scene and the scene itself? Or is that language always open to contestation and questions about its validity? There is no necessary continuity between description of a scene and the pictorial. This does not mean that even given the vagueness of the term, an image cannot be described. Rather, the description must recognize the discontinuities and continuities between language and projection. The apparent symmetry between the statement, "the man hit the ball" and "a close-up shot of a ball, followed by a long shot of a man hitting the ball" is only possible if language is able to stand in a direct and synonymous relationship with images, if the mediations distinguishing the latter from the former are less important than their presumed similarities. In other words, the hierarchical way different levels of discursivity are structured cannot be collapsed without at the same time giving up the very specificity Carroll's approach is meant to reveal.

It is clear that the denotative meaning of the image plays a dominant role in this approach. As Carroll himself puts it, "cinema scenes represent visual events, things that really happen in a three-dimensional world" (Carroll 43) The visual event is what we see. Representation is reduced to a shared code that governs all visual experiences. Similarly, sequential structures in the cinema can be given a systematicity that relates their visual properties to the objective existence of what they reproduce. In the same way the notion of a filmic cut from one scene to another reveals the actual existence of the edit.

Tangled Knots of Yarn

So strong is this impulse toward using denotation as the central frame of reference that Roland Barthes writing some years later (and once again with reference to Eisenstein) says, "the filmic, very paradoxically, cannot be grasped in the film in situation, in movement, in its natural state, but only in that major artifact, the still."[41] For Barthes the still is like a quotation allowing us access to meanings that the flow of projection inhibits, if not destroys. Barthes sees projection as a moment of emptiness that signifies meaning at a more complex level than is immediately apparent. The still allows us access to an obtuse meaning, a signifier without a signified, something he calls a third meaning and which is very closely related to Eisenstein's ideas on collision.

41. Roland Barthes, *Image, Music Text*, tr. Stephen Heath (Glasgow: Fontana/Collins, 1979), 65.

The absent meaning Barthes tries to recover through the still, the obtuseness he feels film has when projected, is there precisely because projections are not literal but mesh the pictorial with the symbolic, producing a mix of systems of enunciation and expression whose effect visually is *not* a direct one. This indirectness, which in part springs from movement and also from the inherent complexity of what Barthes himself calls a permutational unfolding, requires not that we measure the analytical task in terms of the pictorial, but rather that we submit the language of description to a hermeneutic process. What must be recognized is the way an interpretation is a rewriting of experience. Sometimes the film or the image is privileged as a site of entry, but it is only one part of the process of engagement with the medium and with many other media.

The difference between spoken language and a visual construction is so dramatic that even an attempt to reconstruct how meaning has been produced in formal terms must account for the mix between the already named (that which has been created or produced as image), and that which the interpretive process attempts to explain. I am suggesting, in other words, that there are many processes involved in the recovery of meaning from the experience of the cinema. One is the viewing of a film that includes a multitude of conscious and unconscious processes of which language is always a part. Another is the way the discourses surrounding the experience of viewing are subjected to a preliminary interpretation. I would describe this preliminary process as hypothetical. It may or may not be based on the images. There may be a whole variety of hypotheses regarding the specificity of the images themselves at a cultural level, their relationship to the real world as categorized by the viewer, and so forth. The key to so much of this activity will be found in the manner truth surfaces through the encounter of subjectivity and image. This is not truth at an absolute level, but truth as a function of interpretation. It is a deeply felt, though often contingent move, to join the various hypotheses we have about the experience of images with an interpretive framework. This effort often opens a window into the self, into strategies of self-examination. This is why, although the image remains at best a distant apparition, it can be taken so personally and why images can sometimes have such powerful effects.

These questions of form, the relationship of meaning to models based on language as a systems of systems, the role of subjectivity in relation to hypotheses about structural constraints (or codes) all reflect a crisis of legitimation with respect to images. What role does the image play with respect to the experience of viewing? In what follows, I will examine another of the more formally oriented approaches which, even as the language model has receded in importance, continues to haunt interpretive strategies with regard to images.

At the beginning of this chapter I mentioned the work of Sorlin and Ropars. Their work is profoundly indebted to Eisenstein. The authors chose to work on Eisenstein's *October* because in their own words it was "an experimental film designed around the premise that montage produced a specific organization of meaning."[42] I will deal with that section of the book written by Ropars. She created a chart that subdivided a sequence of *October* into shots. Every shot is described in terms of duration, a description of content, movement, and the angle of the camera. For Ropars each edit designates the boundary for each shot. Thus a shot is distinguished from its neighbors by montage, now elevated to the level of a structuring principle with regard to the development and projection of meaning.

Jean Mitry, quoted by Pascal Bonitzer in an article on the notion of the shot describes it this way:

> Originally, all of the images constituted by a single take. A short scene in which the main characters are filmed with one framing and from a single angle, and at the same distance from the camera. These are divided in a totally arbitrary fashion into, tres gros plan (extreme close-up), gros plan, (close-up), plan lointain (long-shot), in proportion as the frame develops a more and more extensive spatial field. Today, because of mobile takes, the shot is no longer homothetic with the take, which may, by its movement, comprise a sequence of different fields of vision and, consequently, of every kind of angle and shot.[43]

To Mitry a shot is equivalent to a field of vision. As Bonitzer says: "This rigourous definition, then, eliminates from the notion of the shot the predicates of duration and mobility. . . . the shot, deprived of the diachronic determinations implied by the term plan-sequence, would now constitute the filmic unit, but as a unit or discrete element of the take considered in its continuity, while the take would constitute the minimal unit from the point of view of the film's montage" (Bonitzer 110).

The question of time is crucial here. Clearly the duration of a shot will in the final analysis be an arbitrary designation. It will depend on the overall interpretive strategy taken by the analyst. The static conception suggested by Mitry is attractive because it apparently simplifies the boundaries separating one shot from another. But it also produces a spatialization of the shot, a way of diagrammatically "picturing" what projection otherwise tends to overwhelm. In a reciprocal manner, that picturing then comes to stand for representational processes, to confirm and validate the choice of boundary.

There is a collapse here between the shooting of a film and the editing process, between the many takes that comprise the raw material for the con-

---

42. Sorlin and Ropars, *Octobre* 9.

43. Jean Mitry, *Esthetique et psychologie du cinéma*, Tome 1 (Paris: Editions Universitaires, 1963), quoted in Pascal Bonitzer, "Here: The Notion of the Shot and the Subject of Cinema," *Film Reader* 4 (1979): 109–10.

struction of a montage sequence and notions of duration and time. All of these constituent parts of film production cannot simply be transposed into the realm of viewing, and I would stress here that the critic and the theorist are themselves spectators, irrespective of the strategies they take to the images they are examining. When a film is finished it no longer has any shots in it. The organization of meaning has moved to a different level. The raw material of the production process has been sifted and refined. Sound has been added or enhanced. Special effects have been inserted. Scenes have been reshot or transformed. The idea of the shot has a convenience to it, but it distorts precisely what it was meant to clarify. It defines a boundary that projection transforms. The careful tracking motion of the camera toward a figure in the distance that becomes in the end a close-up of a face, can have a consistency of duration and space, but because of the multilayered and multileveled interaction of all aspects of what is happening in the motion of the camera, the boundaries can be decomposed in an infinite number of ways. As Bonitzer says:

> In short, the difficulties of any theory of cinema seeking to establish abstractly the minimal unit, the unit of the code of the filmic message, of filmic performance, are a result of getting things backwards. The shot is not that unit, to be discovered after a learned sifting process or postulated by knowledge. The shot does not exist, because it can be different things depending on the relevant feature, the paradigm to which we choose to attach to it. It is not a stable unit, because it is the variable notation of a difference, a value marked by the shooting. (Bonitzer 114)

In contrast to what Bonitzer says, Ropars works with a very limited definition of the unit. The average length of the unit that Ropars uses is about fifty-eight frames. They are subdivided off from each other through the application of two criteria. The first are the pictorial changes that occur. These changes include lighting and the particular properties of the pictorial representation. The second is the position of the camera. She outlines sixty-nine subdivisions that total about 130 seconds. The smallest is .16 of a second and the longest is 7.83 seconds. She justifies the way that she has broken the film down by arguing that the segment she has chosen is governed by one central element which is the statue of the tsar. The statue is destroyed by the end of the sequence. There is one homogeneous unit and sixty-nine shots, each of which are subunits of the whole sequence. Her aim is to understand how the segment produces meaning and how a particular *written intention* governs the structure of the resulting discourse. Her analysis is concerned with the variations in the denotative picturing of the statue. Thus the statue is only partially present in the beginning. By the ninth unit, the statue is fully there. As well, by the seventh unit the statue is identified as that of the tsar, and thus a symbolic unity is created between the statue and the church which is in the background of the image. In addition, she makes one final and important assertion that the six parts that she has analyzed reveal crucial characteristics about the general meaning of the film as a whole, though she never clearly defines what that whole is and never explains why the six parts she chose represent the totality of the film. What began as a reading of a portion of a text becomes a reading of that entire text's structure and production context. This empiricism of the unit, as a distinct entity, confuses intentionality, production, and interpretation.

Ropars's approach to segmentation sees relations of meaning built like building blocks, one upon the other, as if the passage of pictorial elements on the screen can be separated by breaks somewhat like frame dividers on celluloid or like phonetic units in language. The production of meaning is much more complex than the analysis allows for. Movement, camera position, and lighting are the kind of formal properties characterizing all films. But the way they are produced in each film is a mixture of both the specific and the general. The fact that most films are shot with very high editing ratios is a result of the tension between production and postproduction, editing, and projection. This relationship between many levels is one of continual transformation, as the text mutates to the demands of each level. (We may properly describe all of this as montage.) As a result the boundary lines for the production of meaning are not frames but complexes of signification, pictorial elements piled upon pictorial elements, movement upon movement, quickly shifting camera positions, and even quicker changes in lighting and effect.

The communication of meaning in a film is so heavily mediated that what we have is a situation where the projection of a film produces information and ambiguity, contradiction, breakdown; in other words, there is a stress and strain between the desire to communicate and the performance of the communication, between form and information, between meaning and signification. "The understanding and transmission of information in principle demands an effort, since, in particular, it assumes the reverse process of reconstructing the transmitted message. Non-understanding, incomplete understanding, or misunderstanding are not side products of the exchange of information but belong to its very essence."[44]

This happens in speech. Verbal communication can provide the context for an elaboration and clarification of what is being said and exchanged (though of course this is not a necessary precondition for communication). This is not so in film. Clarification must come from speculation and memory, interpretation and reflection upon the experience of viewing. Ropars asserts that it is precisely her analytical strategy, the reconstitution of the text, that allows insights into the structure of the communication. But if we look at the

---

44. Juri Lotman, "The Dynamic Model of a Semiotic System," *Semiotica* 21 (1977): 202.

criteria she chooses and the units she comes up with, there can be no escaping the fact that they are oriented away from projection and performance. Camera position, for example, can only be hypothesized. Even a frame-by-frame look at the film will give only an approximate indication of where the camera might have been. Thus, in what seems to be initially the simplest of her formal designations, Ropars is really talking about the perspective of the spectator. For her, camera position is assumed to be spectator position. But is it? The camera may look but the spectator does not necessarily see, because as I mentioned earlier the line of communication is not simply linear or direct. The act of seeing is also not simply reducible to objects placed in front of vision. To presume that what is on the screen is what is seen, of necessity wipes out the mediators that exist between the screen and the viewer.

Another criterion that Ropars uses is movement in the shot. If a crowd is moving from one side of the screen to the other side, or from the foreground to the background, this becomes a further element in the description of the shot. She amplifies on the movement by describing the lighting, (e. g., exterior day, direct light) and then for example in a 2.5-second shot, she describes an empty staircase whose vertical presence on the screen is bounded by horizontal balconies on which there are crowds of people, running. The question here is not whether the empirical description that Ropars gives is correct or incorrect, but whether the shots that she describes are the result of a system of direct observation, and if so, what theory guides her choices and emphases. Put another way, does she have a theory of explanation for the extensive inventory she makes of the signifying properties of *October*? Her system of classification presumes in the first instance, that an image can be described in and for itself, "*prendre le film en lui-meme*," and that there is an inner logic to the developing relationship between images in a narrative film that only an inventory can reveal. Her second assumption is that a film is like a text and therefore is like writing: the work of the critic is to "read" the presence of ideology in the written work, and it is by breaking a film into its parts that ideology can be surfaced. Her third assumption, and the one that she places greatest emphasis on, is that the motor force of the text is montage, and as a result the breakup of the film into parts must follow, or at least try and recreate, the flow of editing in the film.

The object of inquiry, *October*, therefore becomes a montage-language, one that is constituted by a series of repetitions and transformations of a set of identifiable units dominated by a particular denotative instance. Within this entire process there is an object (statue), whose role is primary in determining meaning. This montage-language in turn has a grammar, which is ideology. The important point here is that Ropars uses both the term ideology and the concept of ideology as grammar interchangeably, without defining ideology itself. She also makes ideology and structure parallel. As a result, the units that she comes up with are explained as reflections of the grammar that she imputes to them, without any explanation or justification being given for how that structure works, and how the grammar generates the parts that she describes. In other words, her explanatory system is placed over the object like a transparency, and she forms and reforms it to suit the exigencies of the transparency.

Ropars designates the system of *October* by quantifying and organizing the ratio of a unit's relationship to an ideologically determined montage structure. The permutations and combinations of the parts become like a series of formulas, the potential basis for prediction. She asks, will Eisenstein continue to use a particular pattern of repetition and alternation? Is not this montage a paradigm for all of his montage? But unlike a piece of literature, a film is neither written nor read (and it is important to point out that Ropars never explains or attempts to explain the role of the viewer, or even herself as a viewer, and certainly does not reveal the conditions under which she viewed *October*), and therefore the method of segmentation applied to it inevitably transforms the film, overemphasizing its parts, and making of the parts the whole, as if the whole did not exist with transformational effects upon its parts.

This brings me to a crucial point. It is precisely the crisis of what is visible on the screen, or how the screen makes objects and people available for sight, that is being responded to by the segmentation process. Ropars responds to the crisis by trying to find a more complete empirical methodology to describe what has happened in the segment of *October* that she has chosen. Her intention is to isolate those parts she feels will summarize the overall meaning of the film. This leads her to presume that montage is the central pivot upon which segmentation as an interpretive strategy should operate. In other words, what is essentially an interpretive method is elevated into being the actual structure of the film. Ropars points out how edited oppositions are the basic characteristic of Eisenstein's work as a way of justifying this choice. (Eisenstein is, of course, your ultimate auteur. Having explained in his writings that montage is the most important aspect of his work and of the cinema, he consequently sets out the critical methodology and analytical framework that most theorists and critics use in relation to his work. His films become examples of what he has written, as if the gap between his own desire as a director and that of the critic did not exist. The collapse here of author and film produces a situation in which the analyst-critic simply tests out whether Eisenstein has succeeded in achieving what he set out to do.) Ropars explains that as the edited oppositions get more complex, what was originally for example just a statue, takes on greater meaning in the presence of the crowd that is set on destroying it. The function of the montage is then to explain the developing rage of the crowd so as to contextualize what will happen later, that is, the destruction of the statue. Montage is thus essentially segmented shots relating to each other under the broad exigencies of narrativity and the order imposed upon narrative by the ideology of the film.

Through the Lens of Montage

There is then a convergence here between the formal analysis suggested by Carroll and the strategy chosen by Ropars. Both reconstruct relations of meaning through an emphasis on montage. Both assume that edits can be extrapolated from a film in a manner not dissimilar to the segmentation process undertaken in linguistics. For Ropars and Carroll, montage is a "system of shot arrangement or shot linkage, a kind of film syntax."[45] The presence of this syntax is used to explain the way meaning is structured and the elements that can be used in a repeatable fashion to ensure that structuration and its relationship to meaning and understanding.

The elevation of montage to the level of syntax is closely linked with a strategy of formal analysis searching for laws and rules to explain the diversity of meanings found in any given film. The aim is to give those rules a relative degree of autonomy so that the equation of film and language can be legitimized at the level of structure. This will then allow the organization of images through montage to become a master code.

This elevation of montage to a mastercode confers a structural power on editing which then becomes a naturalized fact of filmic textuality. The probability that editing is a feature of all films does not justify its elevation to the status of a master code. The problem is that this code takes on the character of a grammar. The task of theoretical work is to construct those categories that appear repetitively in many films. But repetition is not the guarantor of structure and clearly does not mean that grammarlike systems are present. I would suggest that editing is an hypothetical activity. Working from a series of hypotheses about meaning, effect, rhythm, relations of sound and projection, interactions between characters, and so forth, an editor and director try to explore relations of meaning. That exploration is itself conditioned by an additional process; the film once cut must be projected in order to test out hypotheses concerning the communication of meaning. In that way a film undergoes many edits but not, I should stress, to arrive at an ideal or unflawed combination of images. Rather, many different decoupages are produced and each is framed by different hypotheses regarding projection.

45. Boris Eixenbaum, "Problems of Cinema Stylistics," *Russian Formalist Film Theory*, ed. Herbert Eagle (Michigan: University of Michigan Press, 1981), 68.

In an article on textual analysis, David Bordwell describes the approach taken by D. W. Griffith:

> The switch-back is the only way of giving the action in two contemporaneous train of events. Its psychological value is even greater. By the switch-back you show what a man is thinking of or what he is talking about. For instance you see a scene, and then a shot showing a man musing. Then the picture switches back to his sweetheart and then back to the man again. Thus you know what the man was thinking of.[46]

Bordwell goes on to say that Griffith recognized the interrelationship between a subjective element and the event. The "cut may well instantiate a minor but clear convention of the American silent cinema at a certain period; if so the cut cannot display the arbitrariness of Griffith's ecriture, no matter how odd it may seem to us today" (Bordwell 1981–82, 129). And yet in one crucial sense the cut is arbitrary. It reveals an hypothesized and quite theoretical presumption on the part of Griffith. There was of course no way he could have guaranteed that the man's thoughts were now being pictured or even imputed. He chose a representational strategy to satisfy the exigencies of the narrative. Part of what he was responding to was a crisis in silent cinema. How could someone be shown thinking if they could not talk? And if they could not talk how could their activities be animated so that it would look like they were?

This was a serious problem for narrative films. It was made more difficult because Griffith was engaged in researching not only the possible, but the probable effects on audiences of the montage and narrative systems he chose for his films. Equally, he was concerned with remaining faithful to the exigencies of the diegesis so that his stories would have the look and feel of reality. But this too was part of an hypothesis about the way sets *looked*, about the fourth wall of stagecraft, about the constraints of space and time within a shot and crucially about the "visualizations" audiences would both expect and desire. The difficulty in constructing a stage set to fit the exigencies he demanded resulted in massive budgets. There was no way of guaranteeing success here, but to justify the time and money spent, more and more energy was put into the staging. Griffith was famous for his attention to detail and infamous for his rages on the set. Yet all of his efforts at precision increased the formulaic approach he developed. I am using the word *formula* here quite consciously. As Bordwell's article develops it becomes clear that the terms *code* and *subcode* refer to accepted formulas that came into place during the growth and development of the film industry. In fleshing out that history Bordwell assumes that the professional codes of the filmmaker are the logical site for an investigation of the codes of projection and viewing.

46. David Bordwell, "Textual Analysis, etc." *Enclitic* Double Issue, 5-2 and 6-1 (1981-82): 129.

But more importantly, for Bordwell the film text bears its history within it, thus the formulas exemplify the traces of the context of production of a particular film or group of films. In so doing, an extrapolation can be made from text to context. Yet the context of production is itself an area for historical research, and we can only hypothesize about it through the observations of the practitioners, theoreticians, or historians of a given period, in other words through a set of texts bearing the imprint of a variety of differing but related sociohistorical and cultural factors. To back up his point that "classical" filmmaking did not alter most of its fundamental assumptions about narrativity during the period of transition from the silent cinema to the sound cinema, Bordwell quotes Fitzhugh Green, who wrote a book entitled *The Film Finds Its Tongue*: "You could not . . . continue any one shot for a great length of time. It got monotonous. That was the reason the silent picture had become a sequence of dozens of little bits, why it shifted from long-shots to close-ups, why any scene was shown from four or five different angles" (Bordwell 1981–82, 133). The key word in this quote is "monotony," which is a programmatic suggestion about viewing, about desire, and about the relationship between the structure of a text and the possible range of interpretations that can be made of it.

Bordwell repeats Green's mistake when he examines the role of the *master shot* in the development of the narrative cinema after 1931. The master shot follows the approach of traditional proscenium stage presentations in which an entire scene is filmed with as much adherence to real time and space as possible. Then, a number of different actions, close-ups, and medium shots are filmed. This is all done to facilitate and enrich the process of editing, to provide as much variety as possible. "This procedure obviously allows control in the editing; one always has coverage for every action, always has a shot to go back to. This not only yielded a very standardized set of editing choices for producers in putting a film together, but it has obvious textual effects (for example creating a narrower set of paradigmatic choices) and consequently altered the representational norm. What Hollywood filmmaking did not do was systematically explore the possibilities which multiple-camera shooting offered for spatial disorientation and discontinuity" (Bordwell 1981–82, 134–35).

The question is, how do we as viewers and Bordwell as the critic gain access to the master shot? The point about editing is that it rearranges and transforms the shooting. This is not simply a movement from one level to the next. The raw material of a shoot can be altered in an infinite number of ways. The shooting of a film creates a cultural context linked to, but nevertheless different from, postproduction. Films bear the inscription of these processes but in asymmetrical ways. While there may be codes that ground and constrain the production process, they are more often than not part of an hypothetical and contingent sphere of communication and understanding. This operates as much in the filmmaking context as it does in the viewing theater. The result is different and often contesting versions of history, of the way production links up to spectating and crucially, vice versa. The lack of linearity here increases the potential of cinematic communication and comprehension through images to such a great degree that at no point can a fixed formula be put in place for any part of this process.

In some senses the reductive approach toward the segmentation of films exemplified by Carroll, Ropars, and Bordwell cannot deal with the gaps in meaning that the movement from production to editing to performance entails. Segmentation as an analytical tool satisfies a desire to classify and then inventory visual and oral experiences and the interpretations we use to explain our experience of viewing both to ourselves and to others. The attractiveness of a taxonomy of filmic units is its immediacy, the way it can *re*-present and concretize the far more complex processes of viewing. The taxonomy also acts as an illustration. It proposes a referential map which marginalizes the very real problems of viewing images. This taxonomy relies so heavily on montage that editing becomes an all-inclusive code with a constellation of causal relationships that determine meaning. The result are discourses that cannot accommodate the performative characteristics of the projection process. The problem is that the cinema and for that matter most images do not communicate across or within a clearly defined set of boundaries. The continuum within which viewing, projection, and analysis operate does not have, as its primary *site* the screen itself, nor can an adequate extrapolation be made from celluloid. The result is an asymmetry which textual formalism tries to constrain, but which images and viewers almost inevitably transcend, if not undermine.

4 | Projection

A Coup in Thailand

EARLIER IN THIS book I briefly mentioned the story of Neil Davis, a news photographer killed in Thailand during an aborted coup in the middle of the 1980s. His death was broadcast all over the world. He died holding a television camera in his hands. The camera fell to the ground, providing viewers with the sensation of a present-tense experience of his death. For many months afterward, the images were quoted in other news shows and in documentaries about the Asian subcontinent, with parallel comments about the hazards of being a reporter in the field. The dangers were accentuated by the relationship between the attempted coup in Thailand and a variety of wars from the Middle East to Afghanistan. The paradox of course is that Davis wanted to be at the center of the action, that he wanted to film the scene that killed him. It is this desire that must be examined in the light of his death.

What could he have shown us about the attempted coup in Thailand? What did we "see"? How do we explain our fascination with the "visual" aspects of this experience? There is a sense in which Davis's death is about, as David Michael Levin has put it (in a comment on George Berkeley's *An Essay Towards a New Theory of Vision*), "what principally *moves* our eyes is the desire to know, and that knowledge is mastery and control."[1] But do we gain control over his death by watching it? The puzzle here is that there is no fixed way of describing the many levels of thought and emotion that constitute this experience of watching a man die. The attempt at mastery is always confronted by a sliding away, a movement from the seen to the unseen and from recognition to confusion. What we define as the visible (in the form of an image or the act of seeing) never fully contains within it the range of experiences we need to maintain a genuine feeling of control.

Yet this is also the basis upon which a dialogue is established *with* the experience of the visible and the image. Possession reveals itself to be ephemeral, and the only "place" within which some order can be brought into this set of experiences is through argumentation and discussion. The dialogic na-

1. David Michael Levin, *The Opening of Vision* (New York: Routledge, 1988), 69.

ture of this process can be internal or external. It can take the form of a vague series of thoughts (an imagining of the seen) or efforts at articulation between two individuals or among many. The lack of stability encourages the movement from image to speech, from experience to discussion. It encourages efforts at validation, at confirming the truth (or not) of what has been seen. In saying this I am obviously trying to counter the dominant cultural notion that the image (and in particular the televisual image) contributes to, if not creates, an illusory universe of one-way communication. This gives precisely the kind of dominant emphasis to the visual that needs to be examined with great care. There is no numbing moment outside of reaction, outside of the discursive richness within which images operate. Fundamentally, the act of seeing is *always* interactive. This is heightened to an even greater degree by images, which act as intermediaries, between points on an ever-changing compass. Davis's death, which we could in any case only imagine, was nevertheless converted into an image, but that conversion was an act of will, only possible because subjectively we were then able to transform the experience into a meaningful one. In other words, images may operate as if the field of vision they represent totalizes the "seen"—synthesizes the visible into a framed "scene"—but it never works. The image remains susceptible to so many different interpretations and experiences that its framing dissolves at every moment of subjective interaction. I shall return to this point many times in this chapter. Suffice to say for the moment that we will have to examine whether the image can in any case be equated with the visible.

There are further questions we need to ask about the nature of information and the news, about the relationship between information and communication. It will be crucial to link all of these arguments with the presumption that being at the center of the action in any given context provides an entry point into history. There are fascinating contradictions at work here. They include the notion that history can unfold in front of a camera, that history can be the subject of a visual presentation, and that the truths of events can somehow be portrayed through the metaphoric fields of the visual. How have these assumptions been incorporated into notions of the image? Why have they taken on such a forceful presence? Levin, responding to an argument by Heidegger, talks about the "enframing mode of vision" (Levin 74), which has come to dominate Modernism. "Enframing requires total visibility and constant surveillance" (Levin 1988, 74). In Levin's terms the frame represents efforts at constraint and the needless creation of boundaries, while at the same time offering human vision the "objects" it needs to validate the experiences of perception. He worries about the "immediacy" offered to the visual experience by the framing process. Yet it is my feeling that immediacy is a temporary phenomenon. In other words, we no sooner experience the in-*sights* of the visual than we are at the point of reimagining their very boundaries. To me these are fields of contestation.

Arguments about whether images are real or not, for example, are discussions of human experience. They center on what is acceptable and what isn't, on presumptions about the way the world looks and the way it should look. The power attributed to documentary images (for example, that images from the Vietnam War contributed to the growth and strength of the antiwar movement) is essentially just that, an attribution. It must be seen as part of a *cultural projection* about the role of the image in contributing to, but not determining, complex forms of human interaction. Anyone from that period who sat through strategy meetings about what would be effective as political action and what wouldn't, knows that the images could not have worked without many, many other activities going on at the same time. Yet we will have to examine why the image is given such a key role, why it is seen as an arbiter of historical events. The will to control resides precisely in the ease with which the image can be described as playing the role of manipulator. This confers the subjective dilemmas of experience and understanding onto another scene. The image is able to absorb any number of conferrals. It sculpts the moment and can be sculpted. But it doesn't have the *body* to do what we suggest it can, although that doesn't prevent us from attempting to wear images, even to tattoo them into our skins in a paradoxical attempt to become what we see as well as what we imagine.

Davis's death was accentuated when his injured soundman was seen dragging Davis's body to safety. This "view" was made possible by the camera's position on the ground and the angle at which it captured the shot. But was there a viewpoint? What analytical tools are best suited to examine these issues? The question of viewpoint is crucial here. The camera acted somewhat as a robot. "It" filmed the aftermath of the shooting. Of course, the results were then edited into a presentable form, but the death exceeded the capacity of the editors to manage it, exceeded itself as picture. This excess, which may well be a characteristic of all images shot "by cameras" (because of the digital revolution, that caveat will quite soon change the analytical boundaries in place for the interpretation of images), is more than an additional element in Davis's death. It is a space of representation and signification that cannot be so easily categorized. As a result, we may not be dealing with signifying processes that are text based, and even the terms *representation* and *signification* may not clarify the many different ways in which Davis's death was communicated.

The evolution of Davis's story into a miniseries produced by Australian television and subsequently broadcast in the United States parallels the frenetic attempt by many different television producers to capture news happenings and redevelop them for presentation as narratives. Examples abound from Baby "M," to David Koresh, to Amy Fisher, to Nancy Kerrigan and Tonya Harding, to weekly TV productions on everything from child abuse to marital violence and natural disasters. All of these also interface with talk shows. This appropriation of "real" events not only blurs the boundaries between the news and fiction, but also transforms the public and communicative sphere within which notions of the real are manufactured and sustained. In effect, through a variety of media, from newspapers to bulletin boards and from television to radio to cable access, from the Internet to interactive media, "events" take on the character of images, but these are not images in the conventional sense of that term. What we are dealing with here are ritualized interpretations and reinterpretations of the world *and* of the process of viewing. What we will have to examine and question is the very nature of the media used to transmit images. In both cases, the operations of the medium and the images used do not have the same character as traditional images. Part of the challenge will be to explore whether the hybridization of media and image has generated a new language of expression and whether we will also have to create radically different modes of interpretation. This chapter will only hint at the new theoretical ground that will have to be developed. And in keeping with the orientation of this book, it is traditional media that will be examined, although future work will have to research the history of, and the changes being initiated by, computer-mediated communications technologies.

Reading a Wave

On Tuesday, November 21, 1989, the president of NBC news announced that the network would discontinue the use of dramatic recreations on the news and in documentaries because "they confuse viewers about where reality ends and recreations begin."[2] "The new policy mandates that any simulation, recreation or reenactment of any kind in a news broadcast must first be approved by the President of the news division." Viewers, it seemed, disregarded disclaimers about the recreations printed on the television screen before the news and repeated by the announcer just before the item was broadcast. Why did viewers disregard the warnings? Why should they have taken them seriously in the first place? The premise here is that the viewer may not have enough control over his viewing, may not be able to anticipate the effects upon himself of watching fiction and thinking that it is real. Another assumption is that the further away the representation of reality gets from the truth, the less likely the viewer will be able to deal with what is shown and said. As the discussion below suggests, the relationship of viewer and image *begins* within an

---

2. *New York Times*, November 21, 1989, A 8.

already established context of mediation. The truth is at best only one part of a complex and interwoven constellation of meanings, the outcome of which can rarely be judged simply by referring to the representation at hand.

One way of thinking about mediation is to reflect on the storytelling experience. If you have ever listened to a fairy tale being recounted to you, then you will surely remember the rather extraordinary way the words and tone of the storyteller generated a variety of images in your mind. Were those images specific to your experience? Were they derived from a culturally shared body of images? Neither of these questions can be answered in a simple or direct way. Yet what we share is the role of the imagery in completing or enhancing the experience of listening to the narrative. This should be a clue to the richly endowed levels of mediation that influence and sometimes overwhelm any activity of communication. Metaphorically, we might want to think of viewing, for example, as somewhat similar to staring at the horizon while the sun sets. The event is only one facet of a multitiered series of experiences which include the many daydreams and thoughts that tear through the mind as we watch, superimposing images upon each other in a never–ending stream.

The beauty and the simplicity of this process was wonderfully brought to life by Italo Calvino in his novel, *Mr. Palomar*. The first chapter has Mr. Palomar on the beach staring at the ocean. It is entitled "Reading a Wave." It takes four-and-a-half pages to describe the wave(s) Mr. Palomar is watching. He moves from its physical characteristics through to questions about seeing and then about geography and vantage point. "In any case Mr. Palomar does not lose heart and at each moment he thinks he has managed to see everything to be seen from his observation-point, but then something always crops up that he had not borne in mind."[3] Something always crops up, and this is not a negative characteristic of the viewing or listening process. It is the very ground upon and through which Mr. Palomar negotiates the mediations of seeing, listening, thinking, and interpreting. This extraordinary plethora of thoughts and images lives within every viewer. And while there are many conventions and rules that try to constrain this process(ing), they merely circle around the complex and different circuits of meaning and understanding constantly being put in place to subjectify the experience of images. There is no doubt, however, that conventions of image creation and viewing have a history. No doubt that what I am describing as constraints generates the possibility of a dialogic—an interplay between many different elements where the outcome need not be as clear as the framework of the convention would itself suggest. I would prefer to approach what follows without casting the debate in terms of convention versus nonconvention, without, that is, buying into a oppositional structure to

3. Italo Calvino, *Mr. Palomar*, tr. William Weaver (London: Seeker and Warburg, 1986), 5–6.

the debate about meaning and communication. Both processes are part of a continuum within which we are continuously recategorizing and redeveloping our beliefs and value systems. What may be fixed and secure one day shows itself to be ambiguous and even wrong the next. These are processes that cannot be systematically mapped—the mediations exceed our efforts to describe them—because they never exist in the simple sense outside of the human bodies they inhabit. Meaning is both the motor for Mr. Palomar and the result of his research. His words express this sense of embodiment. His ideas are driven as much by what he sees as by the fantasies of sight he has. This refers to a comment I made in chapter 1. Mr. Palomar has a fantasy of control. He must, for the purposes of categorization and rationality, propose both to himself and to others that he understands how the mediations influence what he sees and how he is in control of them. But the ground for all of this activity continually shifts and is so dynamic that, much like the sea, the lay of the land never seems to be quite the same. The desire to bring all of this activity to some sort of synthesis is constantly thwarted by the temporal vortex within which it operates, by the stresses and strains of processes that are often autonomous but nevertheless make their way into consciousness.

Fact Is Always Fiction

On December 9, 1990, John J. O'Connor, writing in the *New York Times* described the potential dangers of the docudrama form in relation to a British-American coproduction about the Lockerbie disaster in 1989 entitled *The Tragedy of Flight 103: The Inside Story.* O'Connor discussed the ambiguity of putting a project together on the disaster when all of the facts were not known by the police. "Granada and HBO officials take pains to point out that their product is not designed as standard entertainment focused primarily on the personalities of the major players. Expert editing highlights the thriller aspects of the docudrama, but the very shape of "Flight 103" does not lend itself to the tidiness of drama."[4] And yet it does and the show did combine all of the elements of high drama with the tragedy of death. The injustice and the pain came through. Here, the mediations center on the event, on its appropriation and the many days and weeks during which the crash was reported and discussed in the media. There can be no simplicity to this multilayered treatment of the terrorist bombing of innocent civilians. Inevitably, as docudrama the show wants to be known for its connections to the event and to history. Why then fear all of these other connections? Why try to discourage the many different and possibly related aspects of fact and fiction as they might be understood by spectators? Why assume that the viewer is incapable of distinguishing for themselves between what is true and what isn't?

4. *New York Times*, December 9, 1990, D3.

The profoundly paternal characteristics of this approach are duplicated in "radical" critiques of the media. In discussing coverage of the Gulf War, Elaine Scarry says the following: "So the result—and this is my fourth framing thesis—is that the population has been infantilized and marginalized; the population can no longer exercise its deliberative obligations over these very grave matters."[5] The confusion here between information and knowledge, between communication and understanding leads to reductive arguments about the many ways images work and how they are understood. One of the most important elements of this chapter then will be to link the richness of images with the even greater richness of spectator-image relations. It will be equally important, however, to talk about how these many layers of meaning production empower those who come in contact with them. I am not simply taking a contrary position here with respect to what Scarry has said. Nor do I want to belittle the critiques made about the limited and often superficial approach that modem media take to the issues they cover. However, I am of the opinion that we are dealing with a dramatically different context for images within which determinate and indeterminate relations can coexist. On the one hand there can be stable moments of meaning, and on the other, the unstable, the ambiguous, and the unconventional can provide a terrain for exploration and interpretation. Yet the easy opposition between conventional and unconventional disguises the many grey zones that filter and infiltrate what finally may not even be an opposition. The various classification schemes to which we have become habituated (those that would distinguish, for example, between radio and photography or between video and telephones[6] as media of communication and exchange) lend themselves to normative and rule-based approaches to the study of images. Yet if we are to take seriously the notion that our image context has in fact dramatically changed, then surely our interpretive strategies must also change.

Documentary Simulations

In 1981, during a public presentation in Paris at La Cinémathèque Française, Jean Rouch said the following:

I am an ethnographer and a filmmaker. I have discovered that there is no difference between documentary films and fiction films. The cinema, which

5. Elaine Scarry, "Watching and Authorizing the Gulf War," in *Media Spectacles*, ed. Marjorie Garber, Jann Matlock, and Rebecca L. Walkowitz (New York: Routledge, 1993), 59.
6. In what is otherwise a brillant piece, Kathleen Burnett suggests a classificatory scheme in which verbal, visual, and combinatory media are distinguished from each other. "Verbal media: telegraph, radio, telephone: Visual media: visual arts media (painting, sculpture, etc.), photography: Combinatory media: offset printing, film, television, video." See Kathleen Burnett, "Towards a Theory of Hypertextual Design," *Postmodern Culture* 3.2 (1993): 5.

is already an art of the double, which presents us with a constant movement from reality to the imaginary, could best be characterized as a cultural configuration which balances between various conceptual universes. In all of this the last thing to worry about is whether reality as such has been lost in the process of creation.[7]

Lest Rouch be misinterpreted by purists of the documentary genre, he went on to say that as a filmmaker he creates the realities he films. He sees himself as a *metteur en scène* as well as someone who has to improvise everything from camera angle to camera movement during the shooting of a film. This process is inspired by the kind of personal choices that inevitably rely on the imagination of the filmmaker. The key to Rouch's approach here is the role he sees artifice playing in the construction of any image or as he put it, the way the filmmaking process, irrespective of genre, is ultimately a sharing of dreams at the level of production and performance. Rouch's statement can be seen as a counterpoint to efforts on the part of documentarists working in any medium to overinvest in the realist enterprise. It could also point the way to an examination of why images that look real have such a seductive appeal, yet why they never work completely to uphold the tenets of realism.

The "look of reality" is the key to the process and is in my opinion part of what Jean Baudrillard means by simulation. Most importantly, what Rouch suggests is that the image doesn't play as important a role in the production of meaning as imagemakers would like to believe. In much the same manner as Chris Marker in *Sans soleil*, Rouch's statement questions the place of referentiality within the documentary form and to some degree looks outside of the image for an understanding not only of the message, but of its relationship to performance and projection.

The worry John O'Connor has that somehow the spectator will be duped into believing that a television show can replace the event and in fact dominate it and the similar feelings of the president of NBC points out the ambivalent and often fearful attitude some viewers and critics have to televisual meaning and to the communication of ideas through images. What needs to be questioned here are the various nodal points that both metaphorically and figuratively represent the perceived failure of images to clarify their own operations. Why would Jean Rouch celebrate the fictional as fact and fact as fiction? Why celebrate what so many others see as evidence of the decline of value and morality, of the fudging of crucial distinctions so necessary to the maintenance of our preconceptions about the real and its representations?

In what follows, I propose to explore many of these ambiguities in order

---

7. From documents presented at the celebrations for the fiftieth anniversary of the National Film Board (Montreal: June 1989), n.p.

to move to a radically different explanation of images. I want to trace out a trajectory in which the image is not so much intelligible (in the sense of a sign system awaiting a reading) as it is a vehicle through which spectators create constellations of meaning in stages, transforming, in an historical and temporal sense, the way images communicate and the many ways we communicate about them. My stress will be on the multiplicity of layers of meaning built into most uses of the image, be it for the cinema, television, or any visual medium, silent or filled with sound. And although there is much that is indeterminate here, the thrust of my approach will be to retain the importance of context and what is shared at a cultural and personal level. Yet these are processes in constant evolution in which what is normative for one historical moment may not be for the next. And my strategy will be to account for these shifts, not to elide their importance because they upset or undermine the interpretive approach I have chosen. I will presume that the visible cannot question itself, that meaning is a site of struggle for human subjects and that images are never in the simple sense the main focus of debate.

Projection

"Images are not in consciousness but are acts of consciousness."[8] In supporting this statement I am concerned with moving away from a simple model of information and communication toward one in which active interpretive strategies are being developed and worked upon by viewers at all stages of their experience of images. I would like to accent the creativity of viewing, the shifting movement from awareness to knowledge, to desire and its negation. There is no required order to this movement through a multiplicity of different levels of apprehension and comprehension. There need be no particular source for the variety of understandings we develop in relation to images. I am aware, of course, that this approach can descend into an anarchic relativism. The loss of specificity is a real danger, as well as the elision of context and often, content. I take seriously the critiques made of postmodern strategies to cultural norms and the obsessive concern of postmodern theory and practice with the new. My aim here is not to reproduce a simplistic notion of polyphony to, in a paternalistic sense, reinstate the right of others to speak in as many voices as they wish. Rather, my assumption is that there are always many voices and many meanings crowding together in sometimes similar and sometimes different contexts, making the effort to be heard and to be seen.

The polyphony I am concerned with grows out of the image into a process

---

8. Paul W. Pruyser, *The Play of the Imagination: Towards a Psychoanalysis of Culture* (New York: International Universities Press, 1983), 7.

symbolically represented by a term and a concept I will explore in this chapter—projection. I believe that even though we are witnessing a radical reconfiguration of imaging technologies, our fundamental assumptions about images as devices of communication have not changed since the earliest days of photography (see chapter 1 for a more extensive discussion of this issue). Although we have moved far beyond the mechanics and engineering of the photograph, we still approach images as if they are representations or facsimilies. We are still concerned with and fascinated by depictive techniques, by the wonder of the real reproduced in other forms and through a variety of different media. Even though it has always been possible to invent new universes through pictures, the primary focus remains the connectedness of the image to a describable real. This dependence on what I will tentatively describe as outmoded notions of the visible has already been overturned by digital technology (morphing is a good example). What is at stake here is nothing less than the language we use to interpret and understand the experience of the visual. This is being challenged at an even more profound level by virtual technologies which raise many questions about our capacity to make sense of new forms of image-based embodiment.

In order to break out of what I see as a vicious circle, I will propose in this chapter that we begin to think of images as one stage in the *projection* process. In a transitional sense I will make use of both terms as has been the case with my use of image throughout this book. But I would like to move away from the conceptual base that has nurtured and sustained the almost universal use made of the term *image*. It is somewhat paradoxical that as we have come to understand the multiplicity of ways various cultures (our own and others) use images, we have not found significantly different strategies of interpretation or analysis.

Projection as a concept has traveled through a variety of conceptual universes from Freud to Melanie Klein and to more sophisticated uses of the term in modern-day object relations theory to its appropriation by the hermeneutic tradition and reader-response theory. My use of the term will explore its potential use for the analysis of images and will not remain beholden to its psychoanalytic roots. And, although a definition of sorts will evolve out of the discussion, I will not try and pin down either the term or my use of it. That said, a tentative approach to projections suggests that they are neither solely a result of the image nor are they simply produced by the spectator. I will describe them as a space in between image and viewer, a meeting point of desire, meaning, and interpretation. The attribution of meaning by viewers then becomes as much a product of this meeting as it becomes a potential arena in which viewers can assert their control over what they have seen. Projections are first and foremost acts of consciousness. They are, in a metaphorical sense, like filters, which retain all of the traces of communication, but are always in transition between the demands made by the image and the needs of the viewer.

In a film theater, for example, the screen sets out a terrain within which projection can operate, but this is not a mapped or predetermined space. Nor is the performance of an image locked into a predetermined temporal structure. The time of a projection is not necessarily located within the confines of the cinema or the moment of watching a television screen. Projections can be found in the daydreams we have as we watch or in what we say after the experience. In all cases my goal is to get away from the simple linearity of screen to viewer, image to spectator, to overcome the notion that images are sources of experience and sources of meaning. Thus I believe we will also have to rethink what we mean by spectator and viewer, terms still locked into linear and mechanical notions of reception (a term retained in even the most sophisticated of analyses[9]).

Not only will our language have to change but so will our notions of information. It is just no longer possible or valid to *blame information for what we do with it*. There is I believe no credibility left in the argument that the media determine the way we see the world. Images can only have so much power if we project or attribute that power to them. How can we explain the process of attribution?

It may seem heretical to make the claim that images do not determine the way we see the world. The contrary argument appears to have been culturally validated over and over again, with a variety of institutions, particularly in Western societies, legitimizing the notion that images control our experience of the environments in which we live. This is not an either/or argument. Clearly, what we do with images effects how we see and what we see. But there is far more flexibility to the relationship than is often suggested—many ways in which images operate to clarify, distort, enhance, and negate the frameworks of understanding within which we operate. This is precisely the polyphony that has enabled if not promoted the rapid movement toward new technologies of imaging. It is as if no one moment satisfies the exigencies of communication, no one image or interpretation, properly speaking, constrains the excess flow of information, and so we need sophisticated instruments to manipulate and handle what we ourselves produce. As we move from media to hypermedia and from text to hypertext, images become more and more layered until they are architectural in design, until their relationship to the context from which they have grown cannot be talked about through the rather simple models offered by referentiality, or by attributions of cause and effect.

9. In an otherwise excellent book, Mark Poster continues the uncritical use of the term *reception* to describe the place of subjectivity. Mark Poster, *The Mode of Information: Poststructuralism and Social Context* (Chicago: University of Chicago Press, 1990).

Yet it is precisely our desire to project so much into the image (and to attribute so much power to it) that makes it necessary to reconfigure our analytical and interpretive strategies.

As the metaphor of cyberspace takes on more and more significance, the screen itself seems to dissolve. "The screens of cinematic and televisual experience become touch sensitive, transforming the gaze and collapsing its vision into the tactile worlds of virtual reality."[10] This argument takes us beyond the screen, even beyond the image. It is an argument for projection in which seeing is no longer framed or presupposed through relations of distance or perspective. Rather, the eye and the visible are embodied as they struggle with positionality in the physical, mental, and emotional conflicts that result when you have to take responsibility for what you see, instead of conferring that responsibility on an-other. This sense of responsibility also takes on greater significance as more and more communities define themselves through the use of the camcorder. For example, there is a cable show in the United States and Canada called "Camnet," which is exclusively devoted to showing videotapes submitted by individuals and groups. This video culture may communicate nothing to anyone, since there is no way of validating the experience viewers in the most disparate of locations and from wildly diverse contexts have when they watch the tapes. But this is precisely why communication may not be the purpose of this semi-institutionalized activity. More to the point, the tapes themselves become the place within which a series of arguments are being made. The counterarguments come from other tapes, and the "discussion" takes place in the realm of projection. If the interactive context being elaborated here is entirely image based, then what happens to human language, to the points of reference with which we are most comfortable, to the sense we have that there has to be some measurable distance between the images we watch and the everyday life we lead? The cyberspace argument would collapse all of these distinctions. And I believe that there is some validity to that position. For the moment, I would like to explore the concept of projection to see if there isn't a valid middle ground here. In what follows, I will use the cinema as a major pivot for my argument. I would also like to draw the reader's attention to the experimental style I will be using in an attempt to break with the discursive boundaries normally in place for this type of analysis.

Dreaming the Cinema

Watching someone else dream is akin to watching the film or television screen. (He turns, he moves, he mumbles.) My attention is drawn not so much

10. Sadie Plant, "Beyond the Screens: Film, Cyberpunk and Cyberfeminism," *Variant* 14 (1993): 14.

by what he does as by the mystery of what he doesn't say. Excess. More than the eye can behold. Thought and vision. Can the mind know what it sees? I have run into an immediate difficulty. Do I attribute my thoughts to what I have seen? Or does the very act of attribution tellingly reveal that my thoughts have overwhelmed sight? And is this then the first crucial indicator that in order to see I have to fudge the boundaries between what I know and what I can't see? Are these boundaries accessible? Must they be? The difficulty here is that any attempt to map the process will lead us further into a subjective sphere, the relationship of sight to what I feel. And this, like the experience of listening to music, doesn't have the concreteness that my language of description projects onto the scene.

In a recent series of essays Claude Lévi-Strauss explores this problem. In discussing the relationship between words and music, he mentions the paradox that although there are notations for a score or an opera or a symphony, the result is not that tangible. We listen and perhaps visualize, but there isn't a dictionary that would correlate the one activity to the other. In that sense music has an autonomy that precludes reductive forms of referentiality. Music works directly on what we would describe as our senses, says Lévi-Strauss, and the result is that we are left, not with a defined set of correlations between fixed meanings, but with relations of meaning that may not be found within any specific set of elements, but across them.[11]

This is close to the notion of projection, which situates meaning in different realms loosely connected with a topography in constant flux. There is no lack of specificity here. It is that there are so many possible arenas of meaning creation that the points of intersection traverse each other. The webs or networks that result can be entered through a variety of doors which we must open and close, for which we set the rules even as others try to break them down.[12]

(His body twists to the right and his left leg swings awkwardly off the bed.) Watching him, I don't try and imitate his sleep; I certainly don't enter a semihallucination of which he is the progenitor. I may listen, as Freud has suggested, to a voice-off, and confer greater meaning on that voice than on my own, but perhaps that is because there are already so many voices within me that I don't know. He smiles. Is he enjoying himself? (But five minutes ago he moaned and I assumed that he must have had a nightmare. Suddenly he sits up—awake or asleep?) I tell a story to describe his experience to myself but

11. Claude Lévi-Strauss, "Les paroles et la musique," *Regarder, Écouter, Lire* (Paris: Plon, 1993), 89–94.
12. For a more detailed discussion of these issues I would refer the reader to a forthcoming essay of mine entitled "A Torn Page . . . Ghosts on the Computer Screen . . . Words . . . Images . . . Labyrinths: Exploring the Frontiers of Cyberspace," in *Late Editions* 3, ed. George Marcus (Chicago: University of Chicago, 1995).

somehow it feels insufficient, which leads me to reject all of my hypotheses even as I am simultaneously being transformed by them. I think for an instant here of the moment in *Tightrope* when Wes Block, played by Clint Eastwood, rejects all of the obvious signs that the killer he is hunting has actually begun to hunt him, and then has a violent nightmare in which he turns into the murderer. Substitution? Metonymy? Condensation? Yes—if we have to accept that the dream the film shows is the dream we have seen and also the dream Block had. The irony is that Block says nothing after the dream, though his hardened exterior softens a bit. Can we so easily see inside his head? And do dreams look like that? Perhaps over the years the cinema has created so many images of the dream that it is no longer clear whether the metaphors are derived from experience or fantasy. The point, however, is that Eastwood can structure his narrative around the impact of the nightmare.[13]

This cinematic visualization around the film *Tightrope* with which I am now engaging exists only as a memory to me. Yet the memories are powerful enough that I can make use of them. The conceptual logic here is really centered on my ability to make my own memories relevant. I organize them into what I describe to myself as an experience and fill them with intentionality. This is a fascinating terrain in which I literally become the dream, in which I take up the challenge of the film to inhabit its narrative, to become the storyteller. I cunningly look both from within the screen at myself and at others, and from outside the screen at its operations and my desire to control what I see and listen to.[14] This is not that different from the long wait in *Weekend* (by Jean-Luc Godard), when a traffic pileup ceases to carry meaning because we have witnessed it as image for so long, a lack is created which is never filled. The question of whether meaning can arise from the ashes of many accidents is not answered until we understand that the passage of time will be the only recognizable quality of the sequence. This lack of information turns the process of seeing into projection.

I cannot enter the scene of the accident which Godard's film offers up to me (although I try, over and over again). In order to deal with all of these contradictions I turn instead toward my own thoughts, a witness to something I can't fully grasp but which I call internal. Internal? The image I have of my own fantasies are that they are inside of me. But inside is an abstract word, often used improperly. Its usage reveals many of the problems inherent in thinking and speaking about relations of seeing and understanding. I cannot

---

13. See an earlier essay of mine on *Tightrope* for a more complete examination of these issues. "The Tightrope of Male Fantasy," *Framework* 26/27 (1985): 32–56.
14. This is a theme that has been taken up and explored by Wim Wenders in his video/film *Lightning Over Water*.

talk about my own brain or body as if there is a definable point of origin for my language of description. Inevitably, *inside* is conceptual, defined by hypotheses, constrained by memories and fantasies, a place that is a nonplace.

At which point in time will my dreams come to represent an inside that I will know? "inner makes sense only as a synonym for mental or psychological"[15] Schafer goes on to say that while we can locate the biological site of certain forms of human activity, "where is a dream, a self-reproach?" (Schafer 1976, 159). This troubles me because I want to understand my dreams by stepping inside of them, by literally assimilating myself into the dream state. I start to think of ways of entering my mind, my unconscious. Of course that is not possible. But why not? As a solution I turn toward my own body, my own fantasies. I take a deep breath, conscious of the feeling in my lungs. I gain pleasure from the sensations of movement and stretching. The images in my mind fragment into pieces. I am obviously looking for a way of bringing my experience and my dreams together in order to visualize the entire process.

The Act of Seeing with One's Own Eyes

Is what I have said above identification? "What is identification? What is the evidence that identification has occurred? What motivates it? Does 'motivates' apply? What is the explanation of the process and its result? Identification, as used by Freud through 1919 (and thereafter, I believe), possessed at least two ambiguities. First, it referred to a process and also to the result of that process. Second, it appeared in descriptive contexts as well as in theoretical contexts. For clarity, it is necessary to distinguish process and product, description and theoretical construct."[16]

The confusion between process and product has been exemplified with the greatest impact by the film *The Act of Seeing with One's Own Eyes* by Stan Brakhage. The images of that film have remained with me since my first viewing of it:

"Bodies in an autopsy room, lifeless, in pieces, skulls cut open, chests parted down the center, organs ripped from their locations, faces and fingers, still, yet straining for identity, lost to decay. . . . Even though the bodies were not the perfect expression of "something" dead—I strained to give them a voice just as their necks were cut open—strained to see their faces just as the scalpel sliced into their cheekbones. And when a man's brain was removed from

15. Roy Schafer, "Internalization: Process or Fantasy," *A New Language for Psychoanalysis* (New Haven: Yale University Press, 1976), 158.
16. Allan Compton, "The Concept of Identification in the Work of Freud, Ferenczi and Abraham: A Review and Commentary," *Psychoanalytic Quarterly* 54 (1985): 214.

his skull, I rejected my fascination by closing my eyes and feeling desperately for the pulse on my wrist."[17]

Where were the borders here between my own fear of death and the "sights" being presented to me? I wanted to see death in the film pushed to a point outside of me. But the sight brought the entire process into my thoughts about myself. Clearly, the screen was not the only place I was watching. Could identification be the realization that one is both the product of a process and simultaneously the creator of that experience? Thus the dead body comes to life because I desire not to see myself as dead. Yet to watch death, I must for a moment engage in the fantasy that I too am dead. The line I draw between inside and outside is not the end product but part of the process of identification. This is a point that all of Brakhage's films make. When I saw one of his earliest films, *Window, Water, Baby, Moving*, which is about the birth of his first child, I found myself in a reverie jumping from film to daydream to shock to pleasure and to tears. I had never seen a birth before. Of course, the film didn't show me one either, not in the literal sense. In fact, Brakhage broke all of the rules of camera movement and editing in order to make as much of an aesthetic statement as an emotional one. In so doing he created so many gaps in the "narrative" that I filled as many of the missing pieces as I could. Does that mean I became the filmmaker? Does it mean that I was in the room when the baby was born? Yes and no, or maybe. The answer as such will not be found in the film itself. I will have to make that decision through an examination of my memories which are suffused with enough fantasies to bring the birth to life as a projection.

"*The Act of Seeing with One's Own Eyes* deals with the Pittsburgh morgue—its title is the etymological translation of the Greek components of the English term, 'autopsy.' "[18] Levoff goes on to talk about distinctions between fiction and reality, replaying the argument that Brakhage's film is real because it took place in a morgue. "There is no possibilty that we are witness to trick photography or elaborate properties and make-up designs. We are in an actual morgue; we are confronted with the actual corpses of murder victims, accident victims, fire victims, suicide victims; we are witness to the intimate processes of autopsy" (Levoff 74). For our purposes here, Brakhage's film explores the body by using a *cinéma vérité* style which throws the whole question of death back on the spectator. In order to watch the film, in order to think about it, in order to interpret the experience, I have to deal with my own fears of the *image of death* as if I too have become disembodied.

17. Ron Burnett, "Inside Brakhage's Eyes." From an unpublished manuscript on the work of Brakhage, 1982.
18. Daniel H. Levoff, "Brakhage's *The Act of Seeing With One's Own Eyes*," *Film Culture* 56–57 (1973): 73.

I began by saying that watching someone else dream is akin to watching a film screen. Now I am not sure about the screen itself. Surely the death is real in Brakhage's film but the screen is not. I mean, the images on the screen are not. It's just a flat surface. It has a rather rough texture. And on the rare occasions when I have touched it the screen has felt more like a thin tissue, a membrane. But the question of truth and reality is quite peripheral. The point is that the images are there for me to see. Or so I imagine. I cannot see, however, to the exclusion of thinking. I am continuously playing between the foreground (my thoughts) and the background (the screen). The screen and its "contents" seem to be very concrete. But the question of materiality and materialization is precisely the problem. The screen is after all the site of an object world. The people I see on the screen are not people anymore. In order to be visible they represent a transformation from life to death, a movement from one kind of space and time to another. Brakhage's film meditates on this double death, leaving me to contemplate and deal with the consequences.

The screen spatializes time and constructs a frame around memory. But what if the objects on the screen are reintegrated into our culture as subjects? They come to represent a process that endlessly overvalues itself, that treats thought as visual, that links the the visual and speech as if each can clarify the other. This is the movement of Clint Eastwood from screen character to the mayor of Carmel or the transformation of Ronald Reagan into a president. On the one hand they become part of the stories they tell and on the other hand they enter the historical process. This ends up dissolving the distinctions that keep the screen somehow separate from what it pictures, but this doesn't give me any more power over the image. It is the projections I control.

The materiality of the screen is only possible if the objects on it have a life outside of the cinema. Thus the star system confirms and legitimates what the screen cannot. This then symbiotically links all of the media with each other, while at the same time creating many possible conflicts. *Madonna* comes to life not only through the screen, not only through music, but through television, radio, the news, rumor, word of mouth, magazines, and other spectacles. (The Tonya Harding-Nancy Kerrigan affair is another good example of this materialization-dematerialization process, of many different kinds of ambiguities and contradictions dancing on the same stage, a stage, I might add, itself subject to dissolution.)

When I see Clint Eastwood on the screen, do I make the assumption that there is more coherence to his presence than when I see a news broadcast about his activities as a mayor? Where do we place the slash between inside the cinema and outside? If both are dramatically different then where are their points of contact? If they are the same then how do we define the differences? To suggest that the Clint Eastwood film is more intelligible and more structured than my experience of him outside of the cinema is to privilege the projected image over my capacity to imagine its content. But here again, where will we place the slash? Am I as viewer producing what I see in both instances? Is what I see merely a tiny fragment of what I imagine? Is what I imagine beyond the screen? There is no simple way of mapping these relations of desire, these arbitrary shifts from negation to truth and back. In part, to displace many of these contradictions I displace my body image into Eastwood's. I substitute my dreams for his. The key question here is whether all of this is possible irrespective of whether Eastwood is an image or not.

This then is one of the starting points for projection. We do not need an external image to create one. We do not need the screen to experience the strength of our own imaginaries. We do not need to be reminded that our imaginations exist or that we dream or daydream. Projections allow us to work on ourselves *as if* our fantasies have been externalized, and we can idealize those fantasies, hate or love them or make the effort to disregard their presence. For example, I might find Madonna repulsive, but by whom am I being repulsed? Where does the heightened sense of repulsion come from? The more I make her responsible for my own feelings the less likely I will understand why I have them. In effect, she has become part of me and I dislike that part. I want to avoid sounding mechanical here, but as I push Madonna away, I of course have to recognize her presence within. This it seems to me is inevitable. The part of me that dislikes her can conveniently discard the notion that I am responsible for my feelings. I can describe all of the characteristics of her public personae that alientate me. But who am I describing?

This problem can be recast as a problem of vision. In talking of the gaze Levin says, "inherent in the nature of the gaze, there is an inveterate tendency to develop only one aspect of its primordial ontological potential, viz., its detached, dispassionate, theoretically disinterested power to survey, encompass, and calculate or categorize with one sweep of a glance" (Levin 1988, 98). The discourse I use in relation to a public person and the very public images that sustain Madonna's presence in the culture, are in large measure dependent on how I go about reflecting on my vision of her. What am I ready to include in my vision and what must I exclude? Why have I even chosen Madonna to focus on? Am I threatened by what she puts into her image? The point here is that I must be prepared to examine all of the implications of my gaze, to explore not just the foreground meanings that come to light as she performs, but the full range of relationships I have with her image.

Let me refer back to *Wavelength* again. Throughout the duration of the film very little happens. The film uses a loud whining sound to compliment or interrupt, as the case may be, its image flow. The film does not explicitly link what it is doing with me. Yet its projection immediately shifts the ground upon which I can develop an analysis of my experience. In a sense the film brings to a crisis point my desire to confer upon it the status of a subject. I want to converse with it and to understand its motivations. But the film per se, has none. *Wavelength* places a question mark around its construction of meaning while at the same time producing a performance. Strictly speaking, there isn't a word or even a phrase that can adequately describe the process of viewing the film, since what it pictures puts me into the position where I have to daydream to view. My thoughts move all over the place. Through a variety of displacements and substitutions, I short-circuit the projection continually. It becomes a tug-of-war. Will I prioritize the shifts and inconsistencies of my own daydreaming? Or will I blame the film for not holding onto me?

I would suggest then that the slow zoom of the camera in the film is a lovely metaphor for the inability I have to simply watch a projection. It is a metaphor for the loss engendered by the activity of viewing. Most importantly it suggests that viewing a film exemplifies a crisis in the experience of images. There is no simple solution to the presence of a gap between screen and viewer and our simultaneous inability to designate, to picture that gap. This rather large chasm, the boundaries of which are never set, and which changes in relation to my role as a viewer, also tends to shift the possible ways the viewer as such can be viewed (in other words the very strategy of this analysis). To convert what I see into a meaningful exchange I have to engage with a variety of experiences. I have to create barriers and then cross them. *Wavelength* is after all only providing me with the bare outlines of a map for which I have to find more than just the key. I recontextualize the map so that its elements will fit into a process the film's original structure could never have created or anticipated. Thus in order to understand my experience, even to see the screen, I must *subjectify* it. The screen becomes not an object of projection but an interactive point of contact within which the very drama of projection is itself worked out. This suggests that one part of the process of subjectification transforms the screen into a potential place for narcissistic pleasure. Now, what does it mean to suggest that the screen as subject (an impossibility) also becomes the site of narcissism? It means that every suggestion, every strategy with respect to the experience of viewing is also and inevitably a strategy of self-definition. The mirrors in this instance are many. They come *into* visibility through the ways they are described and talked about, through the many strategic points of reference we use to watch ourselves *as* viewers. This watching takes the screen and transforms it into a site of projection—a place where the visible plays a far less significant role with respect to the gaze than instrumental analyses of vision make room for.

The Purple Rose of Cairo

These problems of subjectification, interpretation, language, and viewing are brilliantly dealt with in *The Purple Rose of Cairo* by Woody Allen. The main character, Cecilia, loves the cinema. In the midst of the Depression and surrounded by misery and despair, she seeks out the cinema as a place to dream and daydream. There have of course been many characters in the narrative cinema who escape to the medium they are meant to be a part of, but in this instance Cecilia finds a magical world in which the character she loves on the screen turns to her, and from that place addresses her, invites her into a conversation with him. Not only does he interrupt the flow of the story in which he is a participant (the scene he interrupts is one we have seen a number of times and this increases the impact of his gesture), but then he walks from the screen into real life, at least the real life of Cecilia, who is of course on another screen, the one we are viewing. The film revolves around the relationship they have.

Tom Baxter, as he is known in the film, talks in the clichés of someone whose part has been written for him. He is constantly amazed by the difference between the screen and the real world. During a fight with Cecilia's husband, he gets beat up, but when Cecilia rushes to help him he merely stands and says: "We never get hurt." One cannot of course be injured in a film. This is the world of the doppelgänger, in which every character claims a place in a realm already defined by camera, director, and script. Reality is always and inevitably mediated. Declarations aside, no character in the film can claim, in an ontological sense, to be alive. But the film celebrates the wonder of the illusion and suggests that our definitions of the real have been irrevocably altered by having the cinema, having the image as a basis of comparison.

The bridge between Baxter's role as a film actor, his role in the film, his new role with Cecilia, the script he usually follows, and crucially, the language he can use, is never clearly fixed (which is why he is such an exuberant character). Just as he is about to kiss Cecilia, he turns away from her and asks for a fade. When she says, "No, no, this is real life," he is astonished. He takes her out for dinner and tries to pay with the fake money used in the film. When he realizes that it is fake, they run off to a car. He gets in and waits for the car to drive off. Again, Cecilia has to educate him. The joke here is of course the way we view Cecilia, as if she represents an instance of reality, when she is no more real than Tom. Ultimately of course we are viewing Cecilia's own fantasy. Tom's love for her is as instant as her love of him.

To complicate matters, Gil Sheppard, the man who plays Tom Baxter, comes to Cecilia's small New Jersey town and tries to make Baxter return to the screen. This is because the movie cannot continue without him. The various "times" of the narrative become confused. The actor becomes the character and then reverses himself. Of course it is precisely this flexibility that allows Cecilia to enter and then continue playing out the fantasies she is having. What is at stake here are the various grids upon which we have based our assumptions about viewing images. Cecilia lives within the projected universes she constructs. But as with any fantasy it only lasts as long as a dream or day-dream. This lack of permanence means that time must be reversible in order for the fantasies to work as projections. Reversibility challenges the visible and makes it possible for narrative links to be established independent of the image.

Throughout the evolving plot with Cecilia, the original black-and-white film continues to be projected. The other characters talk to the audience in the small cinema, who talk back. The screen here becomes a place of exchange, not to reveal that as its potential, but to highlight the performative role played by the audience. Eventually, the lack of action and the constant complaining and bickering by the remaining members of the cast makes the audience leave. But not before we witness the characters talking about the events of the film as if the narrative cannot continue without Tom. "We want to go and eat at the nightclub," they say. "He has to come back, he must, we cannot go on like this," and so forth. Tom Baxter's scripted language suits the image he has of himself. Tom Baxter, Gil Sheppard, Cecilia, and her husband all balance on a variety of precarious fantasies. Cecilia, pale, sensitive cinema addict, radiates an innocence contradicted by her lifestyle. Gil Sheppard, actor, who wants to play the role of Charles Lindburgh ("I am close to the biggest breakthrough in my career") is clearly an opportunist but is also the victim of his own fantasies. Tom Baxter, whom Cecilia rejects as a lover because he is not real, chooses to go with Gil. Tom is perfect, as is to be expected from someone who is both a star and a projection. He pulls Cecilia onto the screen, into his black-and-white reality, where his fake money is good and they spend the night "doing" the cinematic town.

These many layers of plot, action, fantasy, and self-reflexivity are then amplified by the arrival of the producer of the film, one Raoul Hersch, who fears that a second Gil Sheppard running around wild in the streets of New Jersey will lead him to ruin and destroy his film company. We see him receiving reports of other Tom Baxters in other cinemas trying to leave the screen. Finally they decide that once they get Baxter back, they will burn the prints of the film and the negative. Throughout this series of encounters the real Gil Sheppard slowly wins the love of Cecilia. She compliments him endlessly and he uses her to prop up his desires to be a star, as well as being a vehicle for his own narcissism.

All these collapses between reality and film, between desire and its objects, between the imaginary and its images, all lead not to perfection and truth, but rather toward disappointment and failure. To laugh at Cecilia's naiveté is to laugh at our dreams for her. To presume that she is outside of reality while we inhabit it is to join with her in the illusion that the yearnings we feel in the imaginary are somehow separate from ourselves and our experiences of viewing. The film raises very precise questions about the presumed gap between the screen as a place upon which maps of desire are played out and the viewer. The maps do not come from an unknown world dreamt outside of the rational, of the conscious, but rather from the very relations of conscious and unconscious that make all dreams possible in the first place.

Cecilia returns to that point of primary identification where there is no need to differentiate between one's body, one's consciousness, and what one shares with another. She reveals how any presumption of distance from what you identify with is only a defense against the fundamental role of a viewer, which is to create an emotional tie, projection to/from experience, that reunites the dreamt to dreaming (and brings the full force of the present tense to bear on the activities of seeing). It is of course the slash between to and from that concerns me here. For if the cinema poses itself as a place where what I see is the way a character looks at what he or she sees, then the screen and I have become one. But when I watch Cecilia's eyes watching the screen and then see what she has been viewing, a relay of looks has not, in the simple sense of the word *relay*, been established. For as primal as I might desire my identification with her to be, I am actually involved in an oscillating movement of apprehension, distance, and crucially, projection. If I want, I probably could submerge myself in her. But then I cannot because she as such is only there as a term of my identification with her. A term, in the sense that she is not the site of identification but is rather performing a mediating role with the screen as intermediary. I will not convert myself into her, primarily because I know that she won't convert herself into me. Thus her look, if look is the right word, disrupts my anticipation of what she is thinking. What is she thinking about her relationship with the things and people she is seeing? There is a chasm here broader than the one suggested by screen and viewer. There is a difference between performing the role of viewer and being captivated and then imprisoned by the performance. To be a viewer is also to see oneself *as* viewer, to float in and out of the binds experienced by Cecilia, to desire a "scripted" life, and to recognize the impossibility of the dream. (This is also a theme taken up by Wim Wenders in his film, *Kings of the Road*.)

I do not want to suggest by this that film as such is without effect. But the simplicity of the viewer-screen dichotomy suggests a level of effect only possible within the binary nature of the division. It can also be suggested that Cecilia, Mia Farrow, views herself through the viewer and thus responds as a projection only can, by anticipating herself as there for me while knowing that she is not and never will be. Thus whatever I say about Cecilia rebounds against me as observation. It is as if I were to record my own speech and then listen to it. As often as I assert that Mia Farrow did something, performed an action, spoke, I am confronted with the contradiction that I could have imagined it. But this is also crucially at the center of my own pleasure, the prop for my narcissism, the ground upon which I can imagine myself as a viewer. For while Cecilia acts as a mediator I must struggle to overcome the role that she is playing, struggle to interrupt my need to internalize her. She and I coexist in a contradictory dialogue with few clear boundaries, but which, as dialogue, never collapses into the nonperformative. In the midst of what I believe are my own feelings for the heroine one finds a series of reversals. I imagine I control what I see, but what I see cannot not be controlled without the film operating to create a context for my own performance as an interpreter. What this means, and it is a point to which I will return, is that my eyes do not provide me with the sight I think I have seen. In fact the very question of what I am gazing at or listening to becomes a fundamental part of the identification process. To have asked the question is in a sense to have set out the possible scenario for what will follow. This sense of control and loss often attributed to the film, as if the film creates the space for its own absences, is one of the crucial entry points for the projection process.

Germany, Pale Mother

Dreams can neither be corrected by "internal rigour or external reality."[19] Because of that they are an ideal terrain for a vast number of interpretive strategies, the playground of wish-fulfillment, desire, and the imaginary. In film, the act of magnifying an image into an object many times the size of the original fundamentally alters the way meaning is communicated and then understood. Designed as it is for spectacle, the large screen of the 70mm film displays a wide range of elements. An excess is generated. This excess escapes the boundaries of the screen and of the theater (in a metaphorical sense like the character of Tom Baxter). The screen then becomes not the object upon which a projection is found, or upon which it displays itself; rather, the screen becomes a point of mediation for viewing and projection. The internal rigor proposed by the boundaries of the screen is transformed into a place where sight is not privileged. I will begin this section then, with a question. Could it be that I *see* very little of the films and images that I *watch*? I gain some pleasure from the loss. I forget my own contribution to the projection in order to try and remember it. And I identify with my struggle to remember.

I will use *Germany, Pale Mother* by Helga Sanders-Brahms as an example of projection and loss, of the way a film can actually thematize these issues in order to delve into questions of subjectivity and history as they relate to images of Other and self. Now, if the boundary of the screen is merely the pivot upon which a process of identification is put in place then all we need do is look toward the screen for a definition of what happens to the viewer. But if projections are not pictures precisely because viewers are always recontextualizing

19. Gregory Bateson, *Mind and Nature* (New York: E. P. Dutton, 1979), 221.

the act of seeing, then the film may simply provide the background upon which an activity of interpretation is being created. The viewer sits with his or her paint brush and a very large range of colors struggling to fill in and remove all of the constituent elements of a canvas that the brush is never able to touch. There is no final object. A memory, however, remains. I created something.

Pleasure can come from loss if one can maintain control over the whole process. Or, if the illusion of that control can coexist with the constant effort to let go. Letting go. I cannot merge with a character on the screen unless I internalize her image. However, the degree of internalization contracts and expands at a variety of sometimes related and sometimes conflictual levels. If we begin to think of the screen not as an end point or the end point of a look or a series of looks, but rather as an interruption to looking in which, in a metaphoric sense, the behind of the screen, or the missing third dimension of space combines with a new dimension or formation of time, then the act of seeing has been profoundly altered (though sound tries to recuperate the gaps). The continuum between seeing in the cinema and outside of the cinema is broken and reconstituted. Learning how to view in the cinema generates a deeply conflictual relationship, overwhelming the simple linearity of representation to sight. Interpretation struggles with viewing. We struggle to interpret and even to resolve the various levels of this creative yet complex conflict, but the excitement of the struggle is its unpredictability.

Germany, Pale Mother is about Lene and her daughter, Anna. It takes place between the pre-Second World War and postwar period in Germany. Lene marries Hans before the Second World War begins. She is deeply in love with him and he with her. They move into a new house with white lace curtains and new furniture. Their love has an air of tenderness and innocence to it. Suddenly and as if without warning (though the war has hovered in the background throughout the early part of the film) Hans is called to duty as an active soldier. He is sent to Poland. There we see him killing women and children, in particular a woman who looks very much like his wife. As he and the other German soldiers leave the murder scene, Hans cries. He is criticized for being weak and not being a man. This is taken up again when all of the soldiers are issued condoms. Hans refuses to take one. "I am happily married," he says. The men play a series of jokes on him, and he finds his bed full of condoms. He returns from leave to visit Lene, and within minutes of his arrival tries to make love to her. She refuses gently and sensitively. But he misinterprets her hesitation as evidence of adultery. He lets the frustrations of his experiences with the other men out on her. He hits her. Then he holds her, as a father might hold a child. He feels guilty but the aggression remains. They decide to have a child, and it is here that the story enters a dramatically different phase. Anna's birth increases the degree of separation between Lene and Hans.

Their house is destroyed, and Lene has to go to Berlin. There she stays with some rich Nazi relatives who soon leave for the country. Lene's relationship with Anna is very close, both out of dependence and need. Lene is extremely resourceful. She survives on practically nothing. When Hans visits her at the house in Berlin, their relationship has ceased to have any meaning. He is unable to understand her relationship to Anna. The child does not know the father, and Hans shows little emotion toward both women. They don't make love because Anna has to sleep with Lene. Mother and daughter are not only close but their love provides Lene with her defense against Hans. He returns to fight in Russia, and his wife and daughter leave Berlin for the countryside. Mother and daughter survive the war, survive the rape of Lene by American soldiers, survive the dead corpses they stumble over, and survive the lack of food and housing when they return to the city.

In the immediate postwar period Hans and Lene fight another kind of battle. Hans is unable to find his dignity again. He is insensitive to both to his daughter and his wife. They become increasingly isolated from each other. All the while her lack of desire for him reinforces his own fantasy that she is being unfaithful. Finally one day Lene wakes up with a partially paralyzed face. In response to the paralysis the doctor takes out all of her teeth, a terrible indignity. She begins to live in the darkness of her bedroom and slowly moves toward suicide. Anna tries to take care of her mother but is rebuffed. In the last scene of the film, Hans leaves the house saying that he wants to die and Lene goes into the bathroom and turns on the gas. She locks the door and Anna bangs on it continuously for ten minutes begging her mother to come back. Anna repeatedly says that she is alone in the world and needs Lene. Lene walks out and holds her daughter. But this is not a reconciliation. She has decided to live but it is a living death.

This act of symbolic suicide reveals the degree to which history has destroyed Lene. The act of rejecting the suicide reveals the love she has for her daughter. Both aspects of that event reveal the depth of the repression Lene has undergone—repression of the history she lived through, of the loss of love for her husband, repression of the effects of her husband's loss of love for her. Her body becomes the symbolic map upon which her unconscious finally erupts and upon which is charted the displacements she has undergone both through the war and her husband's role in it.

Hans represents the war and the blind ethos of men and their perpetuation of Nazi ideology. Lene, however, internalizes a whole variety of different guilty feelings. In the first instance she feels a guilt Hans does not. She feels guilty for Anna and what the child has been through and then guilt that she cannot be her husband's lover. Hans, it must be remembered, had already symbolically killed her. Lene reproaches herself continuously and this manifests itself in other forms of repression so that finally, her own child becomes an object of hatred, bearing responsibility as witness for Lene's imprisonment by history.

Lene bears a double burden. She must mother her husband and her daughter. She must allow herself to be the victim of a war she had no role in creating and then permit herself to be raped by the victors.

Simultaneously, Lene stands for all women married to Nazi soldiers who had to bear the guilt their husbands quickly suppressed. In that sense Lene's pain is historical, just as Anna's fear of losing Lene is both historical and personal. Mother-daughter come to stand for the copresence of a past that has destroyed meaning, a present that cannot make room for the future, and a future to be held irrevocably chained to the past. What kind of pain has Hans experienced? At first the war shocks him. He kills women, one with Lene's face. Slowly, as less and less is said, his angst turns to resignation and despair. His obsession with Lene is transformed into paranoia. He disbelieves her and doesn't trust her in order to protect his own illusions about himself. His distrust has no basis in fact, but this is unimportant because his paranoia is a projection of what he has repressed inside of himself—his guilt and his loss of identity. The only way he can recover some dignity is by hurting Lene, by hurting, that is, the projection that haunts him.

Metaphorically, Lene stands for Germany. Not only for division and loss and separation, but also crucially for repression and the necessary conjuncture of repression and history. Her burden is to keep the future alive in her child while evaporating the present and the past. She must work to rebuild (and there is a long scene during which she collects and stacks bricks from buildings that have been destroyed), having been an onlooker to destruction. It is this sense of Lene as a viewer, also a participant, that hints at one of the film's concerns. Can the images of Lene's suffering ever be rendered visually? What combination of narrative elements must the film bring together to arrive at some depth here? Does the war become an image with the kind of power that precludes comprehension, even representation? (This was a problem filmmakers like Fassbinder struggled with throughout their careers, most fully expressed in the film, *Marriage of Maria Braun*.)

While Lene keeps Anna alive, she must also sustain her husband, both sexually and morally. She must displace his slow dehumanization onto herself so as to lessen his angst. Finally, Hans shows so little concern for Lene that she breaks down. But this does not mean that she is unaware of the contradictions. Hans, who can neither love his daughter (she plays a joke on him and he beats her) nor his wife, does not represent the successful Nazi who reintegrated into German life. In that sense, he is a victim as well, but only to the degree that he was unwilling to take responsibility for his own actions. For Hans, the continuum of history has no breaks, no gaps, no instances where some measure of self-reflection can be introduced. Time passes from year to year without meaning. He plays a role he cannot describe and accepts no responsibility for his lack of verbalization. Now there is a dilemma here. If he is just an ordinary individual then presumably in his eyes he can have little influence over the events of history. He represents that kind of individual upon which Nazism depended. Someone able to sublimate contradiction, to see themselves as cogs in a machine they neither contributed to constructing nor participated in sustaining.

Yet, Hans too says at the end of the film that he does not want to live. Does he have the right to say that given what Lene has been through? The word *right* is misplaced because in the morass of postwar Germany, the illusion of reconstruction, the illusion that the immediate past could be quickly forgotten, merely sustained the pain, elevating it to a point beyond the control of people like Hans. What happens when the images and the thoughts you have are appropriated by everyone around you, when the personal scenario you want to write for your life has already been written? You don't test reality with your projected hopes but immediately despair at finding reality itself. Ironically your emotions and your thoughts play with, look for, substitutions and replacements. While for Lene, Anna is both daughter and lover, witness and cause; for Hans, Anna represents the destruction of his identity because she seems to have a future devoid of the nightmares of which he has been the progenitor. She is also the site of what he thought was a pure and innocent moment, though Anna was birthed out of the fears engendered by the war and not out of love, nor really out of need. Anna comes to stand for that generation of children born to participants and onlookers of the war, for whom the war is really a secret of childhood. As with most secrets of childhood, the parents are inside and outside of the fantasy. Anna's scars are such that she is alone with her parents or without them. In that sense history can only become concrete for her through unrealizable fantasies constantly overcome by memories and loss. Her history will always be fictional to her, and she will continuously search for some way of crossing the boundaries from fiction into reality. But Anna also knows that for Germany no fiction will ever do. The war overwhelms, silences, and paralyzes both discourse and the imaginary.

In conjunction with this, the family becomes a massive site of repression governed by a set of rules designed to support and legitimize alienation. Lene's paralysis also stands as a symptom that does not turn into a disease, is not allowed to run its course as a disease, but remains forever as an open wound. It is difficult to look at Lene, difficult to watch her face, to see the pain, and yet the film tries to give some access to the history that the marks on her body have left behind and have come to represent.

In the conflict between the historical and the personal, new and different forms of discourse are created. Even lived history folds over into the various interpretations we make of it, the various and often different representations we develop to explain it to ourselves and to others. The very temporality of the personal shifts the grounds of definition and explanation, broadens and sometimes narrows the choices we have. In all of this we struggle with definition and explanation, with interpretation and description—all with the aim of making sense of the images and experiences we encounter. It is this rather rich constellation of ideas and emotions, of embodied and disembodied feelings that transforms images into projections, that disengages the image from its source, that makes it possible for history to be lived as if events themselves have become part of a film. This is what allows Lene to be both within and outside of the scenes she both creates and is a victim of. On the one hand she is an observer. On other hand it is the very act of observation that overwhelms her.

Narrative—Projection

What *Germany, Pale Mother* cannot do is demonstrate through its structure how I have experienced its narrative development. Crucially, my description of the film and subsequent interpretation are really guides to a combination of different discourses. Simultaneously, the film, my interpretation, my description, the discourse I have chosen, all fit into a multidimensional textual body. A narrative film projection is not a story in the sense that a written text is. This is not to suggest that a story once written is not full of gaps, but what we call meaning expressed through writing is different from meaning expressed through projections.

For example, when I say that "Lene's face is paralyzed," transformed into a projection that potentially becomes for me,// the actress playing Lene expressed, through the use of make-up, tears, careful direction, and the clasp of Anna's hand, the effects of the paralysis on her face and what I experience of that process is not Lene but the pressure of creating Lene, the act of acting (a point of departure for the actress and myself)//.

More of course could and perhaps should be added, but the point is that the projection of Lene is a message about a message and is thus always meta-communicative. Writing out a projection thus involves a writing out of the experience of it, which is also a rewriting of the relationship between identification and knowledge. (Imagine trying to do this with the sound.) Lene is present for me and absent, a creation of the actress and my creation. And the various levels of this experience can never be divorced either from the writing or from the viewing, from the subsequent interpretation or what I say to others about the film. In some respects I cannot divorce my feelings of bitterness toward Hans from the fact that my own family lost most of its members to the Holocaust. Even my choice of this film for discussion reverberates with the impact of my own personal history. The universe of projections is not immediately in "view." I must, in a sense, always probe more deeply. You, the reader, must assume that my viewpoint is governed by more than is apparent, more than is on this page. This was of course the monumental project which Jean-Paul Sartre set for himself when he decided to write the biography of Gustave Flaubert. He discovered that every moment of Flaubert's life was filled with detail and that in order for that detail to be "represented" the biography would also become Sartre's autobiography.

To produce a projection is different from producing a film. //The actress playing the role of Lene was surrounded by an apparatus of production and design that fundamentally altered her perception of the part she was playing. The alteration was so dramatic that what she projected was the anguish of her own past, her own despair at the childhood ripped away from her by the war. In that sense she both identified with the character and was repulsed by having to act out her character's life.//

//The actress began to respond less and less to the suggestions given to her by the director of the film. The narrative converged with her own deeply held and ambivalent feelings about her mother. She felt a growing bitterness inside of her toward the man playing Hans. His weakness, his distance, his lack of real involvement in her anguish made her hate him. But then one evening he broke down and said that he could not continue. The crisis grew deeper when the film crew challenged the director to explain why Hans was being cast in such a negative light. This brought Lene out. "Wasn't it men like him who fought the war? Didn't they kill and maim, murder and plunder and then return to us, to the women, expecting love and affection?" Everyone on the set became very silent. The director then said, "This is only a film. Be careful, however autobiographical it is, we all must not take things too literally."//

Whose voice has expressed all of the above? I, as the writer of this text, have chosen to fictionalize a conflict that developed on a film set. But my fictionalization could not have been possible without the film, and yet the film did not make the fiction, did not produce what I said. Have I broken with the film? Have I altered it to suit the exigencies of the argument I am making? Where can the slide between the two versions be situated? Most importantly, am I perverting the images, destroying their fundamental framework, overwhelming the narrative structure? Am I placing the film into a context where meaning becomes so relative that anything can be said about the film and its images?

These questions indicate a slipperiness, a play on the transitional qualities of words and sentences and images. What I have said so far has another aim. It is to draw you, the reader, into my thoughts, to collapse the distance in space and time between this page and your reading of it. But, more likely than not, you haven't even seen the film I have been describing to you. "You" are not even here as I write to you. This is not a letter. But the contradictions I am relating here are the necessary join upon which the fiction of my communication with you is built and is not dissimilar to the way we view projections. To some degree the act of viewing allows this fictional interplay tremendous latitude. I am thinking here of the obvious way a film like *Jurassic Park* brings its dinosaurs to life. I know, even as the characters say otherwise, that I am viewing digitalized effects, blue screens, magical tricks of foreground motion and background sets (the brillance of digital software and microcomputer design). The dinosaurs can only become characters if I choose to make that possible, and in order to "enjoy" the film I willingly accede to the process. The desires I foreground and try to fulfill are the playground of projection. This is more than just my imagination concretely finding an outlet. This is my desire to tell a story, to free associate, to let go, to make myself feel that the dinosaurs are a real threat to the characters, even as I laugh at the impossibility. This is the lure and the attraction of the film. This is that rather ephemeral yet very real playground where over and over again I play at the same games, oblivious to the repetition, yet comforted by its consistency. (This is also the playground of Game-Boy, Nintendo, Sega, and other computer games.)

Let me contrast what I have been saying with another argument. *Germany, Pale Mother* is a rather conventional narrative. Conventional in the sense that it begins with a situation of harmony out of which a particular problem grows, for which a resolution is slowly found. This is done not to restore the prior situation to its original status, but to nevertheless complete the circularity of closure necessary for the fiction to end. It ends with a qualitatively different level of harmony, which explains the history the film has been recounting.

If I were to pursue the above argument (with all of its Aristotelian implications) with rigor, then I would arrive at a point where the narrative would have exhausted the circular structure I have attributed to it. Presumably, I would arrive at a closure for my argument, having found, so to speak, the boundaries for the production of meaning. But what concerns me is whether a self-critical awareness can be produced through which I can move from one level of expression to another. What ends up happening is that two experiences are translated into a third. This quality of thirdness, however, merely becomes the vehicle for an extended process of conceptualization and debate. More importantly, the gap between myself as an observing, experiencing subject dissolves what I observe, not eliminating it, but replenishing its meanings through the relationship I establish and reestablish with it at sometimes related and other times more distant levels.

Crucially, my usage of the word *relationship* doesn't reveal the many layers at work here. Context and meaning interact in a perpetual undoing of structure, an unraveling that often intensifies the search for some rules of organization. But no equilibrium can be found that will retain meaning outside the shape we continually confer upon it. We are continually bound to the problems and to the potential that results when meanings undergo this shaping and reshaping, when many different possible interpretive arguments and strategies swirl around the same object or experience.

So while it is possible that my interpretation of Lene was designed to talk about historical presence and absence, Lene's role as a projection transforms the direction and content of what I have been saying. I internalized her pain because that pain was already in me. I made a place for her, as it were, and then began to reconstruct the film as an instance of my desire to be her. But why would I want to carry the burden of her anguish? This is a crucial question because I presumably haven't gone to the cinema to relive the pain of Lene's character. But, as I said, I am part of a family that lost most of its relatives to the Holocaust. My predispositions were quite clear to me. I am as concerned with keeping the memory of the war alive in myself as I am in keeping it vibrant in the lives of others. I don't want history (as I understand it) to disappear down a black hole. So my relationship to Lene is one of pain and disgust. I keep on transforming her into a real character and not a projection, keep on wanting her to violently reject Hans and fight him tooth and nail. These desires and needs cannot be divorced from the analysis I have been presenting up until now. The crucial questions are where the substitutions took place in relation to the narrative and how I managed their orientation with respect to myself. Furthermore, what extrapolations am I making with regard to the audience for the film?

"Making a place" suggests that I have chosen the substitution. But what I have done is to transform the fiction so as to be able to allow its entry into me. The transformation is partially in my control and partially not. It is as I reflect on the memory of that struggle that I am able to tell the story of the film. In that sense, I relativize what the film is saying so as to be able to believe its truthfulness. Furthermore, I attribute to the film a level of intentionality that I know the film cannot exemplify. Though the attribution has no "real" existence, without it I would be unable to subjectify my experience of the film. At the same time the projective qualities of the film, its desire to transcend the limitations of being thematically locked, serves to subjectify it further for me. Thus I willingly become a part of Lene's world because the communicative interchange into which I have entered "seems" to be my own. This does not mean that I have entered into a pact to produce an illusion. Quite the contrary—I have become involved in a process that allows me to judge, in a kind of postmortem sense, the exchange as exchange. I test out, define and redefine, name and rename, the various meanings I have encountered and created. The postmortem is going on while I watch and after I have watched Lene's difficult struggle.

The Topography of Projection

This brings up then what is observable in a film and what is not, what can be seen and what cannot be seen. We would prefer to privilege the film as a cause, if not *the* cause for what we see. But the process of viewing is far more complex than that. The supposed continuum between viewing in the cinema and outside the cinema needs to be recontextualized as a *struggle* for sight, for vision, for meaning. This produces a deeply conflictual relationship in which the screen plays a rather indirect role. Film images don't keep viewers in place, don't fix or solidify processes of identification. They prepare the ground for conflict without uncovering the topography or the lay of the land. But a film image also displaces its own ground through projection which alters our capacity to describe what is a potentially *discontinous* relationship between seeing and understanding. What one sees in the cinema is thus subject to much more experimentation than might at first seem possible given the finite level at which the film is operating. I am not suggesting here that the film is without a particular order. But the film as projected is a vehicle of experimentation. It is a fulcrum, allowing certain activities, discouraging others. But at no point can it be the privileged port of entry for looking or for the process of interpretation.

What one observes in a film is from the outset embedded with these sometimes contradictory, sometimes conflictual levels of meaning. However, this doesn't confirm André Bazin's contention that vision in the cinema duplicates vision outside the cinema, "confirming the spectator in his or her 'natural' relationship with the world, hence at reduplicating the conditions of his or her 'spontaneous' vision and ideology."[20] Nor does it support Jean-Louis Comolli's assertion that "film tends to reduce it (film and reality) by proposing itself as adequate to the norms of perception, by ceaselessly restoring the illusion of the homogenuous and the continuous."[21] It is Comolli's inadequately explained "norms of perception" that concern me here. Viewers use those norms to sustain what seems like a natural link between the screen and meaning and understanding. From this Comolli quickly moves to the notion of a representational code which acts upon the viewer to set up the possibility of linear perspective, for example. Perspectival relationships sustain the illusion of three dimensions and thus the "sense" that we are witnesses to reality. But the impression of reality so arrived at via the screen cannot be described outside of the relationship between the screen and the spectator. And it is not a question here of either/or. To suggest that the appearance of reality on the screen is dependent on the spectator who desires the naturalness of linear perspective, gives an empirical force to the screen which privileges its mise en scène. In

20. André Bazin, quoted by Jean-Louis Comolli, in "Machines of the Visible," in *The Cinematic Apparatus*, ed. Stephen Heath and Teresa de Lauretis (London: Macmillan, 1980), 134.
21. Jean-Louis Comolli, "Machines of the Visible," in *The Cinematic Apparatus*, ed. Stephen Heath and Teresa de Lauretis (London: Macmillan, 1980), 134

other words, the "staging" of the scenes in a film, their organization into an aesthetic and narrative form, takes precedence over the rather more ephemeral and less tangible consequences of the relationship of viewer to screen and screen to viewer. This ties in with the notion that films have a "director" who both directs the scenes being filmed and attempts to direct the viewer's attention in a certain way. In a sense, the viewer must buy into the bargain. He or she must be ready to be directed and even then, the traces of that relationship will not be found by any strategic leap to the screen as evidence of the process at work.

Comolli suggests a filmic practice that overcomes this problem: "deep cinematic focus does not slip into the naturalness of linear perspective, but inevitably stresses that perspective accentuates it, indicates its curvature, denounces the visual field it produces as a construction, a composition in which there is not simply more real but in which this more visible is spatially organized in the frame, dramatised" (Comolli 37). What I would like to suggest at this stage of my argument is that the notion of a natural linear perspective that fits the expectations of a set of perceptual norms becomes the basis for the opposition Comolli cites. The differences between deep cinematic focus and close-ups would have to be articulated in much greater detail. For Comolli, irrespective of context, a certain impression of reality is maintained in the cinema through the use of a specific spatial organization of the image. But how is this particular organization of meaning arrived at? If it is there naturally then spectator-screen relations are transformed into a function of the conventions present on the screen. The screen becomes the site for an explanation of viewing and the screen then can represent an abstracted universal spectator. The exchange here is one of pure form in which the viewer ceases to play a substantial role other than responding to various degrees of replacement. The viewer confers his or her identity onto the screen and by extension to the director and actors. The error here is to go from the screen into a model of mind.

The certainty that we always have, in our heart of hearts, that the spectacle is not life, that the film is not reality, that the actor is not the character and that if we are present as spectators, it is because we know we are dealing with a semblance, this certainty must be capable of being doubted. It is only worth its risk; it interests us only if it can be (provisionally) cancelled out. The "yes I know" calls irresistibly for the "but all the same," includes it as its value, its intensity. We know, but we want something else: to believe. We want to be fooled, while still knowing a little that we are so being. We want the one and the other, to be fooled and not fooled, to oscillate: to swing from knowledge to belief, from distance to adherence, from criticism to fascination. (Comolli 139)

The spectator oscillates between knowledge and the lack of it. The fictional deceit converts viewing into a game of pleasure and pain governed by complicity and disavowal. For Comolli the spectator is never passive but works to maintain a deception of which they are aware. Yet the more they know, the more complex the game of disavowal becomes. The viewer engages in an endless process of self-deception and mastery of the illusion, simultaneously blind and yet, like the street beggar who covers his sight with dark glasses, conscious of the artifice, able to see into this structuring disillusion. To enter a cinema then, is to engage in this play, which anticipates the movement from fiction to spectator and from reality to illusion.

"A motion picture is not a summation of shapes, sounds, and quanta differences of various types. It is an organization of relationships whose structures derive from a dynamic intersection of functions."[22] Projections produce ever-increasing substitutions, which means that their performative role is best suited to the inevitable patterns of loss produced by memory. This means that the viewing process is continuously involved in an activity of translation and confrontation. Projections transform the observable and the seeable, making the screen not a site of depiction but the location for a play of interpretations and speculations. The resulting ambiguities produce disjunctures between language, description, and interpretation. These, however, continue to carry information. The links between these disjunctures and viewing cannot be *represented*. And it is here that a large gap protrudes from the screen, a hole as it were, which cannot be filled. This then is the fundamental grounding for a loss that cannot find the measure of its own power. The *contingent* quality of projections can best be illustrated by connecting this analysis with that of a film like *Shoah* by Claude Lanzmann.

The Documentary as Projection: *Shoah, Schindler's List*

Shoah, by Claude Lanzmann, more than any other film since World War II, has fully justified Auguste Lumière's early hopes for the cinema. *Shoah's* power as a representation of the Holocaust has been equated by commentators and viewers to the events of history itself. In fact, all of its very extensive footage, up to one hundred hours worth, is going to be housed in a special archive at Yale University. The film's outakes will thus become another source of historical information on the Holocaust. It is rare for a film to be taken this seriously, and the act of converting the film into an archival document is a fascinating one, conflating as it does the differences between history, representation, and the image. It was Auguste Lumière who launched, though by no

22. Walter Rewar, "Signs, Icons and Subjects," *Ciné-Tracts* 4.2/3 (1981): 2.

means sustained, the idea that images were mimetically dependent upon their referent, thus promoting the supposition that history could be pictured if not reproduced through the medium of film.[23] I would like to explore *Shoah's* impact precisely as historical reconstruction, as image, as picture, and to more clearly situate its position in relation to the cinema as an institution. The formal properties of the film also raise questions about the history of the documentary cinema and the stylistic choices that have to be made when the event to be pictured has, so to speak, *not* been filmed. This lack of an image is a brutal reminder of the frailty of historical representation and the parallel need for projection.

Shoah tries to make the past *so* alive that it attempts to transcend the limitations of the film medium; that is, it tries to overcome the inherent problem that the past in this case can only be imagined, not realistically reproduced. To imagine the past, however, implies more than a rewriting. On a broader scale it means, at least in the case of *Shoah*, reconstructing the way the cinema works both as a medium and as a tool of communication. It means somehow *illustrating* the discourse of survivors for example, a task made difficult by the verbal intensity of what they say and by the difficulty of finding images to more fully express their feelings. It means making a film of such length that its veracity cannot be questioned or contradicted. This moral imperative, the perscriptive properties of which I examine below, often overwhelms *Shoah*, but as I will point out, that may well be the inevitable outcome of Lanzmann's choice to make a documentary film. My concern here is whether the concept of projection will enable us to understand the paradoxical position of the documentary cinema in relation to historical events.

This is made all the more urgent because another film on the Holocaust, *Schindler's List*, by Stephen Spielberg, makes extensive use of *cinéma-vérité* styles in what is admittedly a fiction. This mixture aptly reveals that the boundaries of fact and fiction have dissolved, a contention at the heart of the projection process I am trying to describe. Projection opens up the possibility that there are many different kinds of "looking." Mieke Bal discusses art critic Norman Bryson's analysis of the gaze. "Bryson distinguishes the gaze from the

23. Though as the film historian, David Levy, has pointed out, as early as 1897 so-called documentary films were "manufacturing" scenes of events to enhance both their narrative power and their impact as documents. "For their part, early film producers were quick to realise that one didn't have to be at the scene of an event with a camera in order to capitalize on the popular demand for topical material. The manufacture of Spanish-American war footage and fake championship prizefights are among the better-known examples of the practice. Later ones include Boer war scenes fought in New Jersey scenery, a table-top Boxer Rebellion naval action, Russo-Japanese war episodes, prison escapes, executions, a coronation, murders, robberies, natural disasters and Biograph's 1905 version of *Potemkin* entitled, *Mutiny on the Black Sea*." From a personal letter in 1994.

glance, the involved look where viewers, aware of and bodily participating in the process of looking, engage in interactions of various kinds, put themselves at risk, and do not need, therefore, to deny the work of representation, including its most material aspects, like brush, pen, or pencilwork. The virtue in this mode of looking is that the awareness of one's own engagement in the act of looking entails the recognition that what one sees is a representation, not an objective reality."[24]

The key point Bal makes for our purposes here is that vision as such is a temporal process, that the act of looking involves various sensory and discursive strategies that are mobile and unstable. *Shoah*, *Schindler's List* and *Germany, Pale Mother* provide excellent points of entry into notions of instability as they relate to projection and vision. The lack of a fixed entry point for the gaze may lead to the kind of self-reflexivity suggested by Bal. But it is more likely the case that visual activities are the site of a struggle with representation rather than a recognition with "one's own engagement in the act." These struggles are not the ontological basis for the construction of the real, but precisely the place within which reality and history are transformed into representations. Historical discourses resonate with the remains of this process. The gaze is itself part of these remains and not the instigator of the process. This explains why Roland Barthes searches through his memory for the images of his dead mother in *Camera Lucida*. He cannot *see* the image without creating it, which leads him to question the very nature of photographs and the role which images play in our culture.

Claude Lanzmann initially approached his research into the Holocaust and the Nazi era in what he described as a very traditional way. "For over a year I read every history book that I could find on the subject. I went through all of the written archives to which I could gain access."[25] This preliminary comment reveals the strong *fascination* he had with Nazism. It is this fascination that provoked the following comment. "As the research developed I was asked by the people financing me to explain what I was doing, to explain the direction which I was taking. But to me those questions were absurd. I didn't have a clear conceptual framework for what I was doing. I had a few personal obsessions and I knew that I had set myself a rather difficult task, but the whole question of concept was a difficult one for me. I would characterize my knowledge at that stage as theoretical, almost wholly derived from my reading of books, a clearer way of saying that would be that my knowledge was essentially second-hand" (Lanzmann 18).

24. Mieke Bal, "His Master's Eye," in *Modernity and the Hegemony of Vision*, ed. David Michael Levin (Berkeley and Los Angeles: University of California Press, 1993), 384.
25. Claude Lanzmann, *Cahiers du cinema* 374 (July-August 1985): 18. (All translations mine.)

Lanzmann was faced with a series of contradictory problems. In relation to the Holocaust and in particular the extermination camps, knowledge as such can *only* be secondhand. Yet his way of characterizing the problem points toward a possible solution, as if the history of that period has a large hole in it which he will fill by a process of substitution. In effect, he has undertaken his historical research with the film in mind. As I hope will become clear, this has more than just a passing relevance for the final product. There are important differences between the activity of research per se, that is, the investigation and exploration of a particular period of history, and undertaking that research with the intention of transforming essentially discursive materials into images. Parallel to this is the idea that proper research will anchor the images as historical truths and will make the screen the true site of analysis and interpretation. As we have seen, however, projection precludes that possibility and transforms even the most specific of historical images into unpredictable constellations of meaning and expression.

The notion of secondhand knowledge implies a separation between Lanzmann's fascination with the period and his desire to generate new truths from his research. Irrespective of whether it is firsthand or secondhand, whether it is oral history or legend, text or image, the shape and form he gives to his research cannot avoid the mingling of fiction and fact. The arbiter here is not truth but the *context* within which assertions are made about truth, or put another way, the context within which the secondhand is adjudged or interpreted to be truthful. Of equal concern is how his fascination will shape not only the history he chooses to investigate, but the very act of historical interpretation itself. Lanzmann goes on to explain the way he extricated himself from the vice of secondhand knowledge. First he tried to find out as much as he could from the survivors of the concentration camps. He didn't want just ordinary information or even ordinary witnesses—he wanted people who had been close, very close to the killing and death. (This is of course the impulse behind Spielberg's fictionalization of Schindler's heroism.)

> I was like someone who takes dancing lessons, but never really learns how to dance: I found that the gap between what I had learned via books and what the people told me to be so large that all of my earlier work seemed to be irrelevant. . . . I knew then that the only way I could proceed was by going to the actual sites—the concentration camps—and seeing them for myself. I realized that knowledge was without value if it wasn't combined with experience. To know and understand I had to see. In order to see, I had to know. (Lanzmann 18)

Thus, before he actually made the film Lanzmann encountered a fundamental problem. He wanted to experience history, experience the Holocaust and then crucially reconstruct both his experience and the event. He wanted to be part of a process that would join historical inquiry with reproduction, that would link the past with the present and that would transform the past into a living event for the viewer. The film continually uses the recollections of its inter- viewees as a pivot for this desire, as if their discourse, its intensity, its power, will overshadow the fact that he cannot show what they are talking about. To show, to somehow bring to life, to substantiate, and to make the entire chain of relations evidential: this is the essence of the projection process, which con- tinually weaves through sets of relations that must be imagined as well as seen and for which the evidence is always in some dispute. This is because however clear the relations are between an image and what it is trying to depict, that *relation must be imagined* and all of this happens within a temporal context not necessarily dependent upon or located within the parameters of perfor- mance.

How does that link up with Lanzmann's assertion that knowledge of the Holocaust is inevitably secondhand? In some senses he is trying to produce an empirical history, one that will reflect reality and where reality in turn will be reflected through the image. His film will not only explore death by extermi- nation but will *illustrate* the experiences of those who have died. But note that his illustrations will be unique, will show what has not been seen before: an iconography which will join data, reconstruction, and the imaginary, to make the experience of the past as real as possible. Spielberg tries to do this as well. He uses the site of Auschwitz with the incinerators once again burning, to place a group of female characters we have come to recognize from other scenes in the film inside a disinfection room. The camera moves inside as if they are about to be gassed and we will be the witnesses. It is a frightening moment paradoxically caught up in the impossibility of its staging. This is the moment he opens up for our imaginaries. It is as if he invites us into the very horror we as viewers know we can deny. This is precisely the tentative, almost contingent place we have to inhabit in order to watch, in order to work with and work upon the projection process. The fact that what is real here is our emotions and not so much what we have seen, is the ground upon which fic- tion builds its credibility. Spielberg knows this. In some respects *Schindler's List*, with its sophisticated use of editing and set construction, represents that essential moment of projection where the fragments of the past coexist with their negation. There are too many antecedents to the gas chamber, too many different ways it has been imagined (or not) as an experience, for Spielberg to do anything more than release its victims from their impending death.

Lanzmann's search for primary sources, for what was primary both in the event and in people's experience of it, puts to the side the very difficult problem that no event is outside of the discourse used to communicate what has in fact happened. Thus the event itself is suffused with layers of meaning that have become textual and that cannot be foregrounded unless they are rewritten, retold, or reconstructed. And with that, a measure of indeterminacy is introduced, something which, as we shall see, Lanzmann is desperate to avoid and ironically, Spielberg actually invites.

In the film Lanzmann combines his images of concentration camp locations with scale models of gas chambers. For him this combination reflects an internal pressure or urgency to *understand* an incomprehensible event and to *reproduce* in great detail that which the imaginary and images cannot fully reveal. He did this because he could find no archival images or photographs to *show* him what had happened.

> There were two distinct periods. From 1933–39 we found photos and films of book burnings, news footage of Jews being chased in the streets and persecuted, *Kristallnacht* in 1938, etc. Suddenly the war came. The people and countries controlled by the Germans were cut off from the world. From that period we have a few rather inconsequential propaganda films shot by the Nazis, including a grotesque one from the Warsaw ghetto showing Jews singing in fake cabarets, Jewish women parading the streets wearing expensive clothes etc., all designed to show the Jews as hedonists. As far as the process of extermination goes, nothing—and there was a rather simple reason for this—the Nazis formally prohibited any filming of the extermination in order to keep it a secret. (Lanzmann 19–20)

Lanzmann goes on to describe the monumental effort of the Nazis, Himmler and others, to avoid leaving any traces of the atrocities they were committing. It is Lanzmann's effort to confront this absence that interests me, because what shocked him about the response of audiences to his film was the way his efforts at reconstruction were taken at *face value*. The assumption was that archival footage was being used and one viewer said, "That was the first time I had heard the cry of a child in the gas chamber" (Lanzmann 19–20).

Aside from the reconstructions, he set about interviewing people who lived in the town of Treblinka. He even found the conductor of one of the trains used to bring Jews to the concentration camps.

> After I had talked to him, I found the locomotive which he had used. I told him, "Get on the locomotive and we'll film an arrival at Treblinka." I didn't say anything else. We arrived at the station and he made this incredible gesture staring back towards an imaginary chain of boxcars. He made as if he was going to cut his own throat, meaning of course the throats of the Jews. [This scene was repeated in *Schindler's List* by a child as a train passes on the way to Auschwitz.] To me that was an image of truth which made the archival photos which we had seen completely irrelevant. After that I made all of the peasants repeat the same motion and it became what it had always been, a sadistic gesture directed towards their victims. (Lanzmann 20)

For Lanzmann, *Shoah* is both a fictional film and a fiction of the real. Those people he interviewed became actors, not only telling their stories, but reconstructing their own memories, in a sense redefining their imaginary of history at a personal and social level. "This film was not about memories as such, I knew that right away. Memories scare me. They're just too weak. The film abolishes the past and present. I relived the past as if it were in the present" (Lanzmann 21).

Let me deal in the first instance here with the question of past and present in terms of images, because what is important is the way Lanzmann conceptualizes the relationship of history to the image as a strategy of *explanation*. His search for what has been lost is not in and of itself unusual—examples abound from historical and ethnographic film—but his emphasis on confronting his own imaginary is, and what it points out is the rather difficult problem of "living" the past through the present tense of images. This problem is compounded even further when that past is supposed to be brought to life by images not only meant to reveal the past but to *exemplify* it. *Exemplification* and *verification*—clearly those few archival images Lanzmann found and decided were of no value say something not only about history but also about the *history of images*. How could, how can the Holocaust ever be pictured?

In one sense the Holocaust exists as a frozen sign of human brutality—in another sense it lives through its survivors and the children of those survivors and their felt need to keep the memories alive as a warning for the future. But there is a distinct difference between trying to convert the image of an historical event into an authoritative one, and confronting the rather delicate question of the boundary between fascination and the grotesque. It is here that Lanzmann's *assertion* that the film is both fiction and fact flounders, because it is precisely the setting out of that difference, the difference between fact and fiction that needs to be debated both within the film and outside the parameters of its performance. The various elements of that argument will inevitably be at the center of the cinematic strategy he will choose and will be vital to the audiences for his film. If history, to be relevant, to be understood, must be brought to life, then a special kind of illusion has to be created. To work, the illusion must carefully recontextualize and draw upon the very historical discourses Lanzmann feels are absent. Ironically, the representations Lanzmann wants to find cannot be easily pictured. The blame for that lies not with the event nor with the discourses that have followed it, but with a strategy that assumes that the past can *ever* be recreated and relived through images. Part of the problem with this point of view, which is also reproduced, but far less so, in the Spielberg film, is the desire to lessen the distance between vision and interpretation. Lanzmann wants to shock (with respect to the Holocaust and in the present context of reactionary revisionism, I understand why), but in so doing he misunderstands the way projections work. One can be shocked momentarily by an image, but for the process to take hold, for the creative intervention of the spectator to be seen as meaningful for themselves, there has to be a space and a time that permits and encourages interpretation. That is not possible unless the projection process is allowed to work.

In a superb article entitled, "What Has History to Do with the Semiotic?" Brooke Williams says the following: "To argue that the past does not exist until the historian makes the shots by calling them, that is, to argue that the historian creates the past simply by his or her construction of it, sinks history into a kind of linguistic quicksand which loses all ground upon which to base a semiotically objective inquiry. On the other hand to fail to recognize the power of the word, or power of naming, in the shaping of a thought about the object—in establishing the object's signification—is to fail to recognize the presuppositions built into the naming process itself, and thus to fail to recognize any difference between what really happened and what we call history."[26] I would characterize the crisis that Lanzmann faced as a crisis of the image as projection, a crisis of *finding* an image and crucially naming, representing, conferring meaning through the projection process. His desire to somehow make memory concrete is a contradictory one because memories, even those spoken by participants in historical events, are a site of meaning without the specificity or even clarity, that he so desperately seeks.

No event has so fully occupied modem literature, modern historiography, and modern research as the Holocaust and the Third Reich. Few men have had as much written about them as Hitler. Few events can claim as many films, as many documentaries, as many cinematic reinterpretations, as many grotesque attempts to aestheticize the horror of mass extermination as the Holocaust. Lanzmann clearly does not want to duplicate that cultural history.

What discursive hole, then, is Lanzmann trying to fill? It might be useful to contrast a recent film by Robert Kramer, *Unser Nazi (Our Nazi)*, which tries to explore many of the same problems. Kramer set about videotaping (documenting) a film being made by the German director, Thomas Harlaan, entitled *Wundkanal: Execution for Four Voices*, also about the Nazi period. *Unser Nazi* is as much about history as it is about producing a videotape to explore the effects of history on one's own psyche and imaginary. It is about what happens when the image is inadequate, when it inadequately portrays human conflict and violence, when historical images fail, when sight and the activity of seeing provide no base upon which to analyze what one has felt or understood in viewing a film based on a historical event.

Unser Nazi was shot in a television studio skillfully converted into a courtroom. Robert Kramer uses the documentary form to explore Thomas Harlaan's efforts to confront his own history through images. Harlaan acts out the role of filmmaker, victim, and activist. Harlaan examines his past as the

---

26. Brooke Williams, "What Has History to Do with Semiotics?" *Semiotica* 54. 3–4 (1985): 291–92.

son of a Nazi. The results are explosive. Harlaan invites a man into the studio who is identified as a former member of the SS. The distinctions between fiction and document collapse as Harlaan rushes into the studio and assaults not only the old man, but Germany's past. The event becomes symbolic—the type of experience that brings out the Nazi in all of us, as Harlaan mentions afterward.

This movement toward the symbolic in only possible because the film is itself so layered. *Unser Nazi* is a tribute to the skill of Robert Kramer. It is a film within a film, shot for the most part in video and then transferred to the screen. The contrast between the mediums develops into a statement about history and about images and about the very possibility of recovering the past. Throughout *Unser Nazi*, Kramer worries about discourse, precisely about the fictions of those whose recounting of their memories relies on a careful selection of facts, a careful selection of personal experiences. After all, were it not for that selectivity, most historical discourse would take on precisely the kind of absolute qualities that would preclude any rewriting. The film slowly develops in the present tense, as if Kramer is editing on the run. This is also a quality of Harlaan's film. The two encounter each other in the shadows of history, as players on a scene that they desperately want to control. But it is precisely loss of control that characterizes the Holocaust, an unleashing of evil in which there are endless distortions of the ethical base of civilized behavior. In *Schindler's List* the Nazis play out this evil as if it is the only possible moral ground for their activities. In *Unser Nazi* the question is whether a narrative can ever be constructed from that position. And in the final analysis the film shuts the door and says, no.

In contrast, Lanzmann's fascination is as much with his *own* past as it is with Nazism. He is honest about that. Less obvious though is the way *Shoah* is an exorcism of a pain Lanzmann feels guilty about *not feeling*. For, irrespective of the power of the images, they remain just that, images. Their hold is found precisely in their aesthetic impact, a point well made by Susan Sontag in her article about Syberberg's *Hitler, a Film From Germany*. Images offer horror in much the same way as they offer pleasure, and in a repetitive fashion that horror and pleasure can be denied, because viewing never simply replicates what has been represented nor does the act of viewing respond in a simple sense to the events themselves.

This gap is at the heart of a dilemma for *Shoah*, which wants to have an impact upon history and thus to change the way history has been seen and represented. The film wants to invite the spectator into the gas chamber in order to be more than a witness, in order to become the victim, to feel what we cannot feel; the very moment when life and death are indistinguishable and crucially when language means nothing and is emptied of all possibility of meaning. This problem, that images cannot simply transcend their own limitations, is responded to by Lanzmann at the level of editing. The film is nine hours long. He shot well over two hundred hours of film. This is a ratio of twenty to one. A ratio I might add, about which he was not happy, but which he of necessity had to face if he was to transform his film from a mere mass of images into a presentable theatrical show. And this is exactly the dilemma. Irrespective of his intentions and honesty, the exigencies of the medium are not simply a hurdle to overcome, they are at the center of many questions about how processes of representation work. The exigencies of the medium form and reform the way history can be seen and understood, and thus Lanzmann must bear some responsibility for producing a historical spectacle, a responsibility he would prefer to avoid given his desire to produce truth.

Furthermore, given that so much of what we have of the Holocaust is framed by the relationship between language, criticism, and image, the balancing act between images and what is understood to be the empirical reproduction of an event will always be open to debate. Which set of hurdles is Lanzmann really trying to overcome? He says that only traces remain of the extermination, but he himself found many witnesses to it. He says that his film is about the traces of traces, yet he ended up reducing what he had filmed to the broad outlines of an argument conditioned by the performative demands of the cinema. I am not suggesting here that he should not have done that (nor, would I add, am I suggesting this about *Schindler's List*). Rather, the more fundamental question is whether the cinema, in fact, any image, can do more than just *perform* the histories they so willingly appropriate.

At one and the same time Lanzmann wants to find facts and reshape them. Yet that reshaping is as much a reimagining as it is a retrieval. Ultimately, his faith in the image betrays him, since what he is recreating cannot on its own reveal the imaginary at work, cannot sustain the rather intense contradiction between truth and representation. Thus, he never relived the past as much as he made the past significant for the present. And in so doing he simply filled the *hole* of history with the cinematic equivalent of a phantasm. The imaginary became for him, the real, and in a strangely paradoxical way he repeated one of the crucial processes by which so many Germans adhered to fascism.

It is precisely the phantasm of power, the power to control events, to transform history into a performance that accounts for the enormous popularity of a film like *Heimat* by Edgar Reitz (which like *Shoah* is meant to bring history to life), for it recovers that set of sequential movements in time without which the history of Nazism would seem to be inexplicable. At the same time that recovery reshapes the fascination, conferring power onto both the filmmaker and the viewer so that both can grasp hold of a set of events otherwise governed by rules apparently disconnected from the presumed logic of historical rationality. Foucault has put it quite clearly: "Nazism never gave a pound of butter to the people, it never gave anything but power. Nevertheless, one has to ask oneself why, if the regime was nothing else but this bloody dictatorship, there were Germans up to May 8, 1945, who fought to the last drop of blood, unless there had been some kind of attachment to the people in power."[27]

This raises a further question. Does a film like *Shoah* threaten the historical moment of which it is a part? Put another way, is the film merely one of many, many films, particularly those of Germany in the seventies, which ostensibly concern themselves with history, the history of the thirties and forties, so as to recover not only the past (which will to some degree always remain outside of their grasp), but the *binds* produced by the way the present inevitably recasts and reconstructs the signifying properties of history? *Unser Nazi* is confronted by the same problem. Thomas Harlaan's interview with Filbert (the former member of the Gestapo) becomes violent, because Filbert expresses no remorse, little guilt, and virtually no desire to repent. This infuriated Harlaan, who saw in Filbert a representation of his father but also the problem of guilt *not* being felt. Harlaan is plagued throughout *Unser Nazi* by the pain of not being able to get Filbert to feel guilt. Finally, he physically assaults Filbert and even then can feel no satisfaction. The bind here is that the present has made possible an image of the past, without the past itself rearing its head and producing a *real* enemy. Thus Filbert cannot be killed by Harlaan and yet that is clearly what Harlan wants to do.

Images in films lead toward a past they can conveniently picture and it is the picture that becomes the threat at the level of projection. But changing the picture won't necessarily change the past. And what is more, the past as picture may paradoxically map the ground upon which projections can *replace* that which they were intending to reveal. This led Foucault to say "how could Nazism, which was represented by lamentable, shabby, puritan young men, by a species of Victorian spinsters, have become everywhere today—in France, in Germany, in the United States—in all the pornographic literature of the whole world, the absolute reference of eroticism? All the shoddiest aspects of the erotic imagination are now put under the sign of Nazism" (Friedlander 74).

However, in a context where replacement and substitution are the necessary conditions upon which the Nazi era can be conceptualized, no amount of theater, no aesthetically perfect representation can ever face the substance of that historical moment. Why is it then that the image as projection seems to carry the burden of strategically accounting for the horrors of that period?

Thomas Elsaesser tries to answer this question in the following way:

Syberberg made *Our Hitler* against and in anticipation of Joachim Fest's *Hitler—a Career* as well as NBC's "Holocaust." By structuring his own film

27. Interview with Michel Foucault, *Cahiers du cinema* 251–52 (July-August 1974): 10. Quoted in *Reflections of Nazism* by Saul Friedlander (New York: Harper & Row, 1984), 74.

so much in terms of a critique of showing and seeing, he indicates that Hitler had already, in his appropriation and use of the media, anticipated his own revival and survival as spectacle. The physical destruction of history and of Germany, is redeemed by "Hitler's heirs" through the historically new category of the show—the democratic leveller, according to Syberberg—as we know it from television and advertising, sublating both history and personal experience. In the age of the mass-media, the past itself becomes a commodity, and historical experience cannot be transmitted in any form other than as an object for consumption, as a visual system of identification, projection, mirroring and doubling, which is to say, by short-circuiting the very possibilities of understanding, knowledge and the social processes of passing them on.[28]

I do not fully agree with Elsaesser's characterization of the mass media in part because he is describes a level of instrumentality that mirrors the *desire* for control the media have, but which they can never exercise unless, that is, they "colonize the imaginary"—a phrase I have borrowed from *Kings of the Road* by Wim Wenders. However, it is quite clear that commodification alters the meaning of history if only by suggesting that the past *can* be shown through visual systems. The problem is that media like film provide a mode of explanation replete with a quite specific impact as if, for example, the empty hallways of a faded Auschwitz in *Night and Fog*, by Alain Resnais, can be explained through the voice-over, as if image and word, image and speech can conjoin to reveal a pain both real and metaphorical, both reconstructed and imagined. Is it then an accident that most efforts to deal with Nazism through images, like *Lili Marleen* and *The Tin Drum* turn toward the metaphorical as a way of rediscovering the imaginary of the event? If our language is so woefully inadequate, how can our images escape that inadequacy? In part, they try to escape by elevating evil to an extreme level and thus by exclusion try to prove the point that even our imaginaries have not gotten away from the instrumental effects of the images surrounding us. But this notion of instrumentality—the desire to effectively produce an audience that mirrors the messages sculpted into language or film—is not all that different from the way the Nazis themselves saw their own propaganda machine.

28. Thomas Elsaesser, "Syberberg, Cinema and Representation" *New German Critique* 24/25 (Fall-Winter 1981–82): 144. Shoshana Felman's essay on *Shoah* brilliantly examines the role of testimony not only in the validation of the historical discourses underlying the film, but the way the people interviewed bring their experiences to life. However, she fails to situate the film within the history of the cinema and doesn't recognize the differences between testimony and cinematic forms of testimony. The distinctions here are not arbitrary or peripheral to her argument. Interviews in the cinema are not transparent renditions of truth. They are effective because of the documentary form, because of Lanzmann's editing and understanding of rhythm and aesthetics. See Shoshana Felman and Dori Laub, *Testimony: Crises of Witnessing in Literature, Psychoanalysis, and History* (New York: Routledge, 1992), 204–83.

In an extraordinary book by the psychoanalyst Ernest Kris, entitled *German Radio Propaganda*, we are given the following explanation: "Since the Nazis believe that the immediate sensory experience that participation provides exerts a more powerful influence on man's attitudes than arguments do, they use every verbal propaganda technique that fosters the illusion of immediacy and concreteness. Hence their preference for the spoken rather than the written word, for eyewitness reports rather than summary accounts, for a personalized presentation of the news rather than sober, impersonalized discussion, for illustration rather than explanation."[29]

The German listening audience was to be molded into one by the listening experience, by nine news bulletins a day, by the regularity and seeming normality of that everyday experience. And if people did not own radios then provisions were made to listen in public squares and in factories, and so forth. What is important for our purposes here is the notion of the audience and the rather extraordinary victory claimed for propaganda by the Nazis. Thus it was a case of the German people merging with a collective self defined in national terms by the images and sounds of Nazi ideology. As Kris points out later, the bombing of Germany reminded the people of a possible gap between the message and the truth, and as this gap grew, as hardship increased, the propaganda became more intense and more idealized. He chooses an example: "Over there is a woman worker; her eyes are still red and full of tears; her voice trembled, but on she went with her work. . . . A boy of sixteen was wounded; his arm is bandaged; his head is bleeding under his steel hat. Duesseldorf stood up to it. Every one of its citizens is a hero" (Kris, Speier 192).

This is precisely the clearest indication of the failure of the message. In any case, the message and the way it is comprehended can never simply be identified with the messenger, though it might be the desire of the propagandists to confer that power on themselves. The question is far more complex than that. From our point of view what is important is the perspective from which truth as such can be *ascertained*.

Now it is clear that for Lanzmann, truth will surface through the imagery, through the power of the message to disturb the viewer, to alter the viewer's own self-image and definition of history. But this assumption depends on whether the viewer is willing to accept the claim that the image can speak in truthful terms and whether she can find a place for herself within the framework suggested by the debate and the images.

The problem is that to believe a cry has come from a gas chamber in a film transforms what really happened to what *may* have happened and paradoxically, that is a condition, a fundamental condition of historical imagery, of the

---

29. Ernest Kris and Hans Speier, *German Radio Propaganda* (London: Oxford University Press, 1944), 12.

cinema, and of projection. The collapse of the distinctions between the probable, the possible, and the real is exactly a victory for the propagandist, which
is why in *Unser Nazi*, the construction of a narrative around Nazism is shown
to be a struggle with the distance that has to be taken from the historical in
order to produce it. This distance is, on the one hand, frightening because it
suggests that evil cannot be immediately pictured and thus understood, and on
the other hand, it suggests that distance must be the fundamental ground upon
which the meaning has to be constructed. Thus meaning has to coexist with
its impossibility (and this does not mean that nothing can be said), and with
the difficulty that the past can never be relived in the present, other than
through the representations that guide it.

In one sense this is precisely the source of of our fascination with historical
imagery and links what remains of the past with the present. The filmmaker
as historian realizes the past through his or her phantasms, a relation between
observation, exploration, explanation, and the imaginary. The same can be
said for the historian as filmmaker. Claims of truth, reality, authenticity, set
those phantasms apart from their progenitors and presuppose a kind of collective fantasy that we all share. The significance of the effort to picture the Holocaust is the manner in which it has come to stand for a story that must be
repeated by every generation in order to believe it, in order, that is, to attach
the truth values of the present to it. But this only further reconstructs the gallery of significations that mediate the distance we have to take from it. And the
result is more and more levels of aestheticization till we finally reach *Heimat*,
that is, if the metaphor can be stretched, until we finally find ourselves in the
comfort of our homes watching a televised reconstruction of history through
cliché and kitsch.

History is judged by its *communicability* and by the effectiveness of those
signifying systems most closely linked to the actualization, the virtual reproduction of the past *as* past. I am not suggesting, however, that this particular
contradiction can be avoided, merely that it be recognized precisely as one of
the sites where history and crucially, projection, is produced. What we understand then to be secondhand both as knowledge and as image—*Shoah*—
marks out the terrain of our fascination with the imaginary as a tool for making history real. This is the case even when historical discourse must be
rewritten and even when images can do no more than hint at the memories
upon which they are based. The paradox is an exquisite one, because for every
film that attempts to assert historical truth, another can use the same techniques to turn the truth upside down. *Shoah* is caught by all of the phantasms
it is trying to unmask and would have perhaps been more significant as a film
if it had confronted the way those phantasms govern historical discourse,
rather than trying to reveal how they must be eliminated.

Here then is a contradictory middle ground where art and history conjoin, and where the poetics of historical writing and historical filmmaking reveal a radical discontinuity between events and the way they can be illustrated. That discontinuity, however, is one of the reasons why images can appear to be historical, since what they name, what they give meaning to, are the phantasms that separate them from the past. At the same time, as the mediations grow it becomes more and more difficult to distinguish among the various levels that might differentiate the role of the image from the event. This is most poignantly illustrated by the following story:

> On Martin Luther King Day last month [January 1994], 69 students from Castlemont High School in Oakland, California, most of them Black and Latino, went on a field trip to see *Schindler's List*. An hour into the movie, a small but loud group of the students laughed and joked during a scene in which a Nazi shoots a Jewish woman in the head. When others in the audience stormed out to complain, the theater's management stopped the film and ejected all of the students. Then someone called the press, throwing the story onto the front page and the community into an uproar. 'I've never seen such furious, hurt customers,' Allen Michaan, the theater's owner, told the Los Angeles Times. 'Some were Holocaust survivors, and one woman was sobbing.'[30]

The story has a positive ending because it led to the development of a Holocaust curriculum at the high school and an effort on the part of students to learn more about the history of the Jews, after which they apologized publicly for their insensitivity. They even received an award at the Simon Wiesenthal Center's Museum for Tolerance in L. A. as a recompense for their attempts to reconcile the African-American and Jewish communities in Oakland.

In this, as in many other instances, the image changes through the projection process. Historical events lose their specificity and become appropriated for a variety of different ends. The seemingly transparent relationship of image and history never succeeds in lessening the ambiguities and paradoxes of the communicative sphere into which the image enters and upon which projections depend.

Listening to Projections

How is natural language used in film? When we view an interchange between two characters, what kind of speech are we getting? Rather than assuming that everyday speech is simply present on the screen as a function of a character's use of it, how does projection change speech? A dialogue between two characters is not similar to a dialogue between two people on the street. On the screen the dialogue becomes poetic, stylized, and crucially, interrupted and

30. Frank Rich, "Schindler's' Dissed," *New York Times*, Sunday, February 6, 1994, E17.

mediated by the context of performance. Paradoxically, as fragmented as the verbal encounter between two people might ordinarily be, it is now transformed even further. The presence of natural language on the screen is transformed into a //projection of natural language,// which creates as a result a semantic field where the directness of language is disrupted, mediated, pushed toward the poetic, even the surreal. The synchronicity of voice to lip movement does not mean that there is a synchronicity of speech and projection. What is suggested, however, by the notion of synchronicity is that there is some similarity to what is said on the screen and what should be understood by the spectator.

"But the reproduction of a text by a subject (return to the text, new reading, new performance, citation) is a new and nonreiterative event in the life of the text, a new link in the chain of verbal communication."[31] This crucial insight can be applied to projections and images. Natural language is decenterd by the screen, and the recovery of meaning is no simple task. Through repetition and projection, speech and sound (because the two are rarely separate) in images come to have a set of preexistent meanings. There is no doubting the presence of conventions and the simultaneous tension among the exigencies of style, genre and performance. There is a clash between prior sets of meaning (speech designed to fit the exigencies of scripting and direction) and the context of audience and screen. It is quite possible for the synchronicity of voice and lip movement to exhibit a logical relation between speech and expression. But the character looking out from the screen and talking, or two actors talking to each other, address not an audience, but the apparatus of the cinema. The apparatus functions here, not as a means of confirmation, but as a creative tool in which some portion of what is spoken will be included in the final version of the film. In terms of projection the apparatus vanishes as an intermediary. There is a break between what is spoken and the dislocations necessary for the speech to appear synchronous and logical within the context of the sequence or shot in which it appears.

The overlap of speech and projection, of what is pictured with what is said, recontextualizes communication in the cinema away from resemblance, toward highly stylized forms of presentation. Paradoxically then, synchronicity heightens the paradoxes of projection, producing a contingent link between voice and lip movement. There is thus no immediate moment of denotative strength that enlivens the actor talking to an absent audience. It is not a matter here of a process at one time direct and then indirect. Nor does the immediacy of the voice speaking conjoin with meanings outside of that moment. Rather, projected voice-body relations are so profoundly transformative

31. Todorov Tzvetan, *Mikhail Bakhtin: The Dialogical Principle*, tr. W. Godzich (Minneapolis: University of Minnesota Press, 1984), 27.

that they continually assert new configurations of meaning. In other words, the image process results in a different *type* of intersubjective dialogue on the screen.

Crucially, two actors talking to each other and to an apparatus, and also to an audience simultaneously projecting its own desires onto what it hears, reverses the hierarchy of speech, projection, comprehension. There is then no necessarily analogous identity between the structure of sentences spoken on the screen and their use in everyday conversation and the manner in which they come to be understood as images and projections. (This point has now been more fully understood in music videos, which have no hesitation in dubbing voices, even when the voice-overs are completely asynchronous.)

Another way of approaching this is by examining the fascination audiences have for candid cameras and with seeing themselves as an image in a film or on television. The candid camera reveals people acting and talking as if they are unaware of the apparatus. This is presumably a moment of spontaneous realism and inadvertent truth. They speak naturally without knowing about the effects of the camera on them. The audience laughs at the interplay. It knows the truth, taking pleasure in the secret, in what Peter Greenaway, the English director, has described as a particular type of voyeurism. In talking about his new film *The Baby of Macon* he says the following: "It is about your own voyeurism. A voyeur is not a Peeping Tom. The original French definition applies to anyone who looks. If you think about the world-wide enthusiasm for soap opera, this is only an indication of the modern world's desire to see without being seen. In my film, you watch an audience watch a performance, and eventually you come to the realisation that you are the next audience in line to be watched."[32]

The pleasure is also to be found in the knowledge of the artifice, in the knowledge of the transformational process the projection is making possible. For the laughter in "Candid Camera" is also directed at one's own apprehensions at being caught, the fear of being laughed at. When the people who have stumbled in front of the candid camera exclaim their surprise at what has happened to them, they generally say, "no, no," or "are you kidding?" They appear to be speechless and quite hesitant to discuss what has occurred. This is because they cannot find the words to act themselves. Their speech seems to be divested of the authority they normally give to it.

This disembodiment, though, is a necessary condition for the transformation of spoken language into a projection. To be able to divest oneself of the authority of one's speech and yet at the same time to speak is to lose one kind of voice and substitute another. Speech becomes part of a fantasy of speech and

32. Ken Shulman, "Peter Greenaway Defends his Baby," *New York Times*, February 6, 1994, H18.

communication, a fantasy about being watched and listened to. There is no particular resolution for these fantasies, but the space opened up shifts the verbal into a context where the disembodied self searches for some sort of communicative opening. It is this search which "Candid Camera" sets up and which makes the humor so specific to the context in which it happens.

A further example of this process at work returns us again to Woody Allen's film, *The Purple Rose of Cairo*. Tom Baxter's departure from the screen into real life is centered on a crisis of speech. Everything that he says has a predetermined context attached to it. Thus he is unable to be spontaneous, reverting at every instant to the clichés of the scene within which he finds himself. It is not only a matter here of speech having been written, of the scenario, so to speak, dominating the potential content of every conversation. More importantly, it is the conjuncture of that speech with the verbal that points out its uniqueness. For Baxter, everyday conversation is just not possible. The resulting schism shifts the authority for speaking to Cecilia. Cecilia, for example, tries to clarify Baxter's thoughts and responses for him. She tries to write a new and more real script which he can use. But as the gap grows between Baxter as a fantasy and Cecilia's desire to convert him into a real person, the unidimensionality of his speech becomes more and more self-evident. What must be understood here is that his language is drawn from a limited, cinematic discursive field. His clichés are rooted in the script, and he cannot break out of those restrictions. So when he finds himself in a brothel and begins to talk about his dedication to Cecilia, his unwillingness to be unfaithful, the women find him even more attractive. His romanticism expresses itself at such a pure level precisely because it is a distillation of cultural assumptions about the perfectibility of speech and communication. The gap between what he says as a translation of written text and what is heard as spoken, collapses. But this only furthers the distance between the ideal, which he represents and the screen, which cannot contain that idealism. It is not a matter here of whether he is a real character or not. Rather, what is important is the extent to which Cecilia is willing to invest in him, by eliding her knowledge that all of his speeches have already *been* written.

This gap then between the spontaneity of a character's expressions and the necessity for a script reveals the heterogeneity of the projection process. The screen does not easily open itself up as a site for intersubjective exchange. Rather, it places in question the very possibility of exchange and as a result the presumed dependency of the viewer upon the screen. Cecilia has to enter the world of Tom Baxter, has to go with him into the film itself in order to make what he says about her and their love for each other real. Thus, she not only has to enter his fantasy but has to give up her speech to legitimize the entire experience. She spends the night on the cinematic town and accepts the bizarre contexts she enters. But this serves to destroy the match of speech and experience and fantasy, since the next day she rejects his offer to join him in a kind of perpetual repetition of the dream.

This would suggest that projections are as much the scaffolding for fantasy as they are the cultural nexus within which specific messages find a context. They are not the place where meaning resides but rather represent a potential *model* for imaginary reconstruction. It is this sense of opening, of many possible bridges to cross, that encourages Cecilia to see images as a release from the unrelentless boredom and oppression of her everyday life. Cecilia's desire to enter the screen and destroy its two-dimensionality is a sign of displacement, but without that, the projection would cease to have a spectator. A new and quite flexible discursive context is opened up within which the very terms of the communication are both examined and challenged. This flexibility has often been condemmed, since it suggests a breakdown of the connections underpinning signifying systems. But the projection process encourages the suppleness Cecilia demonstrates, and it must be remembered that even with all of the problems she encounters, she learns a great deal.

While I have been speaking of Cecilia's desire for Tom and the ideal he represents, I have not talked about her as a screen character in her own right. I, as viewer, have to struggle with another and far more complicated relationship. Mia Farrow and all that she stands for cannot be separated from Cecilia and what she develops into. Farrow's appearance in a number of Woody Allen films bespeaks the kind of interchangeability that alters the gap between her role as an actress and the reality of her presence-nonpresence on the screen. She represents a person, a personae, while also representing the screen, the audience, and a woman oppressed by her husband. The layering of the narrative in this case transforms the possible sites of entry for me. Most importantly, the gaps between Mia Farrow and Cecilia represent the very spaces I have to enter in order to experience the story. But just as Cecilia can never become Tom Baxter, I cannot, in a total sense, become Cecilia. This is the ground upon which my contradictory feelings for the projection process come into the foreground of my own experience. The temporal nature of this process is heightened even more by the breakup of Mia Farrow's relationship with Woody Allen. Seeing the film in this light radically alters the focus I as a viewer bring to the experience. There is a sense in which Cecilia's innocence has been taken away from her, even before Mia Farrow has had a chance to bring the character to life.

Listening to Hiroshima

I have in hand a copy of the script of *Hiroshima mon amour*. In her preface Marguerite Duras qualifies what she has written by stressing its fragmentary character. The film is not fully present in the written text, she says. Yet it can serve as an interesting guide to the problems I have been discussing.

> As the film opens, two pairs of bare shoulders appear, little by little. All we see are these shoulders—cut off from the body at the height of the head and hips—in an embrace, and as if drenched with ashes, rain, dew, sweat, whichever is preferred. The main thing is that we get the feeling that this dew, this perspiration, has been deposited by the atomic "mushroom" as it moves away and evaporates. It should produce a violent, conflicting feeling of freshness and desire. The shoulders are of different colours, one dark, one light. A man's voice, flat and calm, as if reciting, says: "You saw nothing in Hiroshima. Nothing."
>
> To be used as often as desired. A woman's voice, also flat, muffled, monotonous, the voice of someone reciting, replies: "I saw everything. Everything."[33]

I do not intend to use this fragment of the script as an exemplification of what happened on the screen. What interests me is the reference to the viewer in the above text. But I am also interested in the presumed link between what the characters say and the viewer. Clearly, any presumption about the feeling the audience is getting from the perspiring skin of the two characters is a reflection of the writer's desire. But this desire is itself a subject-effect born out of the relationship of filmmaker and screenwriter to the process of viewing and creating images. They themselves are not outside of what they are trying to create. In that sense, the conflicts that Duras describes are a metaphor for the projections she would like to generate. They represent her idealization of the identification process. And she will try and accomplish this within the very texture of the image, as an effect of space and time, dialogue and aesthetic organization.

There is a self-conscious irony to what the male character says. He is Japanese and she is European. His qualms about what she has seen reflect the film's concern with perception and history, with the relationship among different cultures and often dramatically opposing strategies for understanding the past. The thesis is that only the Japanese can really understand what the bomb did to them and to their culture and that outsiders can merely identify at a safe distance with an almost unbearable pain. The vessel within which that pain circulates is covered by time, and it is only by probing through the skin and its tissue that a little bit of that pain can escape for others to see and experience.

What does it mean, then, to say that "You saw nothing in Hiroshima, nothing." Is the "you" the character or the spectator or both? If I were to transform that scene into a projection, it might "read" like this:

33. Marguerite Duras, *Hiroshima, Mon Amour*, tr. Richard Seaver (New York: Grove Press, 1961), 15.

//I have seen fragments of your body. You are a voice without a face. I can't *see your partner. I know nothing about either of you. There is hesitation and pain in your voice. Do you mean I saw nothing in Hiroshima? Am I the one you are speaking to? Did I hear you correctly?//*

//Hiroshima has been etched into my memory just as the Holocaust has. I *will never forget the mushroom cloud and the burned anguished faces. Nor can I forget Slim Pickens riding the bomb to victory for America. I have a particularly vivid image of Hiroshima in my memory—a dazed woman rummaging through the ashes looking for a relative. Everything had been incinerated and she still wanted to find some sign of the death, some fragment of her previous life.//*

//But, yes. I have forgotten. Each day I avoid the memory. The pain recedes. *But avoiding memories doesn't mean that they have been erased. The experience remains, somehow not an image, always an image.//*

//The memories circulate within me, the pain and the anguish come and go. *Perhaps I have seen nothing.//*

//Yet, I have listened. I can close my eyes and listen to you talk. I can imag-*ine your face and imagine the look of your partner. I can hear the cries of the dying at Hiroshima.//*

Does this kind of internal dialogue parallel the viewing of a series of images? Is this a clue to the richness of the projection process? Or is the concept of projections just another strategy for enlarging upon the experience of images? Am I simply adding interpretive discourses in a postmortem sense to the experience of viewing? What is the difference between an image and a projection? We see so many images in such a short time. Can or should a particular set of images be designated as the cause for what I have just said?

Hiroshima mon amour poses many of the above questions through the manner in which it tells its story. The director, Alain Resnais, simultaneously interrogates the film's characters as if they are spectators of their own lives and actors in the film. In this way the characters continually watch themselves on a mental screen suffused with their memories of the past. Emmanuelle Riva, who plays the role of a French actress in the film, must submit herself to the inconsistencies and contradictions of her own past and her mode of interpreting it. She must, if she is to understand her memories, abstract her past into a narrative while also communicating the limitations of that narrative. Slowly, Eiji Okada, the male, becomes a vehicle through which she reconstructs her past, through which she recovers the language to speak about the traumas she has experienced. Yet that recovery, of which they are also spectators, is concretized not only in language, but through images of the past. Thus, as Okada imagines Riva's pain, we watch reenactments of the imprisonment Riva experienced as a young girl. She had been locked into a cellar as punishment for falling in love with a German soldier during the Second World War. Her head had been shaved and she had been banished from her house because her parents could not tolerate the shame. There seems to be no gap between what we have seen and what Okada sees through her words. The ease with which that gap disappears is fundamental to projections. Distance coexists with closeness. The past as projection provides a point of imaginary contact with images of history—personal, public. The film points this out as Okada slowly finds himself becoming the German soldier, slowly watches the fissures between past and present disappear. Riva transforms him into a memory while he is still in front of her. I, too, transform them into memories as I watch.

The crucial point to keep in mind here is that these moments of dissolution and creativity are not pictorial and cannot be described as representations, either. They are, so to speak, found in the performance of the relations of meaning, and this of course includes the pictorial and representational. But performances take place in time, and as a result, the various movements of meaning from the presence of a character on the screen to their comments on their lives, shifts the general configuration here away from "seeing" to a process more akin to listening.

Listening in this instance is part of a different context than the one we usually associate with viewing. It would be a major error to suggest that because we listen, so to speak, without being aware of the process, without often imposing meaning on the activity, that we are somehow less aware of what is going on, less self-conscious of the contingent meanings we are working with. The process of projection in this case can best be characterized as a loose association of potential points of contact with many different sets of meanings. There are elements of this that are random and some that are structured, some that work within accepted paradigms and others that contradict the conventions and norms usually associated with images and their transformation into narratives. As with some of the most crucial scenes in *Hiroshima mon amour*, it is possible for the emotions of the actors to transcend the roles they are playing, possible for that to be "visible" and at the same time for the fiction, so to speak, to proceed nevertheless. A possible real can be brought to life without the need to generate a clear pattern of intelligibility. It is possible to daydream and listen and watch, to engage with the many different layers of all of these aspects of viewing and to create and accept the categories of meaning needed to make the entire process understandable.

At one point the actress Riva, seated opposite Okada, stares outside the screen space toward her memory and some of those images come into view. Her memory, of course, is not available in a simple sense and cannot just be recovered at her whim and fancy, nor does an off-screen space really exist. At one and the same time a never-ending chain of references and meanings can be put in place. The off-screen visualization we see is part of a series of sequences she has had to act in as representations of her memories. (She can be both a youngster and a mature adult and represent those aspects of her history simultaneously.) Her memory, then, can be brought to us by voice and image, but at each stage, the creative process lifts the representations into a metacommunicative sphere since their linkage to the scene is only possible through editing. This sense of the future, of the many different ways the scene could be interpreted and reinterpreted through montage, additional sound, even peripheral postproduction shooting, has a crucial influence on the actress. To be Riva, she has to know the role, anticipate the potential location of her acting within the total film, and reflect upon the feelings she has about Hiroshima and about her experience of World War II. Yet this is also the role which the film has designed for her.

The doubling here creates many different layers of projection, many different strategies for images incapable of presenting everything at once. As much as Riva knows that the past need only be filmed to be brought into the present tense of the film, she also knows that the present tense of the film cannot be projected. The possible variations in the description of this activity are never-ending, which is precisely what links them to the imaginary. As you will no doubt have noticed, I have dissolved the difference between Riva as an actress and the role she plays. But this dissolution is really a way of talking about the coexistence of a number of different levels of projection. The actress never collapses into her role, as might, for example, be possible in the theater, in part because the cinema is shot as a series of fragments to be synthesized in editing. This suggests an almost interminable self-reflexivity at work in the creation and production of the character, a continual play with temporal differentiation. The sound then becomes the crucial bridge for projection and for sustaining the sense that the past can in fact be imaged. So precarious are the elements that permit this process to work, it is a wonder that the term *acting* has been transferred from the theater to the cinema.

Insignificance

Let me return to *Insignificance* for a moment. Here the main characters are four people, each of whom represents a particular historical personality. Marilyn Monroe, Joe DiMaggio, Joe McCarthy, and Albert Einstein. Monroe and DiMaggio's relationship forms a pivot for the film. This is complemented by the relationship between Einstein and Monroe, Einstein and McCarthy, and finally McCarthy with everyone. What is crucial for our purposes here is the presumption that an actress could reenact the role of Monroe through her own imaginary and with the imaginary of the audience. A certain autonomy is necessary, an autonomy that will permit the simultaneity of past and present, of acting and history. For Theresa Russell, who plays Monroe, does not look like her. But who after all does Monroe look like? The referential map available to "recover" Monroe as such only exists through processes outside of the screen. And this outside has already collapsed as a barrier. So the projection need not be there to be effective. It need not be concretely perceptible in order for the narrative to work. It need not represent anything but the conditions for its own enunciation. Monroe as such is not an ulterior or past-tense object awaiting the conferral of meaning by the film. Russell represents the struggle to establish the projection of Monroe, represents the struggle of memory as a privileged nonscene. Projections serve the crucial role of distributing the potential gaps across all symbolic processes. So what is finally signified by Russell is the impossibility of Monroe's presence, which in and of itself constitutes the necessity for her imaginary projection.

Wolfgang Iser discusses this point in the following comment on a piece by Virginia Woolf writing about Jane Austen: "What is missing from the apparently trivial scenes, the gaps arising out of the dialogue—this is what stimulates the reader into filling in the blanks with projections. He is drawn into the events and made to supply what is meant from what is not said. What is said only appears to take on significance as a reference to what is not said; it is the implications and not the statement that give shape and weight to the meaning. But as the unsaid comes to life in the reader's imagination, so the said 'expands' to take on greater significance than might have been supposed."[34]

Iser goes on to discuss the tensions between the presence of structure and the recreation of meaning by the reader. Does the same process occur in the cinema and with images? Iser calls the space in between a virtual one (Iser 106), neither present in the text nor in the reader—two poles of an activity that cannot be described in those terms. The virtual is that place the reader builds during and after a reading. It is not graspable in a simple sense through either side of the equation. While the idea of the virtual is interesting (in part because of the resonance with present-day concerns for virtual technologies), Iser's description relies on discursive models and patterns developed by R. D. Laing for interpersonal communication. The difficulty with this movement from conversation to text and reader is that the virtual becomes a far more defined space than the concept of projections I have been discussing up until now. For Iser, "the blank in the fictional text appears to be a paradigmatic structure; its function consists in initiating structured operations in the reader, the execution of which transmits the reciprocal interaction of textual positions into consciousness. The shifting blank is responsible for for a sequence of colliding images, which condition each other in the time flow of reading" (Iser 119).

34. Wolfgang Iser, "Interaction Between Text and Reader," in *The Reader in the Text: Essays on Audience and Interpretation*, ed. Susan R. Suleiman and Inge Crosman (Princeton, N.J.: Princeton University Press, 1980), 110–11.

It is not clear how the blank operates in a paradigmatic fashion. Iser attempts to find some sort of structuring relation which will finally validate the text's influence as an arbiter of the exchange. I would prefer to reflect upon the space in between, the blank, in very different terms. There seems to me to be no problem in talking about a meeting point through and across which a number of interactions turn. Projections are part of an unpredictable process which has a location in the spatial and temporal sense, and this may clearly firm up the fundamental differences between written texts and images. The reciprocity of the projection process places the image and its screen within a specific context historically bound to the activities of viewing, but it is not the image that designates or even contains within it, the "solution" to this interaction. I am not talking here about a random process, but about a shifting ground within which there are so many different possible combinations that what we define as meaning and meaningful will depend on how much weight is finally assigned to the image by the viewer. Even so, this may shift with context, with the state of mind of the viewer, with the performative exigencies of the film theater, with the perceived role of the image outside of the theater, and so on. The result, as has always been the case with images, is memory(ies), within which a variety of narratives, fiction, and realities can be constructed and maintained.

It takes work to balance all of these elements, to organize them into a coherent point of view, perspective, or phrase. It is the work of a radically disembodied spectator who must refind his or her emotions by referring to a body of memories that lack the specificity and immediacy of the experience of viewing. But that specificity is itself a myth, since the screen upon which we watch images contains within it a struggle with projection, the struggle of the people who embody the production process, their struggle with viewing both themselves and the hypothetical audiences they think they are addressing. A great deal must remain unresolved for the producers of images. They can never be sure if their audiences exist and if they do, what they have seen. The projection process lacks the kind of materiality we usually assign to images. There is a great deal of anxiety possible in this situation because we still assume that communication means the linking of like minds or the transformation of difference into agreement.

Projection suggests an entirely different communicative sphere for images. The context of communication for film and television, for example, is the result of a dynamic activity and not a pregiven or preconstituted place into which obedient subjects enter and process themselves. Disagreements, even violent ones, are inevitable, as evidenced by my earlier discussion of the Rodney King affair. The variability here means that we have to rethink our approach to the screen, to its history as a technology. This problematization of the screen leads naturally to an emphasis on what the German filmmaker Alexander Kluge has called the public sphere (and which I would suggest should also be called the communicative sphere) and on modes of communicative interchange that facilitate the surfacing of the many different claims audiences make about what they have seen and understood with respect to images.

> Kluge's strategic focus is on the moment of negation: the empty space between shots (*Leerstelle*), and the emptying out of the image itself, the non-image (*Nichtbild*, rhyming with the German word *Lichbild*, i.e., slide, transparency). Frequently mocking Adomo's apothegm, "I love to go the movies, the only thing that bothers me is the image on the screen," Kluge himself invests in a similar aesthetic of negativity. Over against the flood of images that beckons the spectator of the contemporary Hollywood product, an alternative cinema has to engender a resistance—in the psychoanalytic sense—resistances that provoke the spectator into autonomous co-authorship. Hence the importance of cuts, ruptures, silences, breaks—whatever may counteract the obtrusive referentiality of the image flow; hence the emphasis on a radical practice of montage.[35]

While agreeing with Kluge's emphasis on negation, on rupture and on the central idea of coauthorship, I remain, as much of this book has attempted to elaborate, unconvinced that Hollywood films, if one can in the first instance accept the homogenuous characterization of them, are separate from, in a fundamental sense, that potential process of rupture about which Kluge is talking. This is simply because, unlike Kluge, I see no value in on the one hand depicting the spectator as a victim, and then on the other suggesting that they are capable of transcending their victimization because of the choices in a particular film. What must be differentiated here is precisely the audience and the film, the image and projection. All films and images search for a way of unifying with their audience. But that desire is constantly undermined by the projection process. There are of course degrees of difference here. Some films attempt closure, but I must stress that even though they try, they rarely succeed. What clearly distinguishes the work of Kluge from the Hollywood cinema is his style. What unites him with all cinema is his attempt to find a solution for the problems of communication and exchange in a theater, through the films themselves, as if the object can contain the probable outcome of its propositions, within its own communicative structure.

Performance, Projection, and Intention

Projections are the site of a performance of potential meanings. The time of a film's projection establishes a context not of silent viewing—the transfixed

---

35. Miriam Hansen, "Alexander Kluge, Cinema and the Public Sphere: The Construction Site of Counter-History," *Discourse* 6 (1983): 61.

audience—but of relationship with another viewer. It is not an accident that most audiences are made up of couples or groups of people. The "other" viewer can be understood in Bakhtin's sense as the site of a double movement incorporating that which "cannot unfold on the plane of a single and unified consciousness, but presupposes two consciousnesses which do not fuse; they are events whose essential and constitutive element is the relation of a consciousness to another consciousness, precisely because it is other" (Todorov 99–100). To see these dialogical elements as being outside the designated boundaries of representation and signification in the cinema is to generate an oppositional relationship between the speaking subject and the screen as a device of projection. The screen may act as a mediator for all of these levels of projection and (mis)understanding.

Let me return for a moment to one of the conversations between Riva and Okada in *Hiroshima mon amour*. They are talking to each other in a restaurant and Riva is revealing more of her personal history. Their dialogue, however, is performed, which of course changes the nature of their utterances since they are being listened to and watched by the director and his crew. They are also closely following a scenario. The viewer enters as a third party onto this preestablished "scene." Riva's act of personal revelation helps her to reconstitute her personal history from which she has, up until the scene, been dispossessed. But this dispossession has also been an intrinsic part of her performance, since she is not the person she is acting out.

Her projection of herself into an actress requires her to internalize a script also written with an imaginary actress in mind. Intentionalities crisscross all over the place here, but what is clear is that there are a variety of dialogues taking place between people who are both absent and present, outside the production context and within it. Alain Resnais intervenes as well, rewriting the scenario to suit what he believes are the conditions of projection, the conditions of narrativity that will best express his intentions. No individual scene in the film is divorced from all of the above considerations. The conversation then, between Riva and Okada, takes place against a backdrop of communications about communications and conversations about conversations, most of which have the viewer as an Other in mind. As must be self-evident, we are dealing with degrees of autonomy, a multiplicity of communicative instances governed not by real results but by imagined potentialities.

It would be an error to think that the spectator is excluded from all of the above, an error to hypothesize a spectator unaware of the various levels operative in a film's efforts to create a space for the projection of meaning(s). The cinema has long ago ceased to be a device of innocent internalization, a place where identification occurs simply because a projection appears to follow a mapped-out narrative direction. Seen as a social event, the projection of a film reveals a high degree of indeterminacy. The result is a lack of equivalence between screen and spectator, a time and space of contingency and substitution. But this in no way should suggest a viewing process devoid of the self-reflexive capacity to critique, question, and remake the image.

As Riva and Okada talk, their discussion turns into the equivalent of a psychoanalytic session, with Riva enacting a transference onto Okada. Interestingly, the way Riva transforms Okada into a former lover allows her to find the images in her mind to explain to herself why she had been traumatized. This doesn't lessen the trauma; it merely raises the question of its existence and the strategy she will have to choose to face up to the past. It must be remembered here that transference is as much about the transformation of an Other as it is about the special circumstances generated by dialogue. "Dialogues, whatever their subject matter, are always dramas of self-constitution."[36] Thus Okada, scarred by the experience of Hiroshima as a boy, tells Riva she cannot really understand the depth of the pain he has experienced. In trying, Riva transforms Okada into the German soldier with whom she had had an affair during the war.

Does this mean then that an interpretation of the conversation the two characters have is another form of transference in relation to the viewer? In a brilliant discussion about texts, Jane Gallop argues that the authority imputed to a text is evidence of transference at work. The text is seen as a place where knowledge and meaning reside, which masks what happens between the text and the reader, creating a separation which the very act of reading contradicts. "I am attempting to do a psychoanalytic reading that includes analysis of transference as it is enacted in the process of reading: that is readings of the symptomatic effects produced by the presumption that the text is the very place where meaning and knowledge of meaning reside."[37]

Okada and Riva are viewers of each other and simultaneously, they are projections, waiting for spectators whom they will never see. In all three instances, symptomatic effects are produced through which further projections can be created, which go far beyond the boundaries of the scene or the discourse of the characters. What can be mapped out are a variety of different levels of meaning, some of which may be conflictual and others which may not. For example, Okada is the vehicle through which Riva resurrects her memory of a love she has lost, while conferring upon Okada the concrete role of the lost lover. She holds him in her arms as if he is from the past, as if her memories have become real. It is this virtual place that actresses and actors construct. But the simulation would mean nothing were it not for the projection process. The

36. Vincent Crapanzano, *Hermes' Dilemma and Hamlet's Desire: On the Epistemology of Interpretation* (Cambridge, Mass.: Harvard University Press, 1992), 130.
37. Jane Gallop, "Lacan and Literature: A Case for Transference," *Poetics* 13 (1984): 305–306.

value of transforming a memory into an image is that it then exists as a possible projection and in that sense, opens up the communicative sphere to many variations.

It will be of use here to follow an argument developed by Roy Schafer in relation to introjection and identification so as to explain the number of different levels that can simultaneously work together to produce the possibility of projection. Schafer talks about introjection as distinct from identification, because identification refers "to modifying the subjective self or behaviour, or both, in order to increase one's resemblance to an object taken as a model; it does not refer, as introjection does, to carrying on certain purely internal relations with an object represented as such (the introject). Although identification implies a continuing object relation, in its most developed form it no longer depends heavily on the representation of that relation."[38]

The key point here is that identification need not depend on a particular source, and the discursive and experiential relationships that develops, for example, after an image is viewed may have little if anything to do with the initial stage of viewing the image. To identify with Riva, for example, doesn't create the kind of concrete scenario that might be suggested by the person she represents. The lines of continuity are built upon different premises. They are related to assumptions and hypotheses about the kind of person she is/was, and although the film first established the content of that exploration, it cannot control the direction taken. Even here, my characterization of the temporal flow still has the ring of a building block process. It is hard to avoid thinking of fragments that connect like a chain, hard to avoid metaphors that make those connections have a solidity which projection dissolves. And it is this sense of the material/immaterial as a consistent feature of images that contributes to the need to repeatedly experience them, to view and review, as if that will somehow bring all of the various levels of experience and understanding together.

Self-image, internal space, "my insides"—all of these metaphors operate to legitimize and concretize the social, personal, and intellectual base I use to identify and explain the experience of viewing. But when a spectator is watching images, she must also enhance the activity of viewing by trying to control or understand her imagination. She is faced with the difficulty of finding a means of expressing her experience. These difficulties and gaps are not ones the filmmaker is outside of. The filmmaker is a spectator of his or her own film as well as being its creator. As such, he or she is not in complete control of meaning, and certainly not in control of the many possible interpretive horizons generated by the film. This bind is shared by the spectator in the sense

---

38. Roy Schafer, *Aspects of Internalization* (New York: International Universities Press, 1968), 16.

that words, speech, language, cannot substantiate the fundamentally nonrepresentational and nondiscursive aspects of viewing. This doesn't pull the spectator away from the possibility of historicizing his own viewing. But it points to why there is this special feeling of loss associated with spectatorship.

The loss is about gaps that operate in conjunction with a further set of quite fluid boundaries between conscious and unconscious, gaps not specifiable in a concrete sense and not directly revealed through viewing. These gaps which are very specific to images and projections, nevertheless reveal a struggle among different levels of representation, where what appears to cease as projection reappears as discourse. This grounds the act of viewing in a play of highly speculative constructs and is, I would suggest, the source of much pleasure and anxiety.

If I assume that identification is a process external to myself, then I make it seem as if a map has been written that will guide me toward a defined point of entry for my experience and what I can say about it. If there is a map, then I have helped to create it. Identification is not about a fusion between a "representation of an object and a representation of self."[39] Rather, identification with respect to images is a fragmented, often contradictory pleasure, which continually and quite effectively raises questions about its own functioning. And it is this, I believe, that pushes the viewer further and further into the projection process. The space in between comes to represent a place of potential control and the site of many possible speculations about the sources for the experience. Let me move on to another example of a film that illustrates what I have been proposing.

Memories of Identification: *Scream from Silence*

I would like to delve into some scenes from the film *Mourir à tue-tête* (translated as *Scream from Silence* for distribution purposes) made by Ann-Claire Poirier, a feminist filmmaker from Quebec and a long-time producer at the National Film Board of Canada. In particular, I would like to examine a scene in which a rapist locks his victim in the back of a truck and sets about abusing her verbally and physically. Not only does he swear at her, he cannot divorce his physical brutality from the language he uses. He berates her, screams at her, spits at her, talks about how she is just another tramp, and so forth. This brutalization lasts for fifteen minutes before the scene shifts to an editing room, where the filmmaker and a companion discuss the sequence and critique it. What this reveals is that the event we have just been viewing is not only constructed, acted, edited, but that we would need to recontextualize

---

39. Daniel Widlocher, "The Wish for Identification and Structural Effects in the Work of Freud," *International Journal of Psychoanalysis* 66 (1985): 43.

whatever feelings we have been having for the woman and provisionally see her as acting out our feelings of disgust for the rapist. Whenever the rapist handles the woman, the camera replaces her and is jostled. His spit dribbles down the lens. He is unshaven, ugly, repulsive.

None of what I have just said is different from what the actress playing the filmmaker says, as she reviews the scene in an editing studio (it is one of the brilliant touches of this film that the filmmaker is also a character in it). She herself wonders whether or not she has overdone the portrayal of the male. The camera becomes as much of a violater as the actor. The camera person must endure this duality. Then the filmmaker must edit the scene. It is precisely because the events being depicted are so brutal and the cry of anger on the part of the filmmakers so important, that the images highlight the duality of their role as artifice and document. It is as if the film is exploring projection and pointing out that even an acted rape retains the violence of the real event through the manner in which it is presented and interpreted.

But my voice is not becoming Poirier's or the actress playing the role of a filmmaker. Rather, the ambiguity here raises a series of questions about the activities of viewing and the very possibilities of interpretation and language. This is because viewing is as much an activity of observation of self and other, as it is one of interpretation, identification, and projection. This writing, my memory of the images, my desire to work out and work upon the many aspects of the projection, all lead to a breakage with the film, and yet what emerges are a series of reconstructions that could not have been produced without the film. Identification and mastery, identification and the loss of mastery—these two processes coexist with each other, and a dialogue can be created around them. I may write about the rape in *Scream from Silence* and the horror I felt, but that horror must be understood as emanating from me, since I know at least to some degree that I am watching a reenactment. I write out that horror with the word *horror*, which reveals only part of what I felt. But I have not mastered that horror within me by the act of writing.

To describe *Scream from Silence* I must recognize the particular way projections are immediately a part of memory, immediately open to reflection and forgetting even as I watch them. What I bring forth as a summary then is never outside of the interpretation I have already made as I viewed, forgetting and remembering simultaneously my own role as a spectator. There are therefore at least three levels at work. One is the film itself which has an existence outside of me, has already been "seen," to which I have gone. Another is the film that I have already seen, perhaps many times, from which I exit in tandem with other people. This is the film I talk about, think about, relate to my personal existence, contextualize in relation to the various political, personal, and cultural positions I hold and my own perceptions of myself as a viewer. The third level is what I do with all of the above information, whether I decide to write about, or speak even further about the previous two levels. But what is crucial here is that these levels can interact simultaneously. Together they can never become the film, never match, never contain the process of projection. Their very existence confirms the inherent and never-ending way meanings circulate. I am not suggesting here that a film clearly sexist in orientation and choice, for example, cannot be specifically labeled as such. Rather, what is important is the context of the labeling and the way that labeling is applied. This contextual factor reveals the history of the interpretation without any pretence that the film is somehow outside of that history. "The attempt, however, to eliminate contradiction itself partakes of the contradiction: the affirmation of meaning as undivided is simultaneously one that excludes the position of the opponent; the homogeneity of meaning can be asserted but through the expulsion of its heterogeniety. In precisely trying to unify the meaning of the text and to proclaim it as unambiguous, the critics only mark more forcefully its constitutive division and duplicity. Contradiction reappears with ironical tenacity in the very words used to banish it."[40] Felman goes on to talk about how the critic is playing a "performative" role in his acting out of an analysis of a text, becoming, as a result, not a simple observer of the "text's pluralistic meaning" but the agent for that pluralism.

Scream from Silence begins with a series of men, all obviously the same actor, but playing different male roles from office manager to worker. Each male turns to the screen and looks out at the audience with the same sneer of disrespect, and each is described in the voice-over as a rapist. //Each male turns to the screen.// Am I then, as the voice-off suggests, also the male turning toward the women I see and desiring to rape them? His face, I want to assert, is not mine. He looks too evil. But then do I comfort myself with the knowledge that I am not him? He is also as I would expect him to be, a stereotype. His face is unshaven. His hair is matted and unclean. He seems to be rooted in that other world, personified perhaps by some dark streets in a large city into which I don't imagine myself ever entering. Yet he is also just a projection, acting out my own ambivalence about men. Who is the narrator? She tries to describe him even as I am describing him to myself. I also feel that his story is about to be told, was just told. No tense will do here, for as I write, I have already begun to pressure myself. I want to remember that face.

This same man, now dressed in dirty clothes grabs a nurse outside of a hospital. He puts a knife to her neck and drags her to a truck. He throws her into it brutally, and wraps some rope around her arms tying her up in a corner of the truck. He spreads her legs and spits at her and also at me. I can't "see" her face and instead the camera lens becomes coated with saliva. It drips down

40. Shoshana Felman, "Turning the Screw of Interpretation," *Yale French Studies* 55–56 (1977): 114.

the screen, ugly and repulsive. //I can't see her face.// But I do remember it. Her fear and shock stay with me even as the filmmaker denies me a glimpse of what her expression looks like. I keep superimposing other memories of rapists who have killed, stories from the newspaper, from television. I watch my own narration starting to develop and wonder where it will take me. //My own narration.// Yes. But I nevertheless am moving toward a point far beyond what the film is offering me. There is no fixed point here, no specific narrative moment upon which I am enlarging. But when he sits down and opens a can of beer, burps, even, it seems to me, farts, calls her names, pours beer on her, on the camera, strikes her when she screams out, I want to push him further and further away from me, even as that brings me closer to the horror of the acts he is committing. This is a reenactment!

I am developing a relationship to the images which is removing him as an actor and transforming him into a man I hate. But in order to do that I must also be hating myself. I have shifted the parameters here from acting to projection. Yet, perhaps it is the way it is being filmed. To a limited degree. He is after all such a caricature, so blatantly evil, so overtly sick. But have I not submitted myself to his illness by feeling it with such strength? So perhaps it matters little that the camera is the recipient of his violence. //It matters little?// Of course it matters a great deal. The camera is not there. Strictly speaking, the camera cannot show itself as an image, cannot reveal its own presence. But at a crucial moment when he punches his victim the screen goes red as if a transformation has been effected between his actions and the screen, as if the screen has become a canvas which he paints. But I am not that screen, not, in other words, the victim of his violence. The red screen hides what must be happening behind it, the interlude an editor takes as she decides on the validity of the scene, or the physical motion of intercutting red leader or the feelings of the crew as they try to light the interior of a small space and continually reposition the victim. Must I not negate all of this seemingly peripheral information in order to experience the rapist as evil? He sits down in a corner and talks about women. He's had many, he says. More than she could imagine. He talks about his mother and her stupidity, her protectiveness, and then he says that all women are the same, power hungry and selfish.

//This is a reenactment.// *Scream from Silence* was made at the National Film Board, in many ways the home of *cinéma-vérité*, a living laboratory in which documentary and fiction coexist, sometimes uneasily. The cross-fertilization between the two genres raises questions about their validity as categories. Docudrama is neither a simple mix nor a new form. Yet *Scream from Silence* is shot as if it were a documentary, creating through its metaphoric structure the very space that permits, if not encourages, the fiction. As the male speaks, he is marked by his position as a male and as a male actor. Would I understand him (me) a bit better if I assumed that he was acting out a set of unconscious desires? But then I view him also through a set of relations that are conscious and unconscious. And if I am to stay within the bounds suggested by the previous sentence then I am continually performing those aspects of my unconscious most likely inaccessible to me.

He pulls out his penis and urinates on the woman. His urine straddles the boundary between acting and truth. Slowly her body becomes less and less a site for me to project myself into. I don't want to take her place. My repulsion is mixed with dread and fear. I am paradoxically pushed closer and closer to the rapist. This would presume something rather dramatic, described by Felman as my transformation into the storyteller's ghost, a process through which his unconscious addresses me. I have, by virtue of my reenactment, become the subject of the movie. This is not a concrete place, a specifiable subjectivity. I must struggle to know and understand its implications because what I am seeing cannot be pulled away from my desire not to see, to exclude him, while also excluding the victim. "Freud's analysis of the movement of psychic energies back and forth between sleep and wakefulness via transference seems perfectly tailored to fit precisely the visual dream-like figures of the ghosts. Seeing is thus above all transferring. . . . just as a dream is a transference of energy between the 'day's residue' and the unconscious wish, so does the act of reading invest the conscious, daylight signifiers with an unconscious energy, transfer on recent materials the intensity of an archaic sleep. Seeing, thus, is in some manner sleeping, that is, looking with the very eyes of the unconscious—through the fabric of a dream, reading not literally but rhetorically" (Felman 1977, 137). It would be more proper to say then that a reenactment of a rape is an impossibility. The violence cannot be shown. Nor can it be seen as image. But the possibility of its depiction can begin to play on the performative reality of the audience, viewing a terror that isn't. And so I must substitute myself for the rapist if I am to experience the violation of the woman. This realization is a crushing one and I resist it. When, after much abuse, he finally rapes her, my despair overwhelms me. There is so little symmetry between what I am seeing (she is not visible in the scene) and my own identity as the viewer. What I desire as the scene finally draws to an end is that it remain an illusion, remain, that is, without threat to me.

What would happen, however, if the substitutions I have produced put me in an impossible position because I am so deeply repulsed by the actions of the rapist? In order to find a way out of the ambiguity of my position I may have to assign the responsibility for my own feelings and thoughts to someone in the film or even perhaps the creator of the film. Paradoxically, as the scene reaches a crescendo of violence and brutality, as the rape is completed and the screen flashes between red colors and camera movement, the scene suddenly ends. Of course, it has not ended, because I continue to reflect upon what has happened to the woman, to the rapist, to me. But the interlude comes and it is with great relief that I listen to and watch the editor and director discussing the previous fifteen minutes. They talk about the rapist overacting his part. His violence is too extreme. The director-actress at first agrees and then expresses profound disagreement. She talks about the experience of rape and the difficulty of revealing its true and traumatic effects. Their discussion thus develops into another interpretation of the film, but does not interpret my role in viewing it, though they do mention that they want to shock men into realizing the horror of such a profound physical and mental violation. The film turns from one kind of reenactment to another. The director is acting her role. So their interruption of the film merely anticipates the next section. It forms a part of the performance, struggling with the ambiguity of its own premises. Thus the film also reveals the ambiguity inherent in its conflation of seeing and knowing. It is just not enough to show the rape without also referring to the closure the scene produces. By this I mean that the exclusion of the victim's face is an attempt to limit and contain the range of interpretations I can make. The film can only tell a small part of the story. It cannot and does not delve into the psychopathology of the rapist. His behavior is meant to be a symptomatic map, a guidebook to the incoherence and irrationality of his violence. But the film makes no effort to delve into his past.

The two women at the editing table slowly reposition the victim. She becomes a lost heroine. The next section of the film delves into her deterioration, her incapacity to understand her own fear and shame. She is exposed to further brutalization by the police who question her without any sensitivity to her plight. All the institutions of society are against her.

//His behavior is meant to be a symptomatic map.// Does the rapist by his actions and verbal abuse reveal enough to allow me an insight into his motivations? He speaks through clichés. They guide his behavior. But in order for me to understand those clichés, I must be able to draw upon more than his behavior. It is here that a potential set of discontinuities develop. Can I be simultaneously repulsed by his image and yet position myself in his role? Can I also know him through negation? As a projection he speaks from outside of these contradictory but intertwined levels. Thus in one sense the question of his behavior is crucial. In another sense his behavior acts as a barrier to my understanding of him. If he can be both the role and a witness to it, then which position do I occupy? Between the force with which he acts the role of rapist and the knowledge I have that he is not one, what at first might appear to be a wide gap is revealed to be quite small. Because he knows that he cannot address me, he must look to the screen as if I am there, speaking as a result to my imaginary. At another level he addresses me in general terms as if my imaginary is shared by all of the men around me.

Some further comments on *cinéma-vérité* might help frame the context a bit more. I have mentioned its origins in Canada, and I would refer the reader to a previous piece of mine that tries to explain the historical relationship between Quebec nationalism, the National Film Board and *cinéma-vérité*.[41] In *Scream from Silence* all of the stylistic elements of *cinéma-vérité* are used to heighten the real effect. Thus there is a measure of spontaneity to camera movement. Often it appears to be hand held. The filmmaker is deeply and visibly implicated in what they film. No effort is made to conceal the efforts needed to construct the subject under inquiry. I would stress the notion of inquiry because so much of the effect of *cinéma-vérité* is found in its use of the present tense. Thus we witness the real as if it is being discovered and not as if it has been edited into a particular form. As much as the technical process is made transparent it is also hidden, but this potential contradiction is used to great advantage by trying to foreground its role in producing knowledge. Yet there remains a desire to reveal the real, to make the real speak as if all of the mediating factors play a role, but not a distinctively important one. In the final analysis for *cinéma-vérité* the truth value of the imagery will transcend all of these limitations. The question of truth situates itself right at the heart of the process through which a projection comes to be seen as containing the truth within it. But that container is at the heart of a play of meanings, the performance of which transforms *cinéma-vérité* into the fictional construct it so desperately wants to avoid.

A major portion of the film is taken up with the devastation the rape has wrought on Suzanne. She stops talking and seems to be incapable of communicating with her boyfriend, who on the surface represents a male diametrically opposed to the rapist. He tries to be sensitive. He stays with her. But eventually her pain becomes incomprehensible to him. When she finally does not come out of her depression, he goes to bed with her and forces her to make love to him. This second rape is both the real and symbolic death of their relationship. A few hours later, she commits suicide. Crucially, at this point, we cut back to the filmmaker and editor discussing the progression of the plot. They seem initially uncomfortable with her death but this shifts when the director turns on a videotape of an interview she did with Suzanne, now not an actress but seemingly the subject of the research that the director undertook to make the film. The twist here, video-television, research as if we have witnessed the result of a social scientific project, further heightens the paradoxes of the filmmaking process. Suzanne is both a projection and a real subject. We get a metareading by the film of its own construction of meaning, a statement not only on the message but on its truth and on the manner in which it has been validated.

---

41. Ron Burnett, "Developments in Cultural Identity Through Film: The Documentary Film, The National Film Board and Quebec Nationalism," *Journal of the Australia-New Zealand Society for Canadian Studies* 2 (1985).

The filmmaker sits with Suzanne in a sunny kitchen. The former repositions herself from researcher to therapist. She urges Suzanne to overcome the grief. But Suzanne responds that certain kinds of shame can never be erased and that life for her has become a source of terror and despair. Guilt, a loss of inner strength, silence, the loss of meaning, the meaninglessness of language, all of these elements are combined to explain Suzanne's suicide. //All of these elements are combined.// Let me reconstruct these elements. The research for the film is presented as a document to strengthen the dramatic structure that led to Suzanne's death. But the interview itself is merely another episode of the drama. And Suzanne's tragedy continues through the theatrical format of filmmaker-therapist-feminist trying to help Suzanne overcome an event which it must be remembered, never happened. The darkness of Suzanne's vision, her tragedy, refers to all rapes, to the problem of rape in our society, and the impossibility of simply banishing the effects of rape by urging its victims to overcome their pain. Suzanne is thus defeated by the social forces surrounding her, as well as by the individual circumstances of her own experience of life. As a projection, however, Suzanne is in the privileged position of imagining the rape of all women and reenacting the performance of a rape. She is there on the screen because she *has not been* raped. Ironically then, her acting the role of an interviewee addresses the imaginary of a spectator caught between the truth of rape and the fiction of its dramatic depiction. Yet this type of contradiction is fundamental to the way projections operate. The power to deal with the contradiction lies with the spectator. This is the site for a further but more complex form of identification.

As a projection Suzanne immediately splits into a number of different yet related parts. She is a victim of one man and all men, thus representing the historical condition of one woman and all women. Suzanne must, as a projection, create the possibility of a disjuncture between the identity she has and the identity the viewer will confer upon her. Suzanne is also an actress who must split her "I" to become both victim and witness, both object and viewer. The social setting for her exposition of this process is a further projection of herself into the role of viewer. She is the spectator of her own split which differentiates her from the viewer of a screen, who must repress the knowledge of that splitting to accept her as a victim. It is here that the social setting of the theater plays such a significant role, because it legitimizes the validity of that repression through the collective presence of other viewers. The film brilliantly exposes this through its use of the filmmaker-director as a character because she is at first so unsure of where she is going in relation to a character-actress (Suzanne) presumably under her control. She must view her own creation as if she is a spectator in the audience, but of course she too is an actress who represents the very structuring of projection and splitting that marks the contradictory role of the director.

The actor who plays the role of the rapist seems on the one hand to be laying bare all of his repressed feelings that have turned reality into a hell for him. On the other hand, as a projection, he is trying to include within the context of his improvisation an image that he and the filmmaker share about rapists, a presumption, as it were, of the stereotypical male able to commit an act of violence against women. This presumption, it is assumed, is one the audience will understand. As a projection, the rapist is also teetering precariously between the image he wishes to portray, the stereotype he must imagine, the anxiety and aggression he must express to the actress-victim, and the audience he paradoxically has to alienate in order for all of the above to communicate effectively. He cannot of course achieve a unification of all of the above, but he can and must idealize his viewers so that his destructive impulses will give the impression of being based on reality. That idealization forms part of what the spectator must repossess while simultaneously defending herself or himself against the idea of rape, let alone its possibility. Because the rapist cannot distinguish between what he has done to himself in order to so violently hurt Suzanne and the pain he is actually inflicting upon her, his representation via projection is of someone as split into parts as the audience. For does he not demand of his victim that she view him? He asks her to remain silent and accept his violation of her. He asks her to understand him. This indicates that he is playing a number of roles at the same time. The audience must join his fantasy world to believe that he is capable of rape. In order for his role to work as a projection he must not only represent the rapist, he must also use language that links his actions with his screen imaginary. Suzanne, the screen, and the viewer must represent him so that he can defend against their representations of themselves. It is as if his display of violence is an interpretation of his own fantasy world and not simply an expression of it. And the battle here, between this expulsion of his hatred and violence and the self he does not know, merely reenforces the impossibility of his own position. He cannot fully give life to a person whom he does not know. This is the point at which acting, becoming the role, and being a projection break down.

Clearly then, projection does not reveal the complexities of identity within a character without also revealing all of the above splits. The self cannot be presented through the rapist without destroying the role, yet the role cannot be acted without the presence of the self to play it. Moreover, this dynamic contradiction shifts with the narrative, often clarifying its own development while undermining the logic of its placement for the purposes of identification.

In a similar fashion Suzanne acts a role she knows leads to suicide. She must experience that possibility in order to act out the process that engenders it. She of course places herself outside of the character she is acting. She experiences that character through her own projection of Suzanne, with whom she identifies through her own fear of rape. In order to act the role she has to provide herself with an image of Suzanne's fantasy world, though she would also have to recognize that Suzanne only exists as a projection of the film's script and author. These elements can act autonomously, yet their relationship to each other must find some means of externalization, some way of being acted out. This is where fantasy need not complement identification but can actually transform the various ways representations of self set the stage for projection within the framework provided by the film and outside of it.

The projection-rapist depicts his internal struggle with reality and fantasy. He sees himself, not through a mirror available on the set, but as a consequence of the role he is acting. He need not provide any explanation for all of this because his off-screen history doesn't have to be included in the film. Nevertheless, he could not play the role if that history were not present. There is a major difficulty here. However stark his character may be, the severity of his regression cannot be clarified through the film itself. In order to open up a space for his own acting and for the viewer, he disrupts the narrative, placing it on notice as an incomplete representation. What is so fascinating about this process is that he can manifest both normal and abnormal behavior while watching and evaluating the role he is playing. It is this capacity to be inside of the role and outside of it at the same time that can be a source of pleasure for him and for the viewer. There is pleasure in knowing that the projection can be separate from his own body, that what he says need not be confirmed by what he does or vice versa. We know that his expressions of hatred for women are only temporary, that the "I" he uses is a more or less false and constructed self. Thus the audience joins him to create a context for projection, where a number of hypothetical possibilities can be played out at a variety of different and often not necessarily related levels. This join is not homogenuous. The film does not represent it. The word *join* bears no relationship to the word *suture* as it is used in film theory. Rather, I am talking here about a kind of asymmetry through which splits in personality can be played with by spectators and actors or actresses, as if those very splits are both crucial to a narrative and detached from it. A number of different messages come through at once and in the final analysis, the audience has to finds a means of restricting the process, imposing boundaries, joining meanings, in order to organize the experience.

In one of the scenes before her suicide, Suzanne's boyfriend, Phillip, tries to break what he perceives to be her self-imposed silence. He suggests to her that she should see an analyst in order to "solve" the problems she is facing. She rejects what he says. She feels possessed by the rapist. She cannot simply disavow the experience. Her body has been abused, and her emotions have been trampled upon. She has lost a sense of self-respect, reenforced by the way she was treated after the rape. The police in effect blamed her for getting into the position in the first place, and though she initially resisted their attribution of blame, their effort to induce guilt, she is now unable to wash away the effects of their intrusion when combined with the experience of the rape itself. It is as if the rapist begins to live within her. He becomes a continual presence, announcing his triumph, his defeat of her through her depression. She is unable to gain any distance from the experience she is having of herself and seems to have become catatonic. Even the act of vomiting does not rid her body of the feeling that she has been dramatically altered. She becomes an onlooker to the events of her own life.

Then after her death, she is brought back to life as the research subject upon which the narrative part of the film has been based. Now this is perhaps the best example of the way projections work. The depression we witness is not a psychotic experience over which Suzanne has lost control. Quite the contrary, she reveals through her reappearance in the interview that she controls the past, the present, and the future. She can defy time, defy the effects of the rape, reconstruct her own story, and so forth. This potential to transform history into a vehicle for projection allows Suzanne the pleasure of understanding her own situation while playing the role of a character who has died. She then comes to represent the effects of a social and political structure that dominates women. Though her body is a symptomatic map, she overcomes those effects by examining the social history of her own trauma. Thus Suzanne can share a desire for instant solutions and gratification, instant explanations with the spectator. Suzanne's death carries with it the paradoxes of its own artifice. The spectator can vicariously reproject her into life, play the game of denying her death, and win on all counts. And crucially, the actress who plays the director can appear to be helpless, at the same time as she structures the scenes that reveal she is in control.

Play-Acting

This chapter details the many different ways projections create what D. W. Winnicott has in another context described as "potential space(s)."[42] Winnicott is of course talking about the relationship between mother and child during a period of the child's life when identification processes are put in place.

> In this way, he [Winnicott] came to posit what he called a potential space between baby and mother, which was the arena of creative play. Human play was thus itself a "transitional phenomenon." Its precariousness belongs to the fact that it is "always on the theoretical line between the subjective and that which is objectively perceived." This "potential space" he saw as arising at that moment when, after a state of being merged with the mother, the

42. D. W. Winnicott, *Playing and Reality* (London: Tavistock Publications, 1971), quoted in Peter Fuller, "Art and Biology," *New Left Review* 132 (1982): 94.

baby arrives at the point of separating out the mother from the self, and the mother simultaneously lowers the degree of her adaptation to the baby's needs. At this moment the infant seeks to avoid separation "by the filling in of the potential space with creative playing, with the use of symbols, and with all that eventually adds up to a cultural life." However, the task of reality acceptance is never completed: "no human being is free from the strain of relating inner and outer reality." The relief for this strain, is provided by the continuance of an intermediate area which is not challenged: the potential space, originally between baby and mother, is ideally reproduced between child and family, and between individual and society or the world. This potential space was the location of cultural experience: "this intermediate area," he wrote, "is in direct continuity with the play area of the small child who is lost in play." He felt it was retained "in the intense experiencing that belongs to the arts and to religion and to imaginative living, and to creative scientific work." (Fuller 94)

The displacement of responsibility for the creation of meaning onto the image makes it seem as if the image controls experience. This fantasy of external power cannot come about without identification and projection, without replacing what has been seen and listened to with the subjective transformations and processes that make it possible for images to be understood and experienced. Thus the discursive choices made by viewers to explain what they have experienced tend to bring them together with the image. At the same time, in a dialogical play with meaning and communication, with self and Other, the image is kept at a distance. The tensions here, fundamental to the operations of projection, are not bipolar. They are transitional. They involve maintaining power over certain aspects of the experience, while at the same time creating a variety of contingent operations that are profoundly contextual. One of these is to confer upon the image a measure of control, which seems to remove the "I" from the responsibility of having effected any transformations. This may be what Winnicott refers to as that "intermediate area" where the intensity of identifying with the image also leads to distance, to the ability to recognize "play" and to the creation of a potential space for understanding and experience. This happens because the image never completely fulfills the expectations of the child. The result is a play between identification and loss, between the object as site of that play and all of the other factors that contribute to the process, including what is outside of the play relationship itself.

In extrapolating from this one can hypothesize that the distinctions between self and image cannot be collapsed through identification. Even at its most intense, projection leaves enough room for questions to be asked about the image and this is a play between image and projection, between the needs of viewing and fantasies of control by both the filmmaker and the spectator. This does not mean that identification is a conscious activity. But it also does not mean that it is entirely unconscious. Watching a film is not the equivalent of being in a dream, and certainly bears little comparison to being in a trance. Whatever sense of disorientation develops, the screen remains two-dimensional, remains, that is, a technology situated in a theater constructed to serve a large audience (economic exchange), and capable of being seen from a variety of different viewpoints. However, the perceived lack of differentiation between screen and self is part, in a quite precise sense, of the "transitional" realm described in detail by Winnicott.

This intermediate phase helps us transform images into projections. We know that an actress on television or in a film plays *with* her role, trying to dissolve into it, but always able to exit. Meryl Streep can appear on the screen as a victim of the Holocaust (in *Sophie's Choice*) while simultaneously appearing on television to explain more about the experience she had in the film. Liam Neeson can appear on the "Larry King Show," answer questions about his interpretation of Schindler in *Schindler's List*, and still be viewed the same night at a local theater playing the role. As projections, Streep and Neeson can explore the feelings of someone about to die, and then play-act death. They can jump among many points of history, make history, become celebrities and be the focal point of discussion for a diverse constituency of viewers. As projections they can dissolve all of the differences between themselves and those who view them and still remain locked into the two-dimensional world of the screen. Yet this is precisely one of the reasons why we are so fascinated with them. They elude us even as we work to bring them closer. We master the ability to understand what they are saying and to identify with the characters they have created. At the same time, that mastery defines and explicates the social and personal context within which we pursue them.

The spectator too can play-act with death, can force the boundary between screen and self to dissolve, by thinking that the characters on the screen are him or her. A figure on a screen can be anthropomorphized into a real person, talked about as if she or he has not acted the role but has become it. The viewer can quite tentatively disappear into the screen, negate her or his own disappearance, disavow any responsibility for having disappeared, and then leave the theater as if the film she or he helped create has ended. This suggests an intricacy to the *practice* of viewing which is part play, part control, and on another level we may not be able to account for the many dimensions of the experience, may not want to explain what moved us or what didn't. This silence shouldn't be misinterpreted. Sometimes it involves a choice to swim in the emotional aftereffects of viewing. Sometimes it reflects the need to find a community of people with whom one may wish to talk about the experience. And sometimes, silence is the only way to start or to continue the process of reflection and interpretation. The silence mirrors, but does not duplicate, the viewing situation in a film theater. Even the openly discursive context of television viewing is enframed by moments of silence.

The daily practice of engaging with images in the late twentieth century means that a certain kind of knowledge is built up and maintained, and this is a very practical as well as theoretical knowledge. The manifestations of this richness, its explosive potential with regard to subjectivity and viewing come into play every time we decide to use images for viewing or when we talk about them or as an inspiration for writing, thinking, and so forth. To repeat, we create boundaries between ourselves and what we see with respect to images and we confer the responsibility for the border markers onto the screen. It is that conferral which creates the space for projection. A part of ourselves disappears into the screen, and we rediscover that part in a different way. This is inevitably a self-reflexive process, a strategy of displacement and replacement, with the aim being to discover more and more about who we are and why we feel what we feel.

The experience of images is created by active agents. This is not to suggest that the image doesn't exist. In fact, projection as a concept is based on the idea of reciprocity, on the notion that we are partially in control of what we see in relation to images. In order to make claims about the visible, we must recognize the hypothetical and contingent character of the entire process and crucially, of our conceptions of control. An example of the slipperiness of projections and subjectivity can be found in the contradictory relationship we have with *cinéma-vérité*, a genre of film I see as one of the foundations for the credibility of the news media. Let us take the example of an unemployed teenager who has been filmed in the *cinéma-vérité* style to explore some of these paradoxes. There are countless images of the unemployed on television and in films about our society. Those images don't simply represent the problem they are trying to depict, rather, they signify the translocation of the unemployed into projections. In the particular case of our hypothetical teenager, this shift makes his identity far more complex because *cinéma-vérité* creates an impression of surrogacy in order to comment on the realities it depicts. This surrogacy, which is a further site for projection, conditions the style of *cinéma-vérité*. Thus "John," our teenager, is followed down a city street, the camera moving in tandem with his body. He is interviewed as he walks. This is meant to heighten the spontaneity of his comments and the sense that the filmmakers have just come upon him in the everyday context of his life. The hand-held camera is meant to convey a direct feeling, a sense of being within the event. As a projection on the screen, that very directness must be split off from the event, edited to suit exigencies history may have already transformed. What John says is very important, but the meaning of his comments has a form as much dependent on the context of his performance in front of the camera as it is the raw material for the filmmakers to edit into presentable shape. John is not outside of these problems of image and self-image. He has to master the picture of reality that both he and the filmmakers want to construct. Nevertheless, even though the core of this series of exchanges (filmmaker-John, John-filmmaker, John-projection, projection-John, audience and projection and image, and so forth.) is above all cinematic, projection makes it possible to rearrange all of the elements at work here. To relate to John, the viewer must be convinced that there is some truth to what he is saying. John must believe that he is directing his comments about himself to a spectator who is listening. The filmmakers will organize the information into a form that can open up the possibility of reciprocity. But that form—the interview done on the the run—a priori seems to contain within it all that is necessary to make it work. There is a presumption that John's discourse will transcend all the elements here and provide the viewer with the information she needs to understand his situation. Ironically, it is because all of these levels cannot be choreographed together into a unified whole that the entire process becomes contingent. And the contingencies here maintain the openings necessary for the reconstruction of the meanings being projected. The news, John, unemployment are all displaced and the results lead, through time, to a highly creative practice of viewing. This practice in effect opens up the links through which the viewer can personalize John's situation, understand and perhaps sympathize with his discourse, and in a self-reflexive sense work upon the images he or she watches.

The film *Culloden* (which mixes the genres of *cinéma-vérité*, documentary, and fictional film), by Peter Watkins, makes use of the projection process in order to explore the reconstruction of a battle that happened many hundreds of years ago. The filmmaker interviews soldiers in the midst of battle. The interviews take place as many of the soldiers are dying. Temporarily they overcome their wounds and respond as interviewees. They reveal the depth of their alienation from the war into which they have been forcibly recruited. Projection can assign them the dual role of actor and historical figure. They can be part of the film and entirely bound to the historical role the filmmaker has given them. The paradoxes of the camera as a witness to war are that the historical moment seems to overtake efforts to control the events visually. This parallels the efforts of the viewer to be a witness as well. The viewer finds herself doubled as witness to the representation of the war and the soldier's efforts to act out the battle. This doubling turns on a further series of levels dependent on the filmmaker's voice and the *cinéma-vérité* movement of his camera through the killing fields. Watkins adds even more to this web by creating a surrogate for himself, a historian who sits behind a wall in the middle of the battle zone. His descriptions have an objective tone, although he finally succumbs to the sheer brutality of the better-armed and better-trained English soldiers and begins to comment on their lust for Scottish blood.

Culloden could be approached as a hall of mirrors. There is the sense that we have entered a labyrinth. Watkin's dilemma, and it is not one which the film or even his career has managed to resolve, is that he still wants to persuade the viewer to accept the particular road has chosen. He brilliantly unmasks all of the levels of meaning and expression that make the projection process work, and then he uses more and more intense imagery to drive home the point that the war was unjust, as all wars are. There is of course nothing wrong with the message. It is just that there is so much more historical detail he wants to communicate, and as he points out, images lend themselves to precisely that kind of distillation. It is, however, the spectator who is the final arbiter of the many different levels projection processes make possible. And this introduces a high degree of variability if not flexibility to the very images Watkins wants to restrain, because of his belief in their historical veracity. This is not a negative conflict. It may be a further ground upon which the viewer inteprets and reinterprets their experience. In other words, the viewer is also involved in the same "debate" as the filmmaker. Where is the truth and how can it be understood? Which images work and which don't? This is related to a perceived difference between the "concreteness" of images and the rather more ephemeral and textual nature of historical discourse. Watkins in this sense joins with the spectator in demanding that history be validated through images in order to create at least the possibility of a visceral response to the moment being reproduced. The effort here to bring the sensory experience into the foreground, to "show" the brutality by making the screen drip with the blood and screams of the victims of war, presumes that the image can break out of its limitations, elide time, become timeless. The images can transcend the artifice (even though Watkins's is concerned with revealing its presence), remain truthful, and upset viewers enough to provoke them into rethinking their values and their understanding of history. Investing in images as sites of truth and meaning inevitably decreases if not eliminates the range of dialogues that viewers can have with images. There is a hidden empiricism to the approach chosen by Watkins. Ironically, he wants to eliminate the stream of ideas the process of projection makes possible. He tries to generate a mirroring process (albeit a self-reflexive one)—history can be seen. This effort has its effects. *Culloden* remains one of the most important examples of the kind of postmodern pastiche which combines different styles and discourses into an effort to create a powerful message. The film is almost entirely dependent on projection to fill in all of the gaps. The same style was used to even greater effect by Watkins in his later films, *Privilege* and *Edvard Munch*.

The Body of Projection

The activities of projection involve the entire body. We listen, we feel, there are sounds which bring out the faint residue of smells which we have experienced. We allow, even encourage images to embody our deepest desires. We move about from the conceptual to the physical and from ideas to realities.

The practice of image watching and interpretation, which to some degree is supposed to be expressed by the term *viewing*, never excludes the physical boundaries of the sensate body. Theories of spectatorship have needlessly marginalized the body and in so doing have separated the experience of viewing from sensations of hearing and the physical sensations of fear and ecstasy, love and apprehension, touch and so on. It seems to me that projection, the idea of a space in between seeing and the seen, allows us to explore a variety of meeting grounds which take on a discursive character once we have acknowledged their presence but which never eliminate the role of the body in giving meaning to experience.

Another way of thinking about this is to reflect on the *internal* conflicts we have when trying to make an important, perhaps life-changing decision (like moving from one town to another or from one country to another or ending a relationship, for example). There is a sense in which the internal reflections we experience have to find some point of externalization, but there is no linearity to this process. And it is not as if the internal and the external are separated by defined barriers or fixed borders. Yet we retain the distinction of the inside and the outside as a strategic way of distinguishing among different levels of perception and understanding of the world around us. Even when the evidence is overwhelming, that is, even when we reach the point of realizing that what we have externalized comes back to us through sometimes direct or indirect routes (a mirror, a screen, an image, a look), we disassociate ourselves from the role we have played in producing the experience. This has become a fundamental aspect of the critique of objectivist social scientific research. The recognition of the contradictions at work here has significantly altered the disciplines of ethnography and sociology. Much of the impulse for this critique has come from feminist thought. Yet I believe the critique must go deeper. If we recognize that the body is both an imaginary and a real boundary to the way we evaluate visual experiences, then we are less likely to reduce the feelings we have to one set of causes. We would not perhaps even try and generate the kind of linearity that links visual expressions into an ordered chain, that confers upon them the structure of a sentence or even a paragraph. Why have we collapsed notions of projection into the sometimes narrow forms of a carefully bordered narrativity?

The distinction here is between the storyteller and the listener, between images that surface in a chaotic manner from the simplest of expressions, from words or sounds, and the deliberate, highly developed intentionality of the narrator. Although intentions are fundamental to all forms of human expression, there are obviously degrees of intention built into every activity. Projections in some respects, though not entirely, are like sounds, or as I mentioned before, like music. The creative structure may be precise, even mathematical, but the freedom to work with music encourages an almost endless flexibility, an interpretive phantasmagoria. Projected images are like sounds. They fill our environments with varying degrees of meaning, with many different kinds of expression, and this flow is neither completely linear nor predictable. Much time and work are needed to deal with and understand projections. There is one excellent example of this process—video games. The ability to respond to, challenge, and even master a video game requires repetition, hours of work with the characters until they bend to the will of the player or until the codes that govern the game are completely uncovered. Yet these are simply images. More often than not the characters are surreal and two-dimensional. The landscapes are obviously constructed, digital, and artificial. Why then are the games so attractive? What are the challenges here? I cannot offer a complete answer to these questions because that would require another book. Suffice to say for the moment that the evolution of images on television for example, into video games like Nintendo represent a shift as significant as the one into virtual images and cyberspace. I would stress that although the notion of cyberspace is derived from the fiction of William Gibson, its metaphoric power lies in its suggestion that images can only be controlled if we are ready to accept our own integration into them. In other words, we have to be a part of what we see, and to do that much more is required than acceptance. The energy needed to learn a video game is exacting and requires a mental concentration that shifts the burden almost entirely onto the player.

Images, whether fictional or documentary, experimental or a hybrid of many genres, types, styles, don't so much offer experiences as they create the field within which a whole host of possibilities can be generated. In the same way, but at a different level, the activities of seeing and relations between seeing and understanding are not necessarily dependent upon what we have conveniently defined as objects of perception. Rather than proposing that the imaginary is more or less an interference to all of this, I would suggest that the idea of projection places the imaginary in the forefront of what we do when we think about what we have seen. This introduces such a high level of unpredictability to the multiplicity of ways we understand the world around us that often, in a desperate attempt to constrain the process, we try, by an inversion, to systematize the ground upon which we analyze our visual experiences. Yet, even the word *visual* tends to put brackets around processes that cannot be divorced from thought, from the bringing into being of sensation, from the recognition that to see invokes autonomous as well as recognizable activities, to the awareness that all of this is *inside* consciousness as well as being part of our bodies.

This is not meant to suggest that we see nothing and that the world around us is simply a figment of our imaginations. On the contrary, the struggle here is a dialogic one. For example, as we watch the horizon at twilight we also produce the horizon through our statements about it and our assumptions about our own experience of the sun setting. To the horizon we add our poetry and categories of thought. To the horizon we attribute shades of color and light, which although "out there," are a manifestation of our ability to distinguish among sensation, thought, vision and our fantasies. Add the dream and the daydream to this and it is clear that we are in a constant struggle to actively give structure and meaning to the many aspects of visual experiences. Most of the elements upon which this process depends are just inaccessible. The manifestations of all these relations cannot be boxed into instrumental forms of thinking. There is no simple or transparent picture that can be created here, although it is one of the functions of the image as projection to suggest that there is.

The cultural role of the image seems to confer mastery to the spectator. This conferral is the illusion so often attributed *to* the image. It is not so much that the image is the site of illusion (in the sense of a false vision of the world or one that seems to disregard often discredited universal notions of truth) as it is part of a context in which the image is meant to arbitrate between reality and truth, between the world as it is (or as it is presumed to be) and what images supposedly do to it. The illusion of mastery has more of an impact than the illusory characteristics of the image. This is a far more significant aspect of the documentary movement in the cinema and photography, for example, than presumptions about what is being shown. It is at the heart of the commercial and political use of imagery to try and convince or persuade viewers about the validity of a particular argument or the value of certain products. Yet this form of mastery is precisely an illusion because it proposes the absence of projection. It sets in place subject/object distinctions which projection dissolves. The control of understanding, perception, and sensation that it suggests is continually undermined by the unpredictable nature of fantasy and the independent operations of the imaginary. It is our ability to reflect upon all of these elements, to sometimes organize them and other times "stare" in wonder at their complexity, that contributes to the sense we have that we are viewers.

This "sense" has external and internal features. It comes neither solely from within the viewer, nor from without. It is not situated in a look or a gaze. It doesn't have those qualities of singularity. Rather, to be a viewer of images, for example, combines forms of empathy which we must create, with the recognition of that creativity in our thoughts and feelings about vision. It is one of the ironies of this analysis that in order to talk about the process of projection I must imagine that it has a concreteness that my own suggestions about seeing would contradict. To bring the imaginary or fantasy into the foreground as I have done is exactly the displacement projection encourages. I am faced with the contradiction that unless I am willing to bring my ideas into a discursive form, they will merely exist as thoughts. In the same way a sight I have will never be seen by others, unless I am willing to give that vision the quality of a representation. What happens then if I identify with my own representation of what I have seen? Have I forgotten that I created it? Isn't this forgetting precisely what keeps me looking? Isn't this why I can repeatedly watch the same scene over and over again and forget my role in making the experience significant? This suggests that we are constantly exploring not only what we see but the metaphors we use to explain the sights to ourselves. We may attempt to ritualize the form and shape of the exploration (as in, the movies are the place where we watch images), may even attempt to regularize all the cues and processes we use (which may explain why we want to convert images into objects that can be "read"), but projection pushes all of this over a precipice. The result is a far less mechanistic activity than the term spectator proposes, a far more chaotic positioning of subjectivity than we are often willing to allow for. Crucially, as the image loses some of its strength, projection enhances the possibilities of surprise, the very ground upon which new ways of thinking and seeing can come into being. David Levin:

> The style of vision that I would associate with the hermeneutical discourse of poetizing, and with truth as *aletheia* [Heidegger uses this Greek word, which means truth as unconcealment, not truth as correctness, certainty, reliability, and Levin takes up the Heideggerian usage] is exemplified by the playful gaze, gently relaxed, calm, centred by virtue of its openness to experience, its delight in being surprised, decentred, drawn into the invisible. Perhaps, if we can allow our gaze to wander, to come under the spell of shadows and reflections, and can learn from *their* ways of being a more playful way to *be* with visible beings, we might at long last break the spell of metaphysics, a vision of ontology that has captured our imagination since the dialogues of Plato. (Levin 438)

It is this sense of the unpredictable that encourages fantasies of control over images, efforts at constraint, the need to know that neither the image nor the projection process are entirely beyond who we are. Identity is crucial but identity is an unstable fulcrum for identification. The lure here is precisely to find some measure of stability *in* the image and to disavow projection. This disavowal is a resistance to the idea of the image as embodied. The best example of this process at work are "viewers" who transform themselves into lookalikes of dead movie or rock stars. Their efforts at surrogacy are like a Brechtian play with identification and distanciation. They are neither the star nor themselves. They are a "place" within which a flood of projections can be embodied. Their being encourages the creation of an imaginary world where no one really dies. Their images are sustained not so much by the actors who embody them as by the spectators who come to their performances. This entire constellation of relationships is fundamentally a way in which everyone can be anyone if they are willing to transform their bodies to meet the exigencies of image creation.

Another example is the way in which digital images can bring dead stars to "life"—Louis Armstrong playing the trumpet or Humphrey Bogart reappearing to advertize a soft drink. These "views" are written onto our bodies because of the pleasures they provide, but the categories of visuality they "embody" cannot from the outset be locked into a particular shape or form. One of the filmmakers most concerned with these issues is Atom Egoyan, whose films, *The Adjuster, Speaking Parts* and *Calendar* explicitly examine these problems and debates.[43] Projection processes suggest that images are not the dangerous ground upon which false illusions and hopes are built. They can of course provide the venue within which illusion and simulation can reign supreme. But as I hope to show below, I do not believe that that is the case, nor is it the central issue with respect to images.:

Inside the Dome of Images

At the end of the first chapter of David Levin's book he has a section entitled "The Age of the Image: Triumph of False Subjectivity." In it he sets up an opposition that has proven itself to be the most enduring and powerful of the conflicts surrounding the production, projection, and use of images in everyday life. I must stress that Levin does not establish a dialogue here. The opposition he constructs and the point of view he supports suggest that images have so much power that the cultural, social, and subjective effect is nihilism, despair, and pathological narcissism. On the other hand are many of the assumptions that have guided this book: images in of themselves provide us with only partial evidence of what we do with them; it is only when we recognize the workings of projection that we can move away from linear and quite reductive presumptions of control, manipulation, and loss; much of what is immediately accessible through images is so fleeting that we are forced to work on what we see, moved to examine and go beyond the surface of the experiences we have with them; none of these activities is exclusive to the other and they intermingle to create unpredictable constellations of meaning; the image, both figuratively and metaphorically, represents a new and important site of subjectivity and identity.

Levin's position is very close to Jean Baudrillard's. Both are pessimistic about the role of the image in contemporary society. Both see the image as an external and internal danger to consciousness, as an arbiter between reality and truth. Levin quotes Heidegger:

world picture, when understood essentially, does not mean a picture *of* the world, but the world conceived and grasped *as* picture. What is, in its en-

43. I would refer the reader to Ron Burnett, "Speaking of Parts," in *Speaking Parts: Atom Egoyan*, ed. Marc Glassman, (Coach House Press: Toronto, 1993), 9–22

tirety, is now taken in such a way that it *first* is in being and *only* is in being to the extent that it is set up by man, who represents and sets forth. Whenever we have the world picture, an essential decision takes place regarding what it is, in its entirety. The Being of whatever is, is sought and found in the representedness of the latter. (Levin 119)[44]

The reduction of the world to a picture and the dependence on the picture as the world initially strikes a familiar chord. Since images are produced and controlled by human beings, this suggests a will to power, a need to transform the world into a manageable place. Medium and message become one and they join together as arbiters of the real and as the foundation upon which modernity has built its rather tender cultural infrastructure. Yet what does it mean to collapse the world into a picture? Why do Heidegger and Levin see this as one of the most important problems we face and as evidence of a profound cultural crisis over which we have less and less control?

With reference to the mass media and with a similar tone, here is what Baudrillard has to say:

What characterizes the mass media is that they are opposed to mediation, intransitive, that they fabricate noncommunication—if one accepts the definition of communication as exchange, as the reciprocal space of speech and response, and thus of *responsibility*. In other words, if one defines it as anything other than the simple emission/reception of information. Now the whole present architecture of the media is founded on this last definition: they are what finally forbids response, what renders impossible any process of exchange (except in the shape of a simulation of a response, which is itself integrated into the process of emission, and this changes nothing in the unilaterality of communication).[45]

To Levin, everything around us must become a "re-presentation" if it is to be acceptable, if it is to be real. "In this way, re-presentation manifests the most extreme form of subjectivity, for the imposition of this metaphysics of objects is the work of the will to power, which thrives on setting up situations structured in terms of the relationship between a subject and its object" (Levin 120). For Levin the subject-object relationship is fundamentally a violent one, producing "opposition, conflict, struggle" (Levin 120).

Levin's concerns are that an age dominated by the image is an age profoundly restricted in its vision, both literally and metaphorically. These restrictions turn the activities of seeing into consumption and end up producing a narcissistic subject incapable of going beyond the rather limited boundaries

---

44. Quoting Heidegger, "The Age of the World Picture," in *The Question Concerning Technology and Other Essays*, ed. W. Lovitt (New York: Harper & Row, 1977), 129.
45. Jean Baudrillard, "The Masses: The Implosion of the Social in the Media," *Jean Baudrillard: Selected Writings*, ed. Mark Poster (Stanford: Stanford University Press, 1988), 207–208.

provided by the image, incapable of recognizing the way that the image dominates and then cuts off his capacity to feel, and most importantly, "how our blind attraction to the ontology of the image, and our correlative propensity to restrict ourselves within a mode of vision for which the image is predominant, compel us to take part in the production of human suffering" (Levin 120). Levin also asserts that the image and our relationship to it is responsible for "narcissistic character disorders" (Levin 120), and his chapter on the image develops into a distillation of the characteristics of the psychopathology of narcissism.

Both Levin and Baudrillard are clearly dependent on Heidegger. In Baudrillard's case, as I will examine later on in chapter 6 of this book, the pessimism with regards to images and the media extends into a fatalistic analysis with apocalyptic results. Baudrillard uses many terms to describe this descent, but the one that struck me most was "stupor" (Baudrillard 209). We lose any chance to really control who we are and what we do. Everything is mediated through the lenses and images provided to us by the media. Not only that but as more and more demands are made on us from all sides, as images proliferate, they become the only way we can evaluate and understand the experiences we have. *All* experience in fact becomes media based, because reality can never be separated from "its statistical, simulative projection in the media" (Baudrillard 210). And in a tone similar to Levin's, with an almost equivalent move toward the narcissistic model, Baudrillard says, "the social becomes obsessed with itself; through this auto-information, this permanent autointoxication, it becomes its own vice, its own perversion" (Baudrillard 210).

As with Heidegger, quoted by Levin, "But we do not yet hear, we whose hearing and seeing are perishing through radio and film under the rule of technology" (Levin 121), and because we do not see or hear we have become the worst kind of victim, one who cannot understand his or her oppressor and must labor under the false illusions created by a cultural context that has lost control of its own creations. In what follows I will argue that both Levin and Baudrillard have in fact reified the image into an ideological construct and in so doing have created a model of human subjectivity that precludes the possibility of creative change and intervention with respect to images and the social. In Baudrillard's case this may well be the direction his ideas take anyway, but Levin is genuinely concerned with elaborating a radical new basis upon which human vision can be altered at its very roots. The fact that he falls victim to the pessimism which at another level he is trying to overcome is evidence of the difficulties we face in trying to analyze images.

There are so many impediments here that I cannot hope to distill them all. Suffice to say that one of the symptomatic and more incoherent responses to the flood of images we experience every day has been the visual literacy movement. I mention this because on the one hand it represents a genuine desire to somehow gain control and on the other hand the very notion of visual literacy begs the questions it asks. It is not a matter of learning how to "read" what we see or how to "decode" what we are shown. These we do anyway and we invoke and make use of many different strategies of analysis and interpretation as we grapple with images. There is simply no grid upon which all images can somehow be placed. It is not a matter of becoming literate in the Victorian sense, able to apprehend either by learning or instantly the constellation of meanings and messages that are thrust our way. Neither is it a matter of overcoming the propensity to watch images and gain pleasure from them by reducing them to a series of manageable figures within an easily definable and simplistic semiotic. The visual literacy movement, like Levin and Heidegger, sees images as predators on all expressions of human subjectivity. Thus, although images are fundamental to the ways we see the world around us, they are somehow alien, imported into our everyday activities by forces we cannot control. We can only gain that control by becoming more literate, that is, by more fully understanding the image and how it is created. But this must be done not for the pleasure it might bring but because images are inherently dangerous and their effects need to be neutralized.

Levin uses as one of his central examples the story of a man who tried to immolate himself in Chicago. News reporters witnessed the event, and they did nothing to stop the man, presumably because they were more interested in the images and their dramatic value than they were in the individual's well-being. The result were a series of news images that were transparently brutal and evidence of a gaze, a vision, which in Levin's terms has lost its way. More than that, there is an ambivalence to this loss. It is ambiguously situated in the fact that seeing a human being experiencing so much pain both destroys vision and gives the viewer enormous power. How? The viewer can control their reaction, can avert their eyes, can deny the anguish. But the victim cannot. In Levin's terms the presence of the camera created the event. "Observation has become cruelty. Obsessed with the picture, the image, we take part, whether willingly or unwillingly, in the production of suffering" (Levin 126). In comments that recall the now famous work of John Berger (in particular, *Ways of Seeing*), Levin reflects on the juxtaposition of human suffering with Coca-Cola advertisements and the easy way events become bracketed by "pictures of Calvin Klein asses" (Levin 126). There are links here to Barthes's work in *Mythologies* and Foucault's discussions of the panopticon. In other words, the full force of an argument *against* the image is constructed on a set of assumptions about viewers, about their ability to interpret and critically argue for or against what they watch. Levin's premise is that there can be no counterreaction to all of this because it has an ontological character, which means that the media and images are to a large degree written into our consciousness. They do not so much represent reality in all of its diversity as they create a subject who *is* the image. (This was crucially the position that McLuhan took, although he derived it from the work of the anthropologist Edmund Carpenter in particular Carpenter's book *They Became What They Beheld*.)

The idea that we become what we watch and that our bodies and our minds are inscribed with meanings that we have difficulty reading and understanding, naturalizes the impact of the media. We are therefore less and less capable of locating ourselves in this phantasmagoria. The boundaries between what we know and what we understand, between what we experience and what we see, collapse into the image. This implosion masks all of the borders and distinctions our culture has developed to map itself and in particular provides us with the illusion that we can *be* the representation. As a result, there is no authentic place within which human experience can fully possess itself. There is no place that has not already been defined by the image, no prior moment in which this cacophony can be framed, contextualized. This then is another and far more sophisticated explanation of simulation.

The problem is that both Levin and Baudrillard have taken the notion of the image as the foundation of simulation and naturalized it. They move from the image to the beholder. They talk about images as if images represent the viewer. In other words they collapse their interpretations of the image with *all* interpretations. They would not in any case accede to the argument that what we do with images is transform them, because they feel that the image represents all possible reactions to it. In so doing they freeze the time of the image's projection. They create a timeless sphere in which experience never changes. More importantly, they forget that images do not survive unless they can be interrogated within the context of performance. They have given into an almost medieval argument about the image as an object of idolatry. And in so doing they lock subjective experience into a dispossessed world where "we belong only to others. The image obscures our capacity for authentic existence, true subjectivity, being true to ourselves" (Levin 129).

The force behind this notion of dispossession comes from the image as a representation of false consciousness, not of identifiable subjects, but of subjectivity in general, constrained, blocked, and repressed by its inadequacies. This is subjectivity in the universal sense, unable to recognize either its own power or the way that power is exercised. And lest this argument seem like it is a dispute among philosophers and cultural analysts, we only have to look again at the at the interpretations of the David Koresh–Branch Davidian events in Waco, Texas (see chapter 1), to recognize how useful this model of loss and dispossession has been for the media themselves. The very idea of loss was central to the depiction of the fiery death of so many people. It was not their subjectivities that were in play, but their inability to *be* subjects. They represented precisely that sense of false worship, of idolatry, that symbolically comes to stand for what Levin describes as an epidemic of pathological narcis-

sism. Their activities and their defiance, whatever one may think of them, became further evidence of cultural and social illness. Yet, the Davidians' presumption that they could do and be what they wanted, that they could construct a society in which their values would be enshrined in their daily lives,
was an expression of the principles of American life. Their defiance ridiculed
the illusions and idealism of the will to power of individuals who believe themselves to be outside of the political context they both form and inform. The
outsider, the rebel, the frontier—it was inconceivable that a religious sect, a
cult, could take the romanticism of these fundamental symbolic expressions
and coopt them. How could they test the limits of freedom? How dare they
really go to the edge and make visible, bring into visibility, the iconoclastic
subtexts and eclectic character of all communities? For once the boundaries of
the eclecticism were clear. The images of those boundaries made them seem
pathological. Children abused, women dominated, religion gone mad, brain-
washing, sexual deviance, Koresh as sex king, many wives—all this in one synoptic moment: helicopter images of a blazing inferno and death in the most
horrific way, burned alive, asphyxiated, snuffed out.

As projections these images turn on themselves, they become fragments
begging to be misinterpreted and misunderstood. Their illogic invites debate
and discussion. Their power lies in their incapacity to depict what seems to be
so self-evident. Their weakness is that they cannot *be* pictures. They cannot,
for all of the technology we have constructed and all of the sophistication of
the television cameras, enter and be within the mindset of David Koresh as he
lay dying. In order to deal with this crisis, television turned to fiction, to docudrama, to fantasy, to the imaginary, in other words, to a wide variety of strategies as silly and superficial as the news coverage, but which invited speculation
and questioning. These are, to use Levin's terms, mirrors that neither fail nor
succeed. The duality of truth and reality dissolves. The narcissism challenges
its onlookers. There are too many ridges and gaps in the mirrors.

It seems clear then that Levin and Baudrillard have constructed a theory
dominated by a notion of empirical truth within which the mirror operates to
control the onlooker. Because the media mediate, because images stand between the real and the truth, they are the false world of shadows within which
we, as subjects, are subjected. Baudrillard, however, takes this argument further. The media operate under the illusion that they control the process of
communication. The "masses" absorb all of the messages without producing
a response, and this is ironically an act of defiance (Baudrillard 218). It is an
act seeking to mimic the real desires of the image creators to have a compliant
mass even as the society at large pays lip service to the impulses of participatory democracy. This Baudrillard characterizes as a "double bind," because
there is no clear resolution to the conflict. The double bind forms the basis
upon which simulation becomes acceptable. Simulation is a symbolic level

which we must inhabit and without which we cannot survive the contradictory arguments and irreconcilable conflicts of being participants in the creation of our own conformity.

Nirvana: The Death of Kurt Cobain

Yet it has been my argument with respect to projection (and is one reason why I have introduced the term) that we constitute ourselves as subjects by using images to create a context within which new and unpredictable meanings arise. Our struggle more often than not is with definition and explanation and interpretation. We are so active in this regard that even the most sophisticated of marketing experts cannot predict the outcome of an advertising campaign. More and more money is now allocated to testing prospective consumers. Much of the money budgeted for marketing a film goes toward trying to ensure success, and more often than not that success is far from assured. In other words, the communicative circle never closes. It is fissured and broken.

The configuration of potential meanings here finds its clearest expression in the contradictory symbolism of Kurt Cobain's suicide. Writing in the *Globe and Mail* (published in Toronto, Canada), Jamie Todd, a graduate student at the University of British Columbia, tries to grapple with the paradoxes of Cobain's death.

> And here was a key dilemma: How did one remain the casual flippant icononclast when bank tellers were chirpily nodding their heads to Nirvana in their "beemers" on the way to work? Kurt Cobain hated the fact that frat boys were cranking his song "Smells Like Teen Spirit" at kegger parties. These were the sort of timeless, bullying nobodies who would have pommelled the hell out of him and his friends in high school for being weird. It was an impossible tightrope: writing angstful music when he was a millionaire, trying to write songs which couldn't be co-opted by corporate rock and teeny-boppers, while at the same time avoiding these very pretensions, for he was well aware, that he was, for the music industry, just another stupid rock star."[46]

Perhaps Todd's ruminations are nothing more than a fantasy. Perhaps he is projecting all of these contradictory feelings into a rock icon whom he cannot possibly know. But the point is that he is working with the imagery. He is taking Cobain and subjectifying him. He is making Cobain a part of himself and in so doing is interpreting Cobain in much the same manner as he might interpret his own motivations or character. This join is not just another stage in the massive illusion generating machine of the media. Cobain has moved from im-

46. Jamie Todd, "Why Kurt Cobain's Death Matters," *Globe and Mail*, April 19, 1994, A16.

age to projection and because of this Cobain has ceased to be "visible" in the direct sense and has instead become a useful tool of self-analysis. There will be in all probability be much debate within the "zines" devoted to rock and to Nirvana. There will be films and television shows about Cobain and about the mythological space he inhabited. This cacophony will create as many contradictory stories as have circulated about Elvis Presley. Or perhaps Cobain will become a character in the ongoing fictions of fanzines and join with some "Star Trek" characters in space, perhaps even have a homosexual love affair with Spock or Picard.

Wim Wenders got it right in *Wings of Desire*. The postmodern landscape is littered with a millions of ghosts and they live and die in an arbitrary fashion. They are neighbors and friends. They are JFK conspiracy experts or Prince lookalikes. They are neither the victims of the media nor its progenitors. They are the characters of Robert Altman's *Short Cuts*. They play with video and with images as in *Reality Bites*. They are in your local video store hunting the shelves for excitement and entertainment and for added satisfaction, they watch themselves in *Wayne's World*. They are parodied and are taken seriously. They watch the news and they watch "Larry King." They stare at pictures of dead soldiers in newspapers while eating a sundae at Dairy Queen. They turn their heads from reading the newspaper in a coffee shop and watch a rerun of "I Love Lucy." They walk into a department store and look for clothes which may or may not have been produced by low-paid labor in Taiwan or China, clothes that models and movie stars and rock stars they have never met have modeled to death. Clothes that sit in racks beneath video images of Kurt Cobain singing about the death of consumer society and the fears of being lost in a sewer of commercialism. They listen to his words and they hear what he says and they work upon the contradictions. How can you not? Why would the image of a zombie in a stupor walking hand in hand with Mickey Mouse be a believeable or even justifiable response to all of this?

Although the faint echoes of other epochs can still be heard across the landscapes of our culture, are we not witnessing the explosion, finally, of the paternalism that would restrain our fantasies and make of them some kind of perversion, some kind of aberration of a hitherto locked subjectivity? The irony is that there will always be efforts to constrain, even destroy this shifting paradigm of self and identity and Other. Witness the efforts to mark off an entire generation by the letter X. What could be more ironic? The letter of the illiterate. The letter of the man and woman who cannot write their names, who don't know how to symbolically represent themselves, who face the ignominy of no identity, loss of ego, loss of self. This notion of nothingness, the fantasy of a society without names, the very faceless mass of which Baudrillard speaks, this construction, like all projections, faces its own death through the suicide of Cobain. For it is precisely the frailty and weakness of our culture's efforts to define who we are that creates the gaps within which identities grow and develop. We are never at one with what we see, never comfortable with visions devoid of our own bodies. As sentient beings we are neither the victims of the image nor in the simple sense do we reproduce its symbolic expectations. We are neither Kurt Cobain nor are we Madonna. Our culture's hybridization of truth, reality, fiction, illusion, and pain makes possible a scenario in which our lives will be presented to us as videotapes which we will then completely reedit and which our children will redesign and our grandchildren will format on CD-ROM, so that we can come alive as multimedia presentations. The history of this movement between various forms of image and reality suggests that we are finally in charge of the images we prefer. We will decide where the mediations begin and end and be able to comment upon our own status as projections even as we go about recreating the landscape of feelings and emotions we inhabit.

5 | Reinventing the Electronic Image

Prologue: To Be or Not to Be—Virtual

PORTABLE LIGHTWEIGHT VIDEO cameras and video recorders became a reality in the late 1960s in North America. This chapter will examine video and electronic images in general. Video is a hybrid medium incorporating electronic, celluloid, and photographic characteristics. I like to think of video images as carvings in time. For me, the paradoxes and pleasures of the television monitor are summarized in the rather strange, ghostly images that float across the screen during music videos. On the one hand, with reference to an older technology of synchronous sound, music videos use voice and lip movement to suggest that the singers are actually singing in real time. On the other hand, many of the videos are daring and experimental. Even as experiments, they incorporate the innovations that first appeared in the avant-garde film movements of the 1950s and 1960s and in the public performance styles of early rock stars.[1] It is precisely this hybridization that interests me. The medium encourages a playfulness that is built into ideas of portability. And while most music videos are shot in studios and increasingly are digital and generated through computerized technologies (e.g., Peter Gabriel's videos), they retain the desire to present their material as if the viewer is attending a concert. The temporal juxtapositions and poetic editing are reinforced by the active camera movements used by MTV camerapeople (or as is the case in Canada, by MusiquePlus and MuchMusic). VJs (video disk jockeys) operate within studio contexts where the hand-held camera plays with sensations of movement and the lifelike of rhythms of *cinéma-vérité*. These are instances of mixed media where sounds roar above and beyond the visual in a truly unconstrained process of imagining space, time, and experience. Even repetition doesn't still the shifting parameters within which I, as a viewer, do my work upon music videos. The projections are endless here, and they are manifested most intensely in the quickness with which the videos appear and disappear. They are anthems one day and

1. The best book I have read on this phenomenon is Andrew Goodwin, *Dancing in the Distraction Factory: Music Television and Popular Culture* (Minneapolis: University of Minnesota, 1992), esp. 49–71.

part of a retrospective the next. Memories form around them and are replaced. The video image lives in this perpetually unravelling knot and it encourages if not promotes, expertise and knowledge. I recently asked one of my students, who is an aspiring rock musician, to make an inventory for me of the various musical tendencies in the rock world. He devoted himself to this task for months and came up with 346 different categories worldwide. Then over time and in many conversations he proceeded to argue the validity of his inventory with me.

This is the world of 'zines and counter 'zines, of private videos and micromusic. A city can have hundreds of bands vying for legitimacy and recognition. I see this world as one of contestation, anger, and joy. Images and sounds in this context have generated a vast cornucopia of competing ideas of reality. This is neither virtual nor artificial. There are no prostheses at work acting in a surrogate fashion to replace the body with the machine. Rather, images become yet another tool used to argue about the world. Even the desire to mystify the information highway flounders under the weight of primitive computers which "crash" when they connect. In fact, it is the wreckage that interests me. All around us there are many examples of contradictory and contesting perceptions of "reality"—these come to life as images on a variety of different screens and all of the time, with equal rapidity, more and more tools are being developed to respond to the output. From cable access to local television stations, to informal VCR networks, to an ever-expanding use of radio, to the reinvention of sound across computer networks, to cheap camcorders and desktop publishing, there is an exponential growth in creativity and communication. We do need to step back and examine this phenomenal expansion of media-based technologies and users. Most of all I would like to examine the implications of all this for more traditional forms of political action and cultural creativity. But the point I am making here is that far from disappearing, "subjectivity"—subjects, people—are redeveloping a whole host of strategies to respond to change. These activities are not without their own contradictions, but they do suggest that one has to look at new technologies from within the broader political and social struggles that give them credibility and legitimacy.

Even as video is incorporated into the computer and the computer is incorporated into multimedia, the discourses that I have been addressing and often critiquing in the previous four chapters of this book remain embedded in the critical and popular debates that have been used to evaluate the impact of video images on our culture. Part of the problem is the inevitable gap between the growth and legitimation of new technologies and the critical discourses that can be developed to examine them. Of greater importance is the claim (central to postmodern thinking) that the shift to the electronic symptomatically expresses a revolutionary cultural and social transformation of (in particular) Western culture and human subjectivity. In talking about Paul Virilio, Arthur Kroker has the following to say: "Someday it might be said that the political history of the late twentieth century, the fateful time of the *fin de millenium*, was written under the sign of Paul Virilio. For in his theoretical imagination all of the key tendencies of the historical epoch are rehearsed: the creation of the postmodern body as a war machine; the fantastic acceleration of culture to its imminent moment of collapse in a nowhere zone between speed and intertia; . . . the irradiation of the mediascape by a logistics of perception that work according to the rules of the virtual world."[2] It is in the notion of virtuality that there has been a radical shift not only to a new use of images but to a new level of experience and analysis where "the self mutates into a classless cyborg, half-flesh, half-metal, where living means quick circulation through the technical capillaries of the mediascape" (Kroker, 1993, 21).

I will comment on a few of the ideas in the above quotes: "the creation of the postmodern body as war machine." This refers to Virilio's work on war and speed. Virilio quotes Charles Schreider: "We can imagine for the future a transformation (of reality) into video signals stored on tape."[3] Much has been made of Virilio's comments with regard to the Gulf War and its relationship to Jean Baudrillard's ideas about simulacra. Virilio suggests that consciousness will disappear as a result of the increased speed of technology. Consequently, human beings will have no "direct" perceptions available to them (Virilio 104). Ironically, this resituates the image *inside* the human body and explains Kroker's assertion that people have become part machine, part human. It is a fundamental error, a collapse of levels. Consciousness becomes not only a reflection of the technologies that humans use, but the mind (in this case) evolves into a transparent representation of the machine.

Culturally, of course, this idea circulates with great power and attraction. The *Robocop* film series is only one of many such examples. The film, *The Mask*, represents the apotheosis of special effects from support for narrative into the very substance of storytelling—the human body can be sculpted into any shape or form through digitalization. The attraction of the machine as formulated by Virilio and Kroker is that consciousness is transformed into a programmable semirobotic mechanism. The imaginary becomes the vehicle through which the mechanical-human interface takes on a form and a shape. Hence the metaphors of the nervous system and the blood stream as electrical and the use of terms like "plugged in" to explain our connection to computers. These metaphors increasingly circulate at an autonomous level. They do not

2. Arthur Kroker, *The Possessed Individual: Technology and the French Postmodern* (Montreal: New World Perspectives, 1993), 20–21.
3. Paul Virilio, *The Aesthetics of Disappearance*, tr. Philip Beitchman (New York: Semiotext(e), 1991), 104.

so much "bring to life" as they take on "a life of their own."[4] All of this is cast as Darwinian, as inevitable. This brings up further questions of circuitry and connections; the terminology expels subjectivity into a border zone where the digital language of computer programming creates the context within which human beings respond to their own speech, creativity, and actions, as if they have been dispossessed of the power to remake them.[5]

A further example of this tug-of-war between possession and dispossession are the suggestions by Arthur and Marilouise Kroker in their introduction to *The Last Sex: Feminism and Outlaw Bodies* where they propose a radically new definition of "transgendered" sexuality in which conventional definitions of male and female disappear into "the third sex." "Neither male (physically) nor female (genetically) nor their simple reversal, but something else: a virtual sex floating in an elliptical orbit around the planet of gender that it has left behind, finally free of the powerful gravitational pull of the binary signs of the male/female antinomies in the crowded earth scene of gender. A virtual sex that is not limited to gays and lesbians but which is open to members of the heterosexual club as well and one that privileges sexual reconciliation rather than sexual victimization. Intersex states, therefore, as a virtual sex that is finally liberated from sacrificial violence."[6] They compare virtual sex to anamorphosis (a technique of image distortion through which the image can only be seen and recovered by the use of mirrors at very specific angles to the picture), an "aesthetic space" never full, but whose fragments, nevertheless, yield results. The mirrors of virtual sex are oblique and indirect, but not without effect, not repressive—a form of virtual liberation. Yet there is another definition of anamorphosis I would like to briefly examine. It is the "hidden," even unconscious subtext of the Kroker strategy to virtuality, and it is profoundly beholden to an approach to cultural analysis which priviliges the role of the masculine. Anamorphosis as a term is used in the sciences to talk about the

---

4. See "Out of Control," in *Ars Electronica*, ed. Karl Gerbel (Linz: Landesverlag, 1991), especially the essay entitled "Mechanization Takes Command—Verses from Giedion's Bible" by Paul DeMarinis and Laetitia Sonami, pp. 51–60. The article examines the work of Siegfried Giedion who wrote a book in 1947 entitled *Mechanization Takes Command*. Giedion was very concerned with the way machines become transparent to their users. He has a lovely anecdote about the bathtub belonging to the "category of external ablution." DeMarinis and Sonami respond: "Machines afford us a sort of trinity of dialog among self-as-subject/machine/self-as-object. The barber's chair, the Barbie doll, the desktop computer, the smart bomb—each mute object is a participant in a discussion of which it understands nothing" (57).

5. Sherry Turkle analyzes this phenomenon from an historical and ethnographic point of view in *The Second Self: Computers and the Human Spirit* (New York: Simon and Schuster, 1984), esp. the Introduction and Part 3.

6. Arthur and Marilouise Kroker, "The Last Sex: Feminism and Outlaw Bodies," in *The Last Sex: Feminism and Outlaw Bodies*, ed. Arthur and Marilouise Kroker (Montreal: New World Perspectives, 1993), 18.

gradual evolution of plants and animals, an ascending progression in which there are changes in form and shape. It also refers to the "acquisition in certain anthropods of additional body segments after hatching" (Webster's Third New International Dictionary). Here the full force of the Darwinian paradigm comes into the forefront of the Kroker strategy. It is an approach that privileges not the body, but the eyes as appendages. It is a "perspectival world of the last sex" (Kroker and Kroker 19) in which vision is translated into a new form of bodily expression, where the hands and the arms, the trunk, the legs and the genitalia evolve into receptacles for seeing. The possibly liberating move beyond traditional definitions of gender and sexuality is subsumed under the sign of a body without a past, a body now making an evolutionary jump into a neutral zone where the senses don't clash. How, and why have we arrived at this point with regard to images? Why are electronic images the pivot for this new exploration of human identity and sexuality? As Gerald Edelman puts it, the approach taken by the Krokers (and celebrated in such journals as *Mondo 2000* and *Wired*) sees mind-body relations as if the "software is independent of the hardware" (Edelman 239). If, on the other hand, "the mind is embodied," then the metaphor of consciousness as computer dissolves in the face of a complexity that far exceeds our capacity to handle or control it. If the body becomes an extension of the eyes then relations of mind and behavior are suddenly unveiled as causal. Technology, which, for all of its rich diversity can nevertheless be created and destroyed by human beings, jumps the evolutionary ladder. The mind is unveiled as nothing more or less than a reflection of the way it has been constructed. The theological impulse here is to somehow stand outside of the architectural design, to see oneself plugging the holes, as it were, and to reduce human consciousness almost entirely to a function of behavior. Human consciousness, which far exceeds our capacities of description and analysis *turns into what can be seen.*

Paul Virilio says, "the irradiation of the mediascape by a logistics of perception that work according to the rules of the virtual world." What are the rules of the virtual world? How do we inhabit a "place" that does not exist? For Virilio we become the ultimate viewer, forever sedentary, "the extension of domestic inertia."[7] This is linked to the increasing transparency of the image as we travel from its borders into the eye of the camera. The model of mind here is fundamentally no different from a causal one. The linkage is determined by relations over which subjects have little or no control. In this definition, subjectivity collapses the moment it recognizes how images form the body and the eyes. As I have tried to show, this is actually the traditional model of image-subject relations.

7. Paul Virilio, "The Last Vehicle," in *Looking Back on the End of the World*, ed. Dietmar Kamper and Christoph Wulf, tr. David Antal (New York: Semiotext(e) Foreign Agents Series, 1989), 109.

Ironically, it is the image in all of its forms that nurtures this frenzy of dissolution and recreation, which is the feeding ground for the engineered blood our culture manufactures as nourishment for its simulacra. Yet the electronic image survives in an in-between zone, used for so many different purposes, that it is more difficult than ever to find a vantage point for analysis and criticism. This may well be Kroker's error, to have confused the confusion with reality, and with Virilio, to have assumed that the paths of perception never diverge or contest each other. The apocalyptic tone is a necessary component of this. It encourages a *fin de millenium* despair, tinged by a kind of demonic inevitability about the very ground upon which virtual machinery will be built. It abstracts the Malaysian or Taiwanese components factory and encourages the conflation of the body with the eyes. It looks in upon the domestic scene and blinds itself to conflict and negates the power of language to overcome if not transform the image and the computer program. (Computer hackers are our new frontier adventurers who undermine the "solidity" and integrity of the network. The people who plant viruses play a similar role.) Most importantly, it does not recognize the meeting places in between image and identity, where people struggle sometimes in confusion and other times with great clarity about their encounters with new technologies.

Yet, the questions that come to mind are, why believe that images in any form can ever produce these effects? Why follow a line of thought that reproduces the idea that the virtual means the loss of mind and the body, the loss of self, the conflation of the visual and consciousness? I will examine video and television images over the next two chapters in order to explore these arguments. I am fascinated by the ease with which our culture slips into the total seduction of images and then jumps back in horror. I am reminded of my first experience rollerblading. I took off at great speed, delighted to be able to skate in the summer. But, I had no idea how to stop. The braking system is at best primitive. I flew onto the grass, tumbled and slid, and when I finally came to a stop my body was bruised and my clothes were stained. The subjective boundaries here are fluid and relatively unpredictable. I rejoice in the accident for what it taught me. I threw out the videotape demonstration that came with the rollerblades.

In a memorable scene from his film *Speaking Parts*, the director, Atom Egoyan, has one of the main characters seated in front of an array of video monitors in a television mausoleum. There she looks at images of her dead brother and reflects upon her loss. She can create a field of projections haunted by the ghosts of her memories, and her memories can take on a form. Yet, as she gazes at the televisions, Claire is sad, distant, wistful. The television monitor is within reach; its shapes and forms beckon her. At the same time, her brother's image fades from view. For all of its strength, the video image still departs. The bodies inhabiting the monitor are only as strong as the memories she confers upon them.

This is a place of death and fantasy, a context within which both can be actualized and denied. The simultaneity of being in two worlds at once *is* the world of simulacra. Experiential maps can be traced out and nobody need worry about the crisis of position or politics.[8] The virtual promises precisely this kind of control, but in the end our bodies may resist the loss of the sensuous—the unimagined and unprogrammable consequences of direct contact between human beings and their creations.[9] I will return to these points in my discussion of Jean Baudrillard. For the moment, suffice to say, it is video and electronic images that carry within them many of the contradictions and potential I have been discussing throughout this book, and I must admit to being within this game of seduction and loss, even as I try to take some distance from it.

Video Activism

Portable video use has exploded worldwide. Since its appearance in the late 1960s video has become the medium of choice for larger and larger numbers of people. Community, gay and feminist organizations, environmental and social advocacy groups, mainstream and alternative political and cultural formations in North America and Europe have made active use of video for information gathering, political agitation, artistic experimentation, and the distribution and dissemination of local and transnational debates and ideas. Very powerful claims have been made for this technology. One of the most important has been that portable video has initiated a new era in the use of visual instruments, because its availability and relative cheapness have encouraged radical changes in creative and political work with images both at a grassroots and mainstream level. This claim, accompanied by the idea that portable video is also an instrument of democratization, has been the impulse for much of the written analysis and video production of the last three decades.[10]

In southern or Third World countries, video has been embraced in much the same manner as radio was for a previous generation, as a technology for training, education, organizing, information gathering, political agitation, and cultural preservation. Even more importantly, the appropriation of video has

8. For a fuller exploration of the film, see, Ron Burnett, "Speaking of Parts," in *Speaking Parts: Atom Egoyan*, ed. Marc Glassman (Toronto: Coach House Press, 1993).

9. Manuel De Landa takes a different position from mine. See "Virtual Environments and the Emergence of Synthetic Reason," *South Atlantic Quarterly* 92.4 (1993): 793–816.

10. See Clifford Scherer, "The Videocassette Recorder and Information Inequity," *Journal of Communication* 39 (1989): 94–103; Lili Berko, "Surveying the Surveilled: Video, Space and Subjectivity," *Quarterly Review of Film and Video* 14.1/2 (1992): 61–91; Sean Cubitt, *Timeshift: On Video Culture* (New York: Routledge, 1991); Manuel Alvarado, *Video World-Wide* (London: John Libbey, 1988); John Hanhardt ed. *Video Culture: A Critical Investigation* (Layton, Ut.: Peregrine Smith, 1988); the special issue of *Communications*, entitled *Video*, published by Seuil in Paris in 1988.

been seen as a key way for economically deprived communities to gain some measure of democratic control over information and communication sources now controlled either by the state or multinational corporations. This grass-roots activity has had a profound influence on the way very different communities in many parts of the world have thought about communications. I will only mention a few examples here: Kayapo Indians in Brazil, portapacks on their shoulders, waging politics through the dissemination of information;[11] satellite receivers on the rooftops of houses in India used for formal and informal networks of information and India's broad-based democratic media group, CENDIT, which makes extensive use of video in rural communities; organizations such as Video News Service in South Africa, New Dawn in Namibia, TV for Development in Uganda, Capricorn Video Unit in Zimbabwe, Centro de Trabalho Indilgenista in Brazil and Asia Visions in the Philippines; Vidéazimut, an international video organization that represents the activities of thirty of the major groups and institutions using video in Latin America, Africa and Asia, and so forth.

There are positive and negative aspects to these activities. The diasporic character and history of the vast majority of the world's communities, the relentless problems of the postcolonial era, the environmental and social consequences of overdevelopment and underdevelopment have transformed the context within which new technologies like video operate. There are very few communities in the Third World not involved to some degree with emerging technologies of communication. These links between the old and the new, between societies in transition and communities undergoing a variety of complex changes, has altered the landscape of meanings within which communications technologies operate. However one puts it (the shift from the modern to the postmodern, the movement from the colonial to the postcolonial), this hybridization has overwhelmed the more conventional critical and practical approaches taken to technologies such as video, television, and radio. The crucial question is, what conceptual, theoretical, and historical tools does one have to evaluate these changes and their accompanying practices?

The MacBride Commission in 1980[12] called for "structural changes to equalize and balance the world communication's order. Such balance is necessary, according to the proponents of the new order, if development—econom-

---

11. See the work of Terence Turner, an anthropologist at the University of Chicago, in *Visual Anthropology Review* 7.2 (1991); Michael Eaton, "Amazonian Video," in *Sight and Sound* 2.4 (1992); Judith Shulevitz, "Tribes and Tribulations," in *Film Comment* 26.2 (1990); and *Video in the Changing World*, ed. Nancy Thede and Alain Ambrosi (Montreal: Black Rose, 1991).

12. See the International Commission for the Study of Communication Problems (The MacBride Commission), *Many Voices, One World* (London: Kogan Page, 1980), and *World Communication Report* (Paris: UNESCO, 1989). The latter lists a long series of reports that have come out of various countries and constituencies.

ically, politically, socially and culturally—is to be effectively promoted. This approach sees communication as the infrastructure of and precondition for economic growth, and thus, development."[13] I will argue that most of the *categories* in place for analyzing the work that has grown out of this presumption, ranging from notions of participatory democracy to the horizontal nature of collective work with video, to the various paradigms for understanding the role of mainstream media, have been very weak. There has been a lack of critical and evaluative work, although there are many descriptive examples which end up justifying development and community work with communications.[14]

Artists have also gravitated to video in part because of its low cost and also because the medium encourages experimentation with images. There are now hundreds of video centers, some independent, others run by universities and museums, all engaged in activities that have legitimated video as a preferred medium for a variety of creative endeavors. The advent of multimedia in the middle of the 1980s has increased the hybridization of video and computer technology and has brought a variety of information systems together, with even greater potential for experimentation and research worldwide. One of the central presuppositions of this activity is that it enlarges the base of participants who use and watch the medium, because video incorporates so many different technologies and potential viewing sites. In fact, the term *video* seems to stand for any device that displays an electronic image. In that sense, it encapsulates all other media except television.

I will argue that the video art movement remains marginalized, in part because of its deeply felt antipathy to most forms of popular culture. Although there are many potential and important ways in which political video and art video could connect, they operate in distinct realms, economically, culturally, and at the level of distribution.

At another level, the advent of cheaper and cheaper camcorders with near professional results (especially with Hi-8, which generates near broadcast-quality images from a camcorder) has encouraged the proliferation of informal networks of communication and exchange. An example of this mentioned above is Video News Service in South Africa, which operates through the exchange and placement of videocassettes in small communities throughout the country. These cassettes have become a precious commodity, as they are often proposed as the only source of alternative news for groups of people with limited access to broadcast technology. Video Sewa operates in India and is a

13. Hamid Mowlana and Laurie J. Wilson, *The Passing of Modernity: Communication and the Transformation of Society* (New York: Longman, 1990), 58.
14. See in particular the essay by Sara Stuart, "Access to Media: Placing Video in the Hands of the People," *Media Development* 36.4 (1989): 42–45, and Chinyere Stella Okunna, "Communication for Self-Reliance Among Rural Women in Nigeria," *Media Development* 39.1 (1992): 46–49.

unique example of the grassroots applications of low or narrowcast media which use smaller scale technologies to reach communities from within a local context: "Video SEWA is the video cooperative of the Self-Employed Women's Association, trade union of some 30,000 poor, self-employed women in Ahmedabad, India" (Stuart 45). Vidéazimut or the International Coalition for Audiovisuals for Development and Democracy (located in Montreal, Canada) has grown dramatically over the last four years. It works on the premise that alternative sources of information will encourage dramatic cultural, personal, and political transformations in the societies and people who make use of new technologies (they are now actively pursuing satellite and broadcast media to enlarge the distribution base for their work). Vidéazimut is made up of well over thirty organizations worldwide, from Peru and Mozambique to India and Hong Kong. Each of these often represent regions rather than countries and have a large number of smaller groups with whom they are associated. Vidéazimut has become a clearing house for the distribution of hundreds of videotapes shot by these groups.[15]

There is a need to more fully explore why this type of investment is being made in video and whether it reflects an idealism for which the criteria of evaluation are often self-serving. The active implication of nongovernmental organizations (NGOs) in these efforts to spread the use of video must be analyzed as a Western phenomenon, very much related to notions of development, aid, and economic growth. Most of the NGOs in the field are supported by Western governments and aid organizations, who are managing video in much the same manner as they might approach a project on educating peasant farmers in the better use of their land. In other words, the medium is being treated as if can serve the function of a formal and informal educational tool. In addition video, like radio, is often described by NGOs as one of the most important vehicles for giving a voice to the disenfranchised.[16] The educational and media model in place here is derived from Paulo Freire and his work on the problems of literacy with South American peasants.[17] As we shall see, the political framework for these models developed in Western countries, in particular, Canada.

15. See *Clips*, the newsletter of *Vidéazimut*, No. 4, October 1993: "Founded in 1990, brings together people from the world of independent and alternative video and television from every continent. Together, its members act to promote the democratic practice of communication. They aim to broaden the participation by communities and movements from the South and the North in sound and image production," np.
16. See "Getting Involved: Communication for Participatory Development," by Ad Boeren, 47–60, and "Traditional and Group Media Utilization in Indonesia," by Manfred Oepen, 61–78, in *The Empowerment of Culture: Development Communication and Popular Media*, ed. Ad Boeren and Kes Epskamp (The Hague: Centre for the Study of Education in Developing Countries, 1992).
17. Paulo Freire, *Education for Critical Consciousness* (New York: Seabury Press, 1973).

The philosophy of "giving a voice" was recently critiqued in an editorial in the newsletter, *Interadio*, which is produced by the World Association of Community Radio Broadcasters (also an NGO):

> More than any other mass communication medium, radio is accessible, affordable and easily appropriated by groups of people whose demands have traditionally been ignored by the mainstream media. Many marginalized groups are turning to community radio as a forum for expression, by-passing the corporate and state media rather than fighting to access them. Community radio often speaks of the need "to have a voice" and of the necessity of establishing community stations as independent voices. Community radio has also become known as the "voice of the voiceless" in many parts of the world. However, while the term voiceless may well refer to those who have traditionally been denied access to the media, labelling community radio as the voice of the voiceless demeans the very essence of community radio. The phrase voiceless overlooks centuries of oral tradition which preceded radio technology (traditions which are especially strong in Asia, Africa and among indigenous populations). It can also be interpreted as implying that people do not have a voice in their communities and in their everyday lives unless they have some kind of access to the media.[18]

This is an important caution but the issues it raises are generally overlooked, if not subsumed by the ongoing need to keep producing videotapes and radio shows. In order to more fully understand how cultures in transition interact with new technologies, the communities affected would have to "educate" the outsiders who bring the technology to them. Yet even the distinctions in operation here between the inside and the outside have been undermined, if not overcome, by the rapid spread of communications technologies. The result is that few societies are now without some experience of video, television, and radio. The various distinctions of otherness that have guided the introduction of video have changed almost entirely. The result are social contexts in which communities have developed sophisticated media strategies at an aesthetic and political level, often far removed from the concerns of the NGO groups who bring the media with them.

Yet there is more to the notion of voice than what Vinebohm suggests. One of the main assumptions of community-based media activities in both the northern and southern hemispheres is that of empowerment. Voice stands in for all of the processes that supposedly lead to enhanced notions of community control of information and knowledge. "Dialogue is at the very heart of community access television. For this is a medium that is (or is supposed to be) interactive, user-defined and operating horizontally. A sharp contrast indeed to the centralized, one-way, top-down flow pattern of conventional media. This alternative communications system . . . has enormous potential to liberate the

18. Lisa Vinebohm, "The Power of Voice," *Interadio* 5.2 (1993): 2.

public from the controlled flow of information, experience and thought."[19] This quote summarizes many of the concerns of the alternative video movement worldwide. Aside from the conventional bow to the hegemonic influences of mass media (which foreground notions of dominance, monopoly, and democratic response), there is the key thought of liberation from control, the opening up of hitherto closed spaces of experience, and the unveiling of different ways of thinking.

Goldberg doesn't define the meaning of "community" and the resulting sense she has that people, once empowered in the use of the medium, will gain a new understanding of their own viewpoints on the world, if not of their politics. Why and how does the experience of images create the open-endedness Goldberg proposes? "Like the medical treatments of the barefoot doctors, community television was a shared tool belonging to a community of equals. However, in the community TV model, the distinction between 'doctor' and 'patient' breaks down. The medium becomes a tool of community self-healing" (Goldberg 10). I will return to this central notion (self-healing) when I discuss the therapeutic framework within which so much community media operates.

Empowerment begins with the presumption that something is missing either in the community or in people's lives. The intervention of the videomakers, accompanied by the use of the medium on the part of "ordinary" people, supposedly leads to shifts in identity and further claims of self-determination. As we shall see, these claims must be examined very carefully if we are to avoid idealizing video and its effects. Video activism is framed by an urgency intimately related to the grassroots use that has been made of the medium. The sense that video will somehow break through the smokescreens manufactured by mainstream media and communicate directly to people in the community has played an important role in the way in which commentators, critics, and analysts have responded to video as a *medium*. This deeply felt and quite symbiotic link between theory and practice is what distinguishes the writing on video from writing on other cultural activities. It is also the focal point for practitioners.

Yet how different is the creative and political use of a medium for communicative purposes, from the viewing of videotapes or shows on television? There is an underlying premise that viewing images is somehow less effective than working with the medium and then seeing the results. This is based on the presumption that viewing is a passive activity. A paradoxical bind comes into play here. The activity of creating meaningful messages centers on the fact that they will ultimately be viewed, as much by creators as by outsiders. So the

19. Kim Goldberg, *The Barefoot Channel: Community Television as a Tool for Social Change* (Vancouver: New Star Books, 1990), 6.

practical and theoretical problems of spectatorship, comprehension, and articulation are continually in play both within mainstream and alternative contexts. The assumption that the former is a place of passivity contributes to a poorly thought out anger at the popular cultural frameworks within which all electronic images circulate. Even the appropriation of these images[20] sees television as a cultural aggressor.

In the same Birnbaum volume, Norman Klein imagines himself as Alexis de Tocqueville arriving from France today and quotes a modern version of de Tocqueville: "In America, all political and cultural matters seem to be arbitrated on the lit surface of a convex piece of glass. Americans sit for hours, rather like fish outside their fish bowls. They stay in partial darkness within their homes, and watch faintly resolved images flickering from the glass. Since there is relatively little continuity between one half-hour and the next on these television shows, even between ten minute intervals, one can only wonder what the larger mental process has become for the television viewer."[21] It is this objectification of the viewing process (which has proven itself to be longstanding and fundamental in nearly all of the literature about alternatives to mainstream television) that undermines the creative intervention of artists like Birnbaum. These generalizations produce an audience incapable of dealing with the supposed fish bowl in which it lives. The metaphor itself sits at the edge of a dangerous precipice where the audience often tumbles off into a place without meaning or subjectivity. This is yet another example of the conflation of the mental with the visual and the predictable way the entire process becomes derivative. It is as if the televisual image suddenly opens up a window into mind. This is once again a case in which the medium is not so much the message as we become what we see or look at.

A Resistance to Theory

What makes a politically urgent message more persuasive as an image than other forms of communication? Do all of the contingent factors that govern

20. I am thinking here of the many ways network television, for example, is plundered and then reedited or reshaped in inventive and creative ways. The work of Dara Birnbaum is exemplary in this regard, especially the work which she has done with the "Wonder Woman" television show. She calls this popular image video. "Essentially, I attempted in my videowork from 1978–1982 to slow down the technological speed of television and arrest moments of TV-time for the viewer, which would then allow for examination and questioning. All the videoworks from 1978–80 documented in this book are constructed from TV-fragments, reconstructing conventions of television, deploying them as readymades for the late twentieth century." Dara Birnbaum, *Rough Edits* ed. Benjamin H. D. Buchloh (Halifax: The Press of the Nova Scotia College of Art and Design, 1987), 15.
21. Norman M. Klein, "Audience Culture and the Video Screen, in Dara Birnbaum, *Rough Edits* ed. Benjamin H. D. Buchloh (Halifax: The Press of the Nova Scotia College of Art and Design, 1987), 98.

the production of meaning in a video (as in any image) contribute to the sense that meaningful exchanges can take place? What blockages are there to learning? Is the concept of horizontal participation an idealized projection on the part of the community workers who use video? How can one analyze the social and discursive dynamic that governs, creates, sustains, and sometimes subverts efforts to work collectively or simply to try and understand a particular message?

In asking these questions from a critical rather than a positive standpoint, in no way do I want to belittle or even underestimate the importance of community efforts to use video. Rather, my aim is to show how little time is spent on the issues of empowerment, participation, democratic control, communication, and comprehension, albeit that these words are used in an almost continuous fashion to construct the discourse surrounding video practices. I believe, given the fundamentally intercultural nature of many of the productions now circulating, that these issues must be dealt with if there is to be a more profound understanding of the political implications of the work. Yet, I also believe that after nearly twenty-five years of effort, the utopian presumptions underlying the community use of video have not been evaluated in great depth. To what degree are communities likely to evaluate a technology which, from the outset, potentially reconfigures their own modes of communication? To what degree have the proponents of this technology brought a critique with them? How well has our own culture understood video? Given the "newness" of video, it is somewhat ironic that the critical analysis that should precede its introduction has not played a more significant role in its use in the West and then its placement in the Third World.

Part of the problem I have faced in researching the organizations involved in using and promoting video is that so much of what is being made is treated as information in the most ephemeral sense of the word. Although there is some discussion of aesthetics and form, the discourse is generally quite limited, in part because there is seems to be no critical vocabulary with which to examine and analyze the material produced. Videotapes circulate and are shown to audiences, but the evaluations that follow are short-lived and rarely followed up. In addition, the arguments developed to describe and analyze the production of community or political videotapes don't often concern themselves with questions of *how* or whether images communicate meaning, and to what degree analytical tools were and are in place for explaining the various relationships among different forms of cultural production and discourse.

This resistance to theory and to critical practices, suffuses, if not dominates, the video movement. Can a video stand on its own? Can the "message" be transparently clear, even if the audience the video is addressing supposedly shares the premises of the communication? The videotapes depend upon the electronic image to do the work of revealing, if not creating, discursive spaces within which questions of identity and self can be addressed. But can the image play that role without a creative pedagogical strategy that extends far beyond the boundaries of the image? How can that strategy be enacted without a careful reflection on the history of the medium, on its aesthetic characteristics and formal properties, and crucially on its links to photography, the cinema, and television?

Some of these problems were addressed in a recent article by Kelly Anderson and Annie Goldson, entitled "Alternating Currents: Alternative Television Inside and Outside of the Academy."[22] The authors bemoan the lack of contact between academics and video practitioners. They make the claim that there is very little interest on the part of theorists to examine the history and development of alternative media in the United States as well as elsewhere.[23] Although they clearly underestimate the work that has been done, they pinpoint a serious gap in the thinking about community and alternative media. There is an underlying moral imperative to the notion of alternativity which locates critique and analysis within a framework of oppositions to nearly all aspects of mainstream culture. This becomes the centerpiece of an evaluative strategy which is then applied to the videotapes produced in a community context. In other words, the basis for comparison, the foundation upon which alternatives as such are created relies on the establishment of differing conceptions of the popular.

To what extent, then, is there some clarity with respect to the idea of alternativity? Anderson and Goldson suggest a number of approaches. Their first assumption is that community-based alternative television has a "precarious though binding relationship to the dominant economy of media production" (Anderson and Goldson 59). This refers to the various strategies that alternative producers and practitioners, as well as community workers, engage in with respect to funding, and the acquisition of resources and equipment. This in itself is a fascinating area because it is at the root of an economic activity rarely, if ever, measured. A number of objections could be raised here to

22. Kelly Anderson and Annie Goldson, "Alternative Television Inside and Outside of the Academy," in *Social Text* 35 (1993): 56–71.
23. The authors seem not to be aware of the work of John Downing, whose *Radical Media: The Political Experience of Alternative Communication* (Cambridge, Mass.: South End Press, 1984) attempts precisely to link historical and theoretical concerns with practical experience. Various monographs like *Community Communications: The Role of Community Media in Development* by Francis J. Berrigan (Paris: UNESCO, 1979); *Access: Some Western Models of Community Media*, ed. Francis J. Berrigan (Paris: UNESCO, 1977); short articles such as, "Visual Media, Cultural Politics, and Anthropological Practice: Some Implications of Recent Uses of Film and Video Among the Kayapo of Brazil," by Terence Turner, *Commission on Visual Anthropology Review*, Spring 1990; and the work coming out of the *Group Media Journal* in Germany reflect an ongoing concern to grapple with the various issues that arise out of alternative use of the media. Also see Roy Armes, *On Video* (New York: Routledge, 1988).

the suggestion that we are dealing with alternative production processes. The first is that lowcasting now makes use of increasingly sophisticated equipment. Although not as costly as conventional broadcast technology, the investment can be considerable. Second, any effort to go beyond the immediate availability of basic resources involves grant requests to government or local agencies, corporations or foundations. This issue has been debated before and the argument always is that public or private aid pollutes, if not skews, the political track of advocacy that governs so much of the production at the community level. Yet what seems to be at stake here is precisely the idealizations of the "alternative" which sees itself outside of the very institutions to which it is beholden. This is a circuitous route, full of potholes, but the most important point to keep in mind is that the terrain of practice that can be opened up by relying on an alternativity that tries to operate outside of the conventional economic constraints any technology imposes, may be extremely limited.

Video and the Public Sphere

Yet this could become a more dialogic process, and it could be more sensitive and aware of the institutional nexus within which it must operate, if there weren't such a strong dependence on the central idea of a dominant culture. There is no question that monopolies from Time Warner to News Corporation control the marketplace and recent moves toward consolidation on the part of telephone and cable companies in the United States presage even more complex, though not necessarily uniformly similar worldwide corporations. This is indisputable. But the terrain of communication, the place within which meanings as such are exchanged, interpreted, worked upon, is within the very communities that video activists want to politicize. If the model of dominance were to operate at the level, and with the intensity suggested by the relationship between mainstream and alternative, then the very people who inhabit those communities would themselves not be accessible (nor perhaps even interested in seeing anything different). It is because there is an economy of scale involved in the activity of community video that one can begin to talk about the grassroots and define with much greater precision what is meant by community. In so doing, the convenience of the opposition I have been discussing would dissolve.

In part, this is because there are so many aspects to a community's activities that traverse the boundaries between what is acceptable and what is not, so much heterogeneity to the relationship between institutions and people, that questions of power and how to address the powerful cannot be answered from within the hazy traditions promulgated and supported by the easy dichotomy of "alternative" and "mainstream." In some respects this opposition carries the same weight as the superstructure/base opposition that did so much to undermine creative, theoretical, and critical work on culture from within the Marxist tradition. There is a simplicity to the opposition which cannot be sustained any longer. It is perhaps more necessary than ever to unmask the weaknesses of an approach that cannot account for desire, pleasure, and the contradictory politics of incorporation which, it must be remembered, can be simultaneously experimental and coopted. A large number of distinctions should be introduced which will reinvigorate the meaning of all kinds of media practices, without locking them into an intellectually convenient oppositional structure. This can only be done by recognizing how heterogeneous the work of the media is, how it is possible for a film like *Wayne's World* to present an analysis and critique of community cable television and be, at one and the same time, irreverent and part of the mainstream, a moneymaker and a joke on American cultural values.

Lili Berko has suggested that the advent of the portapack in the late 1960s broke the hold of broadcast television on the technology of electronic images.

> The coupling of the portable videotape recorder (porta-pak) with the advent of the videocassette offered artists and social activists alike an opportunity to participate in the production of images that were to shape their culture. The most revolutionary aspect of the porta-pak was its mobility. Through the porta-pak, television production was not locked into a studio and the confines of the codes of such mediated experience. Through video, the mystique of production was shattered and the streets became equally important sites of textual inscription. Video soon became the vehicle through which the social world could be easily documented, the vehicle which would record the voices and the images of the Newark riots, or a Mardi Gras celebration; as such it proclaimed the public sphere to be its own.[24]

Berko's analysis of a shift to a new public sphere, of the reclaiming of a territory lost to mainstream media, stands at the juncture of an analytic strategy that has defined an entire generation of writers and practitioners in video. There are few texts or articles on video that have not made the claim for this break (which resonates with the symbolism of the sixties), and most have made it with reference to the history of mainstream media. The trajectory of influences and changes launched by portable video certainly foregrounded the need for a reevaluation of the way mainstream broadcasters operated. A debate resulted within the institution of television (primarily, at that point, the networks) and outside, among radically different conceptions of the public sphere and substantively, though not fully articulated differences, with respect to the process of communication. Much remains unexamined in this choice of ap-

24. Lili Berko, "Video in Search of a Discourse," in *Quarterly Review of Film Studies* 10.4 (1989): 289–307.

proach. The most important point is that the analytical framework for the study of television at that time was in its infancy; thus, definitions of mainstream media were quite weak. In fact, there were very few film departments in universities, let alone media or cultural studies. There were, however, a number of crucial "sites" where media like TV were analyzed, and for the most part they were dependent on communications theory as it had evolved from the 1930s[25] and on critical theory represented by the work of Adorno, Marcuse, Benjamin and Horkheimer or literary theory with such influences as Richard Hoggart and Raymond Williams. Additional work could be found in cultural anthropology and psychoanalysis. The period of the late sixties was characterized by efforts to bring this material together in order to create some theoretical parameters for the study of television. The intellectual boundaries for this work remained fluid for many years afterward and paralleled the growth of new imaging technologies.

I make this point because the attitude toward mainstream television underlying Berko's approach is based on a hegemonic view of the role of the media, with the result that porta-pack activity is analyzed as if the practice of alternative image creation was itself a sufficient, if not utopian reclamation of lost territory. This occupation of a new space and time was seen as a political act, with immediate impact upon the environments and people in which video was used and shown. (It was as if postwar grassroots politics had never existed or as if the many community-based movements of the fifties and sixties had not prepared the ground for using video in a more decentralized and local context.[26] Yet, the absence of contexts for the analysis of mainstream media in the late 1960s, (which was in part a result of the "newness" of television itself), suggests that the initial shift to a populist view of portable television technology was based on a fragmentary and often reductive presumption about mass forms of entertainment and learning. This oppositional framework continues to be the premise for much of present-day video practice and theory, which still does not grapple clearly with the problems of audience, performance, and learning with regard to electronic images. There is, therefore, a measure of continuity to the debate, an historical underpinning to the contrasting attitudes taken toward media technologies that address both large and small audiences. The various definitions of impact and change which underpin

25. Two of the most important were Annenberg and the University of Chicago.
26. It is particularly interesting that the evolution and growth of community media in Quebec would not have been possible without the earlier efforts that had grown out of the social work movement. Many of the people who became most active with video had already worked within the context of grassroots politics. See Marc Raboy, *Old Passions, New Visions: Social Movements and Political Activism in Quebec* (Toronto: Between the Lines, 1986).

notions of grassroots activity and democratic access have been used to give credibility to the practice of portable video. These need to be dramatically re-thought in the context of a broader approach to media history.

Media Theory and the Electronic Image

To begin with, some preliminary thoughts on the theoretical approach taken with respect to video: I am concerned with the fact that many of the debates about the media in general (broadcast and lowcast) refer to electronic images as if they are texts. In addition, and to extend the linguistic metaphor even further, most discussions of electronic images talk about the "reading" of image-texts as if there were a continuity, at a formal and content level between image and language (this is usually conflated into notions of coding and de-coding with regards to the viewer). In some respects this is an "old" debate and I have reflected on it with respect to the cinema in chapter 3. But it seems to me as if the semiotic presumptions that underly the appropriation of linguis-tic concepts for the study of the media have been naturalized.[27] This may be the result of the lack of debate about interpretation and audience within dis-cussions of television and lowcast media. It may also be the result of an over-emphasis on the textual properties of the media (although the last thing I want to suggest is that we are ever "outside" of language), simply because we are used to analyzing our own experience of viewing, as if there is an equivalence between what we say and write and what we have seen.[28] It may also be the consequence of the analytical and critical challenge the viewing of electronic images generates. This challenge is partly the result of the way the term *image* stands in for all that is visual—images act as the metaphorical fulcrum upon which the arts and media are conceptually balanced. Images also seem to have a life of their own outside of the constraints and potential of language and discourse. This means that the work of interpretation balances on a variety of tensions. These are centered on the many possible dimensions of response, which range from distinguishing external image from personal experience, to the emotions that flow from viewing. How can sometimes related but often disparate elements at the level of expression, aesthetics, and form be con-nected? Images are the focal point for these processes, but by no means the end

27. A recent example of this is Judith Butler's "Endangered/Endangering: Schematic Rac-ism and White Paranoia," in *Reading Rodney King/Reading Urban Uprising,* ed. Robert Gooding-Williams (New York: Routledge, 1993), 15–22, which raises many fascinating is-sues but rarely addresses the problems of talking about Rodney King as image. Instead, the interpretive strategy privileges textuality to such a degree that the media events surround-ing King's beating are pushed into the background.

28. A recent work by art historian, Barbara Maria Stafford, makes a poignant plea for more analysis and greater depth in the thinking about images. *Body Criticism: Imaging the Unseen in Enlightenment Art and Medicine* (Cambridge, Mass.: MIT Press, 1991)

point. The boundaries are flexible and this makes the challenge of analysis all the more complex.

Of equal importance is the fact that images are hybridized agglomerations of expression, mixing, and sometimes matching a variety of different discursive, visual, and oral elements. As cultural hybrids, images are used as if they simultaneously *block* and *unveil* truth, reality, ways of seeing and understanding. They refer to the general (as in, that is the image of men in the media) and the specific (for example, the image of a gun in the film *Dirty Harry*). They can politicize and depoliticize (e.g., that you are a passive instrument of television if you watch a lot of it). Yet, the question of how images generate this wide variety of possibilities, that is, questions of meaning, comprehension, communication, and use-value, are rarely theorized to a satisfying level. The best example of this contradiction at work can be found in the educational system which simultaneously frowns upon popular culture, accuses its students of illiteracy, and makes extensive use of the media in the classroom. As we shall see, the *ambivalence* if not aggressivity toward popular culture extends across many different activities in our culture (and this may come as a surprise to cultural analysts who think that this particular bias has been overcome). But how for example can films or videotapes be shown in the classroom, if there is a ground-level antipathy toward the images produced by MTV, for example? Where are the cultural connections here and how do they become disconnected? What makes popular culture an enemy in precisely the context where it needs to be discussed?

I would trace the ambivalence to notions of pedagogy as they are used with respect to images. That is, in educational contexts, images are meant to be illustrations and as such they can function much as an overhead transparency does for a lecture. They are the pictures put into textbooks, the diagrams used to graphically illustrate an argument or a piece of research, pictures to point out meaning, a moving blackboard. The point here is that images and language coexist both as a result of their inherent differences and as a consequence of their fundamental similarities. Culturally, efforts to distill the meaning of the visual through words and vice versa is part of an uninterrupted process of appropriation and rejection. Yet care must be taken in transforming both partners in the exchange into mirrors of each other. Without the ability to speak about images there would be little point in watching them, yet nothing is gained if what is said is then made equivalent to what has been seen, or if the image is simply proposed as an illustration for an already existing argument.[29]

---

29. See David James's superb rendition of the contradictions of this debate in "inTerVention: the contents of negation for video and its criticism," in *Resolution: A Critique of Video Art*, ed. Patti Podesta (Los Angeles: Los Angeles Contemporary Exhibitions, 1986), 84–93.

There is an ambiguous link between the movement, in comparative terms, from image to language and back, and notions of authority. The excesses of the visual, the ability of the electronic image to be in many places at once, the impact of special effects—these and many other elements have a logic and an organizational form, which often precludes simple translation from visual experience to discourse (and thus make it hard to identify an author). Given all of this, the assumption that the image is somehow in control of experience remains central to discussions of its effects. How is this connection made? It is often quite difficult to articulate and explain the images that circulate through our culture on an everyday basis. There seems to be a gap among different levels of comprehension and the highly developed intentional and professional frameworks within which most electronic images are created. Rather than allowing for these gaps and recognizing them as an opening onto a terrain of possibly contested meanings, the effort is to close down the "space in between" so as to validate the communicative efficacy of the medium involved.

It is in this sense that electronic images are often described as having a much greater authority than they can possibly have. And it is also in this sense that most images are boxed into a variety of discursive and analytic models that give order and structure to the gaps.[30] This is where the equivalence between language and image enters. The presumption is that if the flow of images can be converted into a sentence, for example, or if the shots of a television show can be broken down into some kind of formal model, then access to meaning will be gained where none seemed possible or where great difficulties of articulation loomed. To some degree, though not entirely, this explains the attraction of the semiotic approach. The danger is that "formalism" eliminates subjectivity. Certainly, with respect to arguments about meaning, which include the communicative within their epistemological framework, it is difficult if not impossible to avoid generating formal models. Yet it is precisely because structures of communication inevitably draw upon *subjects* and are maintained, even at the institutional level, by carefully guarded subjective notions of what is valid as communication and what isn't, that the formal model can become a substitute for subjectivity rather than an explanation. In fact, the subjective can disappear because it is somehow seen as the surface of an effect that must be examined from another perspective.[31] This is of course basic to any scientific approach to the study of various phenomena in our society. But

30. The development of computer imagery changes this slightly, in part because the images are "self-generating" and also because their referential framework is so eclectic.
31. This may begin to explain the highly professionalized approach to image creation within broadcast television. The aim is to create a series of rules that will offset the inevitable breakdowns which occur when the subjective concerns of a camera operator, for example, intervene in the broadcast of the news. This becomes the focus for comedy in shows like *Murphy Brown*.

the impulse to adapt the scientific to the analysis of images leads to a reductive approach to subjectivity which creates what John Searle has characterized as "observer-independent features."[32]

Learning from Video Images

Community video centers itself on "*the* message." This is directly related to the presumption that activist videotapes have to be transparently clear in what they say. The model of communication in use here relies on the audience. If viewers don't understand the message then they haven't understood the intentions of the video—that is perhaps why so many of the videotapes are like political leaflets or billboards. Paradoxically, as I shall discuss in a moment, the tapes share similar notions of pedagogy with leaflets, similar definitions of what works as communication and what doesn't. They depend upon the electronic image to do the work of revealing if not creating discursive spaces within which questions of identity, self, and politics can be addressed.

Another aspect of this debate about strategies of meaning creation is the rather negative (and sometimes justified) response practitioners have to theorizations about the medium they are using. This doesn't just reflect the classical differences between theory and practice. What must be understood with respect to video is that a new process is afoot, for which video is simply a harbinger. This new process(ing), reflected to some degree in the claims made for "virtual" technologies, challenges the activity of "writing" theory. Although media theorists are quite prepared to acknowledge that "something" is different, they very rarely work out those differences within the context offered by the instruments themselves. This is of course being done by media creators, who are in a sense developing theories *through* their practice. On another level, it seems clear that the binary nature of the theory/practice division offers little in the way of clarification about the kinds of breaks, shifts, and changes that I have been discussing. Below, I will examine whether community video (and indeed art video) in fact does offer something new or innovative, which encourages a different approach to the activities of writing theory and practicing, what I will call video politics.

In part, the orientation of video analysis centers on the idea that to use a camera is a "kind" of writing, with all of the contingent elements of speech built into the process as well. ("Video is inherently interactive, it has the technological potential to liberate the spectator from the authorial power of the artist/videomaker as well as the video artist from the regressive production of closed texts, texts whose meaning has been locked by either the artist's own authorial voice or that of the institution through which his/her work is being

32. John Searle, *The Rediscovery of Mind* (Cambridge, Mass.: MIT Press, 1992), 119.

shown" [Berko 1989, 293]). Unlike previous historical periods during which new visual media have been introduced, portable video encourages, by its simplicity and automatic controls, an almost utopian notion of the power to create and speak. In community video this pushes the question of exchange to a different level. It is as if the medium and the uses to which it is put generate an idealization of communication based on groups of people gathering together to view each other's work or the videotapes of creators who purport to represent them. Paradoxically, there is very little discussion in these public situations, because the saying, so to speak, has already happened, through and with the electronic image. This contradiction then, between the idealized version of communication and exchange, and the difficulties of creating public contexts in which discussion will take place, is as much a pedagogical problem as it is a difficulty with the approach taken to the medium and to electronic images in general.

Writing in 1983, at the tail end of the first wave of political activity with video (before the advent of much cheaper technology), Leonard Henny made the following claim: "Thus, video as an organizing tool has proven to be useful, provided that it plays only a part in a well thought-through strategy of community work. 'Instant video' as had happened in the sixties, has less and less of a chance of succeeding, since people have become used to sophisticated video programmes on television. Very few people will now watch a programme just because it is on video (as a novelty). They tend to only really watch it as long as it is watchable and/or relevant to their concerns."[33] The difficulty with Henny's statement is that he is making a series of assumptions about the viewer for which he provides no clear explanation. Assumptions about what is watchable or not are ultimately assumptions about spectator position. Henny suggests a level of subjectivity to the viewer which makes him or her dependent upon the video image within a communicative loop that is self-determining. Although he makes passing reference to the more general work that has to be done in the community, the details of working with video as a pedagogical tool are passed over.

Yet it is *in* the community, among viewers, that many different strategies of analysis of images have evolved. These cannot be accessed through video showings. The discursive framework here is far more extensive than the temporal and spatial limitations of a video presentation would suggest. In fact, this is a problem of teaching and learning, of venues for open discussion, of community halls and schools, in other words, of cultural activity, which so profoundly exceeds the limitations of the politically charged presentation of a video, that the question of how and where to discuss these issues can rarely be

33. Leonard Henny, "Video and the Community," in *Using Video*, ed. P. W. Dowrick and S. J. Biggs (London: John Wiley & Sons, 1983), 175.

reduced to the moment of viewing itself. On the other side of this argument are the extraordinary possibilities offered by the presentation of a video made by the people who are themselves simultaneously playing the role of viewer and critic, analyst and practitioner. Yet this is neither the panacea suggested by video activists, nor is it necessarily the base upon which new ideas and perceptions can be built. The entire process is far more precarious and far less utopian than community activists assume.

The most personal example I have of this are the video production classes which I have been teaching for over twenty years. Although I always encourage, if not demand, discussion, and although I suggest and sometimes impose a variety of interpretive strategies for the videotapes students produce, they rarely say much of substance about their creations. On the other hand, they are quite willing to write journals, to work in groups, to engage in the process of generating a video. Once the tape is finished, however, the need to create a communicative context disappears. The tapes stand on their own. I used to find this very frustrating and to some degree, still do. My frustrations are compounded by assertions from colleagues that this is evidence of "illiteracy" (verbal and written) on the part of the students. Their unwillingness to participate in a critical dialogue is seen as a crucial example of popular culture's impact on their lives. Somehow, their exposure to images has polluted, if not perverted their capacity to engage with and use their discursive abilities. I find this argument not only unappealing, but deeply suspect.

The *resistance* to writing and to talking about video does have a great deal to do with the medium (as well with the way the educational system valorizes traditional language studies over all other forms of expression). I don't want this argument to essentialize video, nor do I want to suggest a specificity to the medium that somehow encourages a discriminatory attitude toward other media, but I do want to suggest that the creation of meaning in this context reflects a profoundly different agenda. The general tenor of arguments around this issue lock electronic images into "low cultural" notions of entertainment and passivity. The presumption of lack and absence, of loss of meaning, both within the communal context of television viewing and within the use of video for personal and public reasons, has blinded critics to the changes that electronic images have engendered. It is meaningless to conflate the act of writing with videomaking or to suggest that the use of the camera is equivalent to the way a pen might be used to write an essay or a story. In both cases there are of course shared experiences, if not shared assumptions, but the results are dramatically different. After nearly forty years of television and three decades of video use, both of which have expanded exponentially within the public sphere, the time has come to look very differently upon the act of image creation, communication, and understanding. It is with that aim in the mind that the following comments attempt to recontextualize the way we view video as a medium. I will return to the question of language and learning with regard to electronic images at a later point. Suffice to say that the resistance to the written word cannot be attributed to one or even many sources within our culture. Nor would I simply want to accede to the simplification that Western cultures are now entering an "oral" and "visual" phase that inevitably marginalizes the written text. What is not "visual" about reading a book?

Video Politics and Communication

The assessments that have accompanied the use of video (not limited to the popular press but also suffusing a variety of journals, television shows, and public policy reports) have concerned themselves primarily with the impact of video on the public at large.[34] They have been guided by a set of presumptions about viewing, images and truth, the role of video as a window onto the world, its special qualities and potential as an artistic and political device, and most importantly as an innovative technology, which has helped launch and sustain a new type of information exchange. The concept of innovation is crucial to the way the medium has been understood and historicized—with an overwhelming emphasis on its newness, and on its potential to fundamentally alter the people and societies it touches.[35]

However, there is also a paradoxical attitude of excitement and wariness when it comes to video. On the one hand, the discourses used to describe the process promote the idea that new technologies like video are somehow able to *outstrip* their progenitors and their users. Subjects, agents, the people who use new technologies are placed into the position of respondents, as if their discourse and their practice will *inevitably* be transcended by the technology. A rearguard struggle is then fought with the technology. An effort is made to rehumanize the machine, though its history is the result of human intervention and creativity to begin with.

On the other hand, video is promoted as perhaps the best way of democratizing processes of communication and providing access to the media, particularly for those presently excluded from power or conventional networks for the production and exchange of information. The literature on video is often apprehensive about its complexity as a medium, from creation to pres-

34. See U.S. Congress, Office of Technology Assessment, *Critical Connections: Communication for the Future*, OTA-CIT-407 (Washington, D.C.: U.S. Government Printing Office, January 1990). Two key chapters in this report are "New Technologies and Changing Interdependencies in the Communication Infrastructure," and "The Impact of New Technologies on Communication Goals and Policymaking."

35. The phenomena of evaluation of new technologies by the media themselves reached its peak with "Nightline," which recently featured an extended documentary entitled *Revolution in a Box*. Ted Koppel narrated the changes which both television and portable video have produced.

entation, and yet it eagerly embraces the potential of video with regard to communication.

The historical origins of this ambivalence can be found in the long and intertwined history of the documentary and ethnographic cinema, which has generally confused the differences between information and communication, as if the creation of the former inevitably leads to a mastery of the latter. To make matters even more complex, there are the influences derived from the use of film for educational purposes, which have shadowed the development of documentary aesthetics (and all media oriented toward learning) since the 1920s. There are powerful links between 1930s Griersonian concepts of didacticism and the presuppositions that have guided the use of film and video in the community. One of the earliest examples of this was a study and project conducted by L. A. Notcutt and G. C. Latham.[36] The work was carried out with the help of the Carnegie Foundation, some large mining corporations based in England, the Department of Social and Industrial Research, the Colonial Office, and the British Film Institute. Latham himself had been the Director of Native Education in what was then Northern Rhodesia. The language of analysis and description in this experiment alternates between empowerment through education and the image, and racist, demeaning comments about the peoples of Africa. In some respects, the book is foundational (in the negative sense) because its presuppositions about the impact of the medium on the peoples of Tanzania echo the modern concern for using images to educate, to change, even to liberate. There are links between this experiment and the early work of Sol Worth and John Adair, although the latter pair were far more progressive and sensitive to the issues of local control and cultural specificity than Notcutt and Latham.[37] The issues raised by Notcutt and Latham regarding the potential use of film for educational purposes are also mirrored in the 1960s and seventies when development organizations made extensive use of video as a tool of training in Third World countries.[38] In fact, many of the documents that purport to deal with the role of media in development rarely, if ever, examine the history of their own experimentation with the cultures and technologies they made use of.[39]

My point here is that the promotion of video as an *accessible* political tool

36. L. A. Notcutt and G. C. Latham, ed. *The African and the Cinema: An account of the Work of the Bantu Educational Cinema Experiment* (London: Edinburgh House Press, 1937).

37. Sol Worth and John Adair, *Through Navajo Eyes: An Exploration in Film, Communication and Anthropology* (Bloomington: Indiana University Press, 1972).

38. See Henry T. Ingle, *Communication Media and Technology: A Look at their Role in Non-Formal Education Programmes*. Washington D.C.; Information Center on Instructional Technology, 1974.

39. A good example of this amnesia is Henri Cassirer, *Mass Media in an African Context: An Evaluation of Senegal's Pilot Project*: No. 69, Reports and Papers on Mass Communication, Unesco, 1974.

for social change and aesthetic experimentation has not been examined with regard to the histories of radio and film, for example, let alone popular theater and performance, or local forms of cultural expression often not dependent on media as defined through European eyes. This disregard for the variety of strategies that communities all over the world have developed with respect to their own cultures is partially the result of an ideology that conflates the development of new technologies and innovation with social change. Over and over again one reads of the excitement of the experimenters as they enter communities or cultural contexts where, almost magically, the appearance of film or video will overcome hitherto unrealized blockages to knowledge, understanding, and communication.

In an experiment during the 1970s with video, the French *vidéaste* Fred Forest used video at a retirement home in France, describing as his theme the stimulation of the creativity of senior citizens *"par une action vidéo non-directive."* He lists the following basic goals:

—to dynamize human relations in the community through the use of video;
—to study how the seniors (who were all former construction workers) react to video and in general to the arrival of new instruments of communication;
—to allow the community to learn from its perceptions of its own activities;
—to modify the relationship between the seniors and their institution;
—to stimulate exchanges between individuals and the group;
—to liberate the creativity and imagination of the seniors;
—to allow them to give expression to their latent, unrealized needs (my translation.)[40]

These seven aims in some respects represented the core of the cultural and community-based expectations of videomakers during the 1970s and up to the present. In all instances, the expectation was that the image would somehow open up discourses and relationships hitherto repressed by the political and cultural situation in which the public found themselves. The personal, interpersonal, and the social would interact, producing a new public sphere and productively reengage participants in an evaluation of their identities and their political outlook.

Let me return for a moment to one of the aims Fred Forest enunciated in the above list. He says that he wants "to dynamize human relations in the community through the use of video." This is a standard theme derived from the use of film in a variety of social contexts since the 1930s. The genealogy of this idea is based on the presumption that to view oneself, one's situation or environment, or the community one is a part of, effectively repositions subjec-

40. Fred Forest, *Art Sociologique: Vidéo* (Paris: Union Génerale D'Edition, 1977), 75.

tivity. There is a sense in which the notion of document as video, video as document, leads to a conceptual link between the electronic image and presumptions about truth, but truth in this instance as a literalization not only of the way individuals in a community see themselves, but the strategic attitude they take to the representations they create. Forest works on the assumption that certain kinds of truth values held by people in the seniors' home will be altered by the arrival of the video and by its sensitive use. But what base is he starting from? In other words, to what degree are the seniors aware of their own identities and to what degree have they articulated that to each other? The expectation of change becomes the guiding principle here and the premise upon which the entire process depends. There is a presumption of continuity between representations of self prior to the arrival of the technology and what is to be learned after the technology has been introduced. This slides into a pedagogical model in which the dispossessed take control of their voice, articulate a voice, a point of view in need of expression. But why does the creation and projection of images redefine identity and worldview in such a dramatic fashion? The central hypothesis here seems to be dependent on the act of viewing, the attraction of the visual as a foundation upon which certain kinds of *re*visualization can take place.

It is of course possible to argue that the video image merely acts as a catalyst for change, foregrounding contradictions that might otherwise remain latent and inaccessible. Ironically, there need not be a transparent relationship between the images and the use to which they are put. Nor can we assume that the use made of them necessarily links up with the content of what has been said. In fact the image as such, like the technology, becomes a found object that can be named and renamed to suit the exigencies of the moment. This loss of specificity creates a laboratory context in which experiments are held to see if communication and comprehension either collide or work together. It comes down to whether or not the image serves a utilitarian purpose, whether a viewer or a community of viewers can engage in the movement from image to discourse and back and then see some usefulness to the exchange.

But how can these effects be evaluated? Which discourses are valid and which are not? There are hundreds of similar examples to the one which Forest has provided us with, examples of video facilities made available to local cultures in the South and in North America. Communities are engaged in taking the technology and trying to make it work—the public use and then display of the results—even the transmission of the final product through informal videocassette networks, cable, and satellite.[41] This community-based activity is at a

41. See the work of Deep Dish based in New York. Their videotapes are "broadcast" over satellite and downloaded to local sites. See also the work and history of the Alliance for Community Media representing the interests of groups involved with video

fever pitch in some parts of Asia, where informal video networks now account for the majority of what is viewed in any medium. Does this "liberate the creativity and imagination" of the people involved? How does it "allow them to give expression to their latent, unrealized needs"? To what degree does it stimulate new "exchanges between individuals and the group"?

Forest's aims are not dissimilar to Manfred Oepen, who works for the German Foundation for International Development as a consultant in communication:

> The three key concepts of community communication—access, participation and self-management—are aimed at minimising possibilities of oppression and abuse of power. Access means the individual's right to communication, interaction between receivers and producers of messages, and active participation during programme planning and production. Participation is the public right to contribute to the formulation and implementation of media plans, policies, objectives and programmes which directly affect certain communities. Self-management is the most advanced form of participation, in which the public would fully manage and produce community media.[42]

In both these instances as well as in the above list, it is clear that there is a democratic spirit at work encouraging participants to discover for themselves not only why they have worked on a project but to evaluate the impact of video upon their daily lives. Yet, there are a series of questions that remain unanswered. What makes the use of video so attractive and why does it seem so naturally attuned to presumptions about change? Why do processes of this kind find the documentary form more attractive than any other genre? Why would the documentary seem to most fully express the desires, needs, and aspirations of both the participants and the videomakers? How are personal changes evaluated? Who does the evaluating? These questions are about the subjective sphere within which the "public" operates, about the ability and desire of communities to engage with often difficult processes of self-examination. It remains unclear to what degree and with what efficacy video enhances

---

and cable access. Patricia Aufderheide explains the guiding assumptions of cable access very clearly: "Congress had intended public access cable to serve a unique free speech function on cable systems otherwise editorially controlled by the operator, or by the operator's lessee in the case of leased access. It was designed to be "the video equivalent of the speaker's soap box or the electronic parallel to the printed leaflet" (The Cable Communications Policy Act of 1984, U.S. House of Representatives, 1984, pp. 21–22). Public access's mandate is thus linked to the implications of the First Amendment: if it works, it is a public forum, a facilitator of public discussion and action." Patricia Aufderheide, "Underground Cable: A Survey of Public Access Programming," in *Afterimage* 22.1 (1994): 5.
42. Manfred Oepen, "Communicating with the Grassroots: A Practice-Oriented Seminar Series," *Group Media Journal* 9.3 (1990): 4.

the arena in which these questions can be addressed. Catherine Saalfield, in an important article on video activism, makes the following comment with respect to another activist group, the Paper Tiger Television Collective: "Paper Tiger's weekly shows—aired citywide on public access television, with roll-ins—have a handmade look and an immediate message. By challenging network forms of television, it represents alternative TV, and can be watched not only at home but also in community centers and galleries, in schools and organizational meetings. Fundamentally, the group maintains that people 'should be able to work in media, so they can be critical of the mass media and not victims of mass culture.' "[43]

Aside from the reproduction of the mass culture versus activist culture paradigm (which I critiqued earlier), the crucial element in what Saalfield is saying centers on the notion of the "handmade look" of activist video. This look is the result of the collective efforts of the people involved (and Saalfield documents the experience she had with the group DIVA TV—Dammed Interfering Video Activist Television—a loose group of people devoted to nonhierarchical forms of organization and political change) and their desire to avoid reproducing the processes of social organization with which they disagree. The struggle here is both with and against modes of representation for a different approach to information and against communicative models that don't address the everyday needs of people in a time of crisis. The evidence for change will be found in the rising tide of activisms that will lead communities to take charge of their own realities, to know whom to fight and when.[44] The very notion of a multiplicity of strategies, of activisms, suggests that each group is struggling with issues related to communication and the public sphere. The book *Queer Looks* is informed throughout by a desire to change both the political and cultural landscape of film and video activism. There is an urgency to the book which comes out of the AIDS crisis and the daily oppression of gays and lesbians. Saalfield, although perhaps overly optimistic about video images and their potential, nevertheless spends a great deal of time discussing the complexities of working in groups, the divisions, the debates and structures that DIVA put in place in order to facilitate its efforts. The participatory forms of communication Saalfield suggests are central to any political effort with

43. Catherine Saalfield, "On the Make: Activist Video Collectives," in *Queer Looks: Perspective on Lesbian and Gay Film and Video*, ed. Martha Gever, John Greyson, Pratibha Parmar (Toronto: Between the Lines, 1993), 24. The quote Saalfield uses comes from "Feminism Does Media Activism: An Interview with DeeDee Halleck," in *Feminisms*, 3.3 (1990): 4.
44. See Stephen Heath, "Representing Television," in *Logics of Television: Essays in Cultural Criticism*, ed. Patricia Mellencamp (Bloomington: Indiana University Press, 1990), 296–98.

video and focus on the group as a site of change. In some respects, a video group becomes a small community, an icon of the local, an image of the potential the group itself is suggesting to other communities. The group's struggle with power and institutions of authority should not, however, be confused with the creation of new forms of communication. There is a contingent but not necessarily a direct relationship between innovation and the profound effects upon individuals of collective work. What must be recognized here are the specific characteristics of group activity and the semiautonomous reality the group engenders. There is a very specific culture that each group has even in those moments when the group feels most connected to the communities it is addressing.

In a recent paper Joyce Hammond described the use of video among Tongan Polynesians in Salt Lake City, Utah. There, the community has been practicing a kind of ethnographic communication in which tapes are made of traditional and everyday activities (and thus preserved for archival purposes) and for transportation to Tonga, so that relatives can exchange information with each other. When Tongans go home they travel with camcorders and bring back material for the community in Utah. A skillful group of part-time professional videographers now shoot images of virtually all of the major events in the community. "Despite certain disadvantages the videographers may encounter as members of the community which call upon their services, they are in a unique position to communicate their own and other Tongans' interpretations and presentations of themselves and their way of life. Although Tongans admire videographers' skills in operating equipment associated with creating videos, they especially value the videographers' abilities to create visualizations that represent their self-images."[45] I would add that this kind of work has been going on for many years in Australia among indigenous peoples.[46] But the crucial point here is that Tongan video culture has a specificity that would have to be understood from a number of vantage points, including the relationship the videographers have with popular culture in the U.S. The local in this instance has a heterogeneity to it that reflects cross-cultural influences that could not have emerged without a group process. At the same time, the possibilities of intercultural communication are severely limited by the specificity of the Tongans' concerns. The hybridization of vantage points, cultural norms, social organization, and the goals of the community means that questions of

45. Joyce Hammond, "Visualizing Themselves: Tongan Videography in Utah," in *Visual Anthropology* 1.4 (1988): 385.
46. See Faye Ginsburg, "Indigenous Media: Faustian Contract or Global Village?" in *Rereading Cultural Anthropology* ed. George E. Marcus (Durham and London: Duke University Press, 1992).

"self-image are not actually present in a complete sense in the videotapes. This process goes far beyond the image into a web of discursive and cultural activities for which images provide the most marginal of windows. This is exciting because it means that new models of analysis and criticism are needed to respond to the work being done. Questions relating to self-image cannot be addressed through conventional analytic strategies that join images and identity in a transparent and causal way. The intercultural becomes a site of contestation on what links and keeps communities apart.

Both Saalfield and Hammond suggest that profound changes take place in the various ways people see themselves or as Hammond puts it, the way they visualize their self-images. Yet, however powerful the images may be and however effectively they may be used, they must be transformed into either verbal or written texts, into discourse and discursive practices, inscribed into the daily life of the people involved or used to extend the boundaries of communication and understanding. This is a shifting ground upon which it is very difficult to build a solid foundation for analysis. There is a continual movement of information and meaning. The perspective that can be taken on all of these changes is dependent on translation, which is itself further enframed by the unpredictable boundaries of communication and exchange. While video may be effective as a pedagogical tool for those who make use of it, our ability to reconstruct that practice and understand its implications is at best limited to the cultural model of communication that we ascribe to the process and to the image. Crucially, all these elements may not necessarily be compatible, nor may they reveal what the community thinks about its own practices of communication.

It is significant that the Tongans in Utah were so convinced about the importance of their videotapes that an archive was created to house the tapes. Video creates what I will describe as a logic of the present while simultaneously producing an image-event in the past. This generates a somewhat different temporal context than we are normally accustomed to—a mixture of present and past that is both, and neither, simultaneously. The disjuncture that results is part of the attraction but also part of what makes the electronic image so puzzling. It suggests that history has already been made while one continues to make it. It is this suppleness that allowed broadcasters for example to repeat the Rodney King beating in Los Angeles over and over again, as if each showing would somehow reconstitute the event, as if to prove that this was not a dramatization, not a fiction. In order to gain control over the many disjunctures, repetition was used. (See chapter 1 for more detail on this issue.) But, this only validates the contradictions, proposing that the disjunctures in time and place can be controlled, that there is some way of gaining authority over the impact of the event as image. Mona da Vinci, a video artist, has suggested that videotapes create an "electronic space"[47] where conventional forms of identification and escape are impossible. The concept of an electronic space is a fascinating one and links video to a radically different architecture, not so much for viewing, but as a place to live in.

For the Tongans to believe it is the image they are archiving, they must recast the activity of videomaking. They will structure their daily lives upon the fulcrum of possible images that the videographers will shoot. In other words, if we are to believe Joyce Hammond's description, the Tongans have moved beyond interpretation into truth—their images have become the community. I visualize my self-image, therefore I am. The problem, as Marshall Sahlins has so acutely characterized it, "comes down to the relation of cultural concepts to human experience, or the problem of symbolic reference: of how cultural concepts are actively used to engage the world. Ultimately at issue is the being of structure *in* history and *as* history."[48] What does it mean to visualize your self-image? In Hammond's terms it means that one begins to see oneself, one's daily activities, *as* image. This presumably objectifies the self in order that a new understanding can be gained, but this is also at the heart of another and more complex contradiction. The activity of symbolization, self as image, can only be achieved through the interplay of givens at the heart of any cultural configuration. Those givens don't disappear because the video process has, so to speak, come on the scene. In fact, the dialogue between the given and the new, between potential change and the hinderances to understanding change, depend on the manner in which the video is spoken about, the context of its performance, in other words, the relationship between performance and speech, interpretation and cultural context.

Video inserts itself into a highly inventive social process in which, to some degree, the cultural assumptions that went into its production are challenged. Unlike an extremely ritualized activity where the parameters for exchange and action are set up to produce a specific result, the electronic image borrows and plays with a wide variety of givens and reconstitutes and recontextualizes them. But this is not just bricolage nor pastiche. Sets of relations are created that far outstrip the original limitations in place. In other words, one can begin to talk about an unstable situation in which the video plays a far less important role as image (in terms of motivation and learning) than is often presumed. The electronic space made possible by video operates from within a wide number of temporal distortions. These distortions make so many things happen at the same time that spectatorship and positionality, information and meaning, shift from the acceptable to the contested and back again. The instability drives the process further and stimulates the production of more and

47. Quoted in Katherine Dieckmann, "Electra Myths: Video, Modernism, Postmodernism," *Art Journal* 45.3 (1985): 199.

48. Marshall Sahlins, *Islands of History* Chicago: (University of Chicago, 1987), 145.

more electronic images, as if this will somehow overwhelm if not interrupt the flow of contingencies that sustain the production of the images in the first place.

Dialogues in Image Form

Göran Hedebro, a Swedish researcher and writer, talks about the proliferation of media technologies in developing countries. He discusses the role of radio and then television in contexts devoid of most media, aside perhaps from radio, prior to twenty years ago:

> We know particularly little about the role of information via mass media in national development. Our knowledge is somewhat better for communication and changes in the village, but here too, it is difficult to use findings from research to make definite assessments as to the outcomes. Now, why this lack of evaluative studies? There are several reasons. First of all, there is no real tradition of allocating resources to this aspect of planned communication activities. It is still more common to use input figures as indicators of the effects of a campaign. Second, evaluations of interventions may be very risky. It is easier to *talk* about the advantageous outcomes than to run the risk of facing figures that show the real results are far from what was desired and expected.[49]

Hedebro goes on to talk about a media campaign aimed at improving local people's understanding of nutrition questions. The campaign was empirical and concrete. It used the media to convey a direct message. Yet the evaluative tools available to assess the project were minimal. Worse, the campaign seemed to have served its own purposes, but was unable to account for the complexity of the environment it was trying to change. This problem of assessment *shouldn't* be at the margins of the project but falls prey to all of the complexities and contradictions of any type of intervention in the community, whether or not it is media based. Hedebro adds to his argument: "As in many industrialized countries, information has been used in the developing countries as a panacea for problems of the most varying kinds. Some of the problems attacked have been of an informational nature, while in just as many other instances the problem at hand has been of another character, and information activities, no matter how cleverly designed and carried out, have had little to do with the solution of the problem" (Hedebro 50).

The question is, what kind of research could have been done with regard to the introduction of media technologies such as video? It is far easier to introduce the technology than it is to anticipate or simultaneously organize the

49. Göran Hedebro, *Communication and Social Change in Developing Nations: A Critical View* (Ames, Iowa: Iowa State University Press, 1982), 43.

assessment procedures that will be needed to examine the impact. Let me return for a moment to Fred Forest and the experiment which I described earlier. Forest, you will remember, wanted to dynamize human relations in the home for seniors. He wanted them to learn from their perceptions of their own experiences, and in particular, he wanted to liberate them from the constraints of daily life in the seniors' home. He anticipated that the video would give expression to a set of latent, unrealized needs.

The model here is clearly psychoanalytic. There is an embedded notion of transference, of the movement from video to patient and back again. Furthermore, this movement will be articulated, developed, and understood by reference to the video image and it is linked to the *idea* that the machine is powerful in its effects, particularly with respect to communication. This confers an even greater sense of importance onto the process of teaching others to use it. This conferral will have an impact on the way the technology is appropriated and the conceptual and interpretive frameworks applied to what is produced. It also leads to an *overevaluation* of the impact of the technology, and to the presumption that change is *inevitably* one of the major outcomes of the incorporation of the machine into local cultural activity.

> What is the meaning of being confronted, not with other people in the flesh but with videotape records of their (or perhaps of one's own) behaviour? Let us consider first the situation in which we notice ourselves being observed. The classic account here is Sartre's [Jean-Paul Sartre, *Being and Nothingness*, (trans. H. Barnes) Methuen, London, 1958] account of noticing—after having been moved by jealousy, curiosity, or sheer vice to glue one's ear to a door or to look through a keyhole—that one is being observed oneself: "what does this mean? It means that I am suddenly affected in my being and that essential modifications appear in my [intentional] structure—modifications which I can apprehend and fix conceptually."[50]

This essentially narcissistic approach has been commented upon by Rosalind Krauss with respect to video art, but her comments are just as applicable to political video. Until recently (gay, AIDS and feminist videotapes have changed this configuration somewhat), political video was obsessed with the documentary form. The desire to communicate both directly and quickly led to the duplication of traditional documentary strategies of social and cultural interpretation. These included the use of speaking heads to process information through the interview format and voice off, as well as voice over, to authoritatively comment upon, or lead the viewer through the stages of the documentary. The primary purpose was to make the information as clear as possible

50. John Shotter, "On Viewing Videotape Records of Oneself and Others: A Hermeneutical Analysis," in *Using Video*, ed. P. W. Dowrick and S. J. Biggs (London: John Wiley & Sons, 1983), 243.

and to give information priority over more marginal concerns for style and form. Even the more self-reflexive efforts with video seem not to have learned from the experiments of Chris Marker, for example (especially *Sunless* but also his more recent work with television) or filmmakers such as Jean Rouch, David McDougall, and Johan Van Der Keuken. My purpose here is not to talk about the way the documentary genre has stabilized over the years, but to respond to the very idea that information can be communicated through visual-aural media such as video, and then applied to contexts that promote various kinds of change.

The narcissism of which Krauss speaks centers on the human body; "these are the two features of the everyday use of *medium* that are suggestive for a discussion of video: the simultaneous reception and projection of an image; and the human psyche used as a conduit, because most of the work produced over the very short span of video art's existence has used the human body as its central instrument. In the case of work on tape this has most often been the body of the artist-practitioner. In the case of video installations it has usually been the body of the responding viewer."[51]

I would add that in the case of political video there has been the tendency to focus on the human subjects under examination as surrogates for the video-maker's point of view. This is a more subtle and less visible narcissism, but it is part and parcel of the desire to transform the viewer of the video into an accomplice in the exchange, to extend the surrogacy as a way of confirming the validity and political impact of the video. This is taken to its greatest lengths when videomakers (and the filmmakers before them) go into various communities to "give the people a voice"[52] An early example of this was the film, "The Things I Cannot Change,"[53] which was made at the National Film Board of Canada and was in many ways an important precursor to the efforts of video and filmmakers to use alternative media for social change. I will not discuss this film at length except to mention that its notoriety at the time was

51. Rosalind Krauss, "Video: The Aesthetics of Narcissism," in *Video Culture: A Critical Investigation*, ed. John G. Hanhardt, (Layton, Ut.: Peregrine Smith Books in association with Visual Studies Workshop Press, 1986), 180–81.

52. See in particular the various newsletters produced by Challenge for Change, the film and video program developed over a number of years at the National Film Board of Canada. In particular, volume 1, number 2 and number 7 in the series.

53. The film was made by Tanya Ballantyne and John Kemeny. It was about the Bailey family, a poor family on welfare in Montreal. Although it made a strong effort to honestly follow the lives of various family members, the resulting images effectively created a scene of such despair that the title became more of an ironic comment on the point of view of the filmmakers than on the family itself. The film was not taken lightly by the NFB, which sent out promotional material to thousands of households to supplement the showing of the film on national television. It was commented on by government ministers and by local politicians.

in part the result of the filmmaker's genuine committment to the poor family, the Baileys, who were the subjects of the film. The fact that the film painted a profoundly negative portrait of the family's chances of changing their own cir- cumstances added to the impression that the filmmakers began and sustained the project without much historical or analytical understanding of the context they had entered.

I would put forth the suggestion that, as with many of the video and film projects that followed (from *VTR St. Jacques* to the *Fogo Islands Project* to experiments in Acadia, New Brunswick, like *Un Soleil*, to experiments as di- verse as the ones held in Drumheller, Alberta, Boston, and Pittsburgh—all in the period from 1967–73), the question of giving a voice was so primary and the seduction of the image as a tool in the process so crucial, that few of the efforts escaped the initial contradictions of the Ballantyne-Kemeny venture. In a similar vein, Benjamin H. D. Buchloh comments on an experiment with video in the streets of New York. The videomaker, Jenny Holzer, wanted to engage in a dialogue with the public about the 1984 elections in the U.S. She set up a truck with a thirty-foot video screen and "displayed more than thirty prerecorded messages and images by artists and authors as well as direct inter- views that Holzer and her collaborators had conducted in the street, asking passerbys about their political concerns and opinions. The project also encour- aged, during open microphone sessions, the direct interference and participa- tion of the viewers in the process of forming a visual and verbal representation of the political reality of the viewers."[54] However, Buchloh goes on to question the "dialogue" between Holzer and her audience. He expresses the concern that notions of self-representation that depend on an "unmediated spontane- ity" don't necessarily lead to political awareness. He critiques the idea of the spontaneous interview on the street because it enhances "the mythical distor- tion of the reality of the public" (Buchloh 224). The difficulty here is with dialogue, since, as I have discussed in chapter 4, projection, the process through which dialogue is established with images, does not necessarily have a transparent relationship to identity. In other words, what an individual may say when a camera is thrust in front of him may have little to do with what he feels. He may or may not have difficulty translating his feelings into words. Buchloh describes the Holzer strategy as an "anarchistic trust in the collective mind."

I would situate many of these problems in the idea of self, of identity, of the projection of self into the status of image. (There are hundreds of examples of the therapeutic language used by critics and practitioners with respect to video. "The emergence of self and the erotic expression of desire are the cen-

---

54. Benjamin H. D. Buchloh, "From Gadget Video to Agit Video: Some Notes on Four Recent Video Works," in *Art Journal* 45.3 (1985): 223–24.

tral concerns of Neesha Dosanjh's, *Beyond/Body/Memory*."[55] "*Acts of Denial* is a selection of films and videotapes that seeks justice and truth. Many of the works attempt to identify the primary sources of misinformation: film and television as the enforcers of racist views. We are shown how these views support the dominant ideology and how they affect those who must live in denial. Included are superb works of investigative journalism, expressive films and videotapes as sites for reclaiming history and identity. These works challenge us to look between the lines and to hold a mirror up to ourselves."[56] Given my own political biases, which strongly support the points of view held by the writers of the above two quotes, why would I even concern myself with the contradictions of the language and aesthetic that surround these politically charged images? The difficulty is that this type of therapeutic discourse suggests a pedagogical framework that images just cannot create nor be held responsible for. In fact, the model of communication here cannot account for the unpredictable nature of performative contexts, even though it is the expressed desire of the creators and critics of the videotapes to allow for as much variation as possible in response to what has been seen. I do not wish to generalize, but even the notion of feedback (with all of its cognitive and cybernetic implications) works on the assumption that communication *must* take place. In other words, a loop or coil, as Krauss puts it (Krauss 186), has to be put in place for the creative process to be validated: "the feedback coil of video seems to be the instrument of a double repression: For through it consciousness of temporality and of separation between subject and object are simultaneously submerged. The result of this submergence is, for the maker and viewer of most video art, a kind of weightless fall through the suspended space of narcissism" (Krauss 186).

The question of feedback takes on, at one and the same time, a mythical and mechanical character. Mythical, because without feedback there would be no validation of the importance of the statement; mechanical, because the focus of concern is the image as source and progenitor of meaning. Once again I would temper the above by saying that this is a cultural and therefore profoundly embedded process. It is not as if the videomakers or filmmakers I have mentioned, or the many others who believe so strongly in the effectiveness of their work, are acting in bad faith or naively pursuing some kind of utopic political process through their use of video imagery. Even the most optimistic of image makers realizes, I think, that variability of response or even denial, reflects precisely the heterogeneity of the communicative context into which

55. Michelle Mohabeer, "The Inside Out Lesbian and Gay Film and Video Festival of Toronto," in *Fuse* 16.5 & 6 Summer 1993: 57.
56. Paul Wong, "Acts of Denial," in *Images 90*, a catalogue of film and video from the *Images Film and Video Festival*, organized by Northern Visions, Toronto, Ontario, 1990.

images enter. But as with most therapeutic processes dependent on the experience of images, it is very difficult to pinpoint exactly where the changes or the communication, so to speak, begins (let alone where it ends). And there is, as a result, a tendency to forgo precisely the kind of historical investigation into the community of viewers that might foreground or even negate the supposedly central role of the image. In addition, I would attribute the therapeutic impulses of alternative media to the creation of an impenetrable and monolithic Other, which can only be countered by an oppositional strategy that presumes that people, viewers, consumers, and so forth, are passive victims of the culture they inhabit. Of course the more monolithic the mainstream is, the less likely it can be changed, let alone responded to, through precisely the very processes of activism and participation that the ideologies of alternativity promote.

Video Bodies/Video Minds

If it seems as if I am less than optimistic about the tendency to characterize video imagery (in narrative and documentary variations) through the lens of an untheorized pedagogical model, a different opinion is held by Gene Youngblood. He describes a tape by Phil Morton entitled, *General Motors*.

> *General Motors* was presented as a personal correspondence to a Chevrolet dealership where Morton had purchased a van. On the most literal level, the tape documented his frustrated attempts to have the defective vehicle repaired. On a metaphoric level, however, it addressed five themes. . . . First was the theme of the amateur versus the professional: the amateur as populist-hero, the professional as mercenary who disavows ethical responsibility ("We are the people and we are producing and maintaining our thing," is a chorus repeated throughout the tape). This pointed to the second theme, that of autonomy and how it is technologically determined. The amateur is empowered in as much as he or she controls personal tools for the construction of audiovisual reality. The idea that television is the environment in which we live, that we are constantly swimming in the electronic soup is the third issue; realising this fact is the necessary first step toward liberation. Morton proposed a fourth metaphor, that of the amateur as electronic nomad or migrant who leaves the material world for the electronic world by living with and through computer video simulations. For those who live in a world of electronic simulations—and that means everyone today—freedom is the ability to construct personal reality. Hence the fifth and all-encompassing metaphor, electronic visualization as a technology of the self. By creating the world in which we live we create ourselves; in *General Motors*, as in all subsequent tapes, Morton simulates the self he wishes to become.[57]

57. Gene Youngblood, "Art and Ontology: Electronic Visualization in Chicago," in *The Event Horizon*, ed. Lorne Falk and Barbara Fischer (Toronto: The Coach House Press, 1987, 328.

Morton has a specific idea of audience and includes his addressee in the video. His video is close to a letter but there is still the desire to communicate beyond the boundaries of the personal. One creates oneself as both public and private; both realms are constructed through artistry and the result is the integration of video into many possible fields of communication. What is at stake in both Morton and Youngblood is a universe in which concept and image combine into a representation of the imaginary—though this is as fleeting as the movement of electronic images themselves. But what does Youngblood mean when he talks about "electronic visualization as a technology of the self?" Is he proposing a radically different notion of the imaginary here? "On the most fundamental level electronic visualization refers to the video signal itself as a plastic medium, as the 'material' of electronic practice. . . . This isn't visual art or picture-making; it is the thing itself, the visible presence of the electronic substance" (Youngblood 334–35). The idea that the electronic process becomes the content, that the "wand of electrons spraying and throwing . . . becomes[s] the complete content that engulfs everything that's going on" (Youngblood 335), is not taken by Youngblood to be an end in itself. Rather, the more synthetic the electronic image becomes, the more closely linked it is to the imaginary of the user, and the more control and intelligence has gone into its creation. In that sense, the creator sees her own movement between perception and the imaginary—the scattered pulsations of the brain now visualized and organized. (Wim Wenders tried to deal with this in his film *Journey to the End of the World*, a dismal failure only highlighted by the attempts of a scientist to visually render memory through a television hookup with the cortex of the brain.) This "closed loop" turns into what Youngblood describes as a technology of the self in which the technology aids and encourages more accelerated forms of learning and produces the equivalent of a "neuroelectronic drug" in which you become both what you visualize and what you desire (the central claim of virtual reality pundits).

"So on another level they're [the videotapes Morton has shot] imaginary models of us electronically visualizing ourselves so much more powerfully, a more powerful spell. What one does is to create pictures that one would like to see oneself in more frequently. . . . It's the conscious election to put ourselves in different worlds—perceptual, conceptual, physical—and process those worlds electronically."[58] Youngblood theorizes that this kind of artistic practice integrates life and technology, creating a pattern of living in which image and experience undergo the kind of mutual exchange that raises the process from simulation to a conversation. The dialogue that results has no end, does

---

58. Gene Youngblood, "Art and Ontology: Electronic Visualization in Chicago," p. 341 quoting Phil Morton (no reference provided).

not have to categorize itself as either fictional or real, and through its intimacy transforms the act of seeing the self into a moment of sharing—precisely the opposite, to Youngblood, of the narcissism pervading mainstream broadcasting. The medium becomes a place of work in which the self is created and recreated—life as art. In this sense the socially constructed self gains the ability to rebuild, and this can be done privately or publicly. The domains become interchangeable with consequences for most forms of human activity. As the camcorder records yet another birth or an interview with a dying relative, potential spaces for critical thinking can be projected into contexts where none may have existed beforehand, and where there was no prior possibility of reaching out to others. At the same time, this kind of practice resists institutionalization and cannot be so easily co-opted into conventional patterns of interpretation and analysis.

Gene Youngblood talks about the development of a new consciousness based on metamorphosis. "The new consciousness seeks the transformation of realities whereas the old consciousness ventures no further than a timid juxtaposition of 'objective' realities that retain their traditional identity. The fact is that there exists no cinematic equivalent of video keying. Tearing a key in greys or colours produces graphic designs of unique character, blending form and colour in a manner virtually impossible in any other medium. Video keying is inherently synaesthetic; such a claim can be made for no other aesthetic medium" (Youngblood 109).

Youngblood had an uncanny ability to predict the future; in 1970 he suggested that portable video cameras would one day be as small as a Super-8 and be capable of producing color images. His presumptions, however, about the arrival of a new consciousness, about different ways of knowing, while similar to many of the claims about video, went much further than most critics and practitioners of the early seventies. His most interesting proposal was that electronic images produced a phenomenon known as synergy. This is a system that cannot be predicted by the behavior of any of its parts because "there is no a priori dependency between the conceptual and design information of the individual parts. The existence of one is not requisite on the presence of another" (Youngblood 109). Thus design and information, the relationship of aesthetics to meaning becomes arbitrary. Youngblood is not simply adopting a linguistic notion here. He is talking about an epistemological break in the way electronic images function, but is also, perhaps unwittingly, linking electronic imagery in an ontological sense to artistic practices well known to surrealists. There is a curious link here as well to many of the utopian propositions that have come out of discussions on the Internet, hypermedia, and cyberspace.

The arbitrariness he openly supports is at the heart of metaphoric operations that cannot be so easily described, let alone interpreted. Lest this be seen as a result of the innovations of the technology—the result of the way the technology itself is constructed—this is what André Breton said in 1936 about the Surrealist enterprise: "a total revolution of the object: acting to divert the object from its ends by coupling it to a new name and signing it. . . . Perturbation and deformation are in demand here for their own sake. . . . Objects thus reassembled have in common the fact that they derive from and yet succeed in differing from the objects which surround us, by a simple change of role."[59]

It can be argued that this link to the surrealist enterprise grows out of the many shared concerns of the avant-garde, which is where Youngblood would in any case situate himself. But, it also points toward the need to rethink the way new technologies are incorporated into existing patterns of thought and use. Moreover, without precisely that sense of continuity, the difference between an oral argument made on video and one made in person becomes insignificant. The presumably significant contrast between images on television and those on a film screen are relegated to the object, a transference that highlights the capabilities of the technology in a sphere devoid of subjectivity.[60]

Throughout his analysis Youngblood assumes that technological change represents a change in viewing, in subjectivity. He follows Buckminster Fuller and Edmund Carpenter[61] in this. Most importantly, for the purposes of this discussion, he presages the work of Jean Baudrillard in assuming that the image "bears no relation to any reality whatever: it is its own pure simulacrum."[62] There is a continuity in thinking here between developments in electronic media and postmodern presumptions about change. The links are profound and they begin with claims for the impact of technological shifts. These have not been examined in any great depth. Methodological paradigms have been borrowed from the social sciences and linguistics without due reflection on their origins.

To some degree video activists have inherited their idealized versions of opposition from the avant-garde in art and media. This is a powerful mix that suggests shifting configurations of media use, structured and maintained by the impulses behind the politics of social change and experimentation with form and modes of communication. Yet more often than not these efforts are carefully circumscribed by the presumed absences in the audiences being addressed. At the root of these activities is a genuinely felt concern for education,

59. André Breton, "Crisis of the Object," in *Surrealists on Art*, ed. Lucy Lippard (Spectrum: New York, 1970), 106.

60. In some senses then, the notion that a new technology might be a found object is very attractive because it allows for and reveals the degree to which any number of assumptions can be made about that technology's relationship to viewing and subjectivity.

61. See Edmund Carpenter, *They Became What They Beheld* (New York: Dutton, 1976), and Buckminster Fuller, *Utopia or Oblivion: The Prospects for Humanity* (New York: Overlook Press, 1972).

62. Jean Baudrillard, *Selected Writings*, ed. Mark Poster (Stanford: Stanford University Press, 1988), 170.

for teaching, for learning. "Activist groups—community organizers, labour unions, artists, health care workers, and so on—have made effective use of media for education and organizing purposes within their own ranks and in the broader community. The stated intention is to educate people about issues and organize efforts for specific or broad social change efforts. This approach has challenged the 'artist' model of the maker and broken down the traditional maker/audience dichotomy—both producer and audience become participants in the localized social struggle" (Anderson and Goldson 59).

This quote suggests another process at work here. The attempt to break down the differences between maker and audience pivots on the idea of a *new* pedagogy (aside from its connections to the avant-garde). The effort is to link the viewing of video images with learning. This may seem like a natural, if not inevitable outcome of any "transmission of information" through the television screen. But it is first and foremost an assumption. The question of what is learned, even of how learning takes place, would involve far more than a passing reference to the response by a particular audience to what they have viewed. In other words, the anecdotal comments of viewers about what they have seen must be examined from within a more historical and critical perspective than is generally the case.[63] This is a difficult problem because evaluating and explaining what audiences have understood after viewing a video often falls prey to quantitative approaches. The empirical measurement of attitude reveals very little and has generally been marginalized in communications study. I have seen little in the ethnography of audiences which points toward a more profound understanding of what viewers do and learn based on the experience of video watching.[64] This would then also suggest that Youngblood's utopian discourse is based on a series of hypotheses about impact and change which he has elevated to the level of truth.

Although there are examples of video being used for educational purposes

---

63. The video activists of the Challenge for Change period refer to many round table discussions of productions created for and by the community. But in general, these center less on the medium than on the issues raised by the videotapes themselves. The question of whether the "issues" have been changed by the appearance and use of video; that is, whether the *way* a discursive community is created affects the role of the medium, is rarely discussed. Ironically, John Grierson makes a series of comments in an issue of the *Challenge for Change Newsletter* (No. 8, Spring 1972, p. 4) which question the very basis of community video: "The cinéastes may make their films *with* the people and *in* the villages, but they are soon off and away *from* the people and the villages to their normal metropolitan milieu. The old unsatisfactory note of faraway liberal concern for humanity-in-general creeps in, in spite of these real excursions into the local realities. What we have is presentation of local concerns without a real representation of local concerns. *Presentation* does not necessarily mean *representation*, much less participatory democracy."

64. An exception to this, although the problem of how viewers translate experience into interpretation is not dealt with in it, is Purnima Mankekar, "National Texts and Gendered Lives: An Ethnography of Television Viewers in a North Indian City," *American Ethnologist* 20.3 (1993): 543–63.

too numerous to count, there is, as Peter Dowrick has suggested, very little evidence that serious evaluative research has been undertaken.[65] It is noteworthy that so many of the assumptions video activists use with respect to pedagogy are in fact standard procedure from within behavioral approaches to learning, and many of these examples are situated in medical contexts. Little serious analysis has been done on the use of video for medical purposes nor has there been any detailed studies of the diagnostic use of electronic images.[66] I bring this point up because more needs to be said about the transparent use of the image to comment on, for example, the behavior of a child in front of a therapist or the video camera's use to enhance self-awareness on the part of mental patients. The use of the video camera to study facial expression[67] or even more simply to "watch" a classroom teacher practicing her craft, suggests a relationship between image and learning, which needs to be informed by more than the intentions of the experimenters.

Yet it would be reductive to argue that the impulses guiding the diagnosis of speech impediments by videotapes of patients talking or the efforts to generate feedback from depressed individuals, who upon seeing their images are sometimes able to articulate their feelings, that all of this activity is somehow wrong. Efforts to approach the many differing ways electronic images are appropriated must account for the desire to make them work, to make them effective instruments of education and/or change. At the same time these impulses must be analyzed historically and placed within the social, political, and cultural context that legitimates the image and the choices involved in *interpreting* images.

Screens of Subjectivity

I can now suggest a preliminary inventory of the linkages that underpin and join video activism, the scientific use of video and video art: (a) consciousness-raising through images; (b) politicization of the community through par-

65. Peter W. Dowrick, *Practical Guide to Using Video in the Behavioral Sciences* (New York: John Wiley and Sons, 1991). See in particular chapter 3, "Instructing and Informing," 49–63.

66. Though a recent issue of *Camera Obscura* goes a long way towards rectifying this absence. See in particular Paula A. Treichler and Lisa Cartwright, "Introduction," in *Camera Obscura* 28 (1992): 5–21, and Carol Stabile, "Shooting the Mother: Fetal Photography and the Politics of Disappearance," *Camera Obscura* 28 (1992): 179–206. From a historical point of view see Barbara Maria Stafford, *Body Criticism: Imaging the Unseen in Enlightenment Art and Medicine* (Cambridge, Mass.: MIT Press, 1991).

67. See in particular the studies of P. Ekman and W. V. Friesen, "Collaborative Studies on Depression" (Washington, D.C.: National Institute of Mental Health, 1981), or an article by Paul Ekman, "Methods for Measuring Facial Action," in K. R. Scherer & P. Ekman, ed., *Handbook of Methods of Nonverbal Behavior Research* (New York: Cambridge University Press), 45–90.

ticipation in videomaking or viewing; (c) video pedagogy; (d) video as a thera-peutic device oriented toward individual and collective change as well as learn-ing; and (e) video as a tool of creativity—an art form.

Let me return for a moment to the questions raised by Dowrick, although I would like to temper them by also referring to a piece by Dan Graham, a well-known video artist,[68] and an article by Keyan Tomaselli and Alison Laz-erus. Dowrick lists five reasons why video works as a tool of instruction and I will refer here to two of them: (1) "Attention" (Dowrick 59), which refers to the "attention-grabbing" potential of the electronic image. He links this to the "close approximation" of the "human presence" in the image, which he de-scribes as a "compelling" stimulus for learning. By comparison, in a piece on community video, Tomaselli and Lazerus set up a chart of differences between mainstream (or as they put it, conventional) video and alternative (read, more politically involved and effective) approaches.[69] Community video empowers and "creates" a more active response on the part of the viewer, while conven-tional video disempowers and "creates" a passive response (Tomaselli and Lazerus 12). Most importantly, community video "facilitates political theory building," while conventional broadcast "prevents theory building" (Toma-selli and Lazerus 12). The link to Dowrick is an important one, because all three authors assume that there is a connection between watching and learn-ing. And all three presume that video has something to offer because of its characteristics as a medium. Yet, what are those characteristics? They are sum-marized in this passage by the author R. E. Clark[70] quoted by Dowrick; "the best current evidence is that media are mere vehicles that deliver instruction but do not influence, (Clark 445). . . . Only the content, he notes, can influence learning, although choice of a medium may influence the cost or extent of dis-tribution" (Dowrick 50).

It seems clear to me that Dowrick, and Tomaselli and Lazerus don't want to consider the relationship between the medium and the discourses used to express differing points of view about its use. In other words, the medium has characteristics, but they are purely functional and not directly related to what is finally produced. The media object, so to speak, retains or regains its status if it can be slotted into a model of communication that precedes its entry into a discursive context. The most serious problem with this approach is that it presumes information circulates from the medium to the viewer or listener (with all of the follow-up presumptions that something has been learned). The

---

68. Dan Graham, "Video in Relation to Architecture," in *Illuminating Video: An Essen-tial Guide to Video Art*, ed. Doug Hall and Sally Jo Fifer (San Francisco: Aperture, 1992), 168–88.
69. Keyan Tomaselli and Alison Lazerus, "Participatory Video: Problems, Prospects and a Case Study," in *Group Media Journal* 8.1 (1989): 10–14.
70. R. E. Clark, "Reconsidering Research on Learning from the Media," in *Review of Educational Research* 53 (1983): 445–59.

word *transmission* sums up the difficulties. It is as if each showing of a video-tape with pedagogical intentions starts with the premise that spectators have never seen electronic images before (this may begin to explain the reliance on voice-over as a technique of instruction with images). What is missing here is the sense of continuity fundamental to use of the medium both by the makers and those people who decide to watch the results. But even here the problem is that the word *continuity* doesn't even partially explain the integrated relationship between image and experience.

It may well be one of the defining moments of postmodernism that any effort to make the distinction between image and experience a fixed one has been recognized as a weak if not ineffectual interpretive and analytic strategy with respect to media technologies. This comes out in the work of Jean Baudrillard and Roland Barthes discussed in chapter 1. And it is not a matter here of raising the specter of a world now unconscious of its moorings in simulation; rather, the question of what distinguishes experience from imagery needs to be discussed, as Geoff Sharp has recently proposed, as an "extended form."[71] Sharp's suggestion is that technological mediation must be thought of as integral to the social and therefore as an inherent part of any human activity. This seems to be common sense. But the approach generally taken to technologies classified as image based suggests a fundamental separation between their presence and their use. (This comes out in its most extreme form when the media are blamed for violence, as if media technologies and the images produced are somehow separate from the public sphere in which they circulate, as if the violence is imported from a context different from where it has been created.) Sharp to some degree follows the arguments of Walter Ong and Marshall McLuhan regarding the history of media technologies, but he extends their insights further when he says, "the phrase 'technological extension' immediately calls to mind telecommunications and television, with radio tending to be an afterthought, being largely encompassed by television. If the question is pressed however, consistency demands that all of the print media, books and daily or periodical publications as well, be included as extended forms. This step pushes the introduction of the mass media back one hundred and fifty years. If the postmodern period is marked by the proliferation of the technologically extended forms, then it is clear that at least the seeds were sown long ago" (Sharp 230, 231). Sharp's major point, however, comes when he notes that extended technologies "unravel the whole complex of direct interaction. Speech, along with vision, is fileted away from the tangible contexts of presence" (Sharp 234). (It should be noted that this is also Heidegger's position. See chapters 1 and 2.)

The confusion that characterizes discussions of images as integral to the

71. Geoff Sharp, "Extended Forms of the Social: Technological Mediation and Self-Formation," *Arena Journal* 1 (1993): 221–37.

social and the psychological can be traced in part to the tensions arising between presence, direct interaction, and absence. Whereas Sharp sees this as a liberation from conventional institutional constraints on meaning, the more didactically oriented approach tries to dissipate the gaps and breaks produced. The aim is not to play with and be influenced by the arbitrary juxtapositions that may result, but to close them down and in so doing keep the image closely linked to the original intentions of its authors and to some sort of preindustrial ideal of nontechnologically mediated communication. This is a paradox to which I will return as I try to work through the many ambiguities that both motivate and restrain the use of media technologies for purposes of advocacy, education, and observation.

A second category invoked by Dowrick is entitled "Personal" (Dowrick 51). "All forms of media allow the audience members the opportunity to project themselves into situations that are being described. [However] a movie is frequently superior in its ability to transport an observer into the depths of the ocean, the height of a family argument, or the sex life of the flea" (Dowrick 51). In this instance, aside from the obvious slippage between film and video, all media bridge the gap between audience and image—with the kind of directness that once again dissolves the viewer into the message and bridges the differences between seeing and learning. It is this notion of directness that is taken up by community video, as the movement searches for more and more ways of teaching in order to be, as Tomaselli and Lazerus put it, "transformative," or to "develop human relations," or to "produce new knowledge" (Tomaselli and Lazerus 12).

Thus we find a paradoxical resistance to more seriously examining the electronic image (as simulation, for example), because to do so would perhaps bring the pedagogical closer to new forms of interactivity than linear forms of information-based communications. There is a terrible fear of formalism when the electronic image is posited as a device of learning. This is not to say that some reference isn't made to the medium and its properties. But it is usually through a reference to the "technical" that we find some mention of technique. Dowrick does this when he draws attention to a variety of potential image techniques to assist in making video information more effective, as well as to "assist self-assessment and self-correction" (Dowrick 103). These include *still frames*, which "draw attention to specific events, allow absorption of multiple aspects by the viewer, and allow time for discussion," and *slow motion*, which "focuses attention and provides more detail" (Dowrick 103). But the problem is with the model of learning in the first place. This brings up questions discussed in greater detail in chapter 2, which deals more specifically with the methodological problems of explaining and interpreting images.

The social context within which electronic images circulate and operate cannot be reduced to the categories Dowrick suggests. Most importantly, how do images draw attention to one idea or another? How do we know whether attention has been drawn in the fashion initiated by the image? There are few analytic models of interaction available here that would explain how the presence of the image fits into the creation or sustaining of knowledge. Rather than acknowledge the degree to which the electronic image may loosen all ties between communication and meaning, the effort is rather to restrain the arbitrariness and in so doing to create a regime where the image means what the maker says it means. This is then understood as a successful instance of communication and education, a validation that learning has in fact taken place. It is here that pedagogue and activist share the same terrain. The more transparent the relationship between communication and understanding, the more likely the medium has served its purpose.

As the shifting terrain of this argument suggests, at no point do these processes of validation lessen the uneasy sense that video activists have that they don't really control the territories of image projection and understanding. Let me turn for a moment to the writing and work of Dan Graham, who has played in an important role in developing a video practice and an analytical framework to explain both his videotapes and the efforts of others. Graham is concerned as much with the creative act as he is with the locale in which his videotapes will be shown or as Lili Berko has put it, he "has conceptualized video as a specifically architectural medium which produces meaning through the alteration/representation of space."[72] In his article entitled, "Video in Relation to Architecture," Graham says: "When observers see their image immediately, continuously replayed on the screen through videotape loops, their self-images, by adding temporality to self-perception, connect their self-perceptions to their mental states (Graham 185). Of course it is not at all clear whether an "observer" has an image of himself or herself; neither is it clear that an observer sees her image immediately. But even more important, the vocabulary in use here suggests a precision that is simply not achievable (nor may it even be desirable). Note the emphasis on "self" and "self-image" as if there are transparently clear explanations of what these terms mean. Even more distressing is the use of "mental states." Although it is not clear, the model of consciousness here suggests a mechanical duplication of the way images themselves work, a collapse of the mental into the visual, and a necessary link between projections of self and identity. Why the vagueness? What is it about theoretical discussions of the video image that encourage this kind of thinking, which rather superficially combines behavioral and cognitive models of mind with aesthetic concerns for effective communication?

Graham goes on: "In the situation of watching/being part of a video feed-

---

72. Lili Berko, "Surveying the Surveilled: Video, Space and Subjectivity," *Quarterly Review of Film and Video* 14.1–2 (1992): 64.

back loop, there is no longer any split between observed (self) behaviour and supposedly unobservable, interior, mental intention. When the observer's responses are part of and influencing their perception, the difference between intention and actual behaviour as seen on the monitor immediately influences the observer's future intentions and behaviour" (Graham 185). The foundations of this argument are centered on a causal notion of behavior. How is the interior life of the observer (a term with which I am also not comfortable) knowable? To what degree and with what accuracy can intention be measured? Crucially, is it possible for the observable and unobservable to share the same terrain? There is of course no necessary relationship between mental states and behavior. In fact, the difficulty is precisely to describe what we mean by the *mental* and to recognize that subjectivity generates a contingent relationship between a variety of sometimes similar and often different modes of experience and expression.

For Graham, the television monitor acts as a third person. "It" symbolizes an objective place within which the scenarios of subjectivity can be witnessed. This is also Dowrick's argument and is crucial to the comments by Tomaselli and Lazerus. The electronic screen unveils the internal as a map with markers and routes to be followed. Stuart Marshall has commented on this: "If the elementary artist/video equipment confrontation results in the medium acting as its own object, the most obvious redeployment takes the form of the medium acting as a feedback system enabling the artist to become an object of his/her own consciousness. Here the artist confronts both equipment and image of the self, and it is at this point that the curiosity of the artist about the medium becomes subverted into a curiosity about the relationship of the subject to its representations."[73]

Feedback unmasks the problems of subjectivity. More importantly, it brings consciousness into the field of the image as a transcendent window into thought. It would be my contention that this argument actually eliminates subjectivity. This is its goal. For, if there were to be a place for the subjective, then there clearly would be little need of the video screen. Whatever it may be, the screen clearly cannot be the person. In order for it to take on that status, an artistic conceit has to be invoked that anchors the image in the mind, as if it is both internal and external at the same time. Yet this is what excites Graham. The temporal collapse, the loss of spatial differentiation brings observation in line with consciousness, melts the mind into the screen of the monitor and in Graham's terms foregrounds "an awareness of the presence of the viewer's own perceptual processes" (Graham 186).

This cybernetic tautology is inviting because it proposes control over the

---

73. Stuart Marshall, "Video Art, The Imaginary and the Parole Vide," in *New Artists Video: A Critical Anthology*, ed. Gregory Battock (New York: Dutton, 1978), 105.

image and identity by anyone who wishes to collude with the process. That is its lure. For example, many recent videotapes about intercultural relations use interviews with individuals as their strategic lure, as their aesthetic base. (See *In Plain English* by Julia Lesage, which is about students of color at the University of Oregon. "African-American, Asian-American, Pacific Islander, Chicano/Latino and Native American undergraduate and graduate students discuss their expectations about college life before they came to the university and the reality they encountered at the University of Oregon, where they have been used in administrative statistics as a token and otherwise ignored."[74]) The interview form has been a dominant feature of politically oriented videotapes. Why? Well, in Graham's terms it allows for, if not encourages, precisely the kind of awareness of self that the sight of an image is meant to promote. That is, as image, the students of *In Plain English* can talk about identities, theirs and the culture from which they come, as if the video will address someone who will listen and watch. Yet, it is only the videomaker who is listening because she is asking the questions and is a participant in the "scene." The discursive address is toward her and a hypothetical audience, which could be made up of anyone.

The loss of specificity here should the affect the image. There is no transparent relationship between what the students say and the people they are speaking to. Yet their video identities are constructed as if there is. This is achieved by denying the importance of the videomaker and emphasizing the speaking heads of the students. They, so to speak, disappear into their words, a phenomenon meant to highlight and legitimate the validity of what they are saying. They are meant to be the authors of their own authority, and their identities surface because they are supposedly in control of what they say. So, the feedback loop is once again put in place. Through it, a specific kind of political experience becomes a means of revelation of self and Other. Presumably (because no one including myself would question the honesty or good intentions of the students or the videomaker), the process allows the hypothetical (or unknown) audience to learn and to change.

As the students discuss their problems and the various solutions they have found, it would be fair to say that they are traversing an internal mental space. They bear witness to the social and personal hurdles they have had to overcome in order to survive the generally discriminatory attitudes they have encountered at the University of Oregon. Shoshana Felman has summarized how this process of testimony works as a mode of address. In a comment on the testimonial elements in films like *Shoah* by Claude Lanzmann and *Hiroshima mon amour* by Marguerite Duras and Alain Resnais, Felman says: "What the testimony does not offer is, however, a completed statement, a totalizable ac-

---

74. Taken from a promotional flyer for the videotape.

count of those events. In the testimony, language is in process and in trial, it does not possess itself as a conclusion, as the constatation of a verdict, or the self-transparency of knowledge. Testimony is, in other words, a discursive *practice*, as opposed to a pure theory. To testify—to *vow to tell*, to *promise* and *produce* one's own speech as material evidence for truth—is to accomplish a *speech act*, rather than to simply formulate a statement."[75]

In this instance, because Felman uses the example of film, I would link testimony more fully to the gaps and fissures of document as fiction, that is, to the many levels through which the discourse of an individual takes on a *form* once it has been placed into the context of an image. Yet in keeping with the different ways the image separates discourse from the anchors of speech, the many aspects of inclusion and exclusion that both limit and expand the boundaries of meaning in an image, Felman's use of the testimonial as evidence for discursive practices of truth holds a great deal of promise. But what must be remembered here is that the power of testimony, as she goes on to describe it, is realized in large measure through her experiences in a classroom. In other words, she has to move from the image to the practice of teaching and learning *before* she can propose that the testimony has worked *as communication*. This is the crucial and untheorized problem here, as it is in Julia Lesage's videotape, and in the various concepts of political advocacy that continue to have a dominant hold in video politics.

The investment of meaning in the image and what we draw from the experience cannot be reduced to the image itself. This generates both a sense of excess and loss and simultaneously proposes a discourse of plenitude and fragmentation. To make matters even more complex, I would describe this process as a continuum which suggests connectivity where none may exist. The lines of demarcation (and I keep invoking geographical metaphors here in part because of the spatial character of the electronic image as opposed to the temporal character of film—a difference which Felman does not take up, since for her, filmic speech is equivalent to spoken discourse), the various terrains covered are only as linked as the specific context into which they fit. Thus it is the place of testimony Felman explores (the classroom) and it is the process of pedagogy that leads her to the idea of the speech act. It is *not* the testimony in and of itself, because testimony only exists as response to the listener or viewer, whether they are imaginary or real.

The students at the University of Oregon testify to their status as image long before they confirm their "reality" as students. This I would characterize

75. Shoshana Felman, "Education and Crisis, or the Vicissitudes of Teaching," in Shoshana Felman and Dori Laub, *Testimony: Crises of Witnessing in Literature, Psychoanalysis, and History* (New York: Routledge, 1992), 5.

as a bind for any act of political communication and explains in part why the content of what is said is always given priority, pushed into the forefront as a validation of the message the videomaker is trying to put across. It may also explain why a feedback loop is seen as so important because it allows for, if not encourages, the idea that the contradictions of the image can be transcended through communicative processes.

There are links between the testimonial character of the interview format in video, and the politically motivated intentions of the pedagogy that underlies its creation and distribution. There are further connections into the avant-garde and the work of videomaker Sadie Benning for example, which in large measure "testifies" to her coming out—to the declarations, explanations, and celebration of her lesbian identity. Furthermore, many of these elements are also present in the experimental efforts of other videomakers to investigate the potential of portable video as a narrative form. The deliberate structuring of a narrative for the electronic media is as much of a response to this set of unknowns (to this potential anarchy of the visual and the mental) as it is a pointer toward the endlessly inventive fictions that accompany the activity of storytelling. For no sooner has the story been told than it has the capacity to be retold again (is this not the paradox of any feedback loop?). And it is in this highly concentrated version of the real as fiction and fiction as real that the video machine intervenes as a purveyor of yet another level of invention, opening up further dimensions in which the testimony makes its appearance. In this "Ocean of Stories" the antistory, as Salman Rushdie has so cleverly pointed out, also has a story, a shadow-self into which the machine fits as a prop. Yet as the main character of Rushdie's novel, Haroun, listens to the tale of stories and antistories wiping each other out, this negation of a negation is at the heart of yet another narrative.[76] There is no way the shadow can be released from its master, no possible way a story can exist without a double; ironically, no way the image (in all of its forms) can escape the fictive (and the question is why should it?). This loosening of the relations between storytelling and being part of the story, this mixture of fantasy and fact, doesn't so much affirm the ontology of virtual systems as much as it reveals the inescapable relationship of the imaginary and the imagined image with language and discourse.

Challenging Change

I briefly mentioned the National Film Board of Canada earlier in this chapter. In the first instance here, I would like to examine one of their most famous experiments in video advocacy at the grassroots level, Challenge for Change.

76. Salman Rushdie, *Haroun and the Sea of Stories*, (London: Granta Books, 1990).

This is not meant to be a comprehensive overview. Rather, the utopian principles put in place during that period (1968–75) have had a longevity that has transformed Challenge for Change from a local experiment in Canada to *the* example used worldwide by video activists as a successful instance of community involvement with the medium. It is also held up as an example of the radical appropriation of video for political ends—all this within the context of a communications model based on democracy and empowerment. Yet, as we shall see, Challenge for Change was based on the same antipathy to mainstream culture that characterized nearly all video activism. It stands as a primary example of that oppositional stance and for the purposes of this chapter further exemplifies the difficult problems of address, audience, and community. At the same time, it certainly took the experiment of video democracy further than any group has since then.

In the late 1960s and early 1970s Challenge for Change was created to engage with processes of social change through the use of video and film. Broadly speaking, this desire to use the medium as an instrument for an activist relationship to Canadian society grew out of the recognition that the Film Board, as well as politically committed cultural workers, needed to be involved in more than the production of films or videotapes. They needed to connect with and better understand the audiences and communities they were addressing. The aim was to extend the process of creation and production from an institutional nexus into a decentralized model, based on an idealized version of community involvement. "Films can teach, they can explain and they can move people to great depths of emotion. Having done all of these things, is it possible for films to move people to action? There is no question for most social scientists, that carefully constructed communications, films for instance, can produce changes in attitudes, in those who adequately receive the communication. The use of adequately is of course a conscious one in that we know that people tend to mis-perceive that which they hear and see, and go through fairly complicated strategies of selective attention and selective perception."[77]

In fact, the audience became an obsession at the Board, with specific people at the institution assigned to develop polling methods and questionnaires for distribution to the populace at large. After certain films or videotapes were shown on television for example, the Film Board phoned people at random to see if they had watched and to pose questions if viewers said they were prepared to participate. The premise of this community-oriented work was pedagogical, political, and cultural, and it influenced an entire generation of activists devoted to the use of visual media for political purposes. This issue of

77. Dorothy Todd Hénaut, "Editorial," *Challenge for Change Newsletter*, Vol. 1 No. 2, (1970): 3.

connectivity to the viewer, to the community—of the relationship between production and distribution is what distinguished the efforts of the Film Board from many similar organizations elsewhere. The traditions developed during the heyday of the Challenge for Change period were improved upon in the late seventies when the Board decentralized and opened up a series of regional centers across Canada in an effort to build closer ties to the communities it was serving.

The idealism of Challenge for Change was based on notions of democratic access, the rallying call for anyone seriously interested in promoting the use of video in the community. The history of that period has not yet been written in great detail. One of the most interesting aspects yet to be explored will be the relationship between the social work movement in Quebec in the early 1960s and the accelerated movement toward media use for educational purposes.[78] The level of advocacy in both education and social work was very sophisticated, with tie-ins to provincial government departments and local municipalities. The use of video for the purposes of empowerment was embedded in a particular political context and surrounded by debates within Québecois culture about the role of the media and its effects on all facets of life in the province. The specificity of this situation not only affected the videotapes being made but the institutions that promoted them. The claims of this period and the video activism that followed were not as easily transferrable to other contexts as was presumed at the time. In fact, it is startling to read the anecdotal comments about Challenge for Change by modern-day proponents of community video,[79] the decontextualized analyses of the films which were made, the lack of understanding about the history of the National Film Board, and in particular that many of the films were the site of conflicts between the English and French sections of the NFB (which had a definitive impact on what the Film Board meant by community). There is little comment on the newsletters produced during that period (about fifteen) documents that obsessively support the notion that grassroots video work has to attack the presumptions of mainstream culture, although there is little depth to those analyses.

Rick Moore, who wrote *Canada's Challenge for Change: Documentary Film and Video as an Exercise of Power Through the Production of Cultural Reality*[80] quotes one of the members of Challenge for Change: "All across Canada (often with the help of Challenge for Change), citizens are picking up half-

78. One of the most detailed explorations of Challenge for Change can be found in Gary Evans, *In the National Interest: A Chronicle of the National Film Board of Canada from 1949 to 1989* (Toronto: University of Toronto Press, 1991) 157–76.
79. See a number of the essays in Alain Ambrosi and Nancy Thede, ed., *Video in the Changing World* (Montreal: Black Rose, 1991).
80. Rick Moore, unpublished Ph.D. dissertation, University of Oregon, 1987.

inch VTR cameras and learning to speak through them."[81] Moore then goes on to say, "the assessment was not an exaggeration, geographically speaking. Challenge for Change had begun numerous projects across the country in which the primary emphasis was citizen access. Over twenty-three major projects were eventually completed, some in urban areas such as Vancouver, Halifax and Toronto. Some were done in rural areas such as Drumheller, Alberta. In many of these communities, Challenge for Change staff took on new titles. For example, 'directors' were no longer directors, but 'media counsellors' in charge of helping the local citizens use the media most effectively" (Moore 119).

Guided by a vague concept of change, firmly believing in the potential of video as a technology to empower people to "talk to each other," engaged in the legitimation of a public sphere with a hierarchy of discourses that workers at Challenge for Change rarely examined, the program nevertheless produced many important experiments in the field of community video. But the operative word here is experiment—and in some senses people and their communities became the site within which many different ideas of democratic involvement were tested. The problem is that the targets for these experiments were as much the members of the community as the image itself—the creation and construction of meaning within the confines of an electronic medium. And the often expressed frustration of workers at Challenge for Change was that no other form of communication adequately responded to the needs of the people as they understood them. But this is a confusion of levels. Experimenting on the image, testing its effectiveness with regard to change, is already fraught with contradiction. Applying these ideas to the relationship between the image and spectator, the image and the community just confuses the issues even more.

If it appears as if I am referring to a historical situation that may not be relevant anymore, here is what a recent article had to say: "Nearly 30 years since the video portapak launched an independent television movement in the United States, a new generation of video activists has taken up the video camcorder as a tool, a weapon, and a witness. Although the rhetoric of guerrilla television may seem dated today, its utopian goal of using video to challenge the information infrastructure in America is more timely than ever and at last practicable. Today's video activism is the fulfillment of a radical 1960s dream of making "people's television."[82] Boyle goes on to talk about the three com-

81. Elisabeth Prinn, "Vive le Videographe," *Challenge for Change Newsletter*, No. 8, (Spring 1972): 18.
82. Deirdre Boyle, "From Portapack to Camcorder: A Brief History of Guerrilla Television," *Journal of Film and Video* 44. 1-2, (1992): 67.

ponents of video activism as they have coalesced in the nineties: "To be a tool, a weapon and a witness" (Boyle 78). These three categories are as consitutive now as they were in the late 1960s and early 1970s. Their longevity is enfra-med by the concept of empowerment. Yet an examination of the literature and research produced in relation to video reveals very little with regard to empow-erment as a process. Terms like *democratization* and *control by the community* appear over and over again, but these are assumed from within the activities of portable video *use*. There is very little about audience or the ways video images work as devices of communication, if at all, or questions that relate representational issues to empowerment, etc.[83]

Care must be taken in discussing the *effects* of portable technologies upon users and viewers. The evaluative tools we have for examining how these tech-nologies have been appropriated and then understood cannot simply be re-duced to an instance of the technology itself, and while it is true that hundreds of groups started to use video in the late 1960s and early 1970s, that by *itself* does not suggest very much. Nor should too many radical conclusions be drawn from the use of camcorders today, since much of the usage is an out-growth of the widespread acceptance of 35mm still photography as an integral part of everyday life—an instance in which families and individuals archive their memories both for themselves and future generations. Of course, still cameras are different from camcorders, but the arguments around that differ-ence must explore the uses to which each individual technology is put. That will only be possible if the historical categories of technological innovation and change are resituated. It will be important to account more fully for the dif-ficulties posed in analyzing the subjective relationship that practitioners and viewers develop with video images. Is it true that advocacy video changes the ways people both analyze and act upon the social contexts of which they are a part? There is little but anecdotal evidence to suggest what these changes are actually about, to what degree and with what depth viewers and/or commu-nities work upon the images they watch or create. This is as much a methodo-logical problem as it is a theoretical and practical one. All the various problems of conflating class, ethnicity, color, and gender come to the fore here in a no-tion of community that seems to rise above all the contradictions and conflicts that are a part of any community's history. Gary Evans quotes John Grierson's comments on Challenge for Change during a seminar which Grierson gave at McGill University, and these complement his early criticisms in the Challenge for Change newsletter:

83. These questions are addressed, albeit all too briefly, by Lili Berko in "Video: In Search of a Discourse," *Quarterly Review of Film Studies* 10.4 (1989): 289–307.

John Grierson was fond of talking about "using art as a hammer" to his McGill University students: it was a radical phrase appropriate to a radical age. But the wiry Scotsman had his doubts about Challenge for Change which he articulated from 1969 until 1971, and his remarks at one session, with Colin Low [a producer for Challenge for Change] as guest and willing scapegoat, might be a good point from which to observe the overall impact of the programme. Using the Fogo Island experiment as his example, Grierson cautioned that the presentation of local concerns was not necessarily the real representation of local concerns, much less participatory democracy. (Evans 172)

Community and Communication

There is a "history" that can perhaps account for the new circuits of communication put in place by the advent of community-based efforts with video and film. In particular, one would have to develop an analysis of the implications of more and more people of vastly different backgrounds becoming comfortable with video and TV in the home. We would have to explore the link between the technology as a structure of possibilities in the political arena and its location within a postmodern context in which new kinds of histories (public and private) are being created in rather unlinear ways. It may appear as if video permits a massive set of variables to be introduced into a world of endless disjunctures, where there is no clear or level playing field for the construction and maintenance of specific meanings. Yet it may be the case that as more and more electronic images are created for very specific contexts, the fragmentation will allow for an interchangeable flux of meanings to be sustained by hitherto undescribed modes of linkage. These have to some degree been described by Hamid Naficy[84] in his book on exile cultures, in which an exile community manages to redefine itself and its sense of "place" through the use of video and music. Yet the mixture of genres, musical styles, and types of images constructed by the Iranian community in Los Angeles could not have been predicted or designed by video activists from outside of the community.

The often expressed desire of video activists to bring the people in the communities they work with together for the purposes of change and social cohesion is situated in a concept of community which is both naive and untheorized. Aside from the difficulties of gaining access to the rather complex and multilayered aspects of community life, their notion of community is based on a denial of difference and on a vague conception of conflict resolution. As Iris Marion Young has put it: "The ideal of community, finally, totalizes and detemporalizes its conception of social life by setting up an opposition

84. Hamid Naficy, *The Making of Exile Cultures: Iranian Television in Los Angeles* (Minneapolis: University of Minnesota Press, 1993).

between authentic and inauthentic social relations. It also detemporalizes its understanding of social change by positing the desired society as the complete negation of existing society."[85]

Young goes on to talk about the efforts of political activists to radicalize and politicize the communities they work in. She claims that the notion of face-to-face relations "seeks a model of social relations that are not mediated by space and time distancing. In radically opposing the inauthentic social relations of alienated society with the authentic social relations of community, moreover, it detemporalizes the process of social change into a static before and after structure" (Young 305). The implications of these claims for political work in the community with video are quite dramatic. They suggest that the assumptions of involvement and participation that video activists so vigorously pursued may have contributed to a static model of human relations from which it was difficult, if not impossible, to build new paradigms of political and cultural activity.

The desire to bring people together around the practice of making video-tapes has a an initial ring of authenticity to it. In the literature of community video, there seems to be an almost apocalyptic result generated when the technology is introduced and then used. The effect is doubled when the images are shown back to the community, with the explicit presumption being that images provide a mirror which would otherwise not be available. Within this environment, the topography of ideas one uses to clarify or support political media activities needs to be carefully thought out. It seems clear that the arguments presently in place for the activity of viewing are strung out along a very thin border between conflicting conceptions of passivity and nonpassivity. This dichotomy cannot account for televisual viewing, so we need an entirely different model. I bring this up because in the context of the arguments developed around the *legitimacy* of video as a political tool, it is television, and by extension all of popular culture, that is the site of a lack, an absence that the community use of video or video advocacy will somehow fill. It is in the context of this notion of a loss of power to the mainstream media and to the consequences of technological innovation that the notion of empowerment draws its strength. Yet the question of empowerment cannot be answered from within the negative parameters of an opposition that promotes such a mechanical model of communication and exchange. So perhaps the very idea of empowerment as it has been theorized up until now needs to draw upon different sources which incorporate many *more* forms of cultural activity, and which accept the diversity of needs, desires, and political priorities that communities, groups, or individuals encourage, create, and respond to.

85. Iris Marion Young, "The Ideal of Community and the Politics of Difference," in *Feminism/Postmodernism*, ed. Linda J. Nicholson (New York: Routledge, 1990), 302.

Underlying the approach taken by the community video movement is an ideology of communication centered on ideas of citizenship, identity, and empowerment through participatory, media-based activities. In fact, there is a need to move beyond generalized metaphors of the media to perhaps address the following question as it is posed by Nicholas Garnham: "Can we identify cultural forms or types of media practice that favour the formation of democratic identities and others which undermine such identities?"[86]

In one respect this seems like a naive question. In another respect it is at the core of the political assumptions that both guide and enframe the use of video as a pedagogical tool. Although these points are not articulated by the institutions that have become the most important purveyors of video (and I should add other new technologies, in particular the computer), there is an assumed link between media practice and the public sphere. The premise is that images will contribute to the growth of social movements—viewers will also fit what they see into what they think about, both with respect to their own identities and their sense of themselves as public and private personae (the contribution they can make to the social context in which they live). This notion of a "public subjectivity,"[87] a term articulated by Benjamin Lee, is essentially proposed as a holistic practice that moves citizenship beyond the narrow parameters of the community or nation-state. In this respect public subjectivity comes to stand for a public sphere and a public culture that stretches far beyond the physical and psychological boundaries of the community as we presently define it. It also stands for strategies of spectatorship dependent on intercultural and therefore more hybridized conceptions of what works as communication and what doesn't. The appropriation of video leads to forms of cultural expression that mix many different aspects of historically *differentiated* types of information. The problem is to what degree can these histories be accessed when their specificity is both overwhelmed and diluted by the movement of ideas across many, often distinctive, cultures in one country or many countries? What are the attractions of different publics for the videotapes presented to them? To what degree and with what depth can public spaces be constructed where the videotapes can be evaluated? Can viewers gain access to their own and their neighbors' experience of media images? Even more important, since so much of the viewing of electronic images is bound up with desire (the desire to know, sometimes combined with and other times offset by the desire to be entertained) and since the discursive articulation of desire is neither easy nor generally speaking, public, (and may even be anti-

---

86. Nicholas Garnham, "The Mass Media, Cultural Identity, and the Public Sphere in the Modern World," *Public Culture* 5.2 (1993): 264.
87. Benjamin Lee, "Going Public," *Public Culture* 5.2 (1993): 165–78.

thetical to the culture involved) what kind of access can we gain to the way viewers learn from and experience video images?

It may be that Garnham's question merely reinforces the idea that instrumental forms of communication can be constructed to promote political involvement and change. Surely the time has come to alter, if not recreate, this kind of argument. Video advocacy, particularly in Third World countries, is in deep trouble. Community video has rarely moved beyond the initial parameters of the debates that established the movement in the late 1960s. The time has come to examine these closed systems of thought and discourse and reflect on why they have played such a dominant role in grassroots work with lowcast media, and why they have been used as the foundation upon which so-called alternative media institutions have been built. If the heterogeneity of "community" and the richness of the "local" can engage with the genuinely important shifts of emphasis represented by video and other emerging technologies of communication, then it may just be possible to redefine the meaning and breadth of alternativity at the creative, political, and discursive level.

6 | Postmodern Media Communities

A Community of Identities

I RECENTLY RECEIVED a superb essay from a student of mine on the history and development of community radio in Canada. He argued for community radio as a tool of liberation, unfettered by the requirements of visual representation, not constrained by the centralized control of modem media monopolies. He talked about participation, about the opening up of a personal space for discourses that are fundamentally oppositional and guided by a sense of alternativity. "An alternative is another. In the sense of alternative media, alternative is perhaps *the* others. In the sense of community-oriented radio, it is the alternative to rigid formatting, highly packaged, regurgitated information, the search for profit and slickness at the expense of content and social responsibility. It is the 'other': the blacks, the women, the gay men, the prisoners, the adolescents, the community centres, the hispanics, the lesbians, and the children. It isn't just things about them, 'for' them—it is by them, and of them."[1]

As we have seen in Chapter 5, this important concept—meaning recovered and then transformed by political and cultural activity—is being found at the margins of an increasing number of social and political configurations. There is a close yet ambiguous link between all of these activities and the growth and development of new technologies. From lowcasting to camcorders, from electronic publishing to facsimile machines, we have entered an era in which the way information is transmitted is of less consequence than the use made of the material created. This proliferation, however, carries with it a number of dangers, not the least of which is an overinvestment in the effects of new technologies, an overestimation of the changes produced through the circulation of ideas within the context of the media and the public sphere. I would characterize this latter problem as an effort to construct a utopian ideology on the rather slippery foundation of communication and exchange. The slippages are

1. Ian Pringle, *Active Culturalism—Cultural Activism: The Advent of Community-Oriented Institutional FM Broadcasting in Canada*, (Unpublished essay, McGill University, 1991), 8.

often the result of vague conceptions of community and how the members of a given community reflect upon their experiences of technological change. How do communities share the knowledge of their individual members? Do video images encourage people of differing genders, classes, and ethnic backgrounds to meet and discuss issues of common concern? For example, one of the central strategies for bringing people together in a community is the meeting. A variety of community members get together who otherwise don't share the same work context or street or even the same specific problems. What they do share is a desire to meet, talk, and perhaps discover some common ground through which communication and perhaps change can be initiated. As chapter 6 progresses, I will reflect on this process and ask to what degree it is constitutive of community, to what degree it encourages the growth and development of community and individual identity.

My emphasis of course, is on images. I don't propose in this instance to do an ethnography of community meetings and the myriad other strategies that individuals use to give meaning and coherence to their daily lives. Rather, my focus will be on the intersection of images and identity. W. J. T. Mitchell asks the following question: "What is the role of art and imagemaking in a public sphere that is mainly constituted by forms of mass spectacle and the mediatization of experience—the world as theme park?" (Mitchell 366). Although I will not attempt to answer this question fully, it is as Mitchell himself suggests, one of central questions of the postmodern period. I am not completely convinced that the public sphere is in fact dominated by the "mediatization of experience," since for the most part all forms of experience are mediated. I believe that our personal and public identities are very fragile, and that there is a constant tension between the demands of the media and our private lives. I don't think that the media on their own provide us with a window into what communities and individuals do with images. Even though there are now many strategies for trying to understand the public (polling and marketing being the most widely used, though they are in some respects the weakest entry point into community), there is, in fact, less and less dialogue among critics and community members. I take the position that dissent, contestation, and the struggle to define meaning and communication do not confer a homogeneous identity upon any community. In this respect, I share with Bill Readings the following formulation of what he describes as the "heteronomous horizon of dissensus."

> Community without identity or consensus is the uncertain experience of being-together which no authoritative instance can determine, a sharing that does not establish an autonomous collective subject that is authorized to say "we" and to terrorize those who do not, or cannot, speak in that "we." Hence a distinction must be drawn between the political horizon of consensus which aims at a self-legitimating, autonomous society and the heterono-

mous horizon of dissensus, in which no consensual answer can take away
that question mark that the social bond (the fact of other people, of language) raises, no universal community can embody the answer, no rational
consensus can decide to agree on an answer.[2]

Readings also proposes that the community cannot name itself and cannot
confer authority onto a process for which consensus is never a driving force.
In this he is arguing against forms of representation that gain their legitimacy
from a conferral of authority over which the members of a community then
lose control. This same principle must be applied to the role of the media. No
community willingly gives itself over to mediatization in the sense of loss and
absence. Images survive when they can serve a purpose, but they neither reflect
nor create a community identity. They are one facet of a struggle to define
meaning, and that struggle makes the social bonds of community possible but
never fixed or unitary in character.

The importance of experiments in community radio is that they encourage
disenfranchised members of the community to enter into the technology of
sound, to engage with the technology, not so much to produce a representation
that communicates, but to participate in the creative process. This may have
unintended consequences, which highlights the spontaneity of groups and the
rather complex way community relations don't follow predictable patterns.
There is as much danger in assuming that communities are not divided by their
differences as there is in assuming that communities will be united by a set of
shared concerns. Equally, room must be made for the patterns of experience
that grow from the microcommunities of family, friends, or simply living in
the same neighborhood for many years.

One of the more interesting ways of thinking about this is to raise questions about the notion of community in relation to national identity. It may be
of value here to discuss the highly localized contradictions of the national debate as an example of the way context links up with community notions of
history. Context is a variable term, moving and changing in response to the
community's views of it. Although the use of the word often suggests the opposite, great care must be taken in avoiding atemporal definitions and applications of the concept of community.

"When we look at ideas about national identity, we need to ask, not
whether they are true or false, but what their function is, whose creation they
are, and whose interests they serve."[3] This central point of White's is at the
heart of many of the criticisms made of nationalists, but it leaves out the cru-

2. Bill Readings, "Be Excellent: Culture, The State and the Posthistorical University," *Alphabet City* 3 (1993): 51.
3. Richard White, *Inventing Australia: Images and Identity 1688–1980.* (Sydney: George
Allen & Unwin, 1981), viii.

cial need that communities feel for some kind of place they can truly call their own. This is perhaps the biggest illusion of them all, but it is also the most powerful. Ownership of place is bound up with an imagined sense of community beyond the more direct relationship to self to the immediate environment in which one lives. Can this territory of the imaginary be described as a context?[4] People living in the Montreal suburb of Outremont do not call themselves Outremonters. People don't identify themselves, in the sense of nationhood, with the street which they live on, or the high-rise they occupy, or even the suburb they inhabit. It would be absurd to do so, and yet these are a few of the most direct instances of attachment to community.

Concretely, individuals coexist with small groups of people in relatively small social and economic configurations. Yet there is a longing to extend that into something greater, a sovereign realm beyond their immediate control. The only way that can be done is through an imagining, through a fantasy of place and then through a conferral of identity from self to another. Concretely this means giving over one's identity to politicians who are meant to incarnate what we ourselves lack, or to cultural figures who are supposedly more in tune with what we share, than what differentiates us. But this conferral also produces a sense of loss, an almost inescapable feeling that *place* is not enough. The national imaginary is rarely satisfied with the geographic and psychological boundaries it finally creates, which may explain its link to expansionism and violence.

Thus what we describe as the local slips into the national and the international: it slips from gender and race to community and back again. Race circles through the histories of exile, both internal to national history and external to community, governed if not determined by the diasporas of groups moved from their homes to alien environments in which they have to learn a new language and a different way of life. These slippages carry within them all of the seeds of their own destruction, yet they are essential, permitting individuals and communities at one and the same time to claim a heritage and to cast about for a new one. This shifting terrain recreates communities. They become hybrid expressions of histories lost and regained, captured and lost once more.

The result should show us how limited our conception of culture and context is. Yet often, identities are transformed into a particular form, within which the notion of community becomes discrete, so local as to defy the other cultural configurations that surround it, yet able from time to time to communicate with them. The postmodern context is one in which there now exist many places almost unknown to each other, tribes whose rallying function is to isolate themselves from each other while at the same time remaining inter-

---

4. The classic work in this area is Benedict Anderson, *Imagined Communities: Reflections on the Origin and Spread of Nationalism* (London: Verso, 1991).

dependent at a macrocultural level. This clearly postmodern phenomenon challenges the boundaries of enclosure while at the same time increasing the number of local contexts. It redefines or at least should redefine how one thinks about the national and the translocal. It reopens the terrain of identity as "traveling" increases and crucially, that traveling takes place as much through the image as it does in the more traditional sense of the voyage. It should by now be clear that if one is ready to accept the notion that there is an inside to every cultural configuration, then the outside must also be operating as the framework for what we recognize and have recognized as community. We come to know who we are through fantasies of otherness, but the crucial point here is that otherness is created and sustained by the activities of local communities and not the reverse.

Yet, otherness may not exist anymore in the manner to which Western culture has grown accustomed. The best example of this is the way the AIDS crisis has been dealt with. Even now the guiding cultural assumptions enframing the epidemic are that it somehow came from elsewhere and not from within the societies it is ravaging. But no one knows how to pinpoint *the* cause and without that theological strategy, without the props that approach can bring to bear, communities have not only become suspicious of each other, but of necessity see the victims of AIDS as alien. This is a strategy of internal dislocation and displacement, where the principles of observation have shifted so dramatically that no amount of cultural analysis produces the necessary sense of difference that might provide some relief.

The filmmaker Dennis O'Rourke encountered this paradox when he went to Bangkok, ostensibly to recover from a failed marriage, and found himself among a culture of prostitutes where AIDS is rampant. He fell in love with one of the prostitutes, Yaiwalak Chonchanakun, and his video-film, *The Good Woman of Bangkok*, is a personal essay-fiction-documentary on the experience. At no point can he as filmmaker and lover see himself outside of the relationship he develops with Chonchanakun. There is an overriding sense that were he to get AIDS he himself would be to blame. He discovers things about himself and his identity that can only partially be related to the context. There is the sense that he is part of a transhistorical moment not outside of time, but where essential differences are open to being crossed at all times. But this in no way solves his crisis. It merely highlights the fact that what he thought was elsewhere is inside—the crisis cannot be transferred.

Chonchanakun refuses to act as a conduit for his needs. The film dwells endlessly on her face shot in video-8, as if she could somehow provide an easy solution to these dilemmas. The differences are sustained even as there is communication between and across them. This absence of reconciliation, governed by the presence of communication, paradoxically creates a structure of community. It allows O'Rourke to enter her life and discover more about himself, but as the film ends, Chonchanakun has not been much changed as a result of the encounter. The seeming fluidity of identity—the ability to move from level to level, the role playing and switches from one culture to another—do not make the differences apparent. Thus it is not only the enemy who is within but that is precisely what is shared between different communities as they struggle to define what the "outside" is. Chonchanakun's resistance to O'Rourke can be seen as a resistance to the image, to video, to the notion that O'Rourke can use Chonchanakun not only to tell his own story, but to justify his role as videomaker and filmmaker.[5]

In the same way AIDS cannot simply be transferred to an Other since it is quite possible that your next door neighbor may be HIV-positive. The theological game falls flat on its face, and what one is left with is a dispositif—a negative from which no prints can be made. This process generates a severe schism in the circularity of identity and Other. It is so unsettling that the only result may be violence and despair. The image of the Other seems lost, out of control. The fulcrum upon which identity can be sustained has been removed. The shared enemy dissolves, and the result is insularity, fragmentary, almost tribal, configurations, defined by their private mythologies and with no immediate desire to share experiences. I am not suggesting that an enemy is needed or that conventional configurations of otherness are necessary. Rather, these are shifts that fundamentally redefine difference and these shifts do not easily offer discursive tools through which identity can be analyzed. But what is most important here is the way context as such cannot easily find a ground upon which to establish a simple window on discourses that might be true or not. Locating the space within which we operate cannot in the obvious sense be narrowed down, yet the local seems to afford that possibility. It is imaginary and real communities defined by what appear to be autonomous languages upon which difference is both built and undermined, and these are contradictions that sustain each other even as they are contested.

How then is it possible to move around in differing spatiotemporal contexts, from one community to another and regain, let alone retain a sense of identity? If from the outset the history of identity is bound up with contextual factors that shift the parameters of meaning and understanding in a never-ending flow, a kind of bubbling fluidity wherein the question always is, who am I? How do assumptions of ownership of place gain their power? Or perhaps this could be put another way. The endless search for ownership may be such an important constituent of subjectivity that the fantasy of place may be the mental framework upon which the self as such is constituted.

5. For an excellent critique of the film, see Martina Rieker, "Narrating the Post-Colonial Everyday: An Interrogation of *The Good Woman of Bangkok*," *Visual Anthropology Review* 9.1 (1993): 116–22.

With reference to both the term and the idea of "Latinos," Román de la Campa has the following to say:

> Perhaps the term "Latino" is just a demographic or political category imposed on various ethnic and racial groups whose past or present includes the Spanish language or the Hispanic culture. Or perhaps we become Latino by virtue of America's need to identify us as a minority at a particularly uncertain moment when our demographic presence has reached critical proportions. Then again, perhaps it is the situational aspect of the rubric to which we should attend: we may be able to identify as a Latino at certain moments while retaining a sense of Latin American national or regional identity. It seems we are at times Latino, at other Dominican, Mexican, Guatemalan, Cuban, depending on the cultural frame. But can we still be an American?[6]

The hybridization de la Campa talks about here is still in search of an essence that may never be found. It is in the postmodern notion of the border, the nomad, cultures struggling with diasporic moments from within and without, that a new conception of place and identity will be found.[7] Gupta and Ferguson talk about a "postcolonial simulacra" in which cultures can no longer identify a clear pattern of origin and place, "familiar lines between here and there, centre and periphery, colony and metropole become blurred" (Gupta and Ferguson 10).

To summarize: some of the discursive practices of identity are found in highly subjective notions of community; the boundaries for the definition of community are fluid and often very inconsistent; there is no singular moment that fully explains or defines the historical relationship between self and Other and this is the motor force for contestation and resistance; communication is possible across all of these boundaries, but it is not at all clear what the results are; the appearance of autonomous or eclectic languages within communities doesn't necessarily mean that difference has been solidified; rather, the question always is, to what degree and by what means can communicative relationships be sustained even when they are in tension? What happens to communities that are constantly in transition, where there are very few markers for identity, little stability with respect to ethnicity in which, nonetheless, the diasporic struggle continues? What happens to notions of space and place? This parallel movement toward tribalism and eclecticism, which generates highly individualized practices, may produce many barriers to the process of communication. This may mean that what we understand as mass communication

6. Román de la Campa, "Latin Lessons," *Transition* 63 (1994): 61–62.
7. See Akhil Gupta and James Ferguson, "Beyond 'Culture': Space, Identity, and the Politics of Difference," *Cultural Anthropology* 7.1 (1992): 7. Gupta and Ferguson are particularly concerned with the "loss of territoral roots" that the increasing mobility of people from often radically different cultures suggests about the makeup of communities.

doesn't exist anymore, but this then raises the far more complex question of why differing communities are still able to communicate with each other.

Local Travels

In a recent article James Clifford works with the idea and metaphor of "Traveling Cultures"[8] as a way of examining the relationship between knowledge, the gathering of information, and the questions raised by the use of informants in understanding "local" cultures. This he explores with respect to the changes in the analysis of culture and society over the last fifteen years, suggesting that the intersection of the disciplines of ethnography, cultural studies, and communications represents a fundamental shift in the parameters we use to *ground* the research we are doing in each discipline. He makes this claim within the context of a transformation taking place in all disciplines as they come to grips with the new agendas generated by the extraordinarily intense intellectual, political, and cultural activities of the last twenty years.[9]

For example, traditional ethnography has begun to confront its own heritage as a traveling profession dependent on the movement of analysis from one location to another, from local cultures to foreign cultures. Analyses from afar now say more about the *locale* of research and institutional priorities within Western cultural traditions—a reversal back on the imperial source—than about the destinations which are their usual focus.[10]

This important shift is more than a move from one emphasis to another. It represents a reorientation at a paradigmatic level, a fundamentally different combination of discursive and research materials and a shift in the way we think about analytically inclined strategies of observation and investigation in *our own culture*. This *return* has highlighted, among other elements, the importance of what people in disparate locations say about each other and to what degree they communicate those statements to local and nonlocal communities. The crucial point here is that the process of gathering information about our own and other cultures can no longer make the claim that reality can be captured and then reproduced by representational tools that are themselves de-

---

8. James Clifford, "Traveling Cultures," in *Cultural Studies*, ed. Lawrence Grossberg, Cary Nelson, Paula Treichler (New York: Routledge, 1992), 96–116.
9. Michael Fischer explores these issues in great depth in "Anthropology as Cultural Critique: Inserts for the 1990s, Cultural Studies of Science, Visual-Virtual Realities, and Post-Trauma Polities," *Cultural Anthropology* 6.4 (1991): 525–37.
10. A recent essay by Anna Grimshaw and Keith Hart provides an interesting historical focus on the changes in the discipline of anthropology. Anna Grimshaw and Keith Hart, "Anthropology and the Crisis of the Intellectuals," *Critique of Anthropology* 14.3 (1994): 227–62.

rived from ideologies trying to sustain changing cultural and national differences. One of the ways of thinking about this is to reflect on the paradox of ever-more-powerful media monopolies making the effort to control everything from satellite broadcasting to local production. These large conglomerates flood the airwaves with competing conceptions of audience and cultural specificity. The result has been further fragmentation, because in so many different ways the productions have no origin. For example, what are the implications of villagers in Southern India watching soap operas from the U.S.? The particular locale for the viewing has ceased to be the village itself. It seems clear that the village long ago gave up the bounded space and territory that even the term *village* suggests. In other words, the openings to new forms, to new media experiences (aside from everything else) was accomplished *before* Star TV began broadcasting "Dallas" in Asia. There is, I think, no other way of explaining the extraordinary receptivity of seemingly foreign cultures to Hollywood.

This suggests that there must be a shift in the terms of media image analysis and says a great deal about new forms of observation, ways of seeing, methods of relating observation to interpretation. It is not a matter anymore of "envisioning" postmodern cultures through the differences suggested by one culture in control of its destiny and history and another that is primitive and somehow lost and in need of recovery. It must be remembered that much of what we describe as the Modern and postmodern are concepts and practices that have arisen in relation to a set of assumptions about our own cultural evolution, our own cultural history as *set against* the supposed lack of development in other cultures. The very notion of the Third World incarnates this opposition. It is sustained even as efforts are made to try and change the term from "Third World" to "South," while what is maintained are crucial suppositions of cultural difference. The problem is not that Western culture and the cultures that surrounding it are the same. They are, in the most radical sense, different. Rather, we are faced with defining and redefining what is meant by "difference." There is and certainly will never be a final moment when the differences will suddenly disappear, and I see this is as a positive historical reality, evidence of resistance and contestation to any notion that history is dead or over. But as the ground for the definition of difference shifts with historical change and development, it is our own culture's explanation of *context* that has altered. If we can no longer define ourselves and our activities in opposition to other cultures, then what is the new terrain we have created in order to map out our own identity? In other words, what are the vantage points we can use to clarify "difference" from within?

Clifford suggests that the movement from the local to the international redefines the local. "My aim . . . is simply to open up the question of how cultural analysis constitutes its objects—societies, traditions, communities, identities—in spatial terms and through specific spatial practices of research" (Clifford 1992, 97; In a footnote after this quote Clifford quotes Adrienne Rich, "A Place on the map is also a place in history").

Context brings up the question of observation, positionality, vantage point. To what degree does our culture provide us with sites of observation, places where we can watch our own activities, our own praxis? Is it useful to think about the inside and the outside? How can links be established between the context seen and understood as "everyday life"—"this is what I do from day to day"—and the broader context seen as history, the public sphere, the political arena? There is, to my mind, no transcendent moment outside of which the question of vantage point can be negated. The very idea of context suggests an endless circularity within which context operates as the anchor, but is nevertheless a constant site of struggle.

This links up with questions of identity—a slippery slope where distinctions of private and public seem absolutely central—a space and time within which gender, race, and class operate as categories of external and internal explanation—the dialectic of self and Other. How do certain categories of identity take on a status, a power that allows them to cross the boundaries of the public and the private? Is it possible for there to be a cultural definition of self? And if there is, can the categories of analysis remain fluid enough to avoid becoming fixed?

These questions are both existential and pragmatic. They are based on an appropriation of the concept of culture as a representative synthesis of all that we do and understand about ourselves and our society. It seems inconceivable that the concept of culture could be discussed without reference to context. Yet to some degree the idea of context is culturally specific to Western thought, steeped in the traditions of Enlightenment thinking, locked into quite specific notions of space and time.[11]

Culture is always an expression of a plurality of voices in any given social configuration. The point is that there is tremendous stress and strain, a dialectic between the fragment(ary) and the whole—which may mean that culture has little to do with consensus, but consensus *may also mean very little with regard to community anyway*. The family, for example, is not a homogenuous unit. It survives or not, through the stresses and strains of conflict, anger, happiness, and so forth. So, the point is not that consensus is needed but that conflict is inevitable, and what families and communities learn to do is manage the conflicts to arrive at some measure of agreement, or even to more fully

11. The historical implications of this specificity have been examined by Elizabeth Deeds Ermath, *Sequel to History: Postmodernism and the Crisis of Representational Time* (Princeton: Princeton University Press, 1992). See especially pages 25–44.

understand what divides them. Irrespective, this may not be the glue that binds.

Plurality, polyphony, multiplicity, all the canonized terms in postmodern discourse are windows into difference, into schisms and conflicts. But they say very little about the management of all these processes, about what allows us to communicate shared and contradictory understandings of the experiences we have. We can then begin to postulate that heterogeneity and homogeneity are interdependent—that differences and similarities operate in tandem—connections are made and then broken—but at no time do we operate outside of the parameters of what joins us. It is more like a shifting platform, where a multiplicity of viewpoints are possible and where the platform can either remain the same or change.

It is the notion of culture that has been posited as that platform, as that which holds the many voices together, which binds and structures the relations that sustain community and communication both through and across what is shared and what is not. If, as some postmodernists suggest, the platform is itself fluid, shifting, impermanent, then where are the vantage points? For a moment at least, in order to make a judgment, some kind of position has to be taken. If no judgments are to be made or if no judgments *can* be made, then don't we just end up with a long list of descriptive comments 'where "location" itself becomes an abstraction?

Recently, a Canadian business publication said the following: "Hyperchange is the new change. It combines the three classical kinds of change—linear, exponential and discontinuous—with a new type, chaotic change that is random, disorderly and unpredictable. A major characteristic of hyperchange is the rate at which things—states, nations, corporations, products, product models, books, magazines, fashions, ideas—abruptly disappear and are replaced by other things. . . . Hyperchange calls for an entirely new mindset."[12]

This means that there is no time for evaluation, let alone interpretation. In fact, it becomes useless to establish evaluative strategies because the object will change so quickly. Yet even the most ardent postmodernist would agree that cultures operate as places, sites, within which and through which particular sets of values are learned (even as those same values are quickly replaced by others). So our ideas of culture include a structural component—the glue that binds—and an active component made up of institutions which operate under certain restrictions and are to some degree based on normative principles that educate its members from generation to generation. Culture is a "site" of learning, although there are many dimensions to the way all of the elements interact. Associated with this is the additional notion that culture somehow is

12. Derm Barret, "Fast Focus: A Manager's Look at TQM Terms and Topics," *The Globe and Mail*, (19 January 1993), B 24.

a representation of the wholeness of the relations constituting it. All of these ideas are often either collapsed into concepts of community or described as the driving force for its development. Culture and community become one and the same.

"For theorists of all persuasions, a cultural formation takes its meaning from its involvement in what Darwin, speaking not of culture, but of nature, called an inextricable web of affinities and it is this presumption that renders the various elements of a way of life systematically *readable* just as the notion of the organic unity in literary texts rendered them readable according to the norms of the discipline of new criticism."[13]

All the parts of the whole have to have some relationship to each other, which means that the *links* have to be constructed. The whole plus the links becomes evidence of structure that often leads to the assumption that there must be some *structuring* going on. Otherwise, how could the process keep itself alive and perpetuate its values? There must also be some way of accounting for the whole, because, it is assumed, each fragment must have some relationship to the next. What is opened up in all this is a "space" for interpretation based on the idea that the parts must be understood in order to comprehend what links them. This strategy has been derived from textual studies and applied to the study of culture as a whole. The circularity is fascinating, because once there has been a movement from the text to the cultural context, there is then a structural principle invoked to explain the text. The interpretation of the text derived from the reading made of it, transferred to the cultural whole, finds itself once again through the text. This is the origin of statements such as "this television show is the product of American culture." The tautology should be self-evident and it is a wonderful example of the frailties attached to the process of reading or postulating the world as text. For if we read culture in the same way we read a text, if culture is text, then how does the structuring occur? The argument might be that it occurs through language—but there again, the fundamental question would be how?

The problems raised by the above can be thought about this way. The drive to discover the various elements of a phenomenon (TV, radio, rock music, music videos, and so forth) as constituent elements of popular culture or of a text (meaning, expression, ideological direction, semiotic properties, and so on) is as much driven by the categories we use as by the historical presumptions that have given rise to the category. If all the elements are seen as related then that alone suggests meaning, pattern, rationality, structure. This then means that it is the responsibility of the interpretive method to somehow close the differences between the elements, in order, at a most basic level, to be able to under-

---

13. Christopher Herbert, *Culture and Anomie: Ethnographic Imagination in the Nineteenth Century*, (Chicago: University of Chicago Press, 1991), 5.

stand the gaps. The point of entry into any cultural analysis is essentially arbitrary. Thus the question of meaning will vary with the point of entry. Do Trekkies watch "Star Trek" as a soap opera? Do talk show aficionados watch "Oprah" as a sitcom? Do news addicts watch CNN as a soap opera?

So, how you enter and the category you choose will have a large impact on the perspective you develop with respect to the "whole" that you are examining, as well the text(s) you have targeted. Just as I believe that our culture has great difficulty in ridding itself of quite limited notions of audience, so I believe that the idea of the "whole" is always present in the form of an imaginary community designed to uphold the notion that people share similar cultural experiences. This I would describe as yet another platform upon which cultural analysis builds its presumptions and upon which the idea of community gains credibility as a strategic explanation for difference. In other words, the process works from the whole into difference. This runs the risk of removing conflict and contradiction and creating a convenient, even credible, set of definitions for difference, thereby introducing an element of predictability into the relationships that constitute community. Yet this is not how the Trekkie community works. Although the community is a carefully constructed one, one of its most important developments has been the many 'zines that develop and redevelop plotlines in unheard-of directions. These range from sexual fantasies (e.g., a homosexual adventure between Spock and Captain Kirk) to bizarre plots involving characters from other science-fiction stories. Over the years, the 'zines have been building on each other so that there are now intertextual references so eclectic that only a small proportion of the readership could possibly know their meaning. At the same time, the television show, "Star Trek" reaches beyond the Trekkie community, and this happens in a variety of ways—there are references in the shows both old and new, which non-"Star Trek" fans would have difficulty understanding. The Trekkie community also interprets the shows in a specific way, linking them to a variety of preconceptions about the characters which are, to say the least, specific to their own interests. Yet for the most part the communities outside of the Trekkie one can come to grips with the shows. This suggests that the way tribalism works in the postmodern era may be quite different from anything we have imagined up until now. The example of Deadheads (followers of the Grateful Dead) is only one of many groupings that transcend conventional definitions of place and space.

Let me emphasize here that simultaneous to this constitution of particularity, community, and difference, our culture continues to churn out an endless procession of images, spectacles, potential sites of experience. So complex is this interlaced network of production that it can in no sense be described simply as consumption. Its heterogeneity precludes any reduction to equation or formula, though it would be useful to examine why one of the abiding myths of popular culture is that we are its victims. This crucial subset of the entire process is a defensive response to the diversity and conflict at the heart of most cultural activity.

Visual Media, Ethnography, and Indigenous Cultures

In order to look more closely at these questions of difference, community political and cultural activity, I will weave through a series of juxtapositions from a number of experiences I have had in the field of media ethnography (my term)—a kind of bricolage—or as James Clifford has put it, an "ethnographic surrealism."[14] These fragments are linked in ways I could not have anticipated before I made the effort to understand the connections. This kind of reconstruction interests me because it is a combination of personal history and field work, evidence of an effort to explore and map the relationship between subjectivity, analysis, experience, and community. More than that, it is a way of specifying and revealing the presence of "theory" within the subjective—a strategy for talking about theory through subjectivity and for linking them together to discuss the role electronic images play in the constitution of cultural communities.

Stephen Tyler has summarized the purpose, as he sees it, of a postmodern ethnography. "A postmodern ethnography is a cooperatively evolved text consisting of fragments of discourse intended to evoke in the minds of both reader and writer an emergent fantasy of a possible world of commonsense reality, and thus to provoke an aesthetic integration that will have a therapeutic effect. It is, in a word, poetry—not in its textual form, but in its return to the original context and function of poetry, which, by means of its performative break with everyday speech, evoked memories of the *ethos* of the community and thereby provoked hearers to act ethically."[15] In Tyler's terms there is no observer and no one to observe. Instead, there is discourse: that which grows out of dialogue and conversation. The dialogic nature of this encounter means that the stories exchanged feed off each other, provoke each other, and are linked by a set of concerns not exclusive to either party in the exchange. This poesis is not tran-

14. See chapter 4 of James Clifford, *The Predicament of Culture* (Cambridge: Harvard University Press, 1988) in which Clifford argues for a redefinition of the history of Surrealism in order to show the close if not parallel development of ethnography and Surrealist thinking.
15. Stephen A. Tyler, "Post-Modern Ethnography: From Document of the Occult to Occult Document," in *Writing Culture: The Poetics and Politics of Ethnography*, ed. James Clifford and George E. Marcus (Berkeley and Los Angeles: University of California, 1986), 125–26.

scendent; it merely suggests a rearrangement of the familiar. It is reconstructive and destructive (in the Surrealist sense). Tyler tries to articulate the meeting ground of projection and experience which I discussed in chapter 4. He talks about the way a text can evoke meanings. "Because its meaning is not in it but in an understanding, of which it is only a consumed fragment, it is no longer cursed with the task of representation. The key word in understanding this difference is 'evoke,' for if a discourse can be said to 'evoke,' then it need not represent what it evokes, though it may be a means to a representation" (Tyler 1986, 129). Evocation is neither present nor absent—it is a coming into being of meaning that need not reflect a moment of origin or an end. Evocation doesn't depend on reference either, because for Tyler that reproduces the visualist impulse to "describe," "compare," "classify," and "generalize" (Tyler 1986, 130). I bring up Tyler here because in what follows I will examine the postmodern ethnography of Eric Michaels, who explored on the frontiers of one of my major interests—the impact of video and television on indigenous cultures. He achieved this by rethinking the notion of "effects"—the ways in which white imperial cultures control and attempt to dominate other societies —and not positing anything like a linear model for what happens when new technologies are thrust upon indigenous peoples. His insights in this regard are very significant, and like Tyler he is concerned with overcoming the bias in Western ethnography for an analytic strategy that conveniently overlooks the very specificity it is meant to be revealing.[16]

In his essay on Hollywood iconography,[17] Michaels points out many of the radical differences in understanding that the Warlpiri have with regards to American films and television. Not only are the plots dealt with differently, but the characters in these films are reinterpreted according to the specific exigencies of Warlpiri culture and social life. Michaels is very critical of "unilinear" approaches to media history and in his article critiques Harold Innis and Marshall McLuhan for their use of indigenous examples (the primitive) as a contrast with the more technologically driven assumptions of Western societies. Michaels is sensitive to the different symbolic systems of aboriginal people in Australia. He suggests that the differences cannot in one sense be bridged, and perhaps shouldn't. Then he talks about the resistance of aboriginal Australians

16. Further details on the history of aboriginal media in Australia can be found in Faye Ginsburg, "Aboriginal Media and the Australian Imaginary," *Public Culture* 5.2 (1993): 557–78, and Faye Ginsburg, "Indigenous Media: Faustian Contract or Global Village?" in *Rereading Cultural Anthropology*, ed. George E. Marcus (Durham: Duke University Press, 1992), 356–76.
17. Eric Michaels, "Hollywood Iconography: A Walpiri Reading," in *Television and its Audience: International Research Perspectives*, ed. Phillip Drummond and Richard Paterson (London: British Film Institute, 1987).

to the literacy program that they were often forced to take. That resistance was as much against the church as it was against the imposition of Western traditions of schooling. Yet what Michaels discovered was that there was far less resistance to the introduction of modern media. In fact, the VCR was appropriated in a variety of different ways, and, as I shall discuss in a moment, with radically different results. He concluded that the effects of Western cultural phenomena upon indigenous peoples cannot be understood as long as there are intellectual models in place that patronize those cultures and deny to them precisely the strength to resist and recreate what they are exposed to. (The current use of video by the Kayapo in the Amazon rain forest is a testament to this creativity, and the impact of their videotapes has been felt worldwide.)[18] To his credit Michaels understood the depth of Warlpiri creativity and also the important political ramifications of their video work. Much of what the Warlpiri did was, as Michaels suggested, context-sensitive—the video images were not immediately accessible to outsiders, although this in no way prevented Michaels from making the effort to interpret and analyze the videotapes.

All of this is of course, in part, the very question of ethnography itself—a question to ethnography—about how to analyze the *strategic choices* that different cultures make in response to the influences they have on each other. The question of vantage point—where and how these choices can be examined—was a central concern of Michaels. He tried to draw upon the experiences of nonprint media and apply them to the process through which ethnographic knowledge is created and transformed into visual and oral documents. In talking about Warlpiri graphics Michaels says, "another way to describe these graphic constructions is as maps. As stories of the landscape they are also images of that landscape" (Michaels 1987, 114).[19] As is clear by the end of the article, the aboriginal response to Western media both in terms of creativity and appropriation could not have been predicted from the outside. Even the reductive notion that aboriginal culture is "oral" and therefore more likely to

18. See the work of Terence Turner, "Visual Media, Cultural Politics and Anthropological Practice: Some Implications of Recent Uses of Film and Video among the Kayapo of Brazil," *Commission on Visual Anthropology Review* (Spring 1990): 8–13.

19. An extended effort to analyze the relationship of aboriginal art to the landscape of Australia appears in Krim Benterrak, Stephen Muecke, and Paddy Roe, *Reading the Country: Introduction to Nomadology* (Freemantle, Australia: Freemantle Arts Centre Press, 1984), 22: "A book has to be a set of traces, words going somewhere. The nomadic reader will then come along afterwards and track things up, deciphering the traces. There will be no general idea of what the whole thing is about, only specific lines to be followed. Singular authority and over-arching general theory will be abandoned in favour of local and strategic movements, where one person's story ends the other one takes off. Nomadic writing writes itself; its authority comes from the territory covered, not the person temporarily in charge of the pen."

use video, for example, cannot explain why aboriginal people enjoy watching Western melodramas while at the same time being obsessed with *cinema vérité* whenever they use the medium. Michaels senses how his role as an ethnographer is undermined by these ambiguous shifts in meaning. The lesson for me is how difficult it is to find a vantage point that also tells a tale.

Michaels elaborates on this contradiction in his article entitled, "How to Look at Us Looking at the Yanomami Looking at Us,"[20] in which he says: "A solution is to address the entire process of visual media as a problem of communication, more specifically in cross-cultural translation" (Michaels 1982, 145). In the article Michaels confronts the dilemmas of trying to understand images that have come from other societies as a central problem for ethnographic inquiry in general. It is in a later piece, however, that Michaels actually explores the work being done by aboriginal people in Australia. The article, "For a Cultural Future: Francis Jupurrurla Makes TV at Yuendumu,"[21] disputes any notions of authenticity and traditionalism as an entry point into the analysis. Instead, Michaels examines the historical construction of a television culture at Yuendumu in the light of state efforts to centralize broadcasting under the guise of a regionalism dictated by government bureaucrats in Canberra. He also links Warlpiri life and art and the appropriation of video with a desire on the part of aboriginal people "to resolve political, theological, and aesthetic contradictions that arise in uniquely contemporary circumstances" (Michaels 1994, 105).

It may be that nothing of value *to* indigenous cultures can be yielded in the process of translation. But this would presume, as Michaels so often pointed out, that colonized cultures themselves have somehow escaped the influences of modern media, which as anyone who has been watching the growth and development of the video cassette recorder, for example, knows is not the case. This still doesn't lessen one of the central dilemmas of ethnographic work with film and video. For the ethnographer it may be more important to uncover both the applicability and effects of the technology than to let the technology work its way through the society in question and let that society find the measure of its own response. I think that it would not be too radical an assertion to say that the response of indigenous cultures to *cultural* phenomena cannot be ascertained clearly until those cultures have devised strategies of response, whatever form those responses might take. The Warlpiri, and in particular Jupurrurla, have used video in so many different ways that one

20. Eric Michaels, in *A Crack in the Mirror*, ed. Jay Ruby (Philadelphia: University of Pennsylvania Press, 1982).
21. Eric Michaels, in *Bad Aboriginal Art: Tradition, Media, and Technological Horizons* (Minneapolis: University of Minnesota Press, 1994).

would have to look with great depth at their culture to understand why electronic images were so easily accepted and how the images have become so useful at a social and political level.

At the same time, there is a tendency, manifest in many ethnographic projects but even more so when film and video are put to use, to presume that what other cultures choose as images can actually be translated, and it is this presumption that I think needs to be contested, because what is inevitably involved are complex sign systems which our own culture has had difficulty in interpreting for itself, let alone for others. This is a fascinating and perplexing problem. It suggests a kind of opaqueness which the universalizing tendencies of modern film and television theory have not grappled with. But the question needs to be asked; otherwise, we may have to accept Marshall McLuhan's predictions about a global village produced through technologies of communications. If we do accept his predictions then the complex and rather different images that the aboriginal peoples of Australia produced, which Eric Michaels documented, simply become part of a transhistorical and transcultural phenomenon.

On the other side of this debate about cultural specificity, what can be said about countries as different as Australia, India, Taiwan, New Guinea, Tanzania, Israel, Indonesia, and the United States sharing a similar and explosive growth in the availability of video cassette recorders and camcorders? Does the presence of video technology—its mere presence—convey a set of similar concerns, a meshing of cultural and artistic traditions? Does the existence of mini-videotheaters throughout Asia showing a mix of tapes from Hong Kong and Hollywood suggest *uniform* modes of understanding and comprehension? (Hollywood's challenge to cultural specificity has yet to be seriously examined by ethnographers.)

Eric Michaels addressed these issues through his work with the Yuendumu, and I am particularly interested in one tape that he analyzes in depth in the article on the Warlpiri. The videomaker, Jupurrurla, set out to make a video about the massacre of aboriginal peoples at Coniston. Briefly, in 1928, a white trapper and prospector, Frederick Brooks, was killed at Crown Creek near Coniston by two members of the Warlpiri tribe. Subsequently, the police massacred over one hundred members of the tribe, and Jupurrurla wanted to go to the site of the killings in order to retell the story from an aboriginal point of view. Aside from the fascinating details of how the tape was actually made, Michaels comments on the use of landscape shots in the video. "The most striking characteristic is exceptionally long landscape pans; indeed there is more attention to landscape than to actors or action. This could easily be dismissed as the result of naive filmmaking in which static landscapes, which prove easier to record than moving people, receive more attention. These extremely long, uninterrupted takes are also associated with unsophisticated filmmaking."[22]

Michaels goes on to discuss how the landscape pans are in fact very complex and how every feature of the landscape has a set of meanings attached to it. The meanings, which are sometimes historical and often symbolic, cannot be understood by viewers unfamiliar with the culturally specific readings that the Warlpiri confer on the image and that they expect the image to contain. It should be mentioned that Jupurrurla made this videotape with a group of Warlpiri and all of the people involved had had extensive exposure to white European culture and in particular to video through rental stores in the district. It is therefore even more fascinating that their experience as viewers wasn't translated in the videomaking and that they worked so hard to make the medium reflect their own cultural interests. "The pans do not follow the movement of the eye, but movements of unseen characters—both of the Dreamtime and historical—which converge on the landscape: This is where the police trackers came over the hill, that is the direction the ancestors come in from. . . . Shifts in focus and interruptions in panning pick out important places and things in the landscape, like a tree where the spirits live or a flower with symbolic value. The camera adopts technical codes to serve a predetermined system of signification in this radically *Yapa* sense of mise-en-scène" (Michaels 1994, 114). I am not entirely convinced by this argument in part because the boundaries between Michaels's description and Jupurrurla seem to have dissolved. For example, to what degree does Michaels's interpretation reflect his own assumptions about Warlpiri history? Are the reports that Jupurrurla gave him about the landscape he filmed the only authoritative way of understanding the result? I ask these questions not to create further levels of difference but to counter the notion that the interconnections can necessarily be sustained in the manner in which Michaels suggests. The hybridization of cultural concerns implicit in the decision by the Warlpiri to use video means that there may not be a specificity to the *Yapa* approach. Furthermore, even though the static shot may represent a resistance to Western ways of filming in Michaels's eyes, how does it do so? There are many examples of static shots in European and American videomaking and filmmaking. It matters little whether indigenous peoples have been exposed to them. What is important here is Michaels's relationship to his own cultural context, since he is mediating our view of the Warlpiri aesthetic. Even his use of the term *cinéma-vérité* defines a boundary between fiction and truth that may not operate within the framework he suggests. The problem here is that images cross many different borders all of the time. This endless "deterritorialization" (Gupta and Ferguson 20) requires another kind

22. Eric Michaels, *The Aboriginal Invention of Television: Central Australia 1982–86* (Canberra: Australian Institute of Aboriginal Studies, 1986).

of mapping and suggests that Michaels's identification of Warlpiri culture is itself problematic. The irony is that even though electronic images borrow from everywhere, they are also able to root themselves in the very particularity that their transnational status tends to dispel.

The availability of video and the use to which the medium is put may not provide us with enough information about its cultural role. In addition, any extrapolation of effect may not be able to account for the complexity of indigenous response. Allen S. Weiss has commented on this in a recent article: "We might remember, as a cautionary tale, the story told by Eric Michaels about the Aboriginal television program where all that 'we' saw was the most banal sort of 'home video' depicting an empty, bleak landscape; but the tribal members observed the confluence of Dreamtime and historical representation, of myth and legend, in a landscape signifying an originary event of their culture. It is precisely within such an ironic intercultural misunderstanding that the 'magic of the earth ' truly escapes us: even if we know of their history, and their gods, we also know that their deities cannot touch us. We can never truly know their art if we do not believe in their gods."[23] My own empathy with the Dreamtime, for example, both as a mode of storytelling and as lived experience, does not mean that I have genuinely understood the way in which aboriginal culture lives the Dreamtime. Only recently Eric Michaels critiqued Bruce Chatwin's book *The Songlines* because of the author's romanticism and clear inability to understand the complex history and use of "dreaming tracks."[24] Michaels was concerned with how authors like Chatwin use aboriginal culture to further their own aims while at the same time disavowing any connection to the forms of anthropological discourse they are creating. Under the guise of fiction/diary Chatwin transformed aboriginal concerns into his own, but that may well be what is most interesting about the book in any case.

There is therefore an inevitable tension between the particular and the general, between the contingencies that make one historical event more important than another, and the ability our culture has to situate our comprehension of forms of symbolic organization external to us. In terms of video this is a very serious problem because the image, and images that come from somewhere else, tend to suggest a kind of transparent directness, an intercultural nexus, which makes it seem as if they can be understood. Put another way, even the *naming* of that portion of the Warlpiri video that deals with landscape may send us off in the wrong direction simply because of the etymological history and cultural weight of the term *landscape*. This doesn't mean that a pan of a landscape is not one; rather, the pan as such means one thing to us and another

23. Allen S. Weiss, "Outside In: Some New Improved Anxieties of Influence," *Art & Text* 35 (1990): 97.
24. Eric Michaels, "Para-Ethnography," *Art & Text* 30 (1988): 48.

to the Warlpiri. As John Von Sturmer has remarked, an ethnographic film or video can attempt to show the truth viewed from the outside *as if* it is operating from within.[25] I would extend his comment to suggest that what attracts us to particular forms of visual expression in ethnography, to particular ways of revealing another culture's concerns and dreams, stories and daily lives, is precisely that we can only *see* what we have already anticipated as visual. This would explain (though not fully) the extraordinary popularity of the film *First Contact*, which uses racist archival films of indigenous peoples in New Guinea as found footage. The result is that it appears somehow to be new even though that kind of footage has been seen before and would under any other circumstances be rejected for its racism. The fascination with the archival material seems to be situated in its apparent innocence, in the mere fact that it exists, and in the pleasure our culture gets from knowing or at least presuming that we have transcended what the footage reveals.[26]

The theories that Western cultures use to explain the media may not be applicable or even useful when applied to what the Warlpiri have done. This raises the rather interesting problem that Michaels may be using what Jupurrurla made to justify his own particular expectations about video: expectations, for example, that using the medium may provide aboriginal peoples with more control over it as a technology. But that is an assumption based on what set of experiences? Community video? The work of Sol Worth and John Adair?[27] Ethnography itself? How do we evaluate the interaction between new technologies and indigenous peoples? What conceptual tools are best suited to dealing with the very particular characteristics of video? Eric Michaels's effort to answer these questions was tragically cut short by his death from AIDS.[28]

I would like to suggest that what Michaels discovered in the viewing experience of the Warlpiri was not their transparent use of the medium or the image, nor the collapse of the real into the pictorial. Rather, the Warlpiri transformed the video image into a complex and multilayered cultural *system*. They presumed no denotative relationship between the picture and the landscape,

25. John Von Sturmer, "Aborigines, Representation, Necrophilia," *Art & Text* 32 (1989): 135.
26. Ron Burnett, "First Contact: The Ethnographic Film as Historical Document," *Papers of the Second Australian History and Film Conference* (Sydney: Australian Film and Television School, 1984), 69.
27. John Adair and Sol Worth, *Through Navajo Eyes: An Exploration in Film, Communication and Anthropology* (Bloomington: Indiana University Press, 1972). For a far more theoretically rigorous extension of the ideas in *Through Navajo Eyes*, see Sol Worth, *Studying Visual Communication* (Philadelphia: University of Pennsylvania Press, 1981).
28. Michaels kept a diary about his experience of AIDS. It is a harrowing journey but also an inspiring one. As one of my students suggested to me, "may we all un-become with such finesse." Eric Michaels, *Unbecoming* (Rose Bay, New South Wales: Empress Publishing, 1990).

because the landscape as such was already defined by a symbolic network of meanings. The crucial question is, why does our culture have so much difficulty in recognizing the presence of the symbolic, the mesh of sign systems, in the landscapes *we* create on film and video? What the Warlpiri teach us is that there is no prior moment before meaning, before the message, before a technology such as video comes upon a scene. So many messages are already there, already in place, that our desire to eliminate that complexity, that layering, bespeaks a paradoxical primitivism with respect to images and meaning. Of course, the intertextuality that is fundamental to the way the Warlpiri transform the visible world cannot so easily be included in the image as it is conventionally defined.

Images of a Strike

In the 1970s I was involved with a political group that used video and film as a tool for the dissemination of information and as a pedagogical instrument in the community. The aim of the group was to create a series of short videotapes that would function as *"actualités"* — brief news-style documentaries for the most part centered on strikes, which would then be used in meetings and on local public-access television. We used half-inch black-and-white portapacks which were cumbersome and technologically quite imposing.

Our most important project was a strike at the local Noranda chemical plant in Valleyfield, a suburb of Montreal. The aim was to make a videotape with the workers that could be used to rally other workers to their cause and that could also be used for purposes of solidarity among the strikers. The video was divided into seven parts: a history of the strike; the reasons for making the video; the history of the chemical plant whose primary purpose was the production of fertilizers; a history of Noranda Corporation; a discussion of how workers organize to resist large corporations; the actual prospects for the strike itself; and finally an overview of the strike in relation to other strikes in Quebec. I will not go too deeply into the video here. For the purposes of this chapter what interests me is the methodology we used to make the video and in particular the way we organized the workers to participate in its production and creation. I am particularly interested in the assumptions we had about messages and about how they communicate through images, if at all.

Our group was divided into two factions. One faction wanted to make a propaganda statement which would communicate at a popular and populist level to a broad and representative cross section of workers. The other faction was less concerned with communication per se and more committed to the content of what could be said. This commitment to content privileged certain kinds of statements over others and in general transformed the video creation process into a support for their ideology, which I would now describe as a diluted form of vulgar Marxism. Over time the latter faction became dominant, and as the coherence of their ideological beliefs grew more sophisticated, the video creation process became a support for the transparent enunciation of that position. As is often the case, the clarity of the message didn't actually produce the anticipated results from the workers who watched the videotapes.

During one shooting session with a group of strikers at a particularly difficult moment of the strike, a conflict developed among the cameraman, a group of us, and three of the workers, who wanted to tell a more personal story about the health effects of the chemicals they worked with. I will not go into the details of that conflict here except to say that the workers set up the scene. The camera was placed on a tripod and simply recorded their statements. In viewing the footage afterward everyone agreed that it was quite unfulfilling and without either aesthetic or ideological impact.

This was the first in a series of similar experiences that began to divide us, both within the video group and between the group and the workers. The divisions were ultimately about different ways of seeing the video medium, about different perceptions of images and how to create them. In the final analysis, it was professionals against amateurs, but the real battle was between different visions. As it turns out the two apparently banal stories told by the workers anticipated a context in which the videotape was merely one part of a more complex process of interaction among viewers, supporters, and strikers. They invested far less in the image than we had anticipated, expected realism, and were gratified with the directness and clarity of what was said. This expectation about the image was not the result of any lack of sophistication. It saw the image in practical terms and didn't see it as a consciousness-raising device. To be blunt, the workers and their supporters already knew the message and were not looking for surprises where none were necessary.

This example highlights the way expectations about communication can in fact become a substitute for exchange. It points out what Eric Michaels so astutely observed among the Warlpiri. Images *seem* to contain within them not only messages but the maps needed to understand those messages. The minute that particular kind of investment in the image is foregrounded, the context of communication takes on greater and greater significance. The result is a rather different message dependent on cultural specificity and local history.

> Comparisons between Warlpiri story form and imported video fictions demonstrated that in many instances content (what is supplied in the narrative) and context (what must be assumed) are so different from one system to the other that they might be said to be reversed. For example, Warlpiri narrative will provide detailed kinship relationships between all characters, as well as establishing a kinship domain for each. When Hollywood videos fail to say where Rocky's grandmother is, or who is taking care of his sister-in-law, Warlpiri viewers discuss the matter and need to fill in the missing content.

By contrast, personal motivation is unusual in Aboriginal stories; characters do things because the class (kin, animal, plant) of which they are a member is known to behave this way. This produces interesting indigenous theories, for example, of national character to explain behaviour in Midnight Express or "The-A-Team." But, equally interesting, it tends to ignore narrative exposition and character development, focusing instead on dramatic action (as do Aboriginal stories themselves). (Michaels 1987, 119)

As chapter 5 discusses, the use of video in the community is full of potential pitfalls. In our case the desire to communicate through images overwhelmed the very people we wanted to engage with, and consequently the video became more important to us than our personal interaction with the strikers. We wanted to create a pedagogical tool and didn't apply that to the manner we used video, hoping instead that the image would somehow smooth out the more serious problems of social and cultural difference. It may be the case, and we just weren't able to confront this adequately, that the strikers and our video group didn't speak the same language, didn't know how to find points of contact, didn't as a consequence know how to engage in the political process. This striking heterogeneity is not a negative; rather, it supports the idea that the use of video within our own culture faces many of the same problems that ethnographers encounter with cultures different from our own.

The Marshall Islands

In November of 1988 I was invited to the Marshall Islands to advise a group of videomakers working under the aegis of the Museum of the Marshall Islands. My primary contact with the Marshalls had been through Denis O'Rouke's film, *Half-Life* and the book *Day of the Two Suns: U.S. Nuclear Testing and the Pacific Islanders* by Jane Dibblin.[29]

The Marshall Islands occupies seventy square miles in what are in reality hundreds of coral atolls and islands. The Marshalls are scattered over a half a million square miles of ocean. They have been used and abused by a variety of colonizers from the Russians to the Japanese to the Americans to the Germans. Many Marshallese are still very ill as a result of American nuclear testing in the 1940s and 1950s. Some atolls remain uninhabitable. The scandal of American colonialism has produced squalor and disease, birth defects and hunger. These once beautiful atolls and islands where the people used to live in a symbiotic relationship with the ocean have become crowded, with inadequate housing and little fresh water. Many of the lagoons have garbage floating in them, partially buried ships whose rust has leached into the sand, and old machinery, abandoned because of a lack of spare parts.

29. London: Virago Press, 1988.

The main island of Majuro is the center of most commercial activity and is where the government has its offices. Recently the Marshall Islands government proposed to take garbage from the mainland U.S. and dump it in the atolls as a way of making some money. Over the last fifty years the islanders have lost a sense of their own heritage and history as they have struggled to survive neocolonialism, one of the highest infant mortality rates in the Pacific, and a bankrupt economy kept going by American grants. Even today, the islands are used for missile testing with long range interballistic missiles sent over from California. One of the atolls continues to have a large American base on it.

The small video unit that operates out of the museum broadcasts on television once a week for a two-hour period. Usually their shows are historical in nature, reflecting a desire on the part of the Marshallese to gain some measure of control over their own past and to develop visual ways of interpreting it. The extraordinary thing about broadcast television in Majuro is that all of the shows come from the U.S. in videocassette form and specifically from Hawaiian broadcasting companies. As a result, conventional television is dominated by advertising from Hawaii. I found it a disturbing, if not disheartening, experience to watch consumer goods being advertised, such as cars and homes and stereos, which clearly few on the island could ever dream of having. But I was really taken aback when I watched the "news" and realized that it was two to three months out of date. The cassettes, I was told, take months to process and then are sent to the American base first. The news came to me in a time warp and contradicted its very purpose, its raison d'être—which was of course to report on events as they happened. I quickly understood the importance of the two hours which the museum crew diligently worked on every week.

I cannot fully detail the rather complex experience I had in the Marshalls. Instead, I will comment on one particular shooting experience to further exemplify and elaborate on the debates I have been discussing in this chapter. The video crew had decided to produce a show on traditional methods of making rope and twine. This used to be a well-practiced craft on Majuro, but now very few people know how to make rope. The crew and I (four people in all) went by car to the furthest tip of the atoll, about twenty-five miles from the town. There used to be many palm trees on the atoll, but now they are confined to small sections of unusually arid earth and are on private land. It is quite a feat to drive on Majuro. The roads are barely that, though you wouldn't know it from the modern airport.

During the hour it took to get to the palms, we discussed how to film the cutting down of thirty or so coconuts, the hulls of which would serve as the raw material for the rope. The cameraman was very concerned with getting some shots of the men in the trees and suggested a slow tracking pan as one of the men climbed up and then a long shot of the coconut being cut down. I asked if he wanted to get a shot of the facial expression of the climber and in fact if he wanted any close-ups prior to the climb, to highlight the happy feelings that everyone had about doing the video. The cameraman felt that because they were shooting a reenactment, it would be more important to shoot it in a straightforward and direct manner.

This approach coincided with a recent show they had done on an upcoming census, during which a government official read from a prepared text. The camera was kept in one position throughout, prioritizing the content of the presenter's discourse over the image. In fact, it seemed as if the image was just a prop for the sound.

A few minutes into the shoot at the palm grove and I realized that the same process was afoot. The crew were anticipating a voice-over which would explain the content of the reenactment. Their shots were very static and often quite random. They rarely zoomed in. The camera was always on a tripod. Could it be, I asked myself, that this static approach was in fact a response to the frenetic kind of television which they were getting from Hawaii? Was the desire to make sound the central experience of viewing a challenge to my preconceptions about images? Now this may not have been as conscious as I am suggesting, but if for the most part, television in the Marshalls is overwhelmingly dominated by gaps—temporal, spatial—then perhaps a static image, effectively a sound-tape with image, might in fact be a strategic way of making a statement and making it differently.

Coconut hulls have to be soaked for a number of weeks before they can be used for ropemaking, and as we buried the hulls at the edge of a beach, I noticed the cameraman slowly panning the area. I asked him why after he had finished, and he explained that he wanted to edit the image of the sea together with the ropemaking. But on the way back to town the crew decided they wouldn't use that shot. We had worked for about five hours and had two full videocassettes. We returned to the studio near the museum which is housed in a small shack adjacent to the main building, and the crew set about editing the video. They worked very quickly. Then quite abruptly they decided that they needed an interview and went looking for one of the researchers in the museum, an elder and one of the few remaining men on Majuro who knew anything about ropemaking. They set him up in the studio, and he began to speak about the process and about how important it was for the Marshallese to know this information. When he finished, the editing began again and this time the interview became the central focus of the tape. In other words, voice would again become the centerpiece of their show.

Now of course this is my perception of their use of sound, my perception of how the crew was juxtaposing visual and oral elements. But that evening I was shown portions of a six-hour tape on a Christmas dance that had been held in the local church. For the most part, the camera was again static. The "scene," so to speak, was oral. After a while the dancing music didn't even illustrate the image. Both the sound and the image disappeared into the background, and a very gentle, almost meditative feeling overcame the tape. I realized that this wasn't meant to be a record of the event. Rather, the camera was incidental to the ceremony—just another part of the scene. The fact that the event was being preserved in some form had little to do with the way it was being filmed. When I asked what was going to be done with the tape, I was told that it would be kept in the museum. Beyond that, not much was exchanged and in some senses nothing needed to be added. This was in part because the tape was far less significant than I had assumed. In fact, the crew videotaped many events and simply turned them over to the museum without any editing, often without even looking at the footage.

I was confronted with a rather interesting paradox. I assumed a kind of directedness to the process. If you make a video you not only have something to say but also intend that the completed video fit into a particular context of communication. Of course, the context I was assuming was not the one crew had decided upon. They knew what was on the tape. Portions of it could perhaps be used at a later date. While I thought that the tape was illustrative, for them the tape was the event. Thus there was no need to add or subtract anything from it. From the outside this might appear as a lack of motivation. Far from it. I had taken for granted the "idea" that videotapes or films, once made, produced, shot, had to be transformed into objects for viewing. In this instance, the viewing had, so to speak, already taken place.

I am reminded here of a very crucial insight by Paul Rabinow in his book *Reflections on Fieldwork in Morocco*.[30] He talks about the common sense or everyday assumptions that guide the way people in a particular culture interact. This infrastructure of shared viewpoints, mutual understandings with respect to meaning, is like a map where all of the elements are in place. Often the direction markers have to be reconstructed, but not every time people talk or have some sort of exchange. As Rabinow suggests, in our *own* culture common sense is a very fragile base upon which to build and sustain processes of communication and social relations. My preconceptions with respect to the museum crew's use of video, my desire to see a more directed and hence more productive use of the images, was situated in my prior assumptions about the medium. Rabinow uses the word *thin* to explain this kind of implosion. Misunderstandings grow out of situations in which the "taken for granted" cross-cultural maps are used without detailed and careful examination.

There is as much danger in mystifying the possibilities of communication and exchange as there is in pointing out the pitfalls. I believe that my interac-

30. Berkeley and Los Angeles: University of California Press, 1977.

tion with the museum crew was mutually beneficial. But as John von Sturmer points out, there is a distinct difference between "intervening" in another society's everyday existence and projects and immersing oneself in their daily lives.

> Is there any intervention in the lives of these societies that is not destructive? Can we envisage such a possibility? In attempting to answer these questions I find it useful to oppose *presence* to *intervention*—a presence that represents a commitment to a life-within, to the maintenance of the community as community, a willingness to be made over in relation to the group, and an unwillingness to concede therefore that an existence separate from the group is possible. Against immersion, intervention is always extraneous. The latter comes from the outside; it presupposes a position of otherness. But immersion itself cannot proceed until a change occurs, not through any internal group demand or necessity, but because some external agent requires it. Intervention may therefore serve as a prelude to immersion, but not necessarily so. One can live within the group and yet attempt to impose one's own standards." (Von Sturmer 137)

The Ceremony

In a recent film (nearly all of it was shot in video) by Canadian filmmaker Atom Egoyan, entitled *Calendar*, many of the issues I have been discussing in this chapter are worked through in a very personal manner.

Egoyan spends a great deal of time in *Calendar* exploring the act of taking a photograph of historical buildings in Armenia (his country of origin), churches and fortresses, for example, within picturesque natural environments. Although these places are beautiful with rich color tones, wildflowers, and sun-baked fields, they are "tourist" images for which some anecdotal history is provided, but from which the depth seems to be missing. In fact, what becomes important as we look at the old buildings is not so much their connection to the past, but the role they play in triggering questions about the two characters on whom the photographer depends for guidance and information. One is a woman with whom the photographer (played by Egoyan) is in love, identified as his wife, and the other is an Armenian driver who acts out the role of the local "informant." The photographs are ostensibly being taken for a calendar, but in essence we are witnesses over time to the breakdown of the photographer's relationship to his wife and by extension to Armenia. Thus all of the monuments we see are themselves evidence of what cannot be seen. There are histories in the buildings, but they only speak through the voice of the driver. In fact, the pastoral setting of the images seems incongruent with the war raging in Armenia and with the breakdown of civil life and the economic devastation brought on by the overthrow of Communism. How then can this place be spoken of as home? How are national borders defined when identity and place are fluid, moveable, and ever changing? Are we the sum total of all of the different nations we now live beside, within? All of the different languages we either speak or listen to? How does this hybridization change the spatial and temporal boundaries within which we normally operate?

"A life-testimony is not simply a testimony to a private life, but a point of conflation between text and life, a textual testimony which can *penetrate us like an actual life.*"[31] *Calendar* is Egoyan's testimony to his past as much as it is a story of the efforts by the film's characters to understand their own ethnic history. The film explores the many dimensions of identity, which in the late twentieth century means far more than a simple relationship to the nation-state or the recovery of ancestral connections. The postcolonial and postimperial history we are now experiencing has scrambled the meanings of home and homeland. In Homi Bhabha's terms, another history is being written from within a crisis of the sign where language and meaning, discourse and identity have no firm anchors. Traditional notions of subjectivity have been transformed, but this is not simply the movement from one stage to another but a fundamental split in the operations of time and history.[32] "Today, the rapidly expanding and quickening mobility of people combines with the refusal of cultural products and practices to 'stay put' to give a profound sense of a loss of territorial roots, of an erosion of the cultural distinctiveness of place" (Gupta and Ferguson 9). Gupta and Ferguson go on to quote James Clifford: " 'What does it mean, at the end of the twentieth century, to speak . . . of a "native land"? What processes rather than essences are involved in present experiences of cultural identity?' "[33]

Hamid Naficy has commented upon the nostalgic desire to return to the homeland and thus to overcome the double loss of "origin and of reality"[34] as a driving force inhabited by imaginary constructions which "remains alluring only as long as it remains unrealised" (Naficy 1991, 286). This is of course the dilemma of the diaspora and exile, of cultures that have lost their roots as they

---

31. Shoshana Felman and Dori Laub, "Education and Crisis, Or the Vicissitudes of Teaching," *Testimony: Crises of Witnessing in Literature, Psychoanalysis, and History* (New York: Routledge: 1992), 2.

32. Homi K. Bhabha, "Freedom's Basis in the Indeterminate," *October* 61 (Summer 1992): 46–64.

33. James Clifford, *The Predicament of Culture* (Cambridge, Mass.; Harvard University Press, 1988), 275.

34. Hamid Naficy, "The Poetics and Practice of Iranian Nostalgia in Exile," *Diaspora* 1.3 (1991): 285.

have been overrun or destroyed, only to be recreated elsewhere, simulated, and I do not mean this pejoratively. In some respects, then, for Egoyan we have all become tourists and in the process we have had to develop new ways of dealing with each other which are more often than not mediated by complex technologies such as the camera and the telephone. Salman Rushdie has commented on this in a wonderful anecdote. "A few years ago I revisited Bombay, which is my lost city, after an absence of something like half my life. Shortly after arriving, acting on an impulse, I opened the telephone directory and looked for my father's name. And, amazingly, there it was; his name, our old address, the unchanged telephone number, as if we had never gone away to the unmentionable country across the border. It was an eerie discovery. I felt as if I were being claimed, or informed that the facts of my faraway life were illusions, and this continuity was the reality."[35]

Some years ago I found myself at a Cambodian ceremony in Melbourne, Australia. There were about eight hundred people in the gymnasium of an old school which had been taken over by the small but growing exile community of Cambodians in Australia. The gym was decorated with the symbols and colors of their homeland. Everyone was dressed up, and the smell of incense was heavy in the air. I remember little of the specifics of the ceremony except for the feeling I had that we were all in a time warp, transported back into a village, participating in the sounds and rhythms and music of a culture many thousands of years old. I understood then how crucial the nostalgia was, how curative and yet how contradictory. As a particular dance reached its peak the people around me began to cry, and as they comforted each other, they seemed to me to be both weak and strong at the same time. This, it seems to me is one aspect of exile—the ability to implicate oneself so strongly in the homeland and at the same time to go on, to carve out a new life, to break out of the boundaries of geography and time and yet to remain bound by a history that remains static even as things change both in one's new home and abroad. This is of course the paradox of loss and the base upon which narratives are built. As Rushdie says, an original moment cannot be reclaimed here with the result that fictions will be created, "imaginary homelands" (Rushdie 1991, 10). But this is precisely what Egoyan is exploring. How do those fictions sustain themselves? What are the markers we accept and what happens to the ones we reject? How do photographs and images operate as fictional bridges that allow people to cross from one culture to another, to communicate and share experiences? I mention this in relation to *Calendar* because of my own background as an immigrant to Canada as someone who was born elsewhere and for

35. Salman Rushdie, "Imaginary Homelands," *Imaginary Homelands* (New York: Viking, 1991), 9.

whom that "elsewhere" has never disappeared from the various ways I define myself. This very fluid sense of identity is made all the more acute by the situation in Quebec, by the personal signposts I have for my own past and the efforts by official culture here to eradicate the importance of that history.[36]

It is in the borders *between* official culture as promulgated by government policy and the displacement (psychological, physical, intellectual) that grows from being both a witness and participant to the diasporas of twentieth-century life that a film like *Calendar* is situated. The film searches for strategies of talking about identity that will not fall prey to the categories of margin or center. It longs for some coherence in the transnational space of exile and community. Through a series of often funny conversations the film tries to locate the way time and distance work to generate a mental geography within which the markers more often than not are unstable and unclear. At the same time one of the most interesting aspects of the film is the difficulty the photographer has in understanding Armenian. Everything his driver says has to be translated. Often we don't get a translation, and conversations take place which we don't comprehend. This is duplicated in the Toronto flat of the photographer, where he meets a number of different women in exactly the same setting (a small dining room table, wine glasses, a bottle of wine). Each time they go off to the telephone and have a conversation with their lovers in their own maternal language. We hear everything from Hindi to German to Spanish to Swedish, and so forth, and depending on our own backgrounds we either understand the conversations or don't. In all instances the women stand near the calendar that had been produced from the Armenian scenes we witnessed the photographer shooting.

The border region inhabited by Egoyan in this film also pivots on temporal displacement. The time is now, but somehow it isn't. The characters seem disconnected from the present, always yearning for something else—for the future, for the past. Yet that is also the paradoxical situation of photography both as an art form and as a means of documenting past and present.

Each encounter Egoyan has with a different woman suffers the same fate. He is left alone to contemplate the love he has left behind in Armenia. In that sense he is locked into a history that is only real within a false kind of romanticism. As in nearly all of his other films the telephone is a device of contact and breakdown, a metaphor for distance and connection. As a technology the telephone is perhaps the most important contributor to the creation of a public space within which the private fantasy of communication and interaction can be sustained and through which it is often denied. This, I think, is also the role

---

36. See the recent collection, *Boundaries of Identity: A Quebec Reader*, ed. William Dodge (Toronto: Lester, 1992).

played by photography. Distance can be overcome, but the photographic print must be narrativized if links between past and present are to be established.

Calendar is a film in twelve movements, built around the photographs accompanying the months of the year. But the film is really about the memories of times past, when an image somehow connected to its referent and when notions of home and church and tradition could be addressed from within a set of foundations as solid as the buildings we see in the film. Ironically, as the Armenian driver becomes the historian and more fully represents all that is missing from the image, from the photograph, Arsinée falls in love with him. Egoyan is left to his devices in the dining room of his Toronto house or in the darkroom trying to reconstruct a world which, as his own images suggest, has long ago ceased to exist.

Michael Jackson, "Seinfeld," and The Super Bowl

Briefly, I would like to bring together a number of elements here that both reflect on the richness of the context made possible by electronic images and on the many different issues popular cultural artifacts actually discuss and depict. In doing this, I am trying to extend the debate begun by Eric Michaels about Western culture. My premise is that I have to keep on returning to a self-reflexive mode with respect to the culture of which I am a part. "In reflexive examination we probe the techniques by which we reflect ourselves to ourselves: our stories and projections, our portraits and mirrors, our journals and novels, our games and pastimes. When we thus turn a mirror on the mirror, to examine mirroring, we create a sense of movement, of resonance, of process."[37]

The phantasmagoria of meanings and performances in popular Western culture represents only one aspect of the context within which images operate. In some respects I am following in a long tradition of analyses that "lace" together those elements of the "popular" in order to make more generalized statements about culture as a whole. However, my premise in this instance is not that popular culture either reflects or opens a window onto a set of latent truths, which, as the writer of this book, I have discovered. On the contrary, my concern is with my own seduction, my own position within a circuit of desires I have, for the purposes of the present discussion, defined as *popular*, although the term and the field it designates are to my mind so fluid and chaotic that the choice of "popular" must be seen as temporary. For the purposes

37. Phyllis Gorfain, "Play and the Problem of Knowing in *Hamlet*: An Excursion into Interpretive Anthropology," *The Anthropology of Experience*, ed. Victor Turner and Edward Bruner (Urbana: University of Illinois, 1986), 209.

of criticism, specific frameworks not only have to be introduced, they have to be maintained. It may be that as they take shape, definitions and hypotheses as well as suppositions will change. In this case my concern with popular culture is based, I would say, on my desire to redescribe if not reinvent the strategic relationship that different forms of political action can have within our culture. Yet even as I say this I am aware that my own use of culture as a concept is highly specific, gendered, and profoundly related to my position as a middle-class male intellectual. This affects how I analyze the political as a sphere of potential change. It affects the critiques and projections I have with respect to social movements and community efforts to make sense of the complex strategies that our culture has developed to both reproduce and sustain itself. There is, I would suggest, no royal road into the approach I have chosen.

Hamid Naficy has put the argument well: "Mass media typically are thought to be homogenizing agents, resulting in loss of ethnic identity and hastening of assimilation. This study, focusing particularly on liminality, the middle phase, demonstrates the power of the media to enhance and consolidate subcultural identities based on location, ethnicity, race, class, religion, politics, language, and nationality. It also shows that the relationship between mainstream culture and subcultures is fraught with ambivalence and contestation on the one hand and enrichment and assimilation on the other."[38] Naficy's book goes on to explore the location of exile culture at the "intersection and in the interstices of other cultures" (Naficy, Minneapolis 1993, 2), and it this space in between that I would claim for most forms of cultural activity. In other words, as the number and types of communities in the First World and the Third World proliferate, more and more points of contact and conflict are created. So many different elements are now mixed together that often the task is to try and disentangle what Naficy aptly calls the "cacophony of transnational media" (Ibid). Can a rigorous analytical context for political discourse be carved out of this phantasmagoria of images, media, and community? In some respects the challenge is to rethink the very terms within which notions of the political have been hypothesized up until now. But for the time being I will look at a variety of different television shows to examine whether or not the claim (so heavily promoted by, among others, Jean Baudrillard) that our cultural context has changed in an apocalyptic way, adds any further information to this complex debate.

I will look at "Seinfeld," in particular two shows dealing with the production of a show on "Nothing"; the Super Bowl of 1993, with an emphasis on the interaction of the following elements: the launch of a new line of men's

---

38. Hamid Naficy, *The Making of Exile Cultures: Iranian Television in Los Angeles* (Minneapolis: University of Minnesota Press, 1993), xvi.

shaving products from Gillette; ads from Pepsi about its new drink, Crystal Pepsi, and the accompanying slogan, "Gotta Have It"; the game itself including the pregame and postgame shows; the crucial role of Michael Jackson as the anchor for the event and the advertising by NBC for one its new shows entitled "Homicide," which was put together by Barry Levinson, the well-known Hollywood director.

It is perhaps not an accident that the Goodyear blimp high above the Rose Bowl in Pasadena allowed us a view of the Hollywood sign, which stands as a symbol throughout the world of Los Angeles and celebrity and wealth and the world of fantasy. This juxtaposition of football and entertainment—the fact that the halftime show was produced by Radio City Music Hall Productions in New York and that the game itself featured all of the elements of a variety show, suggests that if we are to do an analysis, more will be needed than a description such as the one I have just given. Yet to what degree does the relationship between the youngsters in the Crystal Pepsi commercials who scream into the camera that life is exciting and we should live it, combine with the on-field activities of the players, whose every success or failure leads to a close-up shot of them living in the excitement trumpeted, but clearly fictionalized, in the commercial? How can this be combined with the impact of Michael Jackson, who appears as a giant character on an immense TV screen above (like the blimp) the 100,000 people in the Rose Bowl, and then through a sleight of hand pops out of screen onto the top of it, only to tumble back again into the screen and jump out once more? How can this be reconciled with the physical cut to his presence on a stage in the center of the field, when just a split second earlier he had been on the screen?

Michael Jackson is larger than life with the resources to sustain his image or remake it at will: the the superhuman juxtaposition of him in two places at once; his presence on stage totally still and silent for well over a minute as the audience screams both to him and for him; his silence which suggests a mission greater than the man or the great man made for the mission. Jackson has reinvented himself as a defender of children (a role now cast into a morass of negativity as he faces possible charges for the sexual abuse of young boys), and he duplicated the song and routine that he used at the inauguration of Bill Clinton. He starts off with a series of dance gestures for which he is famous, including the overt display of grabbing his crotch, which for the first time I understood not as representing a mastubatory fantasy, but as a conferral—here is my sex—I give it to you as I give everything, because in the most religious sense, "I am here for you," your humble servant. I enact your desires and fantasies, the physical movements and songs that represent your desires, for isn't it your dream to join me as a celebrity, to be on stage with me, to be part of my body, as I want to be part of yours? The natural extension to this conferral is that I have also become your child and sister and brother and parent, mother and father to all children and of course to the child within you. This is Jackson's crucial juxtaposition of public figure and private person. We are all one. This comes out even more in his *Free Willy* songs but is manifested most fully in the fantasy land he has created on his estate, which represents the psychic unity of child and adult and nature (he also has a zoo).[39]

Of course there is the constant implication throughout the Super Bowl itself that although the players are trying to win for themselves, there is more to it. They are trying to win for their coach and their fans—trying to accommodate the presence of each fan in their bodies—trying over and over again (with each on-field play) to represent their own needs and the needs of their fans. What is at work here are reciprocal forms of projection as a result of which the players act as a conduit for the culture as a whole, making and remaking the terms of the arrangement through the construction of a very complex set of identities. This is the clearest indication that what is at stake in the game is not victory per se, but a ritualized fight for the heroic image. This is made all the more complex by the mediations introduced through the personae of Jackson, who has effectively changed his skin color in order to appeal to more cultures or to more fully represent all cultures. His transformation into a fallen idol means that his efforts to become disembodied (and in that sense, a pure image) may have failed.

As an added element to all of this there is the appropriation by Pepsi of the new world of clear drinks and their corporate assumptions about a different generation searching for new commodities to purchase. But the drink seemed less important than the idea that it represents a real departure from the norm, the potential to reconstruct a lifestyle (in the midst of the worst recession America and the world have seen since the 1930s) that is under threat. The advertisements, like the game, dwell on the idea that life can be lived to the fullest, even under duress, even encircled by poverty and destruction. In this dystopia there is at least one kind of activity that may act as a release, that may permit all of the repressed energy that difficult times have engendered, and that is a drink that can liberate those who purchase it from the constraints of time and history. This begins to explain the intensity with which the characters in the Pepsi commercial express their desire to drink clear(ly)—to be clear, to rediscover the *jouissance* of youth and the innocence of unrestricted pleasure.

---

39. All of this must now be juxtaposed with his status as a fallen hero, whose marriage to the daughter of Elvis Presley has been brilliantly parodied on SHE TV—an explicitly feminist "Saturday Night Live" shown during prime time on ABC. SHE TV has a black woman playing Jackson—and here the mythos of his bisexuality is foregrounded for all to see—with the satire being directed at the efforts he has made to extricate himself from any ambiguity regarding his sexuality.

In this they also express the energy of the players on the field and join with them in a celebration of the body that the age of AIDS has so profoundly undermined. The innocence is repeated over and over again through the body of Jackson, through his childishness, through his contact with children.

This also explains the bursts of energy, the fire and smoke emanating from the stage on which we see Jackson. This is more than the appearance of an apparition—this is about control, about the necessity for change—about transcendence. Inevitable comparisons could be made with medieval dramas, with their representation of purgatory and with the man who will survive and lead us out of the decay in which we find ourselves. This might appear frivolous were it not for the fact that NBC's advertisements for "Homicide" take us through the nightmare into its guts, with a camera that is constantly in motion—variances on *cinéma-vérité*. We enter more than the world of death. We enter a perpetual machine of decay in which homicides are listed on a tote board, with some solved, others unsolved. There is more than a sense of despair at work here. The rhythms of life preclude any feeling that solutions are on the horizon. "Homicide" is what the Super Bowl wants to avoid but it represents the reality just outside of the stadium. It is also shot as if camcorders from home have accidently come on the scenes it depicts. This link to portable video is further enhanced by an intentional obliqueness to the dialogue, as if the camcorders are not sophisticated enough to catch everyday conversations with the same reproductive clarity as the image. To see and not to hear. The sounds of the city in crisis overwhelm the pictures.

Paradoxically, this positioning of "Homicide" makes the football game even more exciting, since nothing is really at stake down on the field. This is the paradox of national sport. Nothing is really at stake for the people who watch. In the short term there is the desire to see a winner and to partake of the experience, but in the long term nothing really changes as a result. Everybody in the game knows this. They recognize that they are operating in a relatively autonomous framework—that win or lose they have gained a measure of fame and fortune. But this is not the case for the losers on "Homicide." In one of its episodes that I watched after the Super Bowl, an old man invites a young man to his hotel room to make love and is strangled. A young woman is shot because that may be the only way in which she can get some money. She receives compensation but it is taken away by a relative. As if to emphasize the metaphoric structure here a significant scene takes place in a cemetery where a dead man is dug up and the only comment the cop can make is that the corpse looks like a prune. The level of dehumanization is so intense that one harkens back to the memory of the Pepsi ads a day earlier during the football game for some relief.

Let me introduce "Seinfeld" (winter 1993) into this trajectory of phantasmagoric processes. NBC announced a rearrangement of its schedule on Wednesdays and Thursdays. Wednesdays will be, as they put it, "Arresting Television" — "Unsolved Mysteries," followed by "Homicide," followed by "Law and Order." Thursdays becomes a night of comedy, and Jerry Seinfeld appears to explain his shift to 9:30 after "Cheers," both during the Super Bowl and during "Homicide."

What is interesting here is that three recent "Seinfeld" shows dealt with the problems of depicting nothing. Invited by NBC to produce a show, Jerry and his friend George can only come up with a show on Nothing. Now the joke is that we know this is not possible. But the effect is nevertheless hilarious. Nothing can mean many things. Is it people saying nothing to each other? Is it the show saying nothing to the audience? Can a word ever designate an empty space? What happens when you describe emptiness? And so on. But with respect to television the word *nothing* takes on a completely different meaning. Are they referring to all shows? What do they mean? Are they making the quintessential postmodern statement? Does it all add up to nothing? Does this come down to a critique of popular culture? What are the vantage points when faced with nothing?

If we switch back to the Super Bowl for a moment, there is Gillette—the male body on display as a hinge for this phantasmagoria of images—the new male body, which will use a new kind of aftershave and new shaving cream to reconstitute himself. The new man is of course on the field, fighting for supremacy. He is Michael Jackson, androgynous, who can be morphed into a muscle-bound man just as quickly as he can be reduced to a smiling midget as tiny as the children he holds. The new man is Jerry Seinfeld, who never makes it all the way with women, who lives in the world of coitus interruptus and masturbation.

Into all of these phantasms, we must begin to project the notion of community, because each show may represent either a community itself, a community in formation, or a constellation of interests without which communities could not form. This is both the wonder and puzzle of television. As Naficy suggests television is both transnational (and I would add, translocal) and personal (Naficy 1993, 2). It is this capacity to be part of many different worlds at once that allows for if not encourages the sense that a particular character in a show or even the show itself can be made into a personal experience. There is no pressure to do this. I am not talking about an invasive process here. Rather, my own interpretation of Michael Jackson, for example, has an eclecticism that may or may not connect with the reader of this book. In that sense, there will be some sharing of assumptions or interpretations, but that is not a condition either of the halftime show or of the analysis. The discourse I am proposing is rooted and it is not rooted. The point is that I am attempting to communicate *across* the personal, as if my own position can be shifted by the very discourse I am creating. This is not the consequence of a weakly theorized polyphony of voices to which I am adding my own. This is very much the result of a structural shift in which interpretation as a discursive and creative activity is the ongoing result of cultural and political tensions generated by the nonstop emergence of highly variable communities. So active is this process and so new are its implications for the interaction of various ways of knowing the world (and acting on it), that there are few moments in which it can be subsumed under one or another label. Naficy quotes Zena Pearlstone: "Los Angeles is the second-largest Mexican, Armenian, Korean, Filipino, Salvadoran, and Guatemalan city in the world, the third largest Canadian city, and has the largest Japanese, Iranian, Cambodian and Gypsy communities in the United States, as well as more Samoans than American Samoa" (Naficy 1993, 5).[40] "Some 96 languages are counted as first languages by the student body" (Pearlstone 33; Naficy 1993, 5) of schools in the L. A. school district. Yet this is only a tiny fragment of the diversity redefining cultural analysis. Taken together none of these instances of multivocality can ever be approached from a singular or should I say unilingual perspective. What we are dealing with here far exceeds the conventional parameters, which up until now have defined the work on subjectivity in cultural studies and by extension, spectatorship.

This is where the "Seinfeld" show on Nothing situates itself—in between the layers of the Super Bowl, Michael Jackson, "Homicide" and commercials for men's toiletries. Seinfeld has recognized television images as a site of and for projection. This is the world of the virtual for which there are many maps but no territory. Electronic images remain just out of touch, beyond the eyes and ears, yet a fulcrum for fantasy. A show on Nothing in which everything is at stake remains rooted in a peculiarly traditional form of humor. The show pivots on the physical antics of Kramer, the insecurities of George, and Elaine's warm yet quirky balancing act among all three men. Imagine Jerry Seinfeld in a Gillette commercial or as the quarterback for the Buffalo Bills. Then jump to Elaine and George advertising Pepsi from within the duality of their personae as reluctant stars and the show's characters. In all of this they are everything at once and nothing. They are Jerry Seinfeld's bestselling book (bracketed by magazine images of him with the nine Porsches he has bought) and his jokes about mall culture—the key to his survival, the audience he is addressing. As he says in his book, "Malls are so easy to find, but it's so hard to find anything in a mall."[41] The joke continues with a discussion of mall maps, the impossibility of finding out where you are, and concludes with the suggestion that you climb onto the map in order to orient yourself. Seinfeld's jokes are about the everyday as phantasmagoria. They are about the conflation of im-

40. Zena Pearlstone, *Ethnic L. A.*, (Beverly Hills: Hillcrest, 1990), 27.
41. Jerry Seinfeld, *SeinLanguage* (New York: Bantam, 1993), 141.

ages, identity, and fantasy. They point toward a place, as Margaret Morse has so aptly put it, "without locus, a partially derealized realm from which a new quotidian fiction emanates."[42] His show about Nothing bases itself in the conflicts that arise when you ground yourself within the mall, and as Morse suggests, you are continuously "displaced" into a world where conventional distinctions of fiction and reality are replaced by dreams.

The Reflecting Pool

Bill Viola, the American video artist, has created a piece about these paradoxes of displacement and images. It is entitled *The Reflecting Pool*. A male character approaches a pool set in a forest. He stands at the edge and stares at his reflection. Then he jumps up and is suspended in midair above the water. He is frozen but the pool continues to reflect changes of color and the movement of other characters. Slowly and imperceptibly he disappears from the foreground of the scene. The reflections in the pool seem to have little to do with what surrounds it. There is a clear disjuncture between the story and the storytelling, which is compounded when the male character suddenly climbs out of the pool, naked, and walks off into the forest. This breakdown of narrative causality, the inherent quality of disjuncture, the arbitrary juxtaposition of elements, is located in the doubling of image and character. The man cannot discover his identity, just as the pool cannot reflect what surrounds it, and though he might, like Narcissus, wish to become what he sees, the pool will only permit him to be reborn on its own terms.

The reflection is neither what he expects nor can it be manipulated. The shadow hangs on and what it needs is light. However, in order for the pool to be reflective it must be dark. Neither the story nor the antistory can exist in a separate universe, and this interdependence is both what marks and then constrains the electronic image. The character is a witness to his own inability to control his image, and yet he knows there would be no image were he not part of the scene. The pool becomes a metaphor of his struggle to control what he himself has created. In the final analysis his identity cannot be judged from the outside. Reflections cannot be generated in a vacuum. In the same way, Seinfeld and George do end up presenting an idea to NBC. Their show on Nothing ultimately clarifies their own identities, but like a dialogue that can only be watched from afar, the clarification means very little.

This inseparability of picture and self (and all of the existential binds that come with it), the fact (or fiction) that neither can exist without the other pro-

---

42. Margaret Morse, "An Ontology of Everyday Distraction: The Freeway, the Mall and Television," *Logics of Television: Essays in Cultural Criticism*, ed. Patricia Mellencamp (Bloomington: Indiana University Press, 1990), 196.

vides a framework for but not the content of images. It is as if Viola's pool could evolve in any direction and as if nature itself has become a construct—a primitive utopia, a quintessential melding of image and reality. The electronic image for Viola is the site of a new Garden of Eden, in which the natural is as much a concept as it is a representation, as it is the site of a potential real—contingent, never anything more than a possible step in the direction of action and understanding. Concepts and representations don't have to be linked—the competence to understand each of these reversals lies with the interpretive power of the viewer who has learned to reconstruct meaning from a set of sometimes disparate if not contradictory fragments. The electronic image is attached to an ongoing process of interpretation (*not* interpellation), and this is perhaps why as testimony so many of its elements are open to *mis*interpretation. Yet it may be the case that to misinterpret is what keeps the image in the present tense, keeps it alive as truth. The reflecting pool only permits the illusion of suspension and thus contributes to a contingent discourse of "presence."

This is also the imaginary power that both the students in *Plain English* and the videomaker, Julia Lesage, herself share: The desire to "see" a simulacrum in which response actually premises itself upon the video, because the video represents the moment of argument. Many of the students in the video reflect upon their personal history using a narrative form in part so that they can enter this imaginary world. It is a *function* of testimony as a discourse to propose that the personal can be narrated in the public sphere. But it may not be the role of the image to either reenforce that presumption or to communicate it.

This is also what is so fascinating about the video work of Sadie Benning, in particular, *If Every Girl Had a Diary* and *Me and Rubyfruit*, which are stream-of-consciousness confessionals. There are really no boundaries to what Benning will say. She is very careful to make the tapes present tense, and they look as if we have accidently come upon her talking to herself in her bedroom. She frames all of her shots as if, like a small puppet theater, the eyes of the spectator are just on the other side of the camera. She does this by filming herself close-up, out of focus, sometimes dwelling on her own eyes or mouth, often kissing the screen-camera lens or just screaming at it. It is her voice that holds the scenes together, her nonstop and fascinating monologues on identity and experience, feeling queer, feeling angst, feeling her age, and often not knowing why she has spoken into the video camera as she has. I am not overstating the heterogeneity here, and if I am emphasizing the importance of Benning it is because it is virtually inconceivable that a political video of the kind I have been discussing up until now could have been made using the medium as Benning has. In part it is because Benning doesn't really care if she communicates or not, because she intuitively senses the paradoxes of the electronic image and the many pitfalls that her images and monologues actually enter into. This is not to suggest that the solution to the many different contradictions I have been describing is simply to adopt the attitude that communication is impossible—therefore don't worry about it. Rather, Benning has worked her way into a new aesthetic by not linking formal experimentation with communication. She is willing to risk the consequences of audiences doing their own experimentation. In other words, she dispels the importance of any feedback loop to validate her work.

This is not to say that she doesn't anticipate a response. It is just that the response can take so many forms, and this is what makes the process of communication not only unpredictable but highly contingent. The shifts here will depend on the context in which the tapes are shown. The tapes may help provoke an increase in the gaps between intention and viewing. As these gaps increase, the viewer can recreate the premises of the communication. Benning's tapes are attracted to this fluidity, and I should emphasize that this doesn't represent a breakdown but is the context within which she radically shifts the potential of video images in general.

I see a convergence between these avant-garde experiments in video, and "Seinfeld," the Super Bowl, Michael Jackson, and so on. Morse brings many of these elements together around the trope of transportation. Her suggestion is that the freeway represents an endless movement through many different spaces—images. This is both a private and a public world. Real movement is replaced by destination. The destinations are malls or homes where the television is on. This could be construed as dystopic or, as I will discuss in a moment, freeways may be the foundation upon which Jean Baudrillard's conceptualization of the simulacrum both begins and ends.

Waiting for Baudrillard in Sadie Benning's Living Room

In trying to understand Benning and Viola's extraordinarily rich and creative work with video, it has become increasingly clear to me that they are articulating precisely the kind of analysis of video and electronic communication this chapter is pursuing. They are doing it from within the image, from within the practice of videomaking. But they are operating in a context where that kind of critical intervention has been drained of meaning and impact because of the suspicious if not cynical relationship our culture has developed with images of all kinds. More than anyone it is Jean Baudrillard who has promoted this point of view (which includes the conflation of simulation, perception, and image), and it has come to stand for the very essence of postmodernism, as well as a fatalistic nihilism that has made the analysis of televisual imagery more difficult, not less.

The slippages here between the apocalyptic and analytical, between a context proposed as entirely *of* the image and one where images can be manipulated for creative and political purposes is full of binds and contradictions. This is very much a question of level. If the image, so to speak, *is* the environment, then how can either be changed or even understood? Do we need an ecology of the image? Where are the vantage points for analysis and critique, let alone creative or political intervention, if simulation is the guiding metaphor? Are these critical or analytical options *themselves* without value or relevance in a world where meaning has supposedly disappeared?

I would propose here to take a look at some of the ideas of Jean Baudrillard. His suspicion that images *by definition* don't communicate meaning but create a simulated universe challenges the very basis of what we have come to know as the media and by extension what we have come to understand as culture. It certainly contradicts the impulses of most practitioners as well as critics and viewers. There is a potentially demobilizing aspect to his approach that I will comment on. But for the moment his central notion that the "Image precedes the Real in that it inverses the logical, causal succession of the Real and its reproduction,"[43] needs to be closely examined for its potential relevance to the analysis of video, television, and other cultural forms.

A few years ago when it was suggested to me that it might be useful to write an extended piece on Baudrillard, I readily agreed, in part because at the time I felt Baudrillard was an overrated postmodern theoretician whose work had not been analyzed with rigor or depth. I also had severe misgivings about postmodernism, both as a category for thinking about social and cultural phenomena, and as an intellectual tool for exploring and investigating the political and economic transformations of Western capitalism during the last thirty years. Although I amassed nearly two hundred pages of notes and gave numerous critical lectures on Baudrillard's essays and books, I felt uneasy, and with time, less sure of my feelings about his approach. In fact, I soon recognized but tried to resist the sense that Baudrillard's strategy to the production of ideas (his texts and essays are not written in traditional academic language) and the debates he initiated had tapped into a crucial shift in the way our society examines its own political and cultural direction. This is a fairly general claim and must be backed up if it is to make any sense. Furthermore, I discovered that Baudrillard, far from being a prophet of postmodern thinking, is actually very sceptical about postmodernism. He is, as we shall see, often quite aggressive in his comments about the postmodern and clearly suggests that the shifts we are experiencing at the moment both with respect to technological change and the explosion of mechanisms for information transmittal and exchange

43. Jean Baudrillard, "Beyond Right and Wrong Or The Mischevious Genius of Image," in *Resolution: A Critique of Video Art*, ed. Patti Podesta (Los Angeles: Los Angeles Contemporary Exhibitions, 1986), 8.

have not served Western societies very well. This discovery fascinated me, because it revealed the gap between the circulation of ideas about Baudrillard and what he was actually saying. The same problem exists with respect to Jean-François Lyotard, whose representative status as the high priest of postmodern thinking falls into disarray upon closer examination.[44]

Yet Baudrillard opens a window onto potentially rich analyses of popular culture and, it seems to me, counteracts the simplicity of the alternative versus mainstream dichotomy that informs so much of the work I have been discussing about video. I am going to suggest that if we do not develop critical (and sometimes sympathetic) tools of analysis for popular cultural events, that the public sphere into which radical political ideas can be inserted will neither be accessible nor understandable. My claim, not dissimilar to Baudrillard's, is that the cultural realignment put in place by mass spectacles broadcast for the most part across television channels but also through other media, has not only affected the way political arguments can be understood, but also transformed the basic assumptions we have about political action and political discourse. Thus I have come around not to an acceptance of Baudrillard's position or even of many of his ideas, but to an understanding that he is a barometer of the shifting ground for discourses about social change who must be read, interpreted, and argued about. His work represents the symptoms of the diseases which he analyzes. In order to deal with some of his key ideas and to provide a point of entry into the relationship between video as an artistic and political tool and popular culture, I will examine some of the debates in this complex area. In effect, my concern is with the place, the location, within which video and other forms of electronic media operate. In some senses, any discussion of popular culture becomes a discussion of community, a way of talking about the relationship between culture and context.

In a recent and powerful article in *New Left Review*, Terry Eagleton bemoans the impact of what he describes as "a pervasive crisis of Western culture itself; and though this epochal upheaval is not everywhere dramatically apparent . . . we should remind ourselves of Walter Benjamin's dictum that the fact that 'everything just goes on' *is* the crisis."[45] Eagleton relates the crisis to identity, language, and the questions surrounding nationhood. In arguments that seem like they have been drawn from Herbert Marcuse, he traces out the loss of meaning in modern culture as the symptom of a profound decline in political awareness and a turn toward blind consumerism. The latter phenomenon

---

44. Jean-François Lyotard, *The Postmodern Condition: A Report on Knowledge*, tr. Geoff Bennington and Brian Massumi (Minneapolis: University of Minnesota Press, 1984). The central themes of this work have been critiqued by Meeghan Morris, "Postmodernity and Lyotard's Sublime," in *The Pirate's Fiancee* (London: Verso, 1988), 213–39.
45. Terry Eagleton, "The Crisis of Contemporary Culture," *New Left Review* 196 (1993): 30.

intersects with a public sphere that has ceased to understand the rationale behind its own activities. This image of a culture out of control and less and less in touch with the "symbolic resources" it needs to maintain its "ideological authority" (Eagleton 33) has been a major concern of cultural and political theory since the 1930s and the work of the Frankfurt School. But Eagleton goes one step further and places the responsibility for the crisis squarely on the back of popular culture, which he in no uncertain terms equates with "consumerist desire" (Eagleton 33), and which I will argue is precisely the kind of reductive thinking that has made unlikely soul mates of people like Alan Bloom and Eagleton. This convergence of the Left and the Right, itself an expression of the flattening of political discourse, hinges on the arguments that have been developed around popular culture.

To be fair, there is great complexity to what Eagleton is saying which raises it far beyond the Frankfurt School and is clearly indebted to Antonio Gramsci and Raymond Williams. Yet his argument is filled with paradoxical claims about cultural change and its effects. "So it is that the intellectuals of the New Right, having actively colluded with forms of politics which drain purpose and value from social life, then turn their horror-stricken countenances on the very devasted social landscape they themselves have helped to create, and mourn the loss of absolute value" (Eagleton 33).

The residual effects of Reaganism and Thatcherism will be with us for a long time. Eagleton targets capitalism as *the* cause of the present disintegration of the social fabric (I bring this up because, as we shall see, Baudrillard agrees). And he proposes that it is culture that has become the battlefield of identity in much the same way as religion was for another age. Culture with a big "C"— the sites of contestation are now the charred landscapes of television soap operas and the nostalgia-ridden songs of Madonna. Although Eagleton at one point suggests that the canons of English literary study need to be opened up and disrupted, and, following on from the work of Williams, that certain areas of popular culture are deserving of analysis (Eagleton 37–38), he is less than clear about how this can be done.

"At its most callow, such theories [as postmodernism] complacently underwrite the commodity form, and do so in the name of an opposition to elitism. Nothing could in fact be more offensively elitist, more aloofly academicist, than this cynical celebration of the marketplace, which for ordinary men and women has meant homelessness and unemployment rather than random libidinal intensities, and which globally speaking means war as well as cosmopolitan cuisine" (Eagleton 35). So on the one hand Eagleton looks for a way to open up the discourses of academic disciplinarity which he rightly argues have become increasingly irrelevant, and on the other hand he frames his arguments about popular culture from the vantage points of market analysis, commodification, and consumerism.

I would argue with Eagleton here because popular culture is about commodities and about the differing ways those commodities come to have a "surplus-value" (at numerous levels, the discursive and the imagistic being among the most interesting) far in excess of the original financial or ideological investment made in them. Furthermore, the cynicism of the marketplace, the just-for-profit orientation of large conglomerates such as Fox Television or Time-Warner are minor components of the analysis that must be undertaken. There is a continuing need to analyze and break down—deconstruct, in the popular sense of the term—the differing strategies these corporate giants deploy in the marketplace. There is a place for the study of marketing and the circulation of goods both attached to and dependent upon the cultural fashions of the moment. One must never lose sight of the presumptions of corporate America, the self-images of Hollywood moguls, and the rhetorical strategies of advertising agencies. The problem is not one of gathering information or finding rigorous ways to describe the activities of private and public institutions that see themselves as part of a large and ever-growing circuit of information exchange. The difficulty is that so little of that kind of analysis explains or clarifies *why* popular culture (particularly of the American variety) *works* and why its effects are not simply reducible to the television shows or advertisements that circulate through our culture every day.

We are surrounded by a wall of critics from Neil Postman to Noam Chomsky who detail, in sometimes brilliant fashion, how these industries operate and how they manipulate information for their own purposes. The arguments they pursue, and which Eagleton to some degree supports, tend to equate the Machiavellian intentions of these corporations and *their presumptions about their own effectivity* with the audiences which either buy their goods or watch their productions or read their magazines and newspapers. In this Eagleton is very close to the analytical and ideological framework within which video activists operate and which in the first instance he seems anxious to critique. The question, it seems to me, always is, what do assumptions of effectivity suggest about analyses of the cultural sphere?

It is precisely the communicative bond between audiences and corporate producers that needs to be examined and researched from within a set of interdisciplinary concerns that the present configuration of research tends to discourage. It is this space *in between* that I believe Baudrillard examines and examines brilliantly. These are sites of learning and comprehension based in large measure on desire (the desire to go to a Prince concert, to wear the clothes he wears, to *be* Prince) and need. These are not instances of false consciousness, not simple examples of seduction and loss, and certainly don't reflect the supposed vacuousness of the people who engage in purchasing either the goods or myths to which they are attached.

The communicative bonds of which I am speaking are very real, but in

Baudrillard's terms they are the prime examples of a symbolic universe that has become the foundation for cultural and social activities that are essentially simulations. Thus, to watch "Beverly Hills 90210" and to purchase the Mattel dolls based on the characters in the show allows a child or an adult to create a simulated world where the fantasy of bringing the characters to life can be satisfied. These simulations fit into Winnicott's notions of play and extend the contingent relationship that the viewer develops with television from the screen into the home. There is no easy way of predicting the outcome of this construction of an imaginary world. To some degree, the dolls also facilitate the projection process because they can be used for any number of difference purposes. An analysis of the show may tell us very little about what we *do* with it or with the dolls. This unpredictability is part of projection, a way of controlling what we see in order to give coherence to the simulation. Simulations don't work unless we have invested ourselves in them. The dolls represent an *otherness* that far outstrips their original creation or the show from which they have been derived. This excess is the site within which a series of potential identifications can occur. A recent show on the decline of one of the main characters, Dylan, is a good example of this type of excess. Dylan crashes his car after a night of alcohol and drugs. He lies in a hospital in a coma. We enter his nightmares and dreams, images of death and retribution, decay and injustice. The images are a swirl, repetitive and intensely metaphorical. They are a fantasy of Dylan's dream world. How does his image, the doll, and our viewing of the show come together? Need there be a unity here? Or is this an experience of excess which does not permit a synthesis? The fragments invert subject and object as if the dolls have been brought to life. Yet this is precisely our work, the work of the television viewer, which cannot be equated with passivity.

Instead of the high-minded moralizing symptomatically typified by Neil Postman[46] we need to more fully understand the pragmatic context into which television, for example, is placed *by* the people who make use of the medium. Postman almost suggests that when he says, "the problem, in any case, does not reside in *what* people watch. The problem is in *that* we watch. The solution must be found in *how* we watch. For I believe it may fairly be said that we have yet to learn what television is. And the reason is that there has been no worthwhile discussion, let alone widespread public understanding, of what information is and how it gives direction to a culture" (Postman 160). Following the paragraph in which the above quote appears Postman asks a series of questions about information, the forms it takes, its effects upon viewers, the ways in which information persuades, disuades, and misinforms. Buried within the

---

46. See Neil Postman, *Amusing Ourselves to Death: Public Discourse in the Age of Show Business* (New York: Viking Penguin, 1986), especially the last chapter entitled, "The Huxleyan Warning," 155–64.

paragraph is this question, "What redefinitions of important cultural meanings do new sources, speeds, contexts and forms of information require?" (Postman 160).

I take this to mean that we need new discourses to explain what is happening to us in order to understand why television is critiqued from all sides (to the left and right of the political spectrum) for its vacuity and negative influence. Yet it is precisely the *way* we address popular culture that will have an effect on the discourses, theories, and practical responses we can have. It is the mode of address from within an ill-defined communicative sphere, which may no longer be dominated by a series of simple equations (viewer-television, consumer-culture), that will either open up or close down the the kinds of responses we develop. This is where I see Baudrillard potentially expanding the theoretical and discursive framework for the analysis of cultural forms.

For example, Sadie Benning explores herself through video technology. She is simultaneously viewer and creator, enacting a process that no longer has any clear boundaries of demarcation among the various levels of looking that separate the spectator from the television screen. The dichotomies that have dominated thinking about images, and in particular, the very idea of spectatorship changes dramatically when the images circulating are themselves the central mode and form within which ideas are exchanged. But even the notion of exchange suggests a process of bartering with defined boundaries between subject and object spheres, based on outdated notions of information transfer. Benning's tapes literally melt all of that (or perhaps the better word is *smudge*), such that what we are left with is not the either/or—did her tape communicate a specific meaning or not?—but that meaning will be there if you decide to invest in and interpret your experience of the tape. It may even be there at an unconscious level, beyond immediate comprehension. The question seems to be how to develop an awareness of the differences between self and image, while at the same time recognizing the fluidity of movement *across* those differences. The transitory nature of this process is in part where Baudrillard situates the idea of simulation. He makes the error, I believe, of confusing transitory movements of meaning with loss and absence and thus doesn't recognize how some configurations become stable with time, although this doesn't necessarily mean that they become fixed.

Benning's tapes can be replayed over and over again (this is one of the most important characteristics of video). This can be done for the same or different audiences. The result is that almost inevitably certain metaphors and subjective claims with respect to meanings and messages take on a more defined character. The notion of "replay" is itself a paradoxical point of entry into the variability of communication with images, into the stresses and strains between the transformative and the transparent presumptions of meaning that come with viewing. Time is crucial here. There is a sense that the past and the present are indistinguishable. To replay with respect to images doesn't necessarily mean to resee. It is not the same as repeating the same line from a poem many times in order to understand the nuances and subtleties that went into the writing of the poem. The replay also doesn't necessarily make clear what might have been vague beforehand. To replay in video means to introduce quotation, bracketing, boundaries to what might have seemed continuous. This makes time malleable, plastic, reversible. To Baudrillard this is precisely a sign of loss when it actually *contradicts* his notion that "the vast majority of current images—photographs, cinema, television—are supposed to witness the world with a naive resemblance, a touching fidelity. We spontaneously trust them because of their realism. We are wrong. They pretend to resemble things, the Real, events, faces. Rather, they really conform, but their conformity itself is diabolical."[47]

There is, rather, always an argument around resemblance, an implicit problem with realism, a widely held nihilism about the possibility of ever coming to the truth with images. The proliferation of images is always critiqued as if more has been lost than gained. (There is of course no better example of this than the superficiality of the arguments around the effects of "violent" images on children.) Why did Baudrillard approach his analysis in this way? In part he conflates all media into image. He also removes all of the ambiguity of communicative processes that might contradict his thesis. Underlying this is his notion of the death of the social, the death of meaningful exchange and interaction in a society obsessed with repeating the same story over and over again. Charles Levin has astutely commented on Baudrillard's approach here. "By a curious roundabout route, the argument that symbolization is no longer possible—originally an extension of the Frankfurt theses on the commodification of culture—has turned itself inside out. What was once a kind of morality tale about capitalist reification has, under the influence of poststructuralist objectivist epistemologies, metamorphised into a story about progressive historical revelation: there never was anything but society (norms, rules, regularities, codes). Alienation turns out to be the inevitable consequence of the fact (recently discovered) that the body is a play of social effects, and the psyche nothing more than one of society's circulating myths."[48] It is Baudrillard's assertion that the body in this environment becomes as artificial as the image, which grounds his ideas of simulation.[49]

47. Jean Baudrillard, "Beyond Right and Wrong Or The Mischevious Genius of Image," 8.
48. Charles Levin, "Time and Postmodernism: A Capsule," *Communication* 10 (1988): 323–24.
49. Jean Baudrillard, "On Seduction," *Jean Baudrillard: Selected Writings*, ed. Mark Poster (Stanford: Stanford University Press, 1988), 149–65.

By way of contrast, Benning's crisis of identity and her search for a solution bear a relation to the reality that her tape has constructed. This may have no direct relationship to the "real" world, but that doesn't matter. Baudrillard's central thesis that simulation precedes the real masks both the moral and theological constructs of his theory and would place Benning's questions about her queer identity into a world without bodies. He makes an ontological claim for the image which can neither be proven nor disproven. Since there is no beginning or end to the process whereby simulations and realities intermingle, there is no point at which either can be distinguished from the other. The dichotomy between the real and the simulated is itself a negation of truth, but what does not exist cannot be negated. Thus to Baudrillard's dismay, the body reappears through Benning's questions about feelings, pain, and desire, and asserts a primacy only partially related to the images she shows.

Ironically, Baudrillard's own antipathies toward the simulated universes he describes place him in an ambiguous position with respect to the operative influences and configurations of cultural activities. This is in part because although he appears to be less than clear politically, much of his work has in fact spiraled out of a Marxist base both philosophically and epistemologically. Mike Gane goes even further: "His [Baudrillard's] project must be regarded as an assault on the 'disenchanted' world from the point of view of a militant of the symbolic (enchanted but cruel) cultures. In this he is prepared to appear in theory as a terrorist, as seducer, as devil's incubus."[50]

Gane traces the lineage of Baudrillard's ideas through the influences of Hölderin, Marx, Nietzsche, Heidegger and the Frankfurt school. Of equal importance are Kafka, Bataille, Borges, and McLuhan, (Gane, *Critical*, 1991, 6–7). There would be little purpose here in summarizing the historical development of Baudrillard's ideas. Gane does an admirable job both in the book mentioned above and in another book, *Baudrillard's Bestiary*.[51] In the latter book, Gane makes the claim that Baudrillard is against postmodernism both as a movement and as a way of thinking about social and cultural representations. I think it is worth quoting this argument in full:

> The irony has rebounded for this anti-modernist, and anti-postmodernist: he has been caught in the hype of postmodernism. Everywhere he has been identified as the leader, the spokesman of postmodern analysis: Yet: "As in a general entropic movement of the century, the initial energy is disintegrating ponderously into ever more refined ramifications of structural, pictorial, ideological, linguistic, psychoanalytic upheavals—the ultimate configuration, that of 'postmodernism', undoubtedly the most degenerated, most ar-

50. Mike Gane, *Baudrillard: Critical and Fatal Theory* (New York: Routledge, 1991), 7.
51. New York: Routledge, 1991.

tificial, and most eclectic phase—a fetishism of picking out and adopting all the significant little bits and pieces, all the idols, and the purest signs that preceded this fetishism."[52]

The clearest sense we can get of the ambivalences that Baudrillard has toward the cultural activities he describes throughout his articles and books is in the essay entitled "Simulacra and Simulations,"[53] (hereafter referred to as "Sim."). This short piece offers a snapshot of Baudrillard's strategic relationship to media and culture. At all levels, it is the most carefully reasoned of his essays, although it is also the most confrontational.

Baudrillard's notion of simulation is in the first instance very spatial. It can be visualized as pyramidal, with large circular structures on top of the pyramid, but also running through the other parts of the pyramid stacked on top of each other, intersecting and joining but never forming an homogeneous whole. It is important to understand here that the pyramid is three-dimensional and slippery, if not treacherous. The circular structures have developed a relative degree of autonomy from each other (and here the links of Baudrillard's arguments to those of Althusser are apparent), but there is no doubt that simulation forms the uppermost structural constraint and is at the very least a system of systems.

"To simulate is to feign to have what one hasn't" ("Sim," 167). Baudrillard uses psychosomatic disease as his grounding example of simulation. The hypochondriac generates all of the symptoms of disease while not having it. The result is that the hypochondriac becomes *ill*: "simulation threatens the difference between 'true' and 'false,' between 'real' and 'imaginary' ("Sim." 168). The illness has been produced by an act of will and puts the question of the cure into a quandary. How to respond then to a process that is *not* real but that results in illness? "Neither psychology nor medicine are able to deal with the truth of the illness. For if any symptom can be 'produced,' and can no longer be accepted as a fact of nature, then every illness may be considered as simulatable and simulated, and medicine loses its meaning since it only knows how to treat 'true' illnesses by their objective causes" ("Sim." 168). The problem here is that truth disappears and with it any possibility of grounding the comparison between the symptom and the simulation. In other words, what is Baudrillard's vantage point with respect to the simulation? Where is *he* situated? And how can he disentangle the relationships he describes without himself falling victim to precisely the same problems of simulation and loss?

52. Mike Gane, *Baudrillard's Bestiary: Baudrillard and Culture*, 158, quoting Jean Baudrillard in *Cool Memories* (London: Verso, 1990), 149–50.
53. Jean Baudrillard, "Simulacra and Simulations," in *Selected Writings*, ed. Mark Poster (Stanford: Stanford University Press, 1988), 166–84.

I am in some respects sympathetic to the way he breaks down the conventional parameters of referentiality. But I believe that he has taken the notion of the sur-real, or the real as unknowable, variable, contingent, and created a theological model. It is true that the psychosomatic shows all the symptoms of disease and then as a consequence of the stress can *actually* produce the disease in themselves. And although the process is complex and very difficult to pinpoint (since the hypochondriac may have spent a lifetime constructing the disease), few of the consequences of this process are themselves *indescribable*. This is the paradox of Baudrillard's metaphor. The body may be a canvas upon which a variety of designs can be painted, but medicine nevertheless makes the effort to name them. In the final analysis the disease is itself the sign of a narrative for which there are many possible points of entry. In other words, whatever the consequences, language and discourse do not disappear. Their relationship to the disease is foregrounded or covered over by many layers of social activity and personal challenge, all of which may appear on the surface of the body but none of which has been handed down from a source or a place outside of human intervention or creativity.

I am not suggesting here that we need return to overly causal or deterministic modes of cultural and social analysis. However, even as the real, so to speak, disappears, Baudrillard feels impelled to *talk* and *write* about it. And as he does, he invokes precisely those levels of rationality he feels have become dependent on simulation. It is my own feeling that what he means by simulation is badly served by the psychosomatic model. Yet it also reveals the historical lineage of his ideas and the strong relationship he has to psychoanalysis. In fact, his simulated universe is an effort to make the unconscious speak and to suggest that neither the ego nor the superego have any control over the eruptions of the unconscious into discourse. All forms of speech, looking and seeing, experience itself, now become subsets of unconscious processes that have no history. It is a rather naive response to the observation that language and truth depend on the arbitrary relationship of signifier and signified. "What can medicine do with something which floats on either side of illness, on either side of health, or with the reduplication of illness in a discourse that is no longer true or false? What can psychoanalysis do with the reduplication of the discourse of the unconscious in a discourse of simulation that can never be unmasked, since it isn't false either?" ("Sim." 168).

Baudrillard suggests that the threat posed by the counterfeit, by reproduction, by any mirroring process ("Sim." 182) is that it may take on a life of its own outside of the capacity of individuals to control the results. The reaction to this loss is to further highlight the real, to overemphasize its importance, and to attempt to submerge all of the binds and knots raised by simulation into manageable discourses and practices. "Reproduction is diabolical in its very essence; it makes something fundamental vacillate. This has hardly changed for us: simulation (that we describe here as the operation of the code) is still and always the place of a gigantic enterprise of manipulation, of control and death, just like the imitative object (primitive statuette, image of photo) always had as objective an operation of black image" ("Sim." 182 n.1).

We are now into the sorcery of simulation, into black magic, and most importantly into processes whose autonomy guarantees their power because they cannot be examined from within or from without. There are no vantage points, just as there is no history, and this realization produces another of Baudrillard's crucial suggestions: the hyperreal. It is as if the elements that make up this soup are chemically combined to produce something no one can control—a Frankensteinian monster born of simulated parents with reconstituted sperm and premanufactured eggs. Once the soup has been made it disempowers those who come in contact with it. (Recent successful experiments with human embryo cloning at a hospital in Boston seem to support some of Baudrillard's contentions.)[54] If this sounds metaphysical, it is because Baudrillard's pyramid, like the ancient structures in Egypt, exists in a universe that can only be interpreted and understood from within the codes established to present it. These codes are at the heart of the hyperreal, a place in which categories of knowledge are forced to accentuate the real in order to focus on the supposed divisions between illusion and reality. Fundamentally, his thesis is that the simulated universe is the one we all find ourselves in—we try to use theory and language to distinguish between the simulated and the real in order to ground the pursuit of knowledge in a discourse based on truth. The example he uses to back up this assertion is Disneyland, which is real, while all surrounding it is illusion. Before I turn to his analysis of Disney let me add that Baudrillard provides no examples of psychosomatic diseases. His use of hypochondria is dangerously simplistic. This is precisely one of the problems with his approach that I think detracts from the more positive possibilities of thinking about the *conditions* upon which truth and meaning can be based.

"Disneyland is a perfect model of all the entangled orders of simulation. To begin with it is a play of illusions and phantasms: pirates, the frontier, future world, etc. This imaginary world is supposed to be what makes the operation successful. But, what draws the the crowds is undoubtedly much more the social microcosm, the miniaturized and *religious* revelling in real America, in its delights and drawbacks. . . . The objective profile of the United States, then, may be traced throughout Disneyland, even down to the morphology of individuals and the crowd. All its values are exalted here, in miniature and comic-strip form. Embalmed and pacified" ("Sim." 171).

It is the premise of Baudrillard's analysis that everything outside of Disney-

---

54. See Andrew Wernick, "Baudrillard's Remainder," *CTHEORY: Theory, Technology and Culture*, Review 7, (17 November 1993), 4.

land is not real and that Disneyland has been created "in order to make us believe that the rest is real, when in fact all of Los Angeles and the America surrounding it are no longer real, but of the order of the hyperreal and of simulation" ("Sim." 172).

It is crucial to understand here that Baudrillard's use of the term *hyperreal* retains "real" within it. The hyperreal is that place in which the real becomes as arbitrary as the discourses that surround and define it, and where illusions are not the result of the human imagination but represent its denial. What has changed is that there are no references for this new place within a continuum that has ceased to have a foundation in some prior moment, but instead is looped in an endless spiral, where time and space double back on themselves in a perpetual, unbroken cycle of feedback. Here again the spatial metaphors dominate.

It is this notion of circularity, symbolically represented in Baudrillard's discourse by many references to machines, in which even the negation simply reinforces its opposite, and where opposition becomes what it opposes. This collapse of all the shadings *in between* is best exemplified in Baudrillard's effort to historicize the concept of the image:

1 It is the reflection of a basic reality.
2 It masks and perverts a basic reality.
3 It masks the *absence* of a basic reality.
4 It bears no relation to any reality whatever: it is its own pure simulacrum.
   ("Sim." 170)

This hierarchy must be read downward as a movement toward absolute loss, a fall in the theological sense, from the pyramid to the ground, which itself has become a sign, a moment in a continuum of simulations that refer to nothing other than themselves. "The transition from signs which dissimulate something to signs which dissimulate that there is nothing, marks the decisive turning point. The first implies a theology of truth and secrecy (to which the notion of ideology still belongs). The second inaugurates an age of simulacra and simulation, in which there is no longer any God to recognize his own, nor any last judgement to separate truth from the false, the real from its artificial resurrection, since everything is already dead and risen in advance" ("Sim." 170–71). The crucial axis for this analysis is time—reversible, unmeasurable, nonanalogical. It is Baudrillard's suggestion that loss does not define presence but precedes it. All the efforts to fill the black hole will inevitably lead to implosion, a negation for which there is no visible result, an absence that cannot be described or explained because it ceases to exist just when we think we have apprehended it. Our vantage point is within this gathering storm of blackness, where matter has become antimatter, a substance with mass that cannot be seen, let alone felt. Digital technologies can produce antimatter because there need be no connection to any source, and this *lack*, at the concept of antimatter itself suggests, immediately dissolves the very relations of meaning used to generate the simulation (morphing is a further example of this process). Transistorized switches made technology intelligent, but in Baudrillard's terms, they also transform our relationship to the technology and hide its operations.

I find it ironic that the computer makes use of a video screen and that multimedia is the combination of video technology and computerized signaling. A paradox because the processes involved are always image based. The Macintosh computer I am presently using and the screen on which these words appear rely on video technology. The image is one I continuously read, scroll through, rework; in other words, I am converting the image to my own uses. Convert in this sense means interactive and transformative. The arbitrariness is precisely what keeps the process going, and drives me forward. Yet there is great fragility here because a storm is brewing outside my window. The winds are strong and violent. I am worried about an electrical surge, or worse, a blackout. This could happen in my home or at the hydroelectric plant hundreds of miles away. The electrical linkages that run through a variety of substations and countless cables can break down at any point. The computer simulation depends on the weather and both are connected by a variety of technologies controlled by the workers who run the electrical installations. These are spheres of interacting subjectivities and realities that exceed the control or picturing capacities of the image. I emphasize the plural here to avoid Baudrillard's metaphysics of absence. At some point, the subjective, whether we conceive of subjectivity as image, or as discourse, as practice, or as loss, imaginatively rebuilds itself through exteriorization, and although we tend to call the result *objects*, the will to control the outcome establishes and grounds the communicative and ontological strength of the entire process. This is, after all, what leads a Sadie Benning to believe in the video image, and it is what encourages her to suggest that what she is saying at the verbal and pictorial level is not so much the result of the technology she is using but is a synthetic expression of how she is manipulating it.

This is, I believe, what motivates Sadie Benning's use of video, to at least imagine a cultural and social context of community. Communication is based on this hypothetical placement of meanings into a sphere of potential interaction. However mythic this desire for authenticity might be, Benning never forgets that the video screen is a boundary. In contrast, Baudrillard confuses, quite intentionally, the gaps between images and meaning, because to acknowledge the gaps would deform the simulation, making of it no more than one of many different strategies of subjectivity. Thus what Baudrillard offers discussions and analyses of images is the paradoxical strength of his own position, which doesn't lie out of reach (as he might prefer it) but which symptomatically reveals that any metaphysical collapse of the real and the image generates its own pure reality. And the purification, the distillation, only retains its character as long as it is contained. Down the edges of the bottle comes the distillate. Open the bottle and it becomes steam. Just as the image cannot be created without a technology, so too do the boundaries of the technological process act as the ground for simulation. The phantasm of Disneyland is the way our culture actualizes the imaginary, yet it cannot be contained nor act on its own. Baudrillard's problem—one that Benning laughs at—is that the real was never real in the flattened sense of a comic strip anyway. Baudrillard's conundrum is that he believed, and like all believers who lose their god, he turned to Esalen, or Scientology, or the Moonies, or Disney. For Benning, the simulations are a world to be explored, images that soar above the technologies engendering them. For Baudrillard, simulation is a religious moment, a baptism into the meaning of cultural activity. He falls prey to the image and allows it to determine what he sees. In this sense he is no more or less the dystopic preacher for a social and economic order which resists understanding the impact of its own inventions.

"This vertigo of interpretation" which he alludes to *is* the work of Benning, the exploration of the limits of the image as a device with no pretentious assumptions about results. After all, Benning makes use of a Fisher-Price toy that tried to hand the technology of the portapack to children old enough to hold it. This extraordinary device failed in the market place because its images were blurred, jumpy, unpredictable. Benning makes a virtue of this and uses her voice to transcend its limitations as an instrument. The results are fragmented pieces of sights and sounds which could be described as simulations but which are also moving cubist paintings or collages now more temporal than spatial. The point is that she could be faking when she declared her love for a woman she met, or she could be telling the truth. For Baudrillard this reversibility represents the final evidence of the simulation at work. For Benning, this is the ecstasy, the orgasmic attraction of the image in which, unlike what Baudrillard suggests for the TV image (see "Sim." 183n.3), no closure is possible. The kinetic, the sensuous are never, in Benning's terms, within the image, but outside of it and crucially, there is nothing predictable about the scenario of interpretations and analyses that the audience will perform in relation to the video.

Let me suggest that Baudrillard's rejection of postmodernism doesn't allow him to understand or even make room for the work of someone like Benning. The problem is that he is so suspicious of the image he is unable to recognize its multifaceted and disjointed character as a positive force for creativity. "In this passage to a space whose curvature is no longer that of the real, nor of truth, the age of simulation thus begins with a liquidation of all referentials—worse: by their artificial resurrection in systems of signs. It is no longer a question of imitation, nor of reduplication, nor even of parody. It is rather a question of substituting signs of the real for the real itself; that is an operation to deter every real process by its operation double." ("Sim." 167) Subjectivity moves inside a sealed mirror—reflections create a distorted image of self and identity which seduces and destroys those who take pleasure in images. (Baudrillard thus aligns himself with Jacques Lacan and simultaneously extends the mirror-phase into all aspects of the media experience.)

I started this discussion of Baudrillard by proposing that he offered at least the opening of a terrain in relation to popular culture. I still believe he extends the map we can use in trying to understand what Benning has understood from within the practice of video. He does this because he plays at many opposing positions simultaneously. He is on the one hand deeply suspicious of the cultural artifacts of the late twentieth century and yet revels in their diversity. On the other hand he is a promoter of the idea that we are the victims of the culture of which we are a part. In this he is not dissimilar to many critics (from Alan Bloom on the Right to Christopher Lasch on the Left) who comment on popular culture. The extraordinary thing is that he contains and expresses all of the extremes. He is the high priest of the diseases he thinks ravage the culture. In managing to be a tour guide of his own psyche, he comes to represent the interminable suspicions that most commentators have about popular culture. His hypochondria is a well-marked road into the schizophrenic relationship that postmodern culture has to the products of its own imaginary.

This is why Benning poses such a risk to Baudrillard. She dives into and then swims in her eclecticism, in the sheer diversity of cultural activity that the camcorder (her medium) makes possible. The result is the formation of new collectivities defined by sexual orientation, ethnic background, shared intellectual purpose, who mix up the categories used to name them, as quickly as they reconstruct other frameworks to give coherence to their work and activities. Benning represents that aspect of modern American culture that has produced thousands of 'zines, that makes videotapes for public access, where suburban basement television studios vie with mainstream broadcasters and journalists for attention. The various analytic hierarchies which would distinguish among all of these creative, political, and social efforts, hierarchies dependent on notions of alternativity and mainstream, miss the point. The presumption that there could be a fixed geography for all of this creativity is paradoxically where the notion of simulation takes us, since it puts in place the kind of binarism that of necessity generates cartographies to justify the creation of guidebooks. Baudrillard has recognized that something is going on, but he has remained staunchly entrenched in a Modernist angst that we are somehow traveling along all of these roads as accident victims. In so doing he returns to a very limited idea of communication within which the parameters of understanding and exposition are from the outset generated by the message. In much the same way as Marshall McLuhan, he conflates image and message into meaning and then encapsulates all of this into an often-times devalued model of subjectivity.

The Virtual Printing Press

If, as is so often suggested, the electronic image in its computerized, tele-visual, and multimedia form heralds the advent of a structural transformation of the public sphere[55] then Baudrillard's dystopic simulation of change may well be the first tentative step toward virtual reality. The transcendent leap of cyberspace from the literary pages of William Gibson into a hypothesis about reality suggests that distinctions of all kinds have become dysfunctional. In that sense, there can be no conclusion to this book, because as with electronic mail, there seems to be more and more reasons to continue writing. "What happens," asks Marc Laidlaw, "when the clumsy helmet becomes a snug full-body datasuit, capable of transmitting illusory sensations so convincing that the false reality is indistinguishable from the real? What happens when TV turns invasive, when your Sony Watchman crawls into your eyes and the an-tennae wrap themselves around your nerves? Can fiction possibly prepare us for such breakthroughs?"[56]

I don't believe it can. Reality and illusion are no longer useful terms for understanding the links between the computer screen, the act of writing, pro-cesses of viewing, images, the virtual, and so on. It has been the thrust of this book to explore all of these elements within the context of an "old" medium. These printed words are themselves one of the best ways of "seeing" and also an excellent strategy for challenging the idea that the imaginary can ever be enclosed within the various technologies that any culture creates. It is in this continual smashing of borders, this nonstop poesis within which the real is recognized as just another printed word, another strategy of explanation and interpretation, that new forms of subjectivity arise. Perhaps the best example of this are the hypertext novels circulating in computer disk form. Most of the sentences are starred (*) suggesting that the text leads to other texts and to

55. See Jürgen Habermas, *The Structural Transformation of the Public Sphere* tr. Thomas Burger (Cambridge Mass.: MIT Press, 1989). Michael Warner's rereading of Habermas and particularly his close examination of the colonial revolution in the U.S. as dependent on "men of letters" extends, then goes far beyond Habermas. Michael Warner, "The Cul-tural Mediation of Print," in *Ruthless Criticism: New Perspectives in U.S. Communication History*, ed. William S. Solomon and Robert W. McChesney (Minneapolis: University of Minnesota Press, 1993), 7–37.
56. Marc Laidlaw, "Virtual Reality: Our New Romance with Plot Devices," *South Atlan-tic Quarterly* 92.4 (1993): 648.

images and to thoughts and to other plot lines—all of this within a contingent framework where there are endless levels and for which there is no clear end. The text becomes spatial, and time evolves into play, forever reversible. This is the labyrinth of reading, now given a form. The virtual text switches from image to word and back again as if no amount of peeling will strip the pleasure from the idea. It may be that we are in the midst of an endless rainstorm or that we are giving shape to the pixels of a new digital future. Yet no amount of sophistication to the various technological surrogates that our culture invents will drain the imaginary of its flexibility to reinvent not only itself but the human subjects who nurture and are nurtured by its creativity and energy.

Bibliography

Adair, John, and Sol Worth. *Through Navajo Eyes: An Exploration in Film, Communication and Anthropology*. Bloomington: Indiana University Press, 1972.

Allshouse, Robert H. *Photographs for the Tsar: The Pioneering Color Photography of Sergei Mikhailovich Prokudin-Gorskii*. New York: Dial Press, 1980.

Alvarado, Manuel. *Video World-Wide*. London: John Libbey, 1988.

Ambrosi, Alain, and Nancy Thede, eds. *Video in the Changing World*. Montreal: Black Rose, 1991.

Anderson, Benedict. *Imagined Communities: Reflections on the Origin and Spread of Nationalism*. London: Verso, 1991.

Anderson, Kelly, and Annie Goldson. "Alternative Television Inside and Outside of the Academy." *Social Text* 35 (1993): 56–71.

Armes, Roy. *On Video*. New York: Routledge, 1988.

Aufderheide, Patricia. "Underground Cable: A Survey of Public Access Programming." *Afterimage* 22.1 (1994).

Avedon, Richard. *In the American West*. New York: Harry N. Abrams, 1985.

Bal, Mieke. "His Master's Eye." *Modernity and the Hegemony of Vision*. Ed. David Levin Michael. Berkeley and Los Angeles: University of California Press, 1993.

Barret, Derm. "Fast Focus: A Manager's Look at TQM Terms and Topics." *The Globe and Mail*. 19 January, 1993. B 24.

Barthes, Roland. *Camera Lucida*. Tr. Richard Howard. New York: Noonday Press, 1981.

——. *Image, Music, Text*. Tr. Stephen Heath. Glasgow: Fontana/Collins, 1979.

——. *Mythologies*. London: Jonathan Cape, 1972.

Bataille, Georges. *Guilty*. Tr. Bruce Boone. Venice, Calif.: The Lapis Press, 1988.

——. *Inner Experience*. Tr. Leslie Anne Boldt. Albany: State University of New York Press, 1988.

——. *The Story of the Eye*. London: Penguin, 1982.

Bateson, Gregory. *Mind and Nature*. New York: E. P. Dutton, 1979.

Baudrillard, Jean. "Beyond Right and Wrong Or The Mischevious Genius of Image." *Resolution: A Critique of Video Art*. Ed. Patti Podesta. Los Angeles: Los Angeles Contemporary Exhibitions, 1986.

——. *The Evil Demon of Images*. Sydney: Power Institute, 1984.

——. "The Masses: The Implosion of the Social in the Media"; "On Seduction"; "Simulacra and Simulations"; in *Jean Baudrillard: Selected Writings*. Ed. Mark Poster. Stanford: Stanford University Press, 1988.

Bazin, André. "The Ontology of the Photographic Image." *What Is Cinema?* Tr. Hugh Gray. Berkeley and Los Angeles: University of California Press, 1967.

Bellour, Raymond. "Le blocage symbolique." *Communications* 23 (1975).

———. "Le texte introuvable." *L'analyse du film*. Paris: Editions Albatros, 1979.

Benjamin, Walter. "A Small History of Photography." *One Way Street and Other Writings*. London: Verso, 1979.

Bensmaïa, Réda. *The Barthes Effect: The Essay as Reflective Text*. Minneapolis: University of Minnesota Press, 1987.

Benterrak, Krim, Stephen Muecke, and Paddy Roe. *Reading the Country: Introduction to Nomadology*. Freemantle, Australia: Freemantle Arts Centre Press, 1984.

Berger, John. *About Looking*. New York: Pantheon, 1980.

Berko, Lili. "Surveying the Surveilled: Video, Space and Subjectivity." *Quarterly Review of Film and Video* 14.1–2 (1992): 62–91.

———. "Video in Search of a Discourse." *Quarterly Review of Film Studies* 10 (1989): 289–397.

Berrigan, Francis J. *Access: Some Western Models of Community Media*. Paris: UNESCO, 1977.

———. *Community Communications: The Role of Community Media in Development*. Paris: UNESCO, 1979.

Bhabha, Homi K. "Freedom's Basis in the Indeterminate." *October* 61 (1992).

Birnbaum, Dara. "Author's Introduction." *Rough Edits: Popular Image Video*. Ed. Benjamin H. D. Buchloh. Halifax: The Press of the Nova Scotia College of Art and Design, 1987.

Bishop, Elizabeth. "Insomnia." *Elizabeth Bishop: The Complete Poems 1927–1979*. New York: Farrar, Strauss and Giroux, 1991.

Boeren, Ad. "Getting Involved: Communication for Participatory Development." *The Empowerment of Culture: Development Communication and Popular Media*. Ed. Ad Boeren and Kes Epskamp. The Hague: Centre for the Study of Education in Developing Countries, 1992.

Bolton, Richard. "In the American East: Richard Avedon Incorporated." *The Contest of Meaning: Critical Histories of Photography*. Ed. Richard Bolton. Cambridge, Mass.: MIT Press, 1992.

Bonitzer, Pascal. "Here: The Notion of the Shot and the Subject of Cinema." *Film Reader* 4 (1979).

Bordwell, David. *Making Meaning: Inference and Rhetoric in the Interpretation of Cinema*. Cambridge, Mass.: Harvard University Press, 1989.

———. *Narration in the Fiction Film*. Madison: University of Wisconsin, 1985.

———. "Textual Analysis, etc.." *Enclitic* 5 & 6.1 (1981–82).

Bordwell, David and Thompson, Kristin. *Film Art*. Reading, Mass.: Addison-Wesley, 1979.

Bourdieu, Pierre. *Photography: A Middle-brow Art*. Tr. Shaun Whiteside. Stanford: Stanford University Press, 1990.

Boyle, Deirdre. "From Portapack to Camcorder: A Brief History of Guerrilla Television." *Journal of Film and Video* 44.1–2 (1992): 67–79.

Braudy, Leo. *The World in a Frame: What We See in Films*. Garden City, N.J.: Anchor Press, 1976.

Bryson, Norman. *Vision and Painting: The Logic of the Gaze*. London: Macmillan, 1983.

Buchloh, Benjamin H. D. "From Gadget Video to Agit Video: Some Notes on Four Recent Video Works." *Art Journal* 45.3 (1985).

Buck-Morss, Susan. *The Dialectics of Seeing: Walter Benjamin and the Arcades Project.* Cambridge, Mass.: MIT Press, 1989.

Burnett, Kathleen. "Towards a Theory of Hypertextual Design." *Postmodern Culture* 3.2 (1993).

Burnett, Ron. "Developments in Cultural Identity Through Film: The Documentary Film, The National Film Board and Quebec Nationalism." *Journal of the Australia-New Zealand Society for Canadian Studies* 2 (1985).

———. *First Contact: The Ethnographic Film as Historical Document. Second Australian History and Film Conference.* Ed. Brian Shoesmith and Sally Stockbridge. Perth, Australia: Australian Film and Television School, 1984.

———. "Speaking of Parts." *Speaking Parts: Atom Egoyan.* Ed. Marc Glassman. Toronto: Coach House Press, 1993.

———. "The Tightrope of Male Fantasy." *Framework* 26/27 (1985).

———. "A Torn Page . . . Ghosts on the Computer Screen . . . Words . . . Images . . . Labyrinths: Exploring the Frontiers of Cyberspace." *Late Editions* 3. Ed. George Marcus. Chicago: University of Chicago Press, 1995.

———. "Video/Film: From Communication to Community." *Video in the Changing World.* Ed. Nancy Thede and Alain Ambrosi. Montreal: Black Rose Books, 1991.

Butler, Judith. "Endangered/Endangering: Schematic Racism and White Paranoia." *Reading Rodney King/Reading Urban Uprising.* Ed. Robert Gooding-Williams. New York: Routledge, 1993.

Calvino, Italo. *Mr. Palomar.* Tr. William Weaver. London: Secker and Warburg, 1986.

———. *Six Memos for the Next Millennium.* Cambridge, Mass.: Harvard University Press, 1988.

———. *The Uses of Literature.* Tr. Patrick Creagh. New York: Harcourt Brace Jovanovich, 1986.

———. *The Watcher.* Tr. William Weaver. New York: Harcourt Brace Jovanovich, 1971.

Campa, Román de la. "Latin Lessons." *Transition* 63 (1994).

Carpenter, Edmund. *They Became What They Beheld.* New York: Dutton, 1976.

Carroll, John M. *Toward a Structural Psychology of the Cinema.* The Hague: Mouton, 1979.

Cassirer, Henri. *Mass Media in an African Context: An Evaluation of Senegal's Pilot Project. Reports and Papers on Mass Communication.* Paris: UNESCO, 1974.

Chatterjee, Partha. *Nationalist Thought and the Colonial World: A Derivative Discourse.* London: ZED Books, 1986.

Clark, R. E. "Reconsidering Research on Learning from the Media." *Review of Educational Research* 53 (1983): 445–59.

Clifford, James. "Traveling Cultures." *Cultural Studies.* Ed. Lawrence Grossberg, Cary Nelson, and Paula Treichler. New York: Routledge, 1992.

———. *The Predicament of Culture.* Cambridge, Mass.: Harvard University Press, 1988.

Comment, Bernard. *Roland Barthes, Vers Le Neutre.* Paris: Christian Bourgeois, 1991.

Comolli, Jean-Louis, and André Bazin. "Machines of the Visible." *The Cinematic Apparatus.* Ed. Stephen Heath and Teresa de Lauretis. London: Macmillan, 1980.

Compton, Allan. "The Concept of Identification in the Work of Freud, Ferenczi and Abraham: A Review and Commentary." *Psychoanalytic Quarterly* 54 (1985).

Cornwall, Regina. *Snow Seen: The Films and Photographs of Michael Snow*. Toronto: PMA Books, 1979.

Crapanzano, Vincent. *Hermes' Dilemma and Hamlet's Desire: On the Epistemology of Interpretation*. Cambridge, Mass.: Harvard University Press, 1992.

Crary, Jonathan. "Modernizing Vision." *Vision and Visuality*. Ed. Hal Foster. Seattle: Bay Press, 1988.

———. *Techniques of the Observer: On Vision and Modernity in the Nineteenth Century*. Cambridge, Mass.: MIT Press, 1991.

———. "Unbinding Vision." *October* 68 (1994).

Cubitt, Sean. *Timeshift: On Video Culture*. New York: Routledge, 1991.

De Landa, Manuel. "Virtual Environments and the Emergence of Synthetic Reason." *The South Atlantic Quarterly* 92.4 (1993).

Deleuze, Gilles. *Cinema 1 The Movement-Image*. Tr. Hugh Tomlinson and Barbara Habberjam. Minneapolis: University of Minnesota Press, 1986.

DeMarinis, Paul, and Laetitia Sonami. "Mechanization Takes Command—Verses from Giedion's Bible." *Out of Control*. Ed. Karl Gerbel. Linz: Ars Electronica—Landesverlag, 1991.

Derrida, Jacques. "The Deaths of Roland Barthes." *Philosophy and Non-Philosophy Since Merleau-Ponty*. Ed. Hugh J. Silverman. New York: Routledge, 1988.

Dibblin, Jane. *Day of Two Suns: U.S. Nuclear Testing and the Pacific Islanders*. London: Virago Press, 1988.

Dieckmann, Katherine. "Electra Myths: Video, Modernism, Postmodernism." *Art Journal* 45.3 (1985).

Dodge, William, ed. *Boundaries of Identity: A Quebec Reader*. Toronto: Lester, 1992.

Dowrick, Peter W. *Practical Guide to Using Video in the Behavioral Sciences*. New York: John Wiley and Sons, 1991.

Duras, Marguerite. *Hiroshima, Mon Amour*. Tr. Richard Seaver. New York: Grove Press, 1961.

Eagleton, Terry. "The Crisis of Contemporary Culture." *New Left Review* 196 (1993).

Eaton, Michael. "Amazonian Video." *Sight and Sound* 4.2 (1992).

Eco, Umberto. *Interpretation and Overinterpretation*. Cambridge, England: Cambridge University Press, 1992.

Edelman, Gerald M. *Bright Air, Brilliant Fire: On the Matter of Mind*. New York: Basic Books, 1992.

Eisenstein, Sergei. *Film Form and Film Sense*. New York: Meridian Books, 1957.

Eixenbaum, Boris. "Problems of Cinema Stylistics." *Russian Formalist Film Theory*. Ed. Herbert Eagle. Detroit: University of Michigan Press, 1981.

Ekman, P. and Sherer P. Ekman. "Methods for Measuring Facial Action." *Handbook of Methods of Nonverbal Behaviour Research*. Ed. K. R. and Sherer P. Ekman. New York: Cambridge University Press, 1982. 45–90.

Elsaesser, Thomas. "Syberberg, Cinema and Representation." *New German Critique* 24/25 (1981–82).

Ermath, Elizabeth Deeds. *Sequel to History: Postmodernism and the Crisis of Representational Time*. New Jersey: Princeton University Press, 1992.

Evans, Gary. *In the National Interest: A Chronicle of the National Film Board of Canada from 1949 to 1989*. Toronto: University of Toronto Press, 1991.

Fabian, Johannes. *Time and the Other: How Anthropology Makes Its Object*. New York: Columbia University Press, 1983.

Felman, Shoshana. "Turning the Screw of Interpretation." *Yale French Studies* 55–56 (1977).

Felman, Shoshana, and Dori Laub. "Education and Crisis, Or the Vicissitudes of Teaching." *Testimony: Crises of Witnessing in Literature, Psychoanalysis, and History.* New York: Routledge, 1992.

Fischer, Michael. "Anthropology as Cultural Critique: Inserts for the 1990s, Cultural Studies of Science, Visual-Virtual Realities, and Post-Trauma Polities." *Cultural Anthropology* 6.4 (1991).

Foucault, Michel. "Interview." *Cahiers du cinema* 251–52 (1974).

Freedberg, David. *The Power of Images: Studies in the History and Theory of Response.* Chicago: University of Chicago Press, 1989.

Freire, Paulo. *Education for Critical Consciousness.* New York: Seabury Press, 1973.

Friedlander, Saul. *Reflections of Nazism.* London: Harper & Row, 1984.

Friesen, P. Ekman. *Collaborative Studies on Depression.* Washington, D.C.: National Institute of Health, 1981.

Fuller, Buckminster. *Utopia or Oblivion: The Prospects for Humanity.* New York: Overlook Press, 1972.

Fuller, Peter. "Art and Biology." *New Left Review* 132 (1982).

Gabriel, Teshome H. "Ruin and the Other: Towards a Language of Memory." *Otherness and the Media: The Ethnography of the Imagined and the Imaged.* Ed. Teshome H. Gabriel and Hamid Naficy. Langhorne, Penn.: Harwood Academic Publishers, 1993.

Gallop, Jane. "Lacan and Literature: A Case for Transference." *Poetics* 13 (1984).

Gandelman, Claude. *Reading Pictures, Viewing Texts.* Bloomington: Indiana University Press, 1991.

Gane, Mike. *Baudrillard's Bestiary: Baudrillard and Culture.* New York: Routledge, 1991.

——. *Baudrillard: Critical and Fatal Theory.* New York: Routledge, 1991.

Garnham, Nicholas. "The Mass Media, Cultural Identity and the Public Sphere in the Modern World." *Public Culture* 5.2 (1993).

Giannetti, Louis. *Understanding Movies.* Englewood Cliffs, N.J.: Prentice-Hall, 1990.

Ginsburg, Faye. "Aboriginal Media and the Australian Imaginary." *Public Culture* 5.3 (1993).

——. "Indigenous Media: Faustian Contract or Global Village?" *Rereading Cultural Anthropology.* Ed. George E. Marcus. Durham: Duke University Press, 1992.

Godard, Jean-Luc. "Excerpts from the transcript of Godard-Gorin's *Letter to Jane.*" *Women and Film* 3 & 4 (1974).

Goldberg, Kim. *The Barefoot Channel: Community Television as a Tool for Social Change.* Vancouver: New Star Books, 1990.

Goodwin, Andrew. *Dancing in the Distraction Factory: Music Television and Popular Culture.* Minneapolis: University of Minnesota, 1992.

Gorfain, Phyllis. "Play and the Problem of Knowing in *Hamlet:* An Excursion into Interpretive Anthropology." *The Anthropology of Experience.* Ed. Victor Turner and Edward Bruner. Urbana: University of Illinois, 1986.

Graham, Dan. "Video in Relation to Architecture." *Illuminating Video: An Essential Guide to Video Art.* Ed. Doug Hall and Sally Jo Fifer. New York: Aperture Foundation, 1990.

Grimshaw, Anna, and Keith Hart. "Anthropology and the Crisis of the Intellectuals." *Critique of Anthropology* 14.3 (1994).

Gross, Kenneth. *The Dream of the Moving Statue*. Ithaca: Cornell University Press, 1992.

Gupta, Akhil, and James Ferguson. "Beyond 'Culture': Space, Identity, and the Politics of Difference." *Cultural Anthropology* 7.1 (1992).

Guzzetti, Alfred. *Two or Three Things I Know About Her: Analysis of a Film by Godard*. Cambridge, Mass.: Harvard University Press, 1981.

Habermas, Jürgen. *Moral Consciousness and Communicative Action*. Tr. C. Nicolson and Shierry W. Lenhardt, Cambridge: MIT Press, 1990.

——. *The Structural Transformation of the Public Sphere*. Tr. Thomas Burger, Cambridge, Mass.: MIT Press, 1989.

Hall, Doug, and Sally Jo Fifer. *Illuminating Video*. New York: Aperture Foundation, 1990.

Hanhardt, John, ed. *Video Culture: A Critical Investigation*. Layton, Ut.: Peregrine Smith, 1988.

Hansen, Miriam. "Alexander Kluge, Cinema and the Public Sphere: The Construction Site of Counter-History." *Discourse* 6 (Fall 1983).

——. *Babel and Babylon: Spectatorship in American Silent Film*. Cambridge, Mass.: Harvard University Press, 1991.

——. "With Skin and Hair: Kracauer's Theory of Film, Marseille 1940." *Critical Inquiry* 19. 3 (1993).

Haraway, Donna. "Situated Knowledges." *Simians, Cyborgs, and Women*. New York: Routledge, 1991.

Heath, Stephen. "Representing Television." *Logics of Television: Essays in Cultural Criticism*. Ed. Patricia Mellencamp. Bloomington: Indiana University Press, 1990.

Hénaut, Dorothy Todd. "Editorial." *Challenge for Change Newsletter* (1969): 3.

Henny, Leonard. "Video and the Community." *Using Video*. Ed. P. W. Dowrick and S. J. Biggs. London: John Wiley, 1983.

Herbert, Christopher. *Culture and Anomie: Ethnographic Imagination in the Nineteenth Century*. Chicago: University of Chicago, 1991.

Hirst, Paul. *On Law and Ideology*. London: Macmillan, 1979.

Ingle, Henry T. *Communication Media and Technology: A Look at their Role in Non-Formal Education Programs*. Washington, D.C.: Information Center on Instructional Technology, 1974.

Iser, Wolfgang. "Interaction Between Text and Reader." *The Reader in the Text: Essays on Audience and Interpretation*. Ed. Susan R. Suleiman and Inge Crosman. Princeton, N.J.: Princeton University Press, 1980.

James, David. "inTerVention: the contents of negation for video and its criticism." *Resolution: A Critique of Video Art*. Ed. Patti Podesta. Los Angeles: Los Angeles Contemporary Exhibitions, 1986.

Jameson, Frederic. "Reading Without Interpretation: Postmodernism and the Video-Text." *The Linguistic of Writing: Arguments Between Language and Literature*. Nigel Fabb, Derek Attridge, Alan Durant, and Colin MacCabe, eds. New York: Methuen, 1987.

Jay, Martin. *Downcast Eyes: The Denigration of Vision in Twentieth-Century French Thought*. Berkeley and Los Angeles: University of California Press, 1993.

Kaplan, E. Ann. *Women and Film*. New York: Methuen, 1983.

Kelman, Ken. "Anticipations of the Light." *The New American Cinema: A Critical Anthology*. Ed. Gregory Battock. New York: Dutton, 1967.

Kern, Stephen. *The Culture of Time and Space 1880–1918*. London: Weidenfeld and Nicolson, 1983.

Klein, Norman M. "Audience Culture and the Video Screen." *Rough Edits: Popular Image Video*. Ed. Benjamin H. D. Buchloh. Halifax: The Press of the Nova Scotia College of Art and Design, 1987.

Kostelanetz, Richard, ed. *Moholy-Nagy*. New York: Praeger, 1970.

Kracauer, Siegfried. "Photography." *Critical Inquiry* 19.3 (1993).

Krauss, Rosalind. "Photography's Discursive Spaces." *The Contest of Meaning: Critical Histories of Photography*. Ed. Richard Bolton. Cambridge, Mass.: MIT Press, 1992.

——. *The Optical Unconscious*. Cambridge, Mass.: MIT Press, 1993.

——. "Video: The Aesthetics of Narcissism." *Video Culture: A Critical Investigation*. Ed. John G. Hanhardt. Layton, Ut.: Peregrine Smith Books, 1986.

Kris, Ernest, and Hans Speier. *German Radio Propaganda*. London: Oxford University Press, 1944.

Kroker, Arthur. *The Possessed Individual: Technology and the French Postmodern*. Montreal: New World Perspectives, 1993.

Kroker, Arthur, and Marilouise Kroker. "The Last Sex: Feminism and Outlaw Bodies." *The Last Sex: Feminism and Outlaw Bodies*. Ed. Arthur Kroker and Marilouise Kroker. Montreal: New World Perspectives, 1993.

Laidlaw, Marc. "Virtual Reality: Our New Romance with Plot Devices." *South Atlantic Quarterly* 92.4 (1993).

Lanzmann, Claude. "Shoah." *Cahiers du cinema*, 374 (1985).

Lasch, Christopher. *The Culture of Narcissim: American Life in the Age of Diminishing Expectations*. New York: Norton, 1979.

Lee, Benjamin. "Going Public." *Public Culture* 5.2 (1993).

Levin, Charles. "Time and Postmodernism: A Capsule." *Communication* 10 (1988):

Levin, David Michael. *The Opening of Vision*. New York: Routledge, 1988.

Lévi-Strauss, Claude. "Les paroles et la musique." *Regarder, Écouter, Lire*. Paris: Plon, 1993.

Levoff, Daniel H. "Brakhage's The Act Of Seeing With One's Own Eyes." *Film Culture* 56–57 (1973).

Lotman, Juri. "The Dynamic Model of a Semiotic System." *Semiotica* 21.1 (1977).

Lyons, Nick. "The Age of Betamax." *The Sony Vision*. New York: Crown, 1976.

Lyotard, Jean-Francois. *The Postmodern Condition: A Report on Knowledge*. Tr. Geoff Bennington and Brian Massumi. Minneapolis: University of Minnesota, 1984.

MacBride, James. *Many Voices, One World*. Rome International Commission for the Study of Communication Problems, 1980.

Mankekar, Purnima. "National Texts and Gendered Lives: An Ethnography of Television Viewers in a North Indian City." *American Ethnologist* 20.3 (1993): 543–63.

Marcuse, Herbert. *One-Dimensional Man*. Boston: Beacon Press, 1966.

Marshall, Stuart. "Video Art, The Imaginary and the Parole Vide." *New Artists Video: A Critical Anthology*. Ed. Gregory Battock. New York: Dutton, 1978.

Marx, Leo. "The Idea of Technology and Postmodern Pessimism." *Does Technology Drive History? The Dilemma of Technological Determinism*. Ed. Merritt Roe Smith and Leo Marx. Cambridge, Mass.: MIT Press, 1994.

Metz, Christian. *The Imaginary Signifier: Psychoanalysis and the Cinema*. Bloomington: Indiana University Press, 1982.

———. *Language and Cinema.* Tr. Donna Jean Umiker-Sebeok. The Hague: Mouton, 1974.

———. *The Language of Film.* New York: Praeger, 1972.

Michaels, Eric. *The Aboriginal Invention of Television: Central Australia 1982–86.* Canberra: Australian Institute of Aboriginal Studies, 1986.

———. "For a Cultural Future: Francis Jupurrurla Makes TV at Yuendumu." *Bad Aboriginal Art: Tradition, Media, and Technological Horizons.* Minneapolis: University of Minnesota Press, 1994.

———. "Hollywood Iconography: A Walpiri Reading." *Television and its Audience: International Research Perspectives.* Ed. Phillip Drummond and Richard Paterson. London: British Film Institute, 1987.

———. "How to Look at Us Looking at the Yanomami Looking at Us." *A Crack in the Mirror.* Ed. Jay Ruby. Philadelphia: University of Pennsylvania Press, 1982.

———. "Para-Ethnography." *Art & Text* 30 (1988).

———. *Unbecoming.* Rose Bay, New South Wales: Empress Publishing, 1990.

Mitchell, W. J. T. *Picture Theory: Essays on Verbal and Visual Representation.* Chicago: University of Chicago Press, 1994.

Mitchell, William J. *The Reconfigured Eye: Visual Truth in the Post-Photographic Era.* Cambridge, Mass.: MIT Press, 1992.

Mitry, Jean. *Esthetique et psychologie du cinéma.* Paris: Editions Universitaires, 1963.

Mohabeer, Michelle. "The Inside Out Lesbian and Gay Film and Video Festival of Toronto." *Fuse 15.5 & 6 (1993).*

Moore, Rick. *Canada's Challenge for Change: Documentary Film and Video as an Exercise of Power Through the Production of Cultural Reality.* Ph. D. dissertation. University of Oregon, 1987.

Morris, Meeghan. "Postmodernity and Lyotard's Sublime." *The Pirate's Fiancee.* London: Verso, 1988.

Morse, Margaret. "An Ontology of Everyday Distraction: The Freeway, the Mall and Television." *Logics of Television: Essays in Cultural Criticism.* Ed. Patricia Mellencamp. Bloomington: Indiana University Press, 1990.

Mowitt, John. *Text: The Genealogy of an Antidisciplinary Object.* Durham: Duke University Press, 1992.

Mowlana, Hamid, and Laurie J. Wilson. *The Passing of Modernity: Communication and the Transformation of Society.* New York: Longman, 1990.

Münsterberg, Hugo. *The Film: A Psychological Study.* New York: Dover, 1970.

Naficy, Hamid. *The Making of Exile Cultures: Iranian Television in Los Angeles.* Minneapolis: University of Minnesota, 1993.

———. "The Poetics and Practice of Iranian Nostalgia in Exile." *Diaspora* 1.3 (1991).

———. "The Semiotics of Veiling and Vision: Women and the Cinema." *Arena* 1 (1993).

Nancy, Jean-Luc. "Exscription." *Yale French Studies* 78 (1990).

Nichols, Bill. "The Birds At The Window." *Film Reader* 4 (1979).

———. *Ideology and the Image.* Bloomington: Indiana University Press, 1981.

Odin, Roger. "La sémio-pragmatique du cinéma sans crise, ni désillusion." *Hors Cadre* 7.7 (1988–89).

Oepen, Manfred. "Traditional and Group Media Utilization in Indonesia." *The Empowerment of Culture: Development Communication and Popular Media.* Ed. Ad

Boeren and Kes Epskamp. The Hague: Centre for the Study of Education in Developing Countries, 1992.

Okunna, Chinyere Stella. "Communication for Self-Reliance Among Rural Women in Nigeria." *Media Development* 39.1 (1992).

Osborne, Peter. "Small-scale Victories, Large-scale Defeats: Walter Benjamin's Politics of Time." *Walter Benjamin's Philosophy: Destruction and Experience*. Ed. Andrew Benjamin and Peter Osborne. New York: Routledge, 1994.

Pearlstone, Zena. *Ethnic L.A.* Beverley Hills: Hillcrest, 1990.

Plant, Sadie. "Beyond the Screens: Film, Cyberpunk and Cyberfeminism." *Variant* 14 (1993).

Poster, Mark. *The Mode of Information: Poststructuralism and Social Context*. Chicago: University of Chicago Press, 1990.

Postman, Neil. *Amusing Ourselves to Death: Public Discourse in the Age of Show Business*. New York: Viking Penguin, 1986.

Prigogine, Ilya, and Isabelle Stengers. *Order out of Chaos: Man's New Dialogue with Nature*. London: Heinemann, 1984.

Pringle, Ian. *Active Culturalism—Cultural Activism: The Advent of Community-Oriented Institutional FM Broadcasting in Canada*. Unpublished essay, McGill University 1991.

Prinn, Elisabeth. "Vive le Videographe." *Challenge for Change Newsletter* Spring 1972.

Pruyser, Paul W. *The Play of the Imagination: Towards a Psychoanalysis of Culture*. New York: International Universities Press, 1983.

Rabinow, Paul. *Reflections on Fieldwork in Morocco*. Berkeley and Los Angeles: University of California Press, 1977.

Raboy, Marc. *Old Passions, New Visions: Social Movements and Political Activism in Quebec*. Toronto: Between the Lines, 1986.

Readings, Bill. "Be Excellent: Culture, The State and the Posthistorical University." *Alphabet City* 3 (1993).

Rewar, Walter. "Signs, Icons and Subjects." *Ciné-Tracts* 4.2/3 (1981).

Rieker, Martina. "Narrating the Post-Colonial Everyday: An Interrogation of *The Good Woman of Bangkok*." *Visual Anthropology Review* 9.1 (1993).

Ritchin, Fred. "Photojournalism in the Age of the Computer." *The Critical Image*. Ed. Carol Squiers. Seattle: Bay Press, 1990.

Romanyshyn, Robert D. *Technology as Symptom and Dream*. New York: Routledge, 1989.

Ropars, Marie-Claire. *De la litterature au cinéma: génèse d'une écriture*. Paris: Colin, 1970.

Ropars, Marie-Claire, and Pierre Sorlin. *Octobre: ecriture et ideologie*. Paris: Editions Albatros, 1976.

Rorty, Richard. *Contingency, Irony and Solidarity*. New York: Cambridge University Press, 1989.

——. *Philosophy and the Mirror of Nature*. Princeton, N.J.: Princeton University Press, 1979.

Roy, Sylvia, and Nancy Thede. "An Interview with Luiz Fernando Santoro." *Clips* .0 (1992).

Rushdie, Salman. *Haroun and the Sea of Stories*. London: Granta Books, 1990.

——. "Imaginary Homelands." *Imaginary Homelands*. New York: Viking, 1991.

Saalfield, Catherine. "On the Make: Activist Video Collectives." *Queer Looks: Perspective on Lesbian and Gay Film and Video.* Ed. Martha Gever, John Greyson, and Pratibha Parmar. Toronto: Between the Lines, 1993.

Sahlins, Marshall. *Culture and Practical Reason.* Chicago: University of Chicago Press, 1976.

Said, Edward W. *Culture and Imperialism.* New York: Alfred A. Knopf, 1993.

Sartre, Jean-Paul. *The Psychological Imagination.* London: Metheun, 1972.

Scarry, Elaine. "Watching and Authorizing the Gulf War." *Media Spectacles.* Ed. Marjorie Garber, Jann Matlock, and Rebecca L. Walkowitz. New York: Routledge, 1993.

Schafer, Roy. *Aspects of Internalization.* New York: International Universities Press, 1968.

———. "Internalization: Process or Fantasy." *A New Language for Psychoanalysis.* New Haven: Yale University Press, 1976.

Scherer, Clifford. "The Videocassette Recorder and Information Inequity." *Journal of Communication* 34 (Summer 1989).

Searle, John. *The Rediscovery of Mind.* 2. ed. Cambridge, Mass.: MIT Press, 1992.

Seinfeld, Jerry. *SeinLanguage.* New York: Bantam, 1993.

Sharp, Geoff. "Extended Forms of the Social: Technological Mediation and Self-Formation." *Arena Journal* 1.1 (1993).

Shotter, John. "On Viewing Videotape Records of Oneself and Others: A Hermeneutical Analysis." *Using Video.* Ed. P. W. Dowrick and S. J. Biggs. London: John Wiley & Sons, 1983.

Shulevitz, Judith. "Tribes and Tribulations." *Film Comment* 26.2 (1990).

Silverman, Kaja. *The Subject of Semiotics.* New York: Oxford University Press, 1983.

———. "What Is a Camera? or: History in the Field of Vision." *Discourse* 15.3 (1993).

Sitney, P. Adams. "Structural Film." *Film Culture Reader.* Ed. P. Adams Sitney. New York: Praeger, 1970.

Smith, Merritt Roe. "Technological Determinism in American Culture." *Does Technology Drive History? The Dilemma of Technological Determinism.* Ed. Merritt Roe Smith and Leo Marx. Cambridge, Mass.: MIT Press, 1994.

Snyder, Joel. "Picturing Vision." *The Language of Images.* Ed. W. J. T. Mitchell. Chicago: University of Chicago Press, 1980.

Sobchack, Vivian. *The Address of the Eye: A Phenomenology of Film Experience.* Princeton, N.J.: Princeton University Press, 1992.

Solomon-Godeau, Abigail. "The Armed Vision Disarmed: Radical Formalism from Weapon to Style." *The Contest of Meaning.* Ed. Richard Bolton. Cambridge, Mass.: MIT Press, 1992.

———. *Photography at the Dock: Essays on Photographic History, Institutions and Practices.* Minneapolis: University of Minnesota, 1991.

Sontag, Susan. *On Photography.* New York: Anchor Books, 1989.

Stabile, Carol. "Shooting the Mother: Fetal Photography and the Politics of Disappearance." *Camera Obscura* 25 (1992).

Stafford, Barbara Maria. *Body Criticism: Imaging the Unseen in Enlightenment Art and Medicine.* Cambridge, Mass.: MIT Press, 1991.

Staiger, Janet, Kristin Tompson, and David Bordwell. *The Classical Hollywood Cinema: Film Style and Mode of Production to 1960.* New York: Columbia University Press, 1985.

Stuart, Sara. "Access to Media: Placing Video in the Hands of the People." *Media Development* 29.4 (1989).

Sturmer, John Von. "Aborigines, Representation, Necrophilia." *Art & Text* 32 (1989).

Thompson, Kristin. *Eisenstein's Ivan the Terrible*. Princeton: Princeton University Press, 1981.

Todorov, Tzvetan. *Mikhail Bakhtin: The Dialogical Principle*. Tr. W. Godzich, Minneapolis: University of Minnesota Press, 1984.

Tomaselli, Keyan, and Alison Lazerus. "Participatory Video: Problems, Prospects and a Case Study." *Group Media Journal* 8.1 (1989).

Treichler, Paula A., and Lisa Cartwright. "Introduction." *Camera Obscura* 28 (1992).

Turkle, Sherry. *The Second Self: Computers and the Human Spirit*. New York: Simon and Schuster, 1984.

Turner, Terence. "The Social Dynamics of Video Media in an Indigenous Society: The Cultural Meaning and the Personal Politics of Video-making in Kayapo Communities." *Visual Anthropology Review* 7.2 (1991).

———. "Visual Media, Cultural Politics and Anthropological Practice: Some Implications of Recent Uses of Film and Video among the Kayapo of Brazil." *Commission on Visual Anthropology Review* (Spring 1990).

Tyler, Stephen A. "Post-Modem Ethnography: From Document of the Occult to Occult Document." *Writing Culture: The Poetics and Politics of Ethnography*. Ed. James Clifford and George E. Marcus. Berkeley and Los Angeles: University of California, 1986.

———. *The Unspeakable: Discourse, Dialogue, and Rhetoric in the Postmodern World*. Madison: University of Wisconsin Press, 1987.

UNESCO. *World Communication Report*. Paris: UNESCO, 1989.

Ungar, Stephen. *Roland Barthes: The Professor of Desire*. Lincoln: University of Nebraska Press, 1983.

Vinebohm, Lisa. "The Power of Voice." *Interadio* 5.2. (1993).

Virilio, Paul. *The Aesthetics of Disappearance*. Tr. Philip Beitchman. New York: Semiotext(e), 1991.

———. "The Last Vehicle." Tr. David Antal. *Looking Back on the End of the World*. Ed. Dietmar Kamper and Christoph Wulf. New York: Semiotext(e), 1989.

Walton, Kendall. "Transparent Pictures: On the Nature of Photographic Realism." *Critical Inquiry* 11.3 (1984).

Warner, Michael. "The Cultural Mediation of Print." *Ruthless Criticism: New Perspectives in U.S. Communication History*. Ed. William S. Solomon and Robert W. McChesney. Minneapolis: University of Minnesota, 1993.

Waterman, David. "Narrowcasting and Broadcasting: On Nonbroadcast Media, A Program Choice Model." *Communication Research* 19 (1992).

Weiss, Allen S. "Outside In: Some New Improved Anxieties of Influence." *Art & Text* 35 (1990).

Weschler, Lawrence. "Portfolio: Slight Modifications." *New Yorker* (12 July 1993).

White, Richard. *Inventing Australia: Images and Identity 1688–1980*. Sydney: George Allen and Unwin, 1981.

Widlocher, Daniel. "The Wish for Identification and Structural Effects in the Work of Freud." *International Journal of Psychoanalysis* 66 (1985).

Wilden, Anthony. *System and Structure*. London: Tavistock, 1972.

Williams, Brooke. "What Has History to Do with Semiotics?" *Semiotica* 54.3/4 (1985).

Winnicott, D. W. *Playing and Reality*. London: Tavistock Publications, 1971.

Wiseman, Mary Bittner. *The Ecstasies of Roland Barthes*. New York: Routledge, 1989.

Wolheim, Richard. *The Mind and Its Depths*. Cambridge, Mass.: Harvard University Press, 1993.

Worth, Sol. *Studying Visual Communication*. Philadelphia: University of Pennsylvania Press, 1981.

Young, Iris Marion. "The Ideal of Community and the Politics of Difference." *Feminism/Postmodernism*. Ed. Linda J. Nicholson. New York: Routledge, 1990.

Youngblood, Gene. "Art and Ontology: Electronic Visualization in Chicago." *The Event Horizon*. Ed. Lorne Falk and Barbara Fischer. Toronto: Lorne Falk and Barbara Fischer, 1987.

Index

AIDS, and video, 247, 252, 282–83

Anderson, Kelly, and Annie Goldson: alternative television and the academy, 232

Auferderheide, Patricia: cable access and the public sphere, 246n

Avedon, Richard, 40–43, 46–47, 65

Bal, Mieke, 161–62

Barthes, Roland: and Avedon, 40–47; Bataille, 33; and Baudrillard, 52; Bazin, 56n; and Benjamin, 35–39; McLuhan, 51; and photography, 32–71; projection, 67–71; and Sartre, 33; Susan Sontag, 56; and visual performance, 49–52; *Camera Lucida,* 31, 32, 162; connotation and projection, 95; and frame analysis, 116–17; *Image-Music-Text,* 51n; *Mythologies,* and images, 105, 213; naturalization and artifice, 104–108; sight and meaning, 31; time and history, 52–55

Bateson, Gregory, 149n

Bataille, Georges, 11, 12n, 13, 14, 65

Baudrillard, Jean: and Althusser, 327; and the hyperreal, 329–30; Disneyland and simulation, 329, 332; pessimism and images, 210, 211–12, 214; simulation and images, 52, 70, 71, 134, 213, 215, 224, 263, 310, 318–20, 323–34

Bazin, André, 158

Bellour, Raymond: representation, 79, 114

Benjamin, Walter, 31, 36, 39–40, 56, 61, 63, 320

Benning, Sadie: and video testimony, 269; and video, 317–18, 324, 331–33

Berger, John, 36, 45n, 56, 212

Berko, Lili: the history of the portapack, 234, 235, 265

Bhaba, Homi, 306

Birnbaum, Dara: popular image video, 230

Bolton, Richard, 41

Bonitzer, Pascal, 118–19

Bordwell, David: textuality, formalism, 79, 90, 96, 99, 123–25

Bosnia, and images of war, 14

Bourdieu, Pierre, and photography, 67

Boyle, Deirdre, and Guerrilla TV, 272–73

Brahms-Sanders, Helga, 149

Brakhage, Stan: *The Act of Seeing with One's Own Eyes,* 141–43; *Window, Water, Baby, Moving* and the relationship of fantasy to projection, 142

Brecht, Bertolt, 98

Breton, André, 61n, 65, 258–59

Buchloh, Benjamin: video in the streets, 254

Buck-Morss, Susan, 36

Buddhism, the Vietnam War and images, 62–64

Butler, Judith, 236n

Calendar, 209, 305, 308–309

Calvino, Italo: and storytelling, 75; *Mr. Palomar* in relation to the viewing process, 131

Camcorders, 2, 20–22, 62–64, 218–19, 248–51, 274–77, 299–305; and the Super Bowl, 313

Campa, Román de la: and Latino identity, 284

Candid Cameras, and voyeurism, 176–77

Carpenter, Edmund, 213

Carroll, John: and film grammar, 110–16

Chatwin, Bruce, 297

Chomsky, Noam: and critiques of commodity culture, 322; generative grammar, 112

Cinéma vérité and projection, 142, 161, 194–99, 313; Walpiri video practice, 294

Classical cinema: and the spectator, 97–98; as paradigm, 95–98; rules and textuality, 103; and autonomy, 107

Clifford, James: cultural identity and the nation-state, 306; ethnography and surrealism,

349

Clifford—*continued*
  291; thinking of cultural research in spatial terms, 286–87; traveling and the local, 285
Cobain, Kurt, 215–17
Commolli, Jean-Louis, 158–60
Communication, and information, 20, 46, 128, 137, 243
Community: and a sense of place, 280–81, 284, 287; and interpretation, 315; and popular culture, 290; and the tribal, 281; as a cultural configuration, 289
Computers: and the redefinition of grassroots cultural activity, 219–20
Contingency: and interpretation of images, 39, 160, 164, 202, 203, 266, 317; in dreams and daydreams, 38
Conventions, codes and photographs, 38
Crapanzano, Vincent, 187n
Crary, Jonathan, 8–9, 24n, 37
Crystal Pepsi commercials, the Super Bowl and *Homicide*, 311
Culloden, and cinéma-vérité, 203–204
Cyborgs: images as the body, the body as image, 220

"Dallas": TV in Asia and effects on local cultures, 285–86
Danesi, Marcel: visual metaphors/language, 4
Davis, Neil: death in Thailand and news images, 62–63, 127–28
Deep Dish TV: alternate networks for the distribution of grassroots television, 245n
Deleuze, Gilles, 73n
Deren, Maya, 80
DIVA TV, activist video, 247
Dowrick, Peter: and the evaluation of video images, 261, 262
Dreamtime, aboriginal use of video, 295–99
Dualism, viewer and image, 26
Duchamp, Marcel, 35
Duras, Marguerite, 178–79

Eagleton, Terry, 320–21
Eastwood, Clint, 55, 57, 70, 140, 143–44, 237
Eco, Umberto, 108
Edelman, Gerald: cognition and visuality, 8–9; mind-body relations, 222
Egoyan, Atom, 209, 223, 305, 306
Eisenstein, Sergei: film language, montage, 111–13; and normative theories of textuality, image and idea, 113, 115
Eixenbaum, Boris: film syntax, 123
Electronic communications: and zines, VCR networks, desktop publishing, Internet, 219, 258
Electronic media: and the term image, 236; and truth as document, 245; as text, 236; popular culture and the transformation of political discourse and action, 320
Elsaesser, Thomas: and Syberberg, 170

Fassbinder, Rainer Werner, 152
Felman, Shoshana: interpretation and contradiction, 191, 193; testimony as a mode of address, 268, 306
Film: and abstract expressionism, 80; and narrative, 95, 156; and segmentation, 122; and the use of technical terms for interpretation, 89; celluloid, 84, 87; communication, 93; dreams, 94; editing and suture, 94; textuality and montage, 112–13; montage as master code, 123; perspective, 95, 158; presence/absence, theoretical questions in the classical text, 107–108; projection, 94, 152; editing, 115; sign-object relations, 87; text, codes, laws, 83, 107; science of, 108; time, 80, 83
Film noir, 98
First Contact, 298
Fischer, Michael: disciplinary boundaries, 285
Flaubert, Gustave, 154–55
Forest, Fred: experiments in community video, 244–46, 252
Foucault, Michel: and Nazism, 169; the panopticon and spectatorship, 213
Frankfurt School, analyses of pop culture, 321
Freedberg, David, and images, 23
Freire, Paulo, 227
Freud, Sigmund, 63, 80, 98
Fuller, Peter, 199n

Gabriel, Peter: digital technologies, 218
Gabriel, Teshome, 63, 64
Gallop, Jane: projection as transference, 187
Gane, Mike: on Baudrillard, 326–27
Garnham, Nicholas, 276–77
Germany, Pale Mother, 149–54, 156
Gibson, William, 206
Ginsburg, Faye: on indigenous media, 248n, 292n
Godard, Jean-Luc, 59–60, 66, 95–96, 115, 140

Graham, Dan: video art and video activism, 262, 265–67

Grateful Dead, tribal communities, 290

Greenaway, Peter, 176

Grierson, John: didactic use of film and video in the community, 243, 260n, 274

Griffith, D. W.: and montage, 123–24

Gupta, Akhil, and James Ferguson: on space, identity and the politics of difference, 284, 306

Habermas, Jürgen: communicative action as performance, 50

Hammond, Joyce: Tongan use of video in Salt Lake City, 248, 249, 250

Hansen, Miriam, 10, 15, 185

Haraway, Donna: and positionality, 29

Harlaan, Thomas, 167, 168, 170

Heath, Stephen, 247n

Hedebro, Göran: role of media in developing countries, 251–52

Heimat, 169, 173

Henny, Leonard: video and community, 240

Herbert, Christopher: ethnography and culture, 289; meaning and social practice, 109

Hiroshima mon amour, 99, 178–82, 268

Hirst, Paul: and naturalization, 108n

Hitchcock, Alfred, 92

Hoggart, Richard, 235

Holocaust: and projection, 167, 173; and the cinema, 160–68

Hypermedia: new technologies, media change, 137, 258

Hypertext, and images, 27, 49, 58, 137

If Every Girl Had a Diary, 317

Images: against the arguments of manipulation, 129, 264; and computer-mediated communications technologies, 130; and deterritorialization, 296–97; and digitalization, 129, 156; and discourse, 128, 264, 269; and language, 26, 42, 44, 50, 113, 117, 269; and memory, 27, 30, 64, 166, 170; and Nazi propaganda, 172; and the transformations of meaning by the spectator, 135, 166, 201–202, 264–65, 273; and virtual reality, cyberspace, 138, 206, 220, 258; and visual literacy, 212; as dream, 8–9; as gatekeeper, 9, 56; as hallucination, 8–9; as media and cultural hybrids, 237; as metaphors, 4–7; as projection, 6, 18, 67–75, 78, 85, 88, 154–55, 165,

167, 200–202, 312; as text, 93; everyday experience and discourse in relation to projection, 202; representation, 8, 54–58, 264–65; symbolism in relation to video, 2; the body and sight, 222; time, 77–78, 79, 132, 204

Imaginary: and photographs, 43; and memory, 27, 30, 166, 170; mirroring, 30; optical, 30; and projection, 135, 138–41, 145–49, 157–58, 164, 170, 178, 189, 190–99, 205, 207, 312, 315

Indigenous media: and electronic images, use and appropriation for the community, 248–49, 295, 301–305; and Eric Michaels, 291–93, 294, 295–96

Insignificance, 85–86, 181

Intercultural communications, grassroots video, 248–49

Iser, Wolfgang, 183–84

Jackson, Michael, 309, 311–13, 314

James, David: video criticism, 237n

Jay, Martin, 39n

Jurassic Park, 156

Kaplan, E. Ann: 97, 98, 109

King, Rodney: communities and television, 20–22; images and justice, 20–22, 184, 249

Kings of the Road, 148, 171

Kluge, Alexander: and the public sphere, 184–85

Klute, 81

Koresh, David: 18–19; images and the news, 18–19, 214

Kracauer, Siegfried, 15

Kramer, Robert: and *Unser Nazi* in relation to the history of Holocaust images, 167–69

Krauss, Rosalind: video art and narcissism, 252, 253, 255

Kris, Ernest: on propaganda and radio, 171–72

Kroker, Arthur, 220–22

Kroker, Marilouise, 221, 222

Kubrick, Stanley: and *The Shining,* 87–89

Kuntzel, Thierry, 79

Lacan, Jacques, 17n, 80

Laidlaw, Marc: and virtual reality, 334

Laing, R. D., 183

Lanzmann, Claude, 160–66, 168–70, 172

Lazerus, Alison: community video, 262, 264, 266

Lee, Benjamin: and notions of public subjectivity, 276

Lesage, Julia: *In Plain English,* videos on intercultural relations, 267, 268–69, 317

Letter from an Unknown Woman, 98

Letter to Jane, 60, 81–84, 87

Lévi-Strauss, Claude: music and visualization, 139

Levin, Charles, 325

Levin, David Michael: commenting on Berkeley and theories of vision, 127; on Heidegger, 128, 210–12; projection and the unpredictability of viewing, 208–15

Lightning Over Water, 85

Lili Marleen, and the historical imaginary, 171

Listening and viewing, in relation to projection, 181

Locke, John, 37–38

Lotman, Juri: communication/information, 120n

Lowcast media: and popular culture, 230, 237; as a tool for community activism, 229–32, 274–77, 280; self-healing, 229

Lowcast video: and political utopianism, 231, 273, 298–300; history of video and links to other media, 232

Lumière, Auguste, 59–60, 69, 160

Lyotard, Jean-François: postmodernism and its relationship to video, 320

MacBride Commission, communications in the Third World, 225–26

Madonna: image and projection, 143, 144, 217, 321

Magritte, René: *Ceci n'est pas une pipe,* 92

Mapplethorpe, Robert, 42, 65

Marker, Chris: and *Sans soleil,* 134; self-reflexivity and video, 253

Marnie, 84

Marshall Islands, and indigenous video groups, 301–305

Marshall, Stuart: on video art, 266

McLuhan, Marshall: consciousness as image, 213, 334; global village and new technologies, 295

Me and Rubyfruit, 317

Meaning and the nomadic, 63–64

Media: and the Gulf War, 133; and the question of the docudrama and truth, 132

Media monopolies, and the local, 286

Mediation, storytelling in the media, 131

Méliès, Georges, 59–60, 66

Metz, Christian, 77–78, 93; and textual analysis, 104

Michaels, Eric: on Hollywood iconography in relation to aboriginal culture, 292–93; television culture at Yuendumu, 294, 295–96, 300–301; Walpiri graphics as maps, 293

Mitchell, W. J. T., 34, 279

Mitry, Jean: shot and montage in film, 118

Mohabeer, Michelle: Lesbian and Gay Film and Video Festival, 255

Moholy-Nagy, László: photography, 12–15

Moore, Rick: and Challenge for Change, 271–72

Morse, Margaret: and mall culture, 315–16, 318

Mowitt, John: notions of text in cultural and linguistic theory, 109

Mowlana, Hamid, 226n

Music videos: and dubbing, 176; and projection, 218; and the experimental cinema of the 1950s and 60s, 218

Naficy, Hamid: on exile cultures and media, 11n, 14n, 274, 306, 310, 314, 315

Nancy, Jean-Luc, 16n

National Film Board of Canada: Challenge for Change, video for social change, 253–54, 260, 270–74

N.B.C., 62

Neeson, Liam, *Schindler's List,* intertextuality, 201

Nichols, Bill, 92–94, 96–97

Nintendo, 206

Nongovernmental organizations, in development, 227

North by Northwest, 79

O'Rourke, Denis, 282, 301

October, 111, 121–22

Oepen, Manfred: German Foundation for International Development and grassroots communication, 246

Ophuls, Max, 98

Ozu, 90–91

Paper Tiger Television Collective, 247

Pearlstone, Zena, 315

Performance and meaning (oral, visual), 50, 94, 99

Photographs: and narrative, 46, 75; and realism, 47; and representation, 23, 57–58; and the American West, 41; and the public sphere, 47, 49, 53

Photography: and art, 24; and desire, 17; and language, 25; and newspapers, 19; and subjectivity, 34; and the cinema, 24, 72, 77–78, 88; and time, 48–50, 53; and virtual reality, 59; anthropomorphism, 17; as mirror, 45; as picture, as language, 25; as print, 17, 66–67, 88; as window, 45; camera obscura, 35; Descartes, René, 13, 26, 59; digital, 52, 65; ethnography, 53; fantasy, 17, 51; historical discourse and positionality, 48; illusion/reality, 13–14, 60, 64–65; memory, history, 22, 24–25, 62–64; power, 49, 51; presence, absence, 16, 54, 59, 62; simulation, 43, 45; vision, 12–14, 51

Photomontage, 24

Poirier, Anne-Claire, 189–94

Polaroids, and Barthes, 32, 34–35

Postman, Neil: media manipulation, 6, 322, 323

Postmodern Media Communities, 218–19, 224–30, 233–35, 248–51, 256–61, 289–91, 334–35; technology and change, 278–79

Postmodernity, discourse, conflict and consensus, 278–35

Projection: and acting in relation to theatre and film, 182, 186–87; and cinéma-vérité, 195, 202–204; and communication, 135–37; and computer games, 156, 206; and dreams, as metaphor, as reality, 138–41; and history, 173, 203–204; and identification, 157–58, 190, 312; and new technologies, 136; and perception, 30, 158, 190; and performance, 164; and speech in the cinema, 175–76; and the attribution of meaning, 129; and the camera, 91; and the documentary cinema, 134, 163; and the internal dialogue of the spectator, 180, 190, 205; and the unconscious, 189, 191–99; and *Weekend*, 140; codes and the organization of meaning, 28, 119, 158, 196; disembodiment and speech, 176; editing and textuality, 120; embodiment, 205; fantasies of inner and outer, 140–41; fantasy, thought, sensation and vision, 207; images as surrogates and the need to identify, 208; in opposition to images, 184; in relation to the imaginary, 135, 145–49, 164, 170, 178, 190–99, 312, 315; meaning and the image, 139, 163, 190–94; music, sound, listening, as metaphors for projection, 206; narrative, 95, 205; performance and in-

tention, 185; sound and dialogue in relation to performance, 174; sound, 90; spectators and the narrative cinema, 17, 148; time, reversibility and the visible, 147, 164, 204; video images and dialogue, 254; vision and control, 127, 144–45, 157, 160, 184, 190, 312

Prokudin-Gorskii, Sergei: and landscape photography, 76

Propaganda, radio in the Third Reich, 171–73

Rabinow, Paul: and intercultural ethnography, 304

Raboy, Marc: and grassroots media history, 235n

Readings, Bill: community and consensus, 279–80

Reality Bites, 216

Reflections on Fieldwork in Morocco, 304

Reisz, Karel: and editing, 115

Reitz, Edgar, 169

Resnais, Alain: and *Hiroshima Mon Amour*, 180, 186; projection and *Night and Fog*, 171

Rimmer, David, 88

Roeg, Nicholas, 85

Romanyshyn, Robert D.: effects of technology, 5

Ropars, Marie-Clare: film technique as film language, 110n, 111n, 120–21; filmic images as a form of writing, 113, 118–21

Rorty, Richard: and contingency, 13n, 39

Rouch, Jean: the documentary cinema, 133–34

Rushdie, Salman, 269, 307

Saalfield, Catherine: video activism, 247

Sahlins, Marshall, 250

Sartre, Jean-Paul, 32, 33, 40, 58, 60, 64–65, 67–68, 154

Saussure, Ferdinand de, 44

Schafer, Roy: internalization and projection, 188

Schindler's List, 160, 163, 164, 165, 166, 168

Schopenhauer, Arthur, 37–38

Scream from Silence, projection and viewing, 189–96

Screen: as mediator for viewing and projection, 149; viewing and technology, 92

Searle, John: and notions of subjectivity, 239; text and visuality, 112

"Seinfeld," 309–10, 313–16

Sharp, Geoff: media as extended forms, 263

Shoah, 160–66, 168–70, 173, 268
Short Cuts, 216
Shotter, John: viewing oneself as a video image, 252
Silverman, Kaja, 17n; *langue* and *parole* as models for the classical cinema, 100–103
Snow, Michael, 72
Snyder, Joel: language and images, 18n
Sobchack, Vivian, 16
Sontag, Susan, 45n, 168
Sorlin, Pierre, 110n, 118
Speaking Parts, 209, 223
Spielberg, Stephen, 163
Stafford, Barbara Maria, 236n
Star Trek, fans and community, 290
Streep, Meryl: and *Sophie's Choice,* 201
Sturmer, John Von: aboriginal media and issues of representation, 298, 305
Subjectivity, vision and perception, 27
Sunless, 253
Surrealism, 62–63

Television trials, and Rodney King, 20–22
Text: artifice, naturalization and classicism, 106–107, 110; interpretation and the spectator, 106; performance, 50; and structuralism, 109
The Adjuster, 209
The Baby of Macon, 176
The Birds, 92–93
The Elephant Man, 84
The Empire State Building, 85
The Evil Demon of Images, 52
The Flicker, 79
The Good Woman of Bangkok, 282
The Mask, and digitalization, 220
The Purple Rose of Cairo: and Woody Allen, 145–49; projection and dialogue, 177–78
The Shining, 87–88
The Songlines, critique of, 297
The Tin Drum, and the historical imaginary, 171
They Became What They Beheld, 213
Things I Cannot Change, 253–54
Thompson, Kristin, 86n, 87, 90, 95n, 96
Tightrope, fantasy and projection, 140
Todorov, Tzvetan, 175
Tokyo Ga, 90–91
Tomaselli, Keyan, and Alison Lazerus, in relation to participatory video, 262, 264, 266
Tout Va Bien, 81

Turner, Terence: video among the Kayapo of Brazil, 225, 293n
Tyler, Stephen: postmodern ethnography, 291–92; textuality and the social sciences, 109n

Unser Nazi: and the Holocaust, 167–68, 170, 172

Van Der Keuken, Johan: documentary cinema and video, 253
Vanderbeek, Stan, 88
Vidéazimut: international video organizations, 225, 227
Video: activism and development in the South, 224–31; and innovation, the transformative effects of new technologies, 242, 244, 248, 249; and the creation of an electronic space, 250; art centers, museums, universities, 226; as a hybrid medium and as the base upon which multimedia have been developed, 218–24; in the community and relationship to psychoanalysis, 252, 255–56; language, discourse and politics, 238–39; lesbian and gay activism around AIDS, 247; Rodney King, 20–22; theory and practice, 239; time, present/past, 249, 325; use of the documentary genre, 246
Video activism, 224–77; and strategies of learning, 260–62, 273
Video art, and popular culture, 226
Video groups, as micro-communities, 248
Video images: presence/absence, gaps as productive sites of meaning, 264
Video News Service: use of video at the grassroots level in South Africa, 225, 226
Video politics: and communication, 242–49, 273; and community activism, 240–41, 273–77; and the resistance to theory and writing, 241; as the creation of theory, 239
Video Sewa, grassroots video in India, 226–27
Videodisc, 78
Vietnam War and images, 62
Viola, Bill: and video art, 316
Virilio, Paul: technology, perception and the human body, 220
Virtual reality, and anamorphosis, 221; and video, 218
Vision: and the imaginary, 36; appearances and truth, 36, 61, 64–65; Bataille, Georges, 11–14, 65; embodiment, 10–11; language, 3–4; and visual proof, 80; science, 61, 69; tech-

nology and determinism, 13–14, 273; window, 4–7
Visual media, 37–38
Visualization, 59; and death, 63

Warhol, Andy, 85
Watkins, Peter, 100; *Culloden, Privilege, Punishment Park,* 100, 204
Wavelength, 72–74, 89, 144, 145
Wayne's World, 216, 234
Weiss, Allen S.: intercultural communications and indigenous media, 297
Wenders, Wim, 85, 90–91, 148, 171, 216, 257
Wilden, Anthony, 34n
Williams, Brooke: in relation to history and semiotics, 167
Williams, Raymond, 235
Wilson, Laurie, 226n
Wings of Desire, 216
Winnicott, D. W.: contingency and transitional

realms of meaning, 201; play-acting and projection in relation to images, 199–201, 323
Women and Film, 97
Wong, Paul: video and the reclamation of identity, 255
World Association of Community Broadcasters, 228
Worth, Sol, and John Adair: using film in the community, 243, 298
Wundkanal: Execution for Four Voices, 167

Young Mr. Lincoln, 81
Young, Iris Marion: and conceptions of community, 275
Youngblood, Gene: synergy of consciousness and video, 257–58; video and simulation, 256–58

Zweig, Stephan, 98

RON BURNETT is the Director of the Graduate Program in Communications at McGill University and Associate Professor of Cultural Studies in the English department. He is author of *Explorations in Film Theory*, and essays that have appeared in books and journals internationally. He was the founder and editor-in-chief of the journal *Ciné-Tracts*, and has been making videotapes and films since the early 1970s.